D1713540

Plague Writing in Early Modern England

Plague Writing in
Early Modern England

ERNEST B. GILMAN

The University of Chicago Press : Chicago and London

Ernest B. Gilman is professor of English at New York University. He is the author of *The Curious Perspective: Literary and Pictorial Wit in the Seventeenth Century* (1978), *Recollecting the Arundel Circle* (2002), and *Iconoclasm and Poetry in the English Reformation* (1986), the last published by the University of Chicago Press.

The University of Chicago Press, Chicago 60637
The University of Chicago Press, Ltd., London
© 2009 by The University of Chicago
All rights reserved. Published 2009
Printed in the United States of America

18 17 16 15 14 13 12 11 10 09   1 2 3 4 5

ISBN-13: 978-0-226-29409-4 (cloth)
ISBN-10: 0-226-29409-9 (cloth)

FRONTISPIECE. Detail from the frontispiece to George Thomson's *Loimotomia: or The Pest Anatomized* (1666).

The University of Chicago Press gratefully acknowledges the generous support of the Abraham and Rebecca Stein Faculty Publication Fund of New York University toward the publication of this book.

Library of Congress Cataloging-in-Publication Data
Gilman, Ernest B., 1946–
Plague writing in early modern England / Ernest B. Gilman.
p. cm.
Includes bibliographical references and index.
ISBN-13: 978-0-226-29409-4 (cloth : alk. paper)
ISBN-10: 0-226-29409-9 (cloth : alk. paper)
1. English literature—Early modern, 1500–1700—History and criticism. 2. Diseases and literature—Great Britain—History—17th century. 3. Plague in literature. 4. Epidemics in literature. 5. Diseases in literature. 6. Plague—Political aspects. 7. Plague—Religious aspects. 8. Plague—England—History—17th century. 9. Epidemics—England—History—17th century. 10. Literature and society—Great Britain—History—17th century. I. Title
PR438.D56G56 2009
820.9'3561—dc22   2008029867

An Lotte
zum Andenken

[CONTENTS]

[ILLUSTRATIONS]

FIGURE I.

Giovanni del Biondo, *Saint Sebastian Altarpiece*
(ca. 1379), 76

FIGURE 2.

Jacopo Tintoretto, St. Roche and St. Sebastian
(ca. 1578–81), 78

FIGURE 3.

Jacopo Tintoretto, *Miracle of the Brazen Serpent*
(ca. 1575–76), 80

FIGURE 4.

Carlo Maratti, *Carlo Borromeo Saving Milan from
the Plague* (1650), 81

FIGURE 5.

Anonymous Florentine *ora pro nobis* engraving of
St. Sebastian (ca. 1470–80), 82

FIGURE 6.

Giorgio Vasari, *The Virgin and Child Enthroned
with Saints* (1536), 85

FIGURE 7.

Camillo Landriani ("Il Duchino"), *Carlo Borromeo
Administers the Sacraments to the
Plague-Stricken* (1602), 86

FIGURE 8.

Francesco Solimena, *The Miracle of St. John of God*
(ca. 1690), 88

FIGURE 9.

Nicolas Poussin, *The Plague of Ashdod* (1630–31), 89

[ACKNOWLEDGMENTS]

My first debt is to the current and former graduate students at New York University—especially Dr. Patrick Phillips, Dr. Kelly Stage, and the members of my 2006 plague seminar—who helped to raise, and answer, many of the questions in this book. Among these, my most heartfelt thanks go to Jennie Votava, MD, a PhD candidate at NYU who also happens to be a physician (i.e., a "real" doctor), and whose careful reading of this manuscript saved me from any number of life-threatening medical gaffes. Many colleagues at NYU also offered their advice and expertise along the way; among them I want particularly to thank Richard Hull, Patrick Deer, Gabrielle Starr, John Archer, and Elaine Freedgood. I have profited as well from the papers presented at a seminar on plague literature, directed by Professor Rebecca Totaro, at the 2008 convention of the Shakespeare Association of America. Publication of this work has been supported in part through the generosity of the Abraham and Rebecca Stein Faculty Publication Fund of New York University.

An earlier version of chapter 4 appeared in *Reading the Renaissance: Ideas and Idioms from Shakespeare to Milton*, edited by Marc Berley (Pittsburgh: Duquesne University Press, 2003), and is incorporated here by kind permission.

The staff of the New York Public Library, the British Library, and the Wellcome Library in London were unfailingly helpful in my search for early modern plague materials. The burden of securing permission for the illustrations was lightened by the expert help of Erin Pauwels. My gratitude as well to Alan Thomas and Randy Petilos of the University of Chicago Press; to my copyeditor, Nancy Trotic; and to Gail Kern Paster and Barbara Howard Traister for their scrupulous reading of the manuscript.

Finally there are the people in my life for whom, in the end, this book is written: Lois, Seth, and Eve Gilman, and my mother-in-law, Lotte Seelig Prager, to whose memory this book is dedicated.

The View
from the Mountain

There is no health; Physitians say that wee,
At best, enjoy but a neutralitie,
And can there bee worse sicknesse, then to know
That we are never well, nor can be so?
JOHN DONNE, "The First Anniversary"

This book was begun at New York University's Florence campus, a villa reminiscent of the hillside refuge from which, in 1348, Boccaccio's storytellers could survey the devastation below, famously described at the beginning of *The Decameron* as a city in the grip of the Black Death. Boccaccio's company of elegant young women and men, having retired from Florence to wait out the epidemic, pass the time by amusing each other with lighthearted tales. In Boccaccio's collection—as in *The Thousand and One Nights*, to which it has a distant relation—so long as the stories continue, death is held at bay. That same year, Petrarch's Laura died of the plague, as tradition has it, only to be resurrected in the *Canzoniere* as the inspiration for thousands of Petrarchan mistresses. The final agonies of Laura de Noves, if indeed it was she who stands behind the "Laura" of the sonnets, went unrecorded; but her symptoms as a plague victim would be transmuted into the conventional chills and fevers afflicting subsequent generations of Petrarchan lovers fatally attracted to their lethal mistresses. Seen in this light—whether as the site of compensatory fictions, or of lyric's potent blend of suffering and desire—the European literary Renaissance is marked at its Italian origin by the disease that is the subject of this book.

My purpose is to revisit the plague as matter for the literary imagination of the English Renaissance, focusing on the seventeenth century—a period marked by the devastating epidemics of 1603 and 1625 and the "Great Plague" of 1665. The central question of this study is implied in the title: I ask not only how the plague can illuminate the imaginative writing it provokes, but how, at a crucial historical moment, "writing" and "plague" can be understood as most intimately conjoined. This question may be profitably addressed to the period at hand. If we seek a "plague discourse," we will find it always already there, in three interpenetrating registers: in the large body of writing of all kinds that it provokes; in its poetic representation, both direct and implied; and fundamentally in the belief strongly held (and severely tested) in Reformation culture that plague is itself a form of (divine) utterance, and a form of writing that inscribes itself in the natural world, in the body politic, and in the "tokens" to be read on the bodies of the afflicted. The early modern assumption that the *thing* itself is a *word* grounds our own spurious but persistent conviction—eloquently contested by Susan Sontag—that disease is not only encrusted with metaphor but has a "meaning" beyond, or intrinsic to, its biological nature. That suffering must be purposeful is, of course, an ancient idea; that an understanding of plagues has seemed to require hermeneutic as well as diagnostic skills is more immediately a Renaissance legacy. My own assumption in undertaking this work is that we may be better prepared to reconsider plague writing, and moved to do so all the more urgently, than scholars of an earlier generation.

The difference between our vantage point and theirs can be gleaned from two remarkable quotations. The first is from a well-known essay on the plague in Western literature by René Girard, who, writing in 1974, regards the word *plague* as a metaphor for social discord: a metaphor (and a metaphor only), he says, "endowed with an almost incredible vitality"—incredible because ours is "a world where the plague and epidemics in general have disappeared almost altogether."[1] For Girard, the vitality of plague survives as a figurative way of speaking of other things, but only because plague itself, he understands, has literally become a thing of the past. The second is by John M. Barry, author of a recent book on the influenza pandemic of 1918. As an example of the kind of sobering prediction now regularly issuing from the Centers for Disease Control and Prevention (CDC) and other public health authorities—latter-day, secular channels of seventeenth-century apocalypticism—I quote the heading of Barry's article in the November 1, 2004, issue of *Fortune* magazine: "Viruses of Mass Destruction: The emergence of a pandemic flu virus is not only inevitable but overdue."

Toxic Events

In practice, the understanding of literature always involves a negotiation between what we take a work to mean—in itself, to its author, for contemporary readers, as enmeshed in the web of a "cultural poetics"—and how we appropriate that meaning for ourselves. At times, different facets of the work will seem to come into clearer focus, or to be reconfigured for us as newly interesting or problematic, in light of our own experience and the interpretative templates we lay over the past. Literary history always engages us in a balancing act between an inevitable presentism—how did *they* become *us?*—and the difficulties of recovering *their* world in all its particular difference. How does plague bridge the gap? What do we have to learn now from the plague

---

1. Girard, "*To Double Business Bound*," 138.

literature of the seventeenth century? And, as a corollary, what particular insights and sympathies not available in the 1970s to scholars like Girard can we bring to this literature that might justify the writing of this book? One answer to be developed more fully in this book is that past plagues are still present to us, exerting their pressure as shards of cultural memory, traumatic fragments that still have the power to wound even if—especially if—their substance has been "forgotten." The shorthand answer, however, is that since the mid-1980s we have found ourselves once again living in the shadow of plague, its history and the language in which that history has survived newly unearthed in the present moment. Three decades ago, Girard could not have known that AIDS would be the Black Death of the late twentieth century. At this writing, the disease has killed more than twenty-five million people worldwide, with another forty million living with the infection.[2] Although the availability of cutting-edge therapies has tamed the infection into a manageable chronic condition for those (with medical coverage) in the developed West, its unchecked spread elsewhere remains a cause for the gravest concern. And, as health officials warn, AIDS is almost certainly the harbinger of future global pandemics.

Now, indeed, entering upon our second AIDS generation, in America we have witnessed the burgeoning of an "AIDS culture" in the arts, medicine, and politics. Like the plague discourses of the fourteenth century and the Renaissance, our own engages a chorus of voices that can be heard as a response to, and a symptom of, a profound biosocial crisis. Like those earlier discourses, too, ours evokes and revises traditional narratives and figures associated with infectious disease, while drawing other cultural elements old and new into its orbit. In the longest view, this history of discursive appropriation may be read as a recurrent (and, as I shall suggest, traumatic) narrative of the West stretching back to Thucydides and forward to tomorrow's headlines.

In AIDS America, Larry Kramer's 1985 play *The Normal Heart* paved the way for the eventual Broadway success of *Angels in America* and *Rent* (and for such films as *Philadelphia* and *Forrest Gump*, which were deemed commercially risky at the time). Kramer's title proved an early provocation in the ensuing cultural debate about the normalization of AIDS as the disease, at first stigmatizing a dispensable few, spread into the "general population."

2. Esposito, "AIDS: A Twentieth Century Plague," 16.

In the visual arts, Keith Haring and Robert Mapplethorpe represented the face of AIDS for the eighties. Through them, the Bohemian stereotype of the starving, consumptive artist the tubercular Kafka's *Hungerkünstler*—was replaced by the image of the artist-with-AIDS. More recently, the late writer Paul Monette has figured as the St. Sebastian of AIDS literature, a subject recently institutionalized in critical anthologies, course syllabi on literature and disease, professional panels, and books like this.[3] So pervasive has our awareness of AIDS become, so deeply ingrained in our imagination, that everything tends to darken in its shadow. Like the exegetes of 1603 attempting to connect the reign of Elizabeth with that of her successor over the chasm of an intervening epidemic, we find ourselves rereading our own *fin de siècle* cultural history as a prolepsis. In retrospect, Don DeLillo's 1985 novel *White Noise*—with its "airborne toxic event" depositing the lingering dread of a death sentence in those exposed to it—appears uncannily prophetic of both the reality and the paranoia of AIDS just dimly visible at the time. In 1989 Susan Sontag published *Aids and Its Metaphors*, the sequel to her classic essay of 1978, *Illness as Metaphor*.[4] "More than cancer," she argues, "AIDS seems to foster ominous fantasies" about "individual and social vulnerabilities" to a disease marked, like the plague of old, as a divine judgment on its victims.

Just as Foucault's death of AIDS seemed to supply the final cause in the biography of the postmodern historian, the disease can be seen as the stigma of the postmodern condition itself. In the Renaissance, a Madonna of Mercy or a *memento mori* might be seen anew as a plague image; so, for us, the 1987 film *Fatal Attraction* has since been spoken of as an AIDS allegory, with the homicidal Glenn Close as the personification of an enraged retrovirus threatening both the straying husband Michael Douglas and his wife. In this context, it seems inevitable that in *Eyes Wide Shut* Stanley Kubrick should have chosen to update the Arthur Schnitzler story on which the film is based by including an episode in which Tom Cruise, the physician protagonist, narrowly escapes a "fatal" encounter of his own with a hooker who, as he learns the very next day, has contracted a venereal disease—not syphilis, as in the original novella,

3. Monette is commemorated in the extraordinary outpouring of poetry, fiction, memoirs, and polemical essays he published in his last decade, almost up to the moment of his death in 1995. His autobiographical works include *Afterlife*, *Borrowed Time: An AIDS Memoir*, and *Last Watch of the Night*.

4. The two essays were republished in a single volume as *"Illness as Metaphor" and "AIDS and Its Metaphors"* (1989). The following quotation is from p. 153.

but infection with HIV, the human immunodeficiency virus. For Cruise, the young "Dr. Harford" of the film, the final crisis arrives when he comes home late to discover that his wife has found the mask he had worn to a bizarre erotic costume party the night before. She has placed it on his pillow next to her in bed—where she lies in a deep sleep that may lead the viewer to mistake her, momentarily, for dead. It is the moment of Cruise's unmasking (a particularly poignant moment, given the rumors of the actor's own homosexuality), but in Kubrick's brooding meditation on sex and death—already ill, the director was to die in 1999, the year of the film's release—it also serves as the emblem of the film's shadowy AIDS plot. Like the plague introduced into the ball in Poe's "Masque of the Red Death," AIDS can conceal itself—as it does in the case of Cruise's infected prostitute—under the (death) mask of apparent health, even to the trained eye of the physician. Like Dr. Harford in his nocturnal wanderings, the disease he nearly brings to his own bed behaves furtively, in a kind of insidious charade. If in plague times the window of infection could only be open for a few days at most before the victim was unmasked by the appearance of unmistakable symptoms, the carrier of HIV can secretly deal, and deal with, death for years before he or she is discovered at last, visibly marked by the full-blown effects of the disease. The fear that some covert operatives might, from whatever motives, intentionally spread the infection recalls the paranoia in Italy during plague times, when it was believed that *untori*, "anointers," might be daubing some pestiferous liquid on benches and walls.

In the distant mirror of the bubonic plague, other features of AIDS come into sharper focus. In Thomas Dekker's *The Dead Tearme* (1608), "London" complains that sickness "doth now walke still in a ghostly and formidable shape vppe and downe my streets."[5] Medical advances have not banished the like specter of a liminal AIDS America ambiguously divided between the living and the still-living but already moribund, those in whose life death already lives. The virus's long and slow assault on the individual who harbors it is, however, counterpointed in the rhythm of AIDS by its rapid geographical spread. The Black Death needed almost a year to creep slowly northward from its Italian beachhead in Genoa in January 1348 to Chaucer's England. Today, the travel time by air from Italy to the United Kingdom is little more than two

---

5. Dekker, *The Dead Tearme*, 77.

hours—less than half the time it would have taken back in the seventies for the now-fabled "Patient Zero," the Canadian airline steward supposed at the time to have introduced HIV into the United States on a flight from Paris to New York.[6] No matter where in the world a new infectious agent may be spawned, the realization that we are no farther from its reach than the nearest airport has led to calls for emergency quarantine preparations reminiscent of those once enforced in early modern Venice or London at the first sign of plague.

The history of AIDS also demonstrates that the repertory of infectious diseases is not biologically fixed. Like all other forms of life, microorganisms have their life span as a species. Many species of infectious pathogens, like that responsible for the mysterious "sweating sickness" of the English sixteenth century, have become extinct. Others, including HIV (which now comes in several varieties, and which threatens to mutate into a supervirus resistant to current medications), have transformed themselves—are constantly transforming themselves—in response to changing environmental conditions. The leap from simian to *Homo sapiens* hosts and the consequent dispersal of HIV in the world's human communities was but the first act in a continuing evolutionary drama entirely typical of every species of pathogen. What we now know as syphilis is thought to have been related, in an earlier form, to the skin infection yaws (and in another strain to leprosy), which is spread by casual contact and which causes deep, open sores not confined to one area of the body. As climates chilled and more layers of clothing impeded its transmission, the same spirochete migrated both across continents and into the warmer microclimate of the human genital tract and managed to find a new mode of transmission by which its human hosts became willing, if unwitting, accomplices.[7] Given the complex processes of mutation

----

6. A recent study (based upon genetic testing and the analysis of stored blood samples) suggests that HIV may actually have entered the United States from Haiti as early as 1969, at first causing scattered cases of a "mystery illness" before finally being identified more than a decade later. See M. Thomas P. Gilbert et al., "The Emergence of HIV/AIDS in the Americas and Beyond," *Proceedings of the National Academy of Sciences USA* 104, no. 47 (2007): 18566–70, published online October 31, 2007, http://www .pnas.org/cgi/content/full/104/47/18566. The "Patient Zero" story reinforces the mythology of AIDS as the "gay plague"; the new Haitian evidence would recall an equally opprobrious stereotype of the early 1980s, but it does confirm the African origins of the virus.

7. The most current research into the migration of syphilis finds that "of all the strains [of pathogenic *Treponema*] examined, the venereal syphilis-causing strains originated most recently and were more closely related to yaws-causing strains from South America than to other non-venereal strains. Old World yaws-causing strains occupied a basal position on the tree, indicating that they arose first

that have produced any infectious agent identifiable today—and given, too, the rapidity of microbial evolution in comparison with any human timescale for genetic change—epidemiologists cannot be certain even from Thucydides' detailed description of the symptoms whether the "plague" in Periclean Athens was the bubonic plague, or an ancestor of modern cholera, or perhaps some other disease that has transformed itself into a very different creature or vanished entirely. Indeed, because of the difference in symptoms reported in medieval sources, as well as anomalies in the apparent epidemiology and course of the historical disease compared with those of "modern" plague, some historians remain skeptical that the organism responsible for the Black Death and its successor epidemics in Europe was today's bubonic plague—that is, the same infection caused by the *Yersinia pestis* bacterium first isolated from Chinese strains in 1894 by the Swiss bacteriologist Alexandre Yersin.[8]

In the long view, epidemiologists have identified three global pandemics of the bubonic plague: the Plague of Justinian, which ravaged the Roman Empire in the sixth century; the Black Death of the fourteenth century; and the outbreak of 1894–1903, which spread from Hong Kong and caused millions of deaths across east and south Asia. The remnants of the most recent epidemic are "still with us today."[9] Yersin prepared the first serum to combat the pathogen named in his honor. However, given the continued presence of the bacteria in pockets on nearly every continent, the record of its recurrences,

---

in human history, and a simian strain of *T. pallidum* was found to be indistinguishable from them." The results of this study "lend support to the Columbian theory of syphilis's origin while suggesting that the non-sexually transmitted subspecies arose earlier in the Old World" (Kristin N. Harper et al., "On the Origin of the Treponematoses: A Phylogenetic Approach," *PLoS Neglected Tropical Diseases* 2, no. 1 [2008]: e148; doi:10.1371/journal.pntd.0000148).

8. In *The Black Death Transformed: Disease and Culture in Early Renaissance Europe* (2003), Samuel K. Cohn forcefully argues the minority view that the Black Death of the fourteenth century could have been "any other disease" than modern rat-borne bubonic plague (1). In Cohn's view, the rapid spread of the historical disease, as well as the apparent ability of some people to acquire a natural immunity to it, indicates a symptomology significantly different from that of the disease caused by Yersin's organism (despite the coincidence, as Cohn would see it, that the Black Death very likely originated in China). However, "discovery of *Y. pestis* genetic material in those who died from the Black Death and are buried in medieval graves further supports the view that *Y. pestis* was the causative agent of the Black Death" (Didier Raoult et al., "Molecular Identification by 'Suicide PCR' of *Yersinia pestis* as the Agent of Medieval Black Death," *Proceedings of the National Academy of Sciences USA* 97, no. 23 [2000]: 12800–803, published online October 31, 2000, http://www.pnas.org/cgi/content/full/97/23/12800).

9. Finberg, "A Modern Understanding of the Plague of Fourteenth Century Europe," 18.

and the ability of the organism to evolve, it would be overly optimistic to think there will never be another epidemic.

Even familiar diseases like the flu return year by year with an altered genetic makeup; and, as we are warned, it is very probable that one of these routine annual mutations will again produce a particularly lethal pandemic strain. Viral or bacterial agents thus have a life of their own—almost, we might say, a mind of their own. Inscribing their own histories in the bodies of their hosts over hundreds of human generations, capable of prolonged retreat to withstand adverse conditions, "willing" to wait, they vary their habits and evolve in their chemical makeup, often combining with other microorganisms to adapt to ecological change and take advantage of new opportunities. In the last decade, we have also been alarmed by evidence of apparently new diseases—or of ones that have made the "species jump" by merging genetically with human rhinoviruses—cropping up everywhere. Such was the concern in 1998 when it was feared that the Hong Kong "chicken virus" might leap from the poultry yard into the human population, and again in 2006 with the avian flu. In response to these threats, millions of birds were killed and bulldozed into the ground, but what if the virus had succeeded in contaminating scavenging animals, or even the soil itself? With infectious disease, we are always dodging bullets, while the magic bullets at the disposal of medical science are always aimed at a moving target.

Apart from the fears it raises about the potential wild-card dissemination of a mysterious oriental malady, the appearance of avian viruses in the human population also indicates that, in some or even most instances, such "new" diseases may in reality be very old diseases newly emergent from their secluded ecological niches—or indeed, in the case of smallpox, from unsecured man-made niches in scientific laboratories or bioweapons research centers. Recent newspaper stories warn of the possibility that microbes frozen for eons in the polar ice caps may be released as a side effect of global warming. For the same reason, epidemiologists predict, malaria, encephalitis, dengue fever, and other mosquito-borne diseases may gain a new foothold north of the tropics. In August 2007, dozens of people in the Italian village of Castiglione di Cervia came down with chikungunya, a relative of dengue normally found in the area of the Indian Ocean. Cases of dengue have also been reported in Texas, and the *Journal of the American Medical Association* warns that "widespread appearance of dengue in the continental United States is a real possibility."[10] Other organisms—like the current strains of multidrug-resistant tuberculosis (MDR-TB), which thrive in the weakened immune system of AIDS patients—mutate from more benign or less resistant forms and now threaten to break out once more. In Kafka's day, tuberculosis manifested itself primarily as a lung infection; in its latest varieties, MDR-TB is found in the heart or the brain, and in forms impervious even to the last-ditch cocktail of antibiotics currently in use. Recently, public health workers in Africa have come across an even more robust strain of the disease, dubbed X-TB, which responds to no known treatment and kills in a matter of two to three weeks, especially in individuals whose immune systems have already been compromised by HIV. Physicians are now also finding increasing instances of "reactivation TB" among the elderly, in individuals who have never before been ill with tuberculosis but whose bodies have harbored dormant (and undetected) pockets of bacilli for fifty years or more.

The Black Death offers a historical case study of such opportunistic ecological changes. For centuries before it emerged to follow the trade routes west from the Mongolian steppes, invading the human populations of the Near East and then Europe, the plague bacterium confined itself largely within the stomachs of rat fleas and the bloodstreams of the black rats on which they fed. Typically invading the lymph nodes, at some point it further evolved the ability to cause both septicemic and pneumonic plague in humans—the former increasing its virulence by directly entering the victim's bloodstream, the latter facilitating its spread directly from person to person as an aerosol, as well as through the bite of the flea.[11] Far-fetched as the notion may seem, reputable authorities express concern that bombardment by cosmic rays may cause death-dealing mutations in common microorganisms found in spacecraft—which would then return to earth as the high-tech equivalent of the

10. Elizabeth Rosenthal, "As Earth Warms Up, Tropical Virus Moves to Italy," *New York Times*, December 23, 2007; David M. Morens, MD, and Anthony S. Fauci, MD, "A Potential Threat to Public Health in the United States," *JAMA* 299, no. 2 (2008): 214–16.

11. There are presently known to be seventy-six strains of all three types (biovars) of *Yersinia pestis*: biovar Antiqua, biovar Medievalis, and biovar Orientalis, each endemic to a particular part of the world. These classifications come from studies of modern plague organisms, but their species have been retroactively "dated" based on DNA analysis and linked, respectively, to the Plague of Justinian (mid-sixth century AD), to the Black Death, and to the nineteenth-century plague pandemic. Biovar Antiqua is thus postulated to be the oldest, the other two having evolved from it. See Theilman and Cate, "A Plague of Plagues."

medieval plague ship, with its hidden payload of rats and fleas.[12] Whatever their etiology, today's potential epidemic catastrophes fill the news reports as well as the medical journals with a newly minted and exotic working vocabulary: mad cow disease, hantavirus, MDR-TB, X-TB, Legionnaires' disease, dengue, Marburg virus, "flesh-eating" bacteria, SARS, "super" germs, Ebola, bird flu. African outbreaks of Rift Valley fever represent the threat of fatal infections contracted from livestock—the inevitable consequence of animal domestication—whether through raw milk, a mosquito bite, or other exposure to animal fluids. Mad cow disease—officially, bovine spongiform encephalopathy (BSE) or, in the form transmitted to humans by the ingestion of contaminated beef, variant Creutzfeldt-Jakob disease (VCJD)—raises the novel specter of a class of like "infections" caused by prions rather than by bacteria or viruses.[13] Of this dire catalogue of potential threats to global health, "bird flu" has of late been most alarming. Analysis of lung tissue from victims of the 1918 flu outbreak suggests that the H5N1 avian virus now smoldering in the human population is genetically related to the 1918 strain that killed some fifty million people (perhaps as many as one hundred million) worldwide.[14]

In some places in the American West (among other hot spots around the globe), the bacterium responsible for the plague has now reemerged from the underground rodent reservoirs in which the organism still survives— and from which it can never be completely rooted out. Every year, some

---

12. On the latter possibility, see Groopman, "Medicine on Mars" (39): "Cosmic rays could also cause dangerous mutations in the bacteria and fungi that normally colonize our skin, mouth, and intestine, as well as the ambient ones within the spaceship.... Microbial flora could change into virulent pathogens that might not respond to antibiotics." Less far-fetched is the suspicion, now confirmed by the connection between peptic ulcers and *Helicobacter pylori* bacteria, that such "plagues" as cancer and coronary artery disease may in some forms be caused by infectious agents; see Judith Hooper, "A New Germ Theory."

13. Mad cow disease, or VCJD, appears to be caused by "naked protein particles, without a stitch of nucleic acid." These particles are physically "misfolded" in an abnormal way and can impose their "brand" of misfolding on the normal protein by simple contact" (Grady, "Ironing Out the Wrinkles in the Prion Strain Problem"). The newly discovered cause of this class of bizarre afflictions forces us to rethink the basic definition of infectious disease on two counts. The prion is, strictly speaking, not alive; and its "infectious" property seems to work by physical contact alone, in the way that crystals will cause new crystals of the same configuration to form around them. One implication of such evidence, suggesting as it does that the idea of infection must be extended to nonliving substances and nonbiological processes, is that we must rethink the distinction in kind between computer viruses and viruses proper.

14. Gina Kolata, "Experts Unlock Clues to Spread of 1918 Flu Virus," *New York Times*, October 6, 2005.

thousands of unlucky individuals worldwide fall ill after coming into contact with infected prairie dogs, ground squirrels, or other rodents. Today's victims are in no less peril than their medieval forebears unless promptly diagnosed and treated with the right antibiotics. As if to complete a pattern in disease history now clearly revealed as cyclical, a 2008 scientific article entitled "Plague: Past, Present, and Future" reports on three recent international meetings in which it was concluded that "climate change might increase the risk of plague outbreaks where plague is currently endemic and new plague areas might arise"; that "remarkably little is known about the dynamics of plague in its natural reservoirs and hence about changing risks for humans"; and, therefore, that "plague should be taken much more seriously by the international community than appears to be the case."[15]

A New Perspective

The obscure origins and sheer numbers of these new, old, and previously unrecognized diseases, coupled with what we are soberly advised is the very real threat that any one of them could ignite a massive conflagration if given the tiniest spark, have radically changed our perspective on the "plague," then and now. The "gay cancer" of the early 1980s—first thought to be the peculiar affliction of homosexuals in San Francisco and New York, and then improbably redefined as a disease of homosexuals, hemophiliacs, heroin addicts, and Haitians (the "four H's")—expanded into the national affliction of the late eighties, at which point we also came to realize the major role of HIV infection on the world stage of infectious disease. Despite important advances in the treatment and prevention of AIDS in the United States and western Europe, HIV infection continues to spread at alarming rates in Africa, Asia, and the former Soviet Union, accounting yearly for over three million deaths worldwide. According to a Web site that keeps a running tally of AIDS deaths in sub-Saharan Africa, by mid-2008 more than thirty-five million people in the region had died of the disease, and more than fifty million others had contracted it.[16] In comparison, combat deaths on all sides

15. Nils Chr. Stenseth et al., "Plague: Past, Present, and Future," PLoS Medicine 5, no. 1 (2008): e3; doi:10.1371/journal.pmed.0050003.

16. See http://www.kwanzaakeepers.com/africa-aids-death-count/africa-aids-death-count.htm.

in the two world wars of the twentieth century are estimated at twenty-five million. At a moment when postmodern theory has taken up the banner of "globalization," we realize that the microbes were there before us.

None of this will be unfamiliar to Africanists (not to mention the people whose history they write) or to students of such phenomena as Europe's early modern expansion into the New World. African political history has always been a kind of palimpsest with an underlying history of epidemic and endemic disease. The HIV infection now pandemic in much of the continent has joined (and in some cases complicated) the suite of persistent diseases that claim millions of African lives every year: viral or bacterial diseases such as dengue and infant diarrhea; parasitic infections causing malaria, schisto-somiasis, and onchocerciasis (river blindness); and a host of others. We tend to think of Africa today as a disease exporter. But in the nineteenth century, along with imported human infections, the "cattle plague" rinderpest raced ahead of the Europeans who inadvertently introduced it to the continent. By wiping out the vast herds of sub-Saharan Africa, this enzootic paved the way for the Dutch and English occupation, not only by starving out native peoples, but by unraveling the fabric of cultures whose economic and ritual life was based in the possession of cattle. Thus, rinderpest offers a comparative case study of the social disruption caused by plagues past and to come.

In Africa, as elsewhere, disease has also been the avant-garde of military occupations and the perennial camp follower of human (and animal) population movements.[17] We know that Rome was weakened as much by a series of devastating epidemics as by any other cause to which the fall of the empire is attributed.[18] It should no longer come as a surprise even to those schooled to believe that the Spanish Americas were "conquered" by a few stalwart *conquistadores*, or the North American colonies "settled" by tiny bands of the devout, that in fact the native Americans they displaced fell by the millions to diseases that accompanied the Europeans on their voyages, chiefly smallpox, to which the indigenous populations had no im-

---

17. On the impact of disease on the colonial history of Africa, see Scott, "The Murrain Now Known as Rinderpest": : "The pandemic that changed the fauna of Africa entered the continent in 1887 at Massawa with Indian cattle for the Italian army. The cattle were infected and the disease swept from the Horn of Africa west to the Atlantic and south to the Cape of Good Hope. The Ethiopians lost 95% of their cattle and most of the human population starved to death."

18. See Karlen, *Man and Microbes*, 69–77.

munity.[19] It is now believed that, remarkably, the native population of the New World—a region containing some of the world's largest cities in pre-Columbian times—was reduced by as much as 90 percent between 1492 and 1600, a loss in absolute terms of about one-fifth of the total number of humans on the globe before the explorers set sail.

To see our own vulnerability reflected in these historical events—to realize that we cannot maintain the comforting distinction between "us" and "them"—is to regain a basic knowledge of the human condition that the advancement of Western medicine had allowed us, for a time, to forget. Unobstructed by borders, as by cultural and economic differences, infectious disease creates for itself a level pathogenetic playing field, consolidating its territory into a global village of potential victims. Just as geologists know that the earth is in an interglacial period, epidemiologists argue on no less certain grounds that in the *longue durée* of epidemiological time, we may be nearing the end of a (historically brief) intermission between global pandemics.[20] The lesson for us, however, is not merely that our health may be imperiled, or indeed that in large parts of the world, even now "there is no health." More fundamentally, we have been compelled by events to revise the narrative of medicine itself.

Revising the Narrative

Although more details have come to light in the research of medical historians, the fact of the plague in its early modern recurrences is amply documented in the historical record, including in the meticulous account of the number of its victims as recorded in the English bills of mortality. These have been long known, and it is not my intention (or within my expertise) to offer new evidence. Yet if plague occurs, necessarily, in the realm of wordless agony for those afflicted by it, and if its depredations are said to be

19. An authoritative survey is McNeill, *Plagues and Peoples*, chap. 5, "Transoceanic Exchanges, 1500–1700."

20. John M. Barry's *The Great Influenza* concludes, like most other Cassandran works in the field (e.g., Richard Preston's 1994 book *The Hot Zone*), that "another pandemic not only can happen. It almost certainly will happen" (449)—unless the World Health Organization and governments remain vigilant and respond promptly with massive resources (a fond hope). In the same vein, Wendy Orent warns that "the potential for a lethal weapon, another Black Death, is still there, in the stocks and storehouses of the former Soviet Union" (*Plague*, 227).

unspeakable, so, too, historical narratives have until recently left it largely unspoken. As Hayden White has taught a generation of his (sometimes reluctant) colleagues, historians seek to accommodate the facts to the orderly structures of narrative.[21] Their purpose classically has been to find the threads running through the fabric of events: the achievements of great men, lines of cause and effect, logics of development and principles of change, patterns of growth and decay, generic templates (epic histories, tragic histories), stories with a beginning, a middle, and an end whose unfolding reveals the success or failure of human initiatives. What counts as evidence is what fits into the shape of the story; what doesn't fit tends to drop out of the account as insignificant or merely coincidental. By their nature as forms of consequential narrative, historical accounts cannot easily accommodate the disruptive, the quirky, the inexplicable—in short, events that have not been coded as properly historical and that can only be read, or ignored, as an interruption in the order of things. Medieval and Renaissance narratives fit epidemics into history, however problematically, by subsuming them into an overarching providential design; they are imagined to be extraordinary in origin but inserted (by God) into the natural order, enlisted as the effect whose cause is sin, and whose function is both punitive and therapeutic. That such accounts will no longer seem sufficient (to most readers of this book) reflects both the fragility of the theological argument—a theme I will pursue below—and the subsequent de-theologizing of disease by medical science. But the erasure of epidemics as a historical subject in the older sense has also left them little place in post-Renaissance, secular historiographies. Classical historical narrative cannot easily deal with the extraordinary because its purpose is to find an order, even if no longer to reveal a purposive design, in the historical record, and disease no longer fits into that order.

I overstate White's case, but it is worth noting that the two tropes White considers fundamental to historical narrative, metaphor and metonymy, are both figures of connection. Whether by similarity or adjacency, they draw things together, leaving no empty space in the account for the (unaccountably) disjunctive. The proof of White's contention lies in the absence of infectious disease from older histories of the rise and fall of empires. Whig

---

21. See White's *Metahistory: The Historical Imagination in Nineteenth-Century Europe* (1975); and *The Content of the Form: Narrative Discourse and Historical Representation* (1987).

histories chart the gradual perfection of human institutions, a teleology that would be impeded by too-close attention to epidemic calamities. Military histories record victories and defeats while acknowledging at most coincidentally that in all European wars up to and including World War II, more combatants were felled by disease than by sword or gun. Closer to the concerns of this book, literary histories of the English seventeenth century seldom note that nearly every author in the period from Shakespeare to Milton lived through (or died from) a major outbreak of the plague.

Now, under a revised historical paradigm—one that brings infectious disease into the realm of the ordinary—epidemics count as historical forces, drawn into the matrix of explanation from which they were previously excluded except in histories of medicine as such.[22] Machiavelli's view of history presages this development insofar as his narrative is open to the significant operations of fortune. In *The Prince*, the arc of Cesare Borgia's brilliant career is suddenly deflected by the untimely death of his father, and then, as unlucky chance would have it, by his own illness. Rather than regarding the latter misfortune as an anomaly (or a divine punishment), Machiavelli regards Cesare's disease as a historical event, ordinary and consequent, foreseeable even if unpredictable as to the moment of its appearance. Machiavelli (and, indeed, Montaigne, who befriends his kidney stone as an important co-author of his life history) can be enlisted as a precursor of postmodern disease historians. Disease historiography proper—in practice, an amalgam of social history and historical epidemiology—would, however, have to await the invention of narrative forms crafted for that specific purpose. The "triumph of modern medicine" underwrites one such narrative, only just discredited; more recently, as we have seen, "the coming plague" provides its ironic or apocalyptic counterpart. None of these forms bears the stamp of necessity, and the ones that today seem most congruent with reality will themselves be reconfigured in time. Catastrophe theory, chaos theory, and ecology, as well as new horizons in epidemiology itself, are likely to offer scientistic models for new forms of disease narrative. Needless to say, literary

---

22. Among the latter, the indispensable works include Roy Porter, *Disease, Medicine and Society in England, 1550–1860*; and Nancy G. Siraisi, *Medieval and Early Renaissance Medicine*. See also A. W. Sloan, *English Medicine in the Seventeenth Century*; and Ole Peter Grell and Andrew Cunningham, eds., *Medicine and the Reformation*.

theory can usefully enter the conversation only if it remains aware that its own narratives are implicated in the same process.

In the history of disease narratives, the ancient role of the Galenic physician had been to restore the balance of the body's humors to a harmonious stasis—to preserve the "neutralitie" of which Donne speaks. Diseases ran their own courses, culminating in the Hippocratic "crisis," the peripety that would determine whether in the unfolding plot of his illness the patient recovered or died. Whatever his ministrations, the physician was foremost an interpreter of the signs of the disease, offering a diagnosis and then a prognosis as his reading of its outcome. Correlating the plague of Athens with its political peril, Thucydides extends the idea of a crisis to the health of the state. In the Renaissance the Paracelsian, and then the Baconian, physician assumed a more active practice, in which the strongest weapons available—mercury salts, for example, in the treatment of syphilis—were brought to bear on the hostile forces that had invaded the body. Observation, itself a kind of political neutrality on the part of the physician who saw his role as mediating among the humors of the body, gradually gave way to intervention, *praxis* rather than *gnosis*. Although the plague had overwhelmed all the resources of early modern medicine, this newly militant spirit would eventually score its first triumph in the discovery of inoculation for smallpox in the eighteenth century. In the fullness of time, penicillin would conquer sepsis on the battlefields of World War II, and then, in just a few years following the introduction of streptomycin in 1947 and isoniazid in 1952, the White Plague of tuberculosis would fall before the sword of pharmaceutical research. Vanquished by medicine's steady march toward "the cure," TB suddenly seemed to evaporate like one of those blustering but ultimately powerless giants in *The Faerie Queene*. Contemporary accounts marveled that patients seemingly at death's door were dancing on their beds after a few days on the new "wonder drug." The magic mountain proved to be a magical place after all. The prisoners were all released, and the castles in which they had been confined were dedicated to other purposes—in the case of the Colorado sanitarium in which my father had been a TB patient in the 1930s, to an institute for cancer research, where the battle line would be redrawn to face the next opponent.

As a result of this campaign, each new enemy would be defeated in turn before the Tamburlaines of medical science, and the names of these heroes would be commemorated in their discoveries—Salk and Sabin joining the ranks of Lister, Pasteur, Jenner, and Koch. In the pantheon to the new learning imagined in Bacon's *New Atlantis*, statues would have been erected in honor of these explorers near that of Columbus as heroes of an ongoing epic of discovery. The "flu shot" seemingly guaranteed that influenza epidemics like that of 1918–19 would never recur. Some of us who are now senior enough to have worn the badge of the "Polio Pioneer" will recall visiting a slightly older schoolmate in an iron lung and feeling relieved that the new vaccine would protect us from the same fate. Our own children, in turn, have grown up in a time when the once inevitable childhood afflictions of measles, mumps, and chicken pox, like the former child-killer smallpox, have all been subdued by routine inoculation. All these developments added up to a profound and dramatic improvement in public health (though, once again, only in the first world), reinforcing the triumphalist narrative that gave an overall shape to American history. Was there not good reason to hope that even more powerful discoveries might lead to the eradication of disease itself?

In the last twenty years, however, what had seemed to be the capstone of a Baconian program of medical "advancement" toward a conclusive victory over infectious disease has collapsed under the weight of its own ambition. As I have noted, tuberculosis has returned with a vengeance, and in a form that resists all the usual antibiotics; so has polio, manifesting itself in a variety of debilitating symptoms in patients now in their sixties and seventies who were thought to have recovered from mild cases of the disease in childhood. It is even possible that such residual symptoms are caused iatrogenically, by early forms of the polio vaccine. Ironically, a recent controversial book by the British science writer Edward Hooper argues that the simian immunodeficiency virus first entered the human bloodstream as HIV in the late 1950s by way of a contaminated vial of experimental polio vaccine concocted of monkey's blood and administered to almost a million individuals in the former Belgian Congo.[23] The physician supervising these trials, Hilary Koprowski, was soon overshadowed by Albert Sabin, who licensed the first oral polio vaccine in 1962. If Hooper's allegations were ever to be proven (most AIDS researchers remain skeptical), Koprowski would be credited in

---

23. Hooper, *The River*.

the new *Dunciad* of medical science with inadvertently unleashing a far greater horror than the one he hoped to curb. In the age of AIDS and the growing army of even more formidable adversaries, the epic is revealed to have been a mock-epic all along.

What is required, however, is not only to deconstruct the mythologies of medical science—the last bastion of a Baconian belief in the ameliorative progress of technology—or to revise our calculus of health and disease. So much has already been done for us by circumstance. It is true that on average, we live much longer than our early modern forebears, except if we live in sub-Saharan Africa, where life expectancy has already fallen below forty-five years and is expected to go lower still in the coming decade. In "The First Anniversary," Donne compared the Methuselan years granted to the biblical patriarchs with the brevity of life in his own day. His belief that this decline presaged the death of the world was read as a witty hyperbole by critics a generation ago. Sharing Donne's perspective, we are compelled not only to readjust our view of the human life span, but to reimagine our investment in our "own" bodies—bodies that can be claimed and horribly transformed with catastrophic suddenness. The bounded, proprietary subject of the liberal imagination is more likely to be violated by microbial incursion than by state surveillance. We rediscover our "elements," as George Herbert writes in "Church-Monuments," in this form of elementary schooling, "which dissolution sure doth best discern."[24] Like those self-possessed but exquisitely vulnerable Vesalian figures with their entrails exposed, we are "open" to infection. When the fragile wall of the immune system crumbles, as it does in AIDS patients, the integrity of the body is threatened with not only foreign invasion, but domestic subversion by organisms with which we normally live on friendly terms. Our "individual" well-being now seems no less precarious than in an age when infectious disease constantly threatened to transform death from an isolated experience—the final demarcation of "individuality" itself—into a communal event. In the long view, it may turn out that the period of apparent improvement in world health between the seventeenth century's plague years and our own will prove to be an anoma-

---

24. Herbert, *Works*, 65. See also Michael Neill on the plague as a terrifying force of indistinction and undifferentiation, collapsing "all differences between high and low, kinsfolk and strangers, humans and animals, and ultimately between people and things" (*Issues of Death*, 20).

lous blip in the history of epidemic disease. Thus, we are also compelled to reimagine our connection to the rest of the human community, including historical communities such as that of Donne and Jonson. Beyond that, we must acknowledge our citizenship in the microbial community, where, we now realize, we have always lived in an uneasy symbiosis. If anything, understanding this mode of interspecific citizenship should be a mission of a plague ecocriticism.

I say "reimagine" where the scientist would say "rethink" to emphasize that a crucial dimension of this project lies in the province of the poet rather than the physician (although frequently, as in the case of Thomas Lodge or Sir Thomas Browne, the two inhabit the same person). The literary examples entwined in the brief narrative I have just given are not meant to be decorative. They are meant to suggest that bits and pieces of imaginative invention have formed the very substance of the "story of medicine." Infectious disease "presents" itself (to use the medical term) symptomatically, as the outward sign of some mysterious kernel of being beyond our immediate perception or understanding. All attempts to penetrate it, even the professional efforts of medical investigators, involve the imaginative effort to represent it to ourselves. Not only does it demand interpretation by a trained reader of the body, of the microscope slide, or, more recently, of the computer-generated simulation. Itself unspeaking, it demands to be *spoken for*, to be accommodated in a discursive framework before it can be addressed by the human community at large. The imaginative interface between the human and the microbial populations will be one object of my inquiry: a medium that I will want to regard less as an open window onto the "real" nature of disease than as a speculative mirror of our own fears and desires.

We cannot be sure what story we will tell ourselves now that the very conditions of our experience have changed so radically for the first time in recent decades. It may be that, in time, our narrative about the conquest of disease will seem as overtly factitious as that by which early modern Europe confidently interpreted every "dreadful visitation" of the plague as punishment for sin. One rather startling perspective is suggested by the title of a 1996 lecture by Stephen J. Gould, "The Accidental Presence of the Humans in the Age of Bacteria." The late paleontologist reminded his audience that bacterial life on this planet has a history that long precedes, and that in all likelihood will long outlast, our own unlikely appearance as a species. In the bacterial chronicles, the human race would figure, briefly, as a set of opportunities and obstacles to the propagation of their own culture (which has, since the origins of life, constituted the largest biomass on the planet). Disease historian William H. McNeill notes wryly, but with an underlying seriousness, that given the invasive and exploitative tendencies of our own species over the past half millennium or so, "it is not absurd to class the ecological role of humankind in its relationship to other life forms as a disease."[25] We must assume that these chronicles, unlike ours, would have no particular teleological end in view except the survival of their own kind in an ever-changing and unpredictable environment. Bacterial visitors to the American Museum of Natural History in New York would immediately appreciate the exhibit on the evolution of life as it has been redesigned under the influence of Gould and his like-minded colleagues, to allow one to wander at will among various interlinked chains (or claddings) of evolution without forcing upon the viewer any particular path leading from "lower" forms of life to "higher" ones (i.e., us).

But our master narratives are not so easily displaced, even by such decentering provocations as Gould's alternative bacterial history. Deeply rooted, overdetermined, and (as science would say of its own theories) capable of great explanatory power, such narratives are not *merely* fictive in the sense that they can be exposed as the figments of a whimsical imagination and replaced by truer stories when they are confronted by a new set of facts. We have understood since Kuhn that in the history of science, disturbing facts are more likely to be retrofitted into existing paradigmatic narratives—a process not simply mistaken or motivated by sheer stubbornness, but one that engages a basic algorithm of human understanding. Seventeenth-century theological narratives are especially revealing when, put to their last and most challenging test, they begin to crack under the strain, to be absorbed and succeeded, though never entirely replaced, by the secular heroic narratives more congenial to a later age. In the nineteenth century, tuber-

---

25. McNeill, *Plagues and Peoples*, 19. The point has been made even more forcefully by Jared Diamond in *Collapse: How Societies Choose to Fail or Succeed* (2005). The processes of deforestation and desertification, the extinction of animal species, the destruction of millions of people by war and the importation of disease, and more recently the acceleration of global warming—for all of which humankind has been intentionally or inadvertently responsible—are indistinguishable in their results from a planetary pandemic.

culosis was accommodated as the "White Plague" into the history of the "Black Plague." The hunt for "the cure"—or, in the case of syphilis, for the "magic bullet"—refashioned scientific research into a romance quest. Even Boccaccio's famous "eyewitness" description of the plague in Florence at the beginning of *The Decameron* may be borrowed from Lucretius, who would likely have based his own account on that of Thucydides. As such, it would not necessarily be a misrepresentation, willful or otherwise, by an author who preferred Lucretius to his own observation, but a revealing case study of what Ernst Gombrich called "making" by "matching." By characterizing Ebola, Marburg, and other modern plagues as "new adversaries," my own account also participates in the very narrative of epic conquest from which it otherwise tries to maintain a safe distance. Our own implication in these ancient and durable stories may serve as a reminder that, in fact, any attempt to recuperate the imagined forms of infectious disease must itself grow out of a sympathetic and self-reflective engagement of the critical imagination.

The Atomic Virus

As I was beginning this book in Florence, a newspaper headline caught my eye: "Aids, flagello del terzo millennio"—AIDS, the scourge of the third millennium. The story announces that in response to the rampant epidemic in his country, the president of Kenya had (finally) declared a state of national disaster and instituted wartime emergency measures.[26] Written in a city with its own vivid cultural memory of the Black Death, the article condenses our cultural narrative of AIDS into a fascinating account whose tangle of associations leads us back to the foundational narratives of this book. The explosion of AIDS—like an "atomic virus," as the article goes on to say—comes at a time when we also face an uncertain number of other, equally volatile viral, bacteriological, and (perhaps even more mysterious) crystalline agents ready to produce a tragedy of global proportions. The headline proposes a historical scheme in which every millennium must have its "scourge." The *flagello* reattaches our current imagination of pandemic disease to its medieval predecessor and recalls the memory of those Florentine flagellants by whose self-inflicted penance the city was to be freed

---

26. *La Nazione*, November 27, 1999.

of the plague. The *virus atomico* envisages pandemic disease as the coming apocalypse, the third-millennial successor to the second-millennial threat of nuclear war. In this context, the hybrid specter of an atomic virus immediately evokes an older Christian reading of the plague as the scourge of God: *non c'è arresto il flagello*, "the scourge has not ceased." Reviving a further medieval association between bubonic plague and leprosy, the article goes on to declare that Africa, Asia, and even the republics of the former Soviet Union have become *lazzaretti a cielo aperto*: in Italy, plague victims were often quarantined in leprosariums, but in the mind of the correspondent, vast regions of the earth have now turned into "open-air leper colonies." The otherwise pointless connection serves to stigmatize the third world as backward and unclean; Kenya is the scene of a *danse macabre* where Epidemic Death, transplanted from medieval Europe to a still-medieval Africa, "reaps" (*sta falciando*) five hundred souls a day. Beyond that, the connection seems based on the unspoken fear that the contamination, unconfined in these poor and teeming countries, could affect the atmosphere itself, producing a kind of bio–nuclear winter that would be an updated version of the early modern theory of the miasmal medium of infection.

The implicit logic of an "atomic virus," furthermore, depends not only on the mass destruction of which these tiny particles (atoms, viruses) are capable, but on the idea common to both of their uncontrolled global proliferation that must be "arrested." As we have tended to believe that the spread of nuclear technology should be restrained by international law, we find the same double meaning lurking in the Italian verb *arrestare* as in its English cognate. If AIDS has not been stopped, then there must be a crime somewhere; someone must be responsible for its rampages, someone who deserves to be "arrested," and who, as the guilty victim of the criminal disease, will have been duly "arrested" by it. This thought surfaces in the article's analysis of the circumstances that are said to have caused a dramatic increase of HIV infection in the former Soviet Union: unemployment among the young and the closing of factories, leading to depression and intravenous drug use, leading in turn to the spread of AIDS. Depression prompts our sympathy, but drug use casts blame as much on the infected as on the economic system that failed them. The retribution seems just if we are convinced that the Soviet Union, before it became "former," bore a large responsibility for expanding the nuclear club to include the West's potential enemies in Asia and, perhaps, Africa as well. It is as if, in the third millennium, the cold war will finally have been won through the destruction of Russia and its clients—not by the atom bomb, but by its viral equivalent.

It does not seem coincidental in this context that the article printed in the same newspaper just below the one I have been discussing, also unsigned but likely written by the same correspondent covering events in the third world, reports on clashes that "have exploded" again (*sono riesplosi*) between Catholics and Muslims in Ambon, the capital of the Indonesian province of Maluku. The news of yet another disaster in that part of the world is familiar and unremarkable, and except for the inadvertent echo of "exploding" violence and the cataloguing of the resultant death toll, the article has nothing to do with the AIDS story above it. The atomic virus is exploding in some parts of a medievalized third world, and sectarian conflict in others. Yet what reader of the two articles can fail to be struck by the photograph illustrating the second story: a scene of bodies being removed from *una fossa comune*, a common pit into which the victims of the massacre were thrown? Symbolically, what is being unearthed here in the powerful (and, as I will argue, traumatic) image of the pit are the pictorial remains of other mass burials, narratives reminding us of the common fate of Holocaust victims and victims of the plague, as well as that of Christians and Muslims in the killing fields of Indonesia. For U.S. readers, the image of full body bags thrown in a heap, particularly in an Asian setting, inevitably recalls the waste of human lives in the Vietnam War, itself staged as a latter-day crusade against the spread of communism. This war, like the concurrent "war" against infectious disease on the medical front, was to prove in the end that even the most advanced Western technology was—is, as the "war on terror" now demonstrates anew—helpless in the face of an insidious and determined opponent. Indeed, a cursory glance at the page in *La Nazione* may yield the initial impression that the photograph is intended to illustrate the havoc of AIDS, rather than the scourge of religious warfare, on a virulent third-world battlefield resistant to any therapeutic intervention.

From the point of view of medieval and Renaissance plague times, these very contemporary news accounts resolve themselves into a strange but powerful historical transparency. To explain the force of such narratives, whether in our period or in their early modern origins, should be one of the chief aims of studying plague literature. The following chapters attempt to construct their own tentative narrative about seventeenth-century English plague writing and the political and theological contexts from which it emerges. My purpose is to engage a selection of familiar literary works (by Jonson, Donne, Pepys, and Defoe) in those contexts, and my assumption in doing so is that, taken together, these texts can be read more productively as instances in a discursive history of the plague than in other generic configurations. My discussion develops three related arguments. The first is that the strenuous (and ultimately hopeless) project of elaborating a consistent and psychologically satisfying plague theodicy can be read as a traumatic symptom of the plague experience itself. Second, the imaginary of the plague in England is markedly different from that found in Catholic Europe insofar as the Reformation deprives its adherents not only of the legion of saints whose role was to mediate and ameliorate epidemic disease, but of the entire pictorial regime by which their therapeutic interventions could be represented. The consequence, I argue, is in this respect a "darkened," unmediated theology that confronts the plague as an infliction of God's Word. The plague is inscribed in the Word, and in a word understood as etymologically identical with the (word for) divine speech—but a word finally and impenetrably mysterious. Finally, I argue that the crisis thereby provoked at the heart of Reformation plague theology will issue, in Pepys and Defoe, in the beginning of our own wrestling with epidemic disease in an increasingly secular mode, yet one that still bears the marks of its theological origins.

CHAPTER 1

Diagnosing
Plague Narratives

The Dog died on the Spot, and we left the Doctor
endeavoring to recover him by the same Operation.
JONATHAN SWIFT, *Gulliver's Travels*

When the philosophers of the last age were first congregated
into the Royal Society, great expectations were raised of the
sudden progress of useful arts; the time was supposed to
be near when engines should turn by a perpetual motion, and
health be secured by the universal medicine. . . . But improvement
is naturally slow. The society met and parted without any visible
diminution of the miseries of life.
SAMUEL JOHNSON, *Idler* 88 (1759)

This book stems from, and responds to, our impending crisis of faith in the ability of medical science to conquer epidemic disease. As I have noted above, I take this to be a Kuhnian as well as a spiritual crisis. In the last twenty years, the "normal science" governing our assumptions about disease (including the way historians write about disease) has been disrupted by worrisome anomalies outside the comfort zone of "problem solving." Once-firm distinctions—as, fundamentally, between sickness and health, or between diseases of the first world and the third world—seem increasingly fragile, as does our ability to demarcate an advancing "frontier" between the known and the unknown, between the natural realms under our control and those beyond the mandate of our rule. By ignoring a large blind spot in its own history as a disease exporter, the colonial West was once able to congratulate itself on pursuing the mission of bringing the benefits of modern medicine and sanitation to pestiferous regions of the globe. Now we find ourselves at a postcolonial moment when—as H. G. Wells foresaw in *The War of the Worlds*—the West lies open to devastating bioinvasions immune to (indeed, abetted by) advanced technology. The exhaustion of a dominant triumphalist paradigm thus brings us nearer a Hippocratic "crisis" in the case history of infectious disease, a skeptical *epoché* in the face of our imperiled confidence in the knowledge whose promise of "victory" seems less and less likely to be fulfilled.

In the case of "The First Anniversary," Donne offers a starting point both more and less skeptical than ours today about the state of our knowledge of disease: "And can there bee worse sicknesse, then to know / That we are never well, nor can be so?"[1] To say that there is "no health," that "we are never well," may be taken as a candid statement of the normative human condition in a premedical age. But to be sick is not the worst of it. According to Donne, there is no "worse sicknesse" than to *know* that we are sick: not only to be knowledgeable about disease (to know what "Physitians say"), or to have the experiential knowledge of our own sickness, or even to suffer the anxieties that attend such knowledge, but to know (as Bacon would also assert, but with a remedy) that knowledge itself is sick. In this light, sickness is itself symptomatic of a more profoundly diseased mode of being, the token of not only the individual's illness, but the infirmity of all things. "When thou knowest this," goes Donne's

---

1. *The Poems of John Donne*, ed. Grierson, 1:234, ll. 93–94. All quotations from Donne's poetry are from this volume and will be given parenthetically in the text by page and line number.

refrain, "thou knowest" the paltriness and corruption of our knowledge of the world, as well as of the world itself.

Yet such knowledge is, paradoxically, both deficient and perfect: deficient of any real power to explain disease, but perfect in the skeptical lesson it teaches us about our limited ability to know. The knowledge that we are "never well" serves as a corrective to our arrogance; we realize that we can know nothing certain even about such mundane matters as, to echo Donne's example, what makes our fingernails grow. Insofar as knowledge recognizes its own diseased state, however, its own inability to know truly, it truly knows the state of human disease. Individual sickness is, for Donne, both the reflection and the consequence of man's original "ruin," when the body and mind fell together. The ruined body and the ruined mind are thus a perfect cognitive match. In the "essential joy" of heaven, the "object" of our knowledge—that is, the knowledge of God—will be "one" with the "wit" by which we come to know that object: "it is both the object, and the wit" ("The Second Anniversary," 264, l. 442). Ironically, amid the essential misery of a fallen, plague-ridden world, the same conditions of knowledge prevail. Our corrupt thinking is perfectly suited to thinking about the state of our own corruption, evident in the physical diseases to which we are prone. In this version of the *docta ignorantia*, disease(d) knowledge is that of a lack, of the absence of the "health" we may find only when disease carries us off. In such a view, furthermore, disease must be seen not as one object of knowledge among many others, but as *the* fundamental subject, the subjective (and subjected) condition from which all other objects are seen, an epistemological as well as a biological infirmity—and at the same time, the source of a somber and unillusioned spiritual strength. It is in this mood that Montaigne approves the first lesson the Mexicans teach their children: "Child, you have come into the world to endure; endure, suffer, and keep quiet."[2] Insofar as the language of medicine and disease underwrites other Renaissance discourses, then plague and the fear of its recurrence—the miasmal cloud under which the Renaissance lives—shadow the experiential ground of that language. Except for the few remaining survivors of the generation of the "Spanish flu," we cannot (yet) "know," as Donne and his generation did, what it was like (or will be like) to live and write in the shadow of a pandemic; but my hope in what follows is to reconstruct at least part of that knowledge.

---

2. "On Experience," in Montaigne, *Complete Essays*, 835.

As another document in the case history of the plague, this book positions itself at the point of unknowing what we thought we knew, or of not yet knowing how any argument made now will be read (or, perhaps, who will be around to read it) in the future. Under our present circumstances, it cannot speak above the fray from a secure vantage point; it must descend from the mountaintop to what Milton called the "subjected" plain, in which we are as much subject to the history we survey as we can claim it as our subject. It must risk being speculative. It seeks to mark its spot by returning to another historical moment uncannily similar to our own, and with a sense of the "miseries of life" among the microbes closer to that of Swift and Johnson than to the optimism of Salk and Sabin. My purpose in this chapter is, first, to bracket the historical period of this study between the London plague epidemics of 1603 and 1665, and then to explore more fully the critical paths that may lead us back to the future.

Plague Times

The Black Death of the fourteenth century, long recognized as a calamity leading to "the transformation of the West," has been the subject of extensive critical investigation in all fields, from religious and economic history to demographics, the law, historical epidemiology, and the history of literature and art.[3] In comparison, and as an object of specifically literary study, the impact of bubonic plague in early modern England has received less attention than it warrants, although the pestilence there and then was by every measure the most pernicious of Renaissance, as well as medieval, infectious diseases—and its consequences were, arguably, no less profound.[4] The epi-

---

3. The phrase quoted is taken from the title of David Herlihy's *The Black Death and the Transformation of the West*. See also, among the vast literature on this subject, Philip Ziegler, *The Black Death*; and Norman F. Cantor, *In the Wake of the Plague: The Black Death and the World It Made*. Authoritative for England is J. F. D. Shrewsbury, *A History of the Bubonic Plague in the British Isles*. Since its publication in 1951, Millard Meiss's *Painting in Florence and Siena after the Black Death* has provoked an ongoing literature on the effect of the medieval plague on Italian art.

4. Two notable contributions to the study of the plague and early modern literature are Michael Neill, *Issues of Death*; and Jonathan Gil Harris, *Sick Economies: Drama, Mercantilism, and Disease in Shakespeare's England*. I am indebted to both, but as these two studies deal primarily with drama, and from points of view different from my own, I see the present study as a complement to theirs in a still-developing field.

demiological facts of the plague are well-known, and stark. Between 1348 and 1370, its first pandemic appearance in Britain (as in the rest of Europe) claimed at least a quarter and perhaps as much as two-thirds of the population, with the highest proportion of deaths in London. It would not be difficult to imagine Chaucer's pilgrims near the end of the century as survivors on their way to the shrine of St. Thomas Becket, who "hem hath holpen, whan that they were seke."[5] Petrarch's outcry in a letter to his brother, "Oh happy people of the future, who have not known these miseries," proved to be shortsighted.[6] The Black Death was succeeded over time—such is the natural history of epidemic disease—by aftershocks of varying intensity. On average, plague deaths tended to peak in London every fifteen or twenty years, the infection reasserting itself once its stock of potential victims had been replenished by births and immigration from the countryside with a new (non-immune) generation, and once the density of the city's population had again reached the necessary threshold for a new epidemic to take root.[7]

---

5. The nine-year-old Chaucer and his parents survived the Black Death unscathed in 1349, but most of his mother Alice's family was wiped out. In Christ Church Cathedral, Canterbury, one of the "miracle windows" in the north aisle of Trinity Chapel shows St. Thomas Becket curing plague victims.

6. Quoted in Deaux, *The Black Death*, 94.

7. See the tables of English epidemic years in Slack, *The Impact of Plague on Tudor and Stuart England*, 61–62. The remarkable resurgence of London's population after each onset of plague was the consequence of immigration as well as natural increase. Between the plague years of 1563 and 1625, the estimated population of London (city and liberties) more than doubled, from 85,000 to 206,000. During the same sixty-year period, London recorded more than 80,000 deaths from the plague. Thus, rather than as a smooth curve, the graph of London's population growth is better imagined in sequences of drastic loss and robust recovery—each spike in the numbers representing the demographic staging area for the next epidemic. See Slack, *Impact of Plague*, table 6.1, p. 151. Those who had been exposed to the pathogen (as nearly every Londoner was) but who had either recovered or never fallen ill would have some degree of immune protection. The mystery of why some escaped unscathed, even in plague houses or attending plague victims, was a vexing theological problem to the age. It is now argued that a genetic mutation that leaves the body unable to produce a protein called CCR5 conferred immunity from *Y. pestis* during the European plague years. That same mutation also seems to provide immunity against HIV infection by closing one of the protein "doors" through which the virus enters white blood cells. That the CCR5 mutation is now much more prevalent in the population of Europe (about 10 percent of Europeans have it) than in other populations suggests a historical link between immunity to the plague and immunity to HIV infection, since over a long period of bubonic epidemics there would have been a significant selective advantage for those individuals carrying the mutation. See S. R. Duncan et al., "Reappraisal of Historical Selective Pressures for the CCR5-Delta 32 Mutation," *Journal of Medical Genetics* 42 (2005): 205–8. Among other suspected grounds of genetic immunity, it is now known that hemochromatosis—a rarer inherited disorder leading to harmful levels of iron in the blood and organ tissues, and present in about .05 percent of the European Caucasian population— also protects against bubonic plague.

It became endemic in the sense that some plague deaths were recorded almost every year between major epidemics, while scattered outbreaks suggest that pockets of infected rats and their fleas could always be found. It appears, however, that new epidemics were imported from the Continent through such ports as Great Yarmouth and Hull. In its recurrences after the initial European pandemic of the fourteenth century, plague joined the ranks of typhus—the "spotted fever" with which it is sometimes confused in contemporary accounts—malaria, syphilis, smallpox, dysentery, influenza, and other, unspecific (or now extinct) fevers and agues, such as the "sweating sickness," that smoldered and periodically flared over the centuries.[8]

Yet among the maladies in this dismal catalogue of early modern suffering, the pestilence held a special terror. The "tertian ague" (malaria) and the pox could be endured, their symptoms at least ameliorated. Syphilis, once it was domesticated in its milder form after its calamitous appearance the century before, provoked an endless number of bad jokes about "French crowns" and missing noses, but even these stigmata could be worn with a certain smug pride as badges of amorous conquest. The "small" pox could leave its survivors horribly disfigured, and few came through unmarked by its scars; but with (only) a 30 percent mortality rate among those who fell ill, the chances of survival were good. Like smallpox, with which the plague was often associated in Renaissance medical discourse, the pestilence was one of many diseases violent in their onset. Its staggering mortality rates tend to conceal the fact that not everyone fell ill—whether through the luck of inhabiting a relatively plague-free parish, or surviving quarantine, or fleeing, or (as was rare) having a natural immunity to the disease. Others fell ill and recovered, whether through the strength of their constitution or the luck of having contracted the infection

---

8. On the importation of plague into England, see Slack, *Impact of Plague*, 66. *Endemic* organisms are those that have reached a modus vivendi with their (human or animal) host populations, neither killing them off completely (which would be tantamount to suicide) nor being themselves killed off by whatever adaptive mechanisms the host may devise. Syphilis, which at first cut a broad swath of destruction across Renaissance Europe, is the classic example of an epidemic disease that evolved into such a less (immediately) destructive relation with its host. The microbiological relationship between an endemic pathogen and its host depends upon a continuing negotiation between the evolutionary ingenuity of the one and the immunological resources of the other. Whether, or when, the *Y. pestis* bacterium will flare into a full-blown epidemic depends on a complex mesh of environmental and demographic factors, including the chance importation of a fresh stock of rats and their attendant fleas from abroad. For example, a decline in the population of rats, whose blood is the preferred food of the fleas carrying the bacterium in their gut, will lead these insects to turn to humans instead for their meal.

in a milder form such as may appear in the latter stages of an epidemic. These fortunate ones could expect a long period of debility before regaining their strength. Compared with its companion diseases, however, plague was overwhelmingly and, for most of its victims, almost immediately fatal.

Plague may attack its victim in three distinct ways, the first two by way of the bite of an infected flea. In its *bubonic* form, it first invades the lymph nodes of the groin, throat, and armpits, producing excruciatingly painful swellings—the characteristic buboes. In its *septicemic* form, it kills more quickly by entering the bloodstream directly from the infected bite. As a *pneumonic* infection, it is transmitted from person to person by the breath, immediately overwhelming the lungs and leading to an even more drastic collapse. Among the malign family of gram-negative rod bacteria to which it belongs, *Y. pestis* replicates with alarming rapidity, producing a new generation every twenty minutes. After a three- to four-day period of incubation, its assault on the body is swift and overwhelming. The patient might linger for several agonizing days or even for a week in some cases, but (as the wits had it) a man might dine with his friends and sup with his ancestors. In one of his plague pamphlets, Thomas Dekker claims to have heard of a man about to send his wife to market who "felt a pricking in his arme, neere the place where once he had a sore, and vpon this, plucking vp his sleeue, he called to his Wife to stay; there was no neede to fetch any thing for him from Market: for, see (quoth he) I am marked: and so shewing Gods Tokens, dyed in a few minutes after."[9] Such stories are common: an apparently healthy individual begins to reel and drops dead in the street, or a traveler retires in good spirits to his bedchamber at an inn, only to be found dead in the morning. Nowadays, plague is treatable with antibiotics if caught in time. Then, in whatever form it struck, mortality rates verged toward 60 percent or even higher. Recurrences always held a unique terror, as much for the thousands of victims they could quickly fell as for the ghastly suffering they brought to the individual.

For reasons still unclear, the major epidemics of the seventeenth century, both in England and on the Continent, were more devastating than any since the Black Death. England was spared the worst of the Italian epidemic of

---

9. Dekker, *A Rod for Run-awaies*, in *The Plague Pamphlets of Thomas Dekker*, ed. Wilson, 159–60. Dekker published six plague pamphlets between 1603 and 1630. All quotations from Dekker are taken from this edition and are cited parenthetically in the text by page number.

1630–31, commemorated in Alessandro Manzoni's great historical novel of 1827, *I Promessi Sposi*. Occasional spikes in plague deaths, as in 1637, were sufficient to close the theaters but did not develop into full-scale epidemics. But major outbreaks in 1563, 1593, 1603, and 1625—the last two coinciding, ominously, with the death of the monarch—decimated the London of Shakespeare, Donne, and Jonson. In 1603, 25,045 plague burials (out of a total of 31,861 burials) were recorded in the city and liberties. As London's total population is estimated at 141,000 for that same year, the plague claimed one in five. In 1625 there were 26,350 plague burials out of a total urban population of 206,000.[10] As one historian notes, a Londoner who, against the odds, succeeded in reaching old age at the time of the Restoration would have witnessed seven such visitations in his or her lifetime.[11] The last and most severe English epidemic struck in 1665. Over that summer, the weekly bills of mortality in London ran into the hundreds and then into the thousands—in all, a casualty list of more than 50,000 that dwarfed the number of fatalities on both sides of the Anglo-Dutch war in that same year. By mid-September, the bills reported a weekly total in London's parishes of 7,165 dead, a figure that "all observers agreed to be a ridiculous underestimate."[12] This is the plague chronicled firsthand in Pepys's diaries and reimagined fifty-seven years later in the docufictional account of Defoe's *Journal of the Plague Year*. As a matter of luck or the protection of providence, everyone who lived to die of other causes between 1348 and the end of the seventeenth century was a plague survivor—just as every American alive in the spring of 1919 could be counted as a survivor of the "Spanish flu," which killed more than half a million people in the United States the previous fall and winter.

We have always known that the plague was there, reflected in the literary as well as the medical record, relentlessly taking its toll in England for more than three hundred years. After what proved to be its last cataclysmic gasp in 1665, it subsided as suddenly as it had appeared—again, for a complex of reasons not completely understood—retreating from the human population

---

10. Slack, *Impact of Plague*, table 6.1, p. 151.

11. Hutton, *The Restoration*, 225. In addition to those mentioned above, another outbreak, slightly less severe, struck London in 1636; and between 1592 and 1665, no year passed without at least some recorded plague deaths, as the infection continued to smolder.

12. Ibid., 226.

into its steady-state enzootic habitat of vermin and fleas.[13] For us, however—
that is, for those of us living in a post- (or pre-) plague age—the force of its
presence in the early modern period and its continuing impact even in periods
of intermission have been difficult to gauge. We know that an epidemic, or the
fear of one, would close the theaters on the presumption that their densely
packed audiences would turn the public playhouses into cesspits of contagion.
Mercutio's curse of "a plague on both your houses" conjures up the specter
of domestic quarantine, one of the few weapons available to public health
authorities: at the first sign of the disease in a household, all would be shut in
under guard, the (temporarily) healthy as well as the stricken, to rot together.
As if in fulfillment of Mercutio's wish, the tragedy of the Montagues and the
Capulets is precipitated when the messenger dispatched to Romeo by Friar
Lawrence is waylaid by the "searchers" and "[s]eal'd up" in a house where it was
suspected that "the infectious pestilence did reign" (5.2.8–11).[14] At this moment, Shakespeare's playgoer might well recall the "star-cross'd lovers" of the
prologue to Act I, since in the 1590s it is still possible to believe that the pestilence is caused by some disastrous conjunction in the heavens. Plague also
rages, offstage, in Jonson's *The Alchemist*; onstage, the household is turned upside down because the master, like all who could afford to do so, has fled to the
relative safety of the countryside. The intramural carnivalesque in Lovewit's
house reflects the larger social disorder feared by the authorities. Plague also
provides the sad occasion of Jonson's most heartfelt epigram, on the death of
his seven-year-old son in the outbreak of 1603—my subject in chapter 4. By a
pun that is no mere trope of rhetoric, plague is said to be "communicable," like
poetry, through the breath. In "The Canonization," Donne's speaker invokes,
even as he facetiously dismisses, an underlying anxiety about the mysterious
sources of bubonic infection by insisting that his own Petrarchan "heats" have
added no new victims "to the plaguie Bill" (14, ll. 14–15).

---

13. Reasons advanced for the cessation of the plague after the seventeenth century (excluding the
epidemic of 1720 in Marseilles, which prompted Defoe's *Journal of the Plague Year*) are all tentative: im-
proved sanitary conditions and more effective public health measures; the replacement across Europe
of the black rat by the brown Norway rat, a creature much less susceptible to bubonic infection; and,
in London, the salutary effects of the Great Fire—which consumed a city of wood and thatch, ideal
habitats for rats and fleas. These were replaced by a relatively inhospitable city of brick and stone.

14. All quotations from Shakespeare are from *The Riverside Shakespeare*, ed. Evans et al., and are
cited parenthetically in the text by act, scene, and line number.

While Renaissance literary historians have in the past tended to treat such evidence anecdotally, if at all, it has long been understood by social historians, economists, and demographers on the basis of more systematic studies that not only the Black Death but its epidemic recurrences throughout the early modern period were the cause of deep upheavals in England.[15] In these fields, as well as in the history of medicine, the bibliography on the plague has grown exponentially in the past ten years. Historians of medieval and Renaissance art have always been made aware of the plague, if only by the images of its horrors preserved everywhere in the visual record.[16] Stage historians have written of it as a defining circumstance of Elizabethan theatrical life.[17] Yet the broader effect of the plague on the English literary imagination of the seventeenth century—not just on the dramatists but on More and Bacon, on the poetry of Donne and Jonson, or on the work of later writers like Milton and Pepys—is only now being taken into account, by critics like Jonathan Gil Harris, Rebecca Totaro, Margaret Healy, and Bryon Grigsby.[18] These studies take up a variety of texts and deploy a diversity of critical interests, but together they fill in the portrait of an age and its literary production marked by the threat and the reality of the plague. Offering what follows as a contribution to that ongoing project, I ask my own question: At our remove, with what critical instruments are we to gauge the deep impact of a long-gone cataclysm in its literary remains?

"Construct Plague"

As a cultural phenomenon, the plague makes itself known to us only by the images and narratives, the poetry, the medical reports, and the theological

---

15. The most authoritative recent source for the later period in England's plague history is Slack's *Impact of Plague*. For a broader European perspective, see Braudel, *The Mediterranean and the Mediterranean World in the Age of Philip II*, vol. 1, especially 332–34.

16. On Italian art and the plague in the Renaissance, see Bailey et al., *Hope and Healing*.

17. See especially Barroll, *Politics, Plague, and Shakespeare's Theater*, chaps. 3 and 4.

18. Most recent accounts of Tudor and Stuart plague refer back to F. P. Wilson's pioneering *The Plague in Shakespeare's London* (1927), which has a great deal to say about the archive of plague documents—some of it disputed by more recent historians—but very little about Shakespeare. The works I cite have all appeared in recent years, most of them as this book was in progress: see Harris, *Sick Economies*; Totaro, *Suffering in Paradise*; Healy, *Fictions of Disease in Early Modern England*; and Grigsby, *Pestilence in Medieval and Early Modern English Literature*.

disputes through which it is mediated. These are the objects of our study, the incomplete and depleted fossil records of plague as a lived experience. Whatever its microbial nature (except to modern bacteriologists and epidemiologists, and arguably even to them), the significance of infectious disease, including the very assumption that disease has a significance, is embedded in the history of its cultural construction. Insisting that "the infected individual is never value-neutral," Sander Gilman sees the symptoms of disease as a "complex text" read, and to be read, "within the conventions of an interpretive community" and "in the light of earlier, powerful readings of what are understood to be similar or parallel texts."[19] In Gilman's view, diseases are coded so as to represent our own deepest fears of dissolution and contamination, and to contain these fantasies by projecting them onto the body of the sufferer as a demonized "other"—or by framing them within the boundaries of art. A recent book by Sheldon Watts insists on speaking of "Construct leprosy" and "Construct yellow fever" to emphasize the sense in which our understanding of such diseases is *made*, a thickly elaborated *poesis*, while remaining still at a representational remove from the thing itself.[20] For Dekker and other seventeenth-century plague writers, as we shall see, plague is read as a tragedy played out in the city at large, as if with the closing of the theaters the "drama" had moved to a larger venue and enrolled all of London in the cast. Strict constructionist arguments will assume (with a Donnean skepticism about the limits of our knowledge) that the thing-in-itself cannot be seen, or rather can be seen only *as* and *through* the cumulative archive of its representation.

Indeed, that archive takes on a life of its own. Descriptions of epidemics and even "firsthand" accounts may be indebted more directly to stories of the same kind than to immediate (and unmediated) experience—whether because (as I shall argue below) these "unspeakable" events recur in the form of unassimilable traumatic reenactments or, more generally, because even reports of direct experience have a generic history. Thus, each subsequent account of a plague—including accounts of smallpox, tuberculosis, or AIDS—will, self-consciously or not, register the history of topoi, sentiments, descriptions, moralizations, and so forth that characterize plague narratives in general. A scoffer is secure in his own safety, or refuses to assist a plague victim, and then is

---

19. Sander Gilman, *Disease and Representation*, 7.
20. Watts, *Epidemics and History*, xv.

himself struck down. An impious reveler stumbles drunkenly into a plague pit, and his cries from the grave terrify the sexton. One study notes that such anonymous, and suspiciously similar, accounts during the 1665 epidemic often begin with stock phrases like "As Told by a Citizen who continued all the while in London, never made public before."[21] Such "true stories" migrate from text to text; some made their way into Defoe's *Journal* decades later. Ann G. Carmichael finds that Renaissance Italian plague anecdotes ("a hermit encounters an old woman whom he recognizes as the plague personified . . .") and xenophobic origin stories (the plague is introduced by an itinerant merchant or a fugitive from someplace else; a widow sees a suspicious man in a dark cloak seemingly smearing some substance on a wall) are retold as late as the twentieth century. According to one cautionary tale, a servant in a plague infirmary seduces a young girl and, as a punishment for his lapse, dies of the disease two days later even though he had long worked among the stricken with no ill effects. The details may vary, and the disease may itself change from plague to cholera, but the basic stories persist. Carmichael argues that such mini-narratives—of which the plague-guilt of the Jews is the most pernicious—"permit continuity in the collective memory of plague between epidemics, even if they are widely separated in time."[22] Often passed down from mouth to mouth as part of an oral plague tradition, these "memories" linger "in the less secure space of unwritten tradition, retaining a power that official memories could not always control." Carmichael sees Defoe, too, turning such "urban legends" into "official history." They infiltrate and supplement the written record of successive epidemics to produce a retrospective "narrative order on a past plague, assigning its beginning, middle and end, and selecting which facts and memories are needed to capture the essence or meaning of the plague."[23]

Since antiquity, infectious disease has always been seen as harboring an essence, its visible symptoms the sign of some possession, impurity, or lack otherwise undisclosed. It inscribes itself on the body from without, or breaks through the wall of the body from within in order to "speak for" some inner secret ("never made public before"). Especially in earlier periods when the actual processes of disease were a matter of conjecture, their "meaning" could only be

---

21. The "anonymous account" is cited in Moote and Moote, *The Great Plague*, xix.
22. Carmichael, "The Last Past Plague," 132–33, 146–47, 156.
23. Ibid., 134, 159.

woven from the threads of available narratives. Seventeenth-century divines preached that the symptoms of the bubonic plague (whether the victim's swollen lymph glands or the black and purple skin blotches that characterized the latter stages of the infection) were the "tokens" of God's anger. These black marks were taken as the evidence and proof of that anger, though not, evidently, of the reasons for it. Plague was the instrument of retribution for some sin otherwise unaccounted for—and, as will become clear, a form of writing that both demands and resists interpretation. Revising the later Romantic narrative that associated the "White Plague" with a heightened artistic sensibility, Kafka believed that his illness was "not primarily tuberculosis, but a sign of my general bankruptcy."[24] Even in the 1980s, the deep-seated belief that infectious disease must have a providential meaning made it possible (for some) to see AIDS as the consequence of, and punishment for, a closeted sexual deviance brought to the light by the cancerous lesions of Kaposi's sarcoma. By the same token(s), hemophiliacs and children who contracted the infection were "innocent" victims falsely indicted by those same outward marks. The persistence of such built-in judgments, along with the tendency to regard the symptoms of disease as a site of moral revelation, is perhaps the most enduring legacy of pre-modern plague theology in our current disease culture.

Conventional (and inevitable) as such a constructivist view may be, it places us in the same diagnostic position as that of early modern physicians, working only with the visible tokens of plague culture. Yet this necessary framing of the material makes it possible to interrogate the language of infectious disease at an even more basic level, beginning with the word "disease" itself as the binary partner of "health." If, in Donne's terms, there is no health, then there can be no disease. In other terms—those of the evolutionary biologist—the very origin of complex cellular life can be characterized as an infectious process. Prokaryotic bacteria (i.e., those lacking a nucleus) evolved into eukaryotic bacteria (nucleated cells, and the building blocks of all more advanced forms of life) between 1.6 and 2.1 billion years ago, when these more primitive forms were "invaded" by viruses and other smaller particles that took up residence in the "host" organism. This same symbiotic ecology on a much larger scale facilitates the digestion of our food, which feeds a "healthy" supply of bacteria in our gut before we ourselves can take nourishment from the leavings of their

---

24. Quoted in Sontag, *"Illness as Metaphor" and "AIDS and Its Metaphors,"* 44.

repast (resident bacteria also help produce certain vitamins, such as vitamin K, riboflavin, and pantothenic acid). These bacteria become agents of peritoneal disease only if a breach in the digestive system unleashes a transmural plague—the intrasomatic version of a pathogen suddenly finding itself able to take advantage of a new ecological niche—allowing these formerly harmless residents to "invade" other parts of the body unacclimated to their presence. A similar and remarkably benign, perhaps even mutually beneficial, symbiosis exists between humans and a single-celled parasite called *Toxoplasma gondii*. This organism infects more than half the people on the globe, including more than fifty million Americans. Its remarkable success seems due to its having negotiated a modus vivendi with its host population. We harbor it—often in the brain, without ever being aware of its presence, and for the rest of our lives once infected—and it generally does us no harm. Except for individuals whose compromised immune systems disrupt the otherwise peaceful coexistence between our *T. gondii* and ourselves, their presence in the body is an infection only in the technical sense of the word.

At a higher order of magnitude, the endemic codependence between our bodies and their "domesticated" intestinal bacteria also defines our relationship as a species to the herds and flocks that supply our animal protein. Again, the proximity of human and animal, and the digestive processes that work to the mutual advantage of both (we feed them, they feed us), also facilitates the exchange of pathogens. *Toxoplasma gondii* is transmitted to humans through undercooked meats as well as by way of the litter boxes of our pet cats. As Jared Diamond has written, and as the recent examples of mad cow disease and bird flu demonstrate, infectious disease in humans very likely originated (from our point of view, rather than that of the pathogens that thereby pioneer their own new vectors of communicability) as a toxic by-product of the interspecies partnership between humans and animals formed millennia ago.[25] To invoke the familiar anthropological distinction between the "raw" and the "cooked": just as an uncultivated plant becomes a "weed" when it "threatens" (i.e., moves in among) the "flowers" in our garden, so the semantic distinction between pathogenic and eugenic processes dissolves into a vast, interdependent ecosystem, one whose imbalances and readjustments, whose benefits and calamities alike, are the paradigm of life on this planet on every

---

25. Diamond, *Guns, Germs, and Steel*, especially chap. 11, "Lethal Gift of Livestock," 195–214.

scale, and not a violation of its rules. There is no reason to believe it can be, or ever will be, otherwise.

Plague Politics

If we call this ecosystem a commonwealth, we can construct a frame that brings us closer to one key feature of early modern (and current) narratives: a politics of infectious disease. The analogy between the human body and the body writ large as a model for the polis is, of course, very ancient, running from Plato's *Republic* to Hobbes's fundamental assumption in the *Leviathan* that the commonwealth "is but an Artificiall Man; though of greater stature and strength than the Naturall."[26] For English plague writing in the seventeenth century, infectious disease strikes the city and the kingdom as well as the individual and can be understood only as it is triangulated within these three "bodies." London plague, as Ian Munro argues, is an "urban signifier"—both a "spatial disease" that "refigures the lived and symbolic space of the city," and a temporal disease, "recalling and recycling a long historical and literary tradition of urban dissolution": "London under plague is haunted by Florence, Rome, Jerusalem, Athens, Thebes, and the cities of the plain."[27] Munro sees the plague as opening, on the one hand, a "panoramic city" imagined from above as a single suffering organism or as a form of theater playing itself out on the urban stage; and on the other (here citing Michel de Certeau's *The Practice of Everyday Life*) as a form of narrative, or a confluence of narratives, composed of individual trajectories through the streets of the plague city.[28] The "panoramic" imagery of London as the "scene" of the plague (as imagined in figs. 14–15, pp. 114, 115, below) would thus have its counterpart in the alternative mode of configuring the experience of urban plague—from the street-level point of view of Defoe's H. F., the individual observer whose forays through London provide him with the observations for his *Journal*. The shift in perspective from an overarching, providential viewpoint to that of the walker in the city will be one of my concerns in what follows. In the early modern formation of an English national consciousness, moreover, the vulnerability of the kingdom as

---

26. Hobbes, *Leviathan*, 9.
27. Munro, "The City and Its Double," 242–43.
28. Ibid., 248.

a single victim—its constitution as a suffering individual (in the older sense, still current through the seventeenth century, of "indivisible") body—serves as a means of conceiving the state as such, and of symbolizing the forces that threaten it. With the "city" (the mayor and aldermen of London) and the "kingdom" (the monarch and the Privy Council in Westminster) in such close proximity, plague also foregrounds the overlapping and contested jurisdictions of these two "bodies." Under the pressure of a health crisis that is also necessarily a crisis in the political order, plague writing reveals underlying social tensions and anxieties less obvious in more normal times.[29]

We might think of the "state"—the state of nature, the state of the individual, and in relation to these the political state—as a multicultural society, with equal citizenship granted perforce to its constituent microbial and macrobial communities. To pathogens, as well as to higher-level floral and faunal opportunists, legal boundaries mean nothing. For early modern theology, the pestilence and a relentless marauder like Marlowe's Tamburlaine could both be seen as the scourge of God. Increasingly in a globalized world, "infestations" by any of these opportunists may threaten the state itself, as can be seen not only in human epidemic emergencies, but in the case of the infamous rabbit proliferation in Australia, or of cattle zoonotics in the Horn of Africa. In this global polity, as in the little world of the individual body, the distinction between our "selves" and others—"our" distinction, in every sense of the word—is radically compromised: we live in their realm, and they live in ours. Our bodies (our "selves"?) must now be imagined not as definitive enclosures but as microbial reservoirs, their walls fragile partitions that can be ruptured from within or penetrated from without like an infected cell. That fragility in turn mirrors and exposes the fragility of the larger political order.

This conception of the earth's biosphere as a global village recuperates an early modern sense of our unbounded vulnerability. When in a carnivalesque mood Hamlet imagines the corpse of Polonius as the site of "a certain convocation of politic worms" (4.3.20), the prince's mordant wit, collapsing all distinctions between high and low, plays off the similarity between the corruption of bodies politic and natural, the imperial Diet of Worms and Polonius as a tasty diet for worms. The early moderns have a more vivid sense than ours of the

29. Tensions between the city and the court over "control" of the plague are documented in Freedman, "Elizabethan Protest, Plague, and Plays."

sores, the pustules "rotten with thick slime," and the putrid discharges that disfigured the victim of infectious disease—what Bacon would call, in the context of his dissection of the diseased body of learning, "vermiculate" questions.[30] Their pervasive analogizing of the body and the body politic turns on both the necessity of maintaining the distinction that makes the analogy possible in the first place (a distinction also reinforcing the due subordination of the one to the other) and the threat of dissolution (of the two bodies, and of the distinction between them) figured by infectious disease. Thus, in his famous dying speech, Shakespeare's John of Gaunt imagines "this little world" of England as a "fortress built by Nature for herself / Against infection and the hand of war," and protected by the sea as by a wall or a "moat defensive to a house" (*Richard II*, 2.1.45–48). His English fortress recalls the imagery of sixteenth-century manuals of medical self-government, such as Thomas Elyot's *The Castel of Health* (1534) or William Bullein's *Bulwarke of Defence* (1562)—the latter described by its author as a "little Fort . . . against sickenes."[31] Gaunt's point is that due to Richard's corruption of his royal office, the island body, though safe from another foreign plague as from military invasion (as the providential defeat of the Spanish Armada had demonstrated to Shakespeare's audience), has now been eaten out from within. The "inky blots and rotten parchment bonds" (2.1.64) that contaminate the kingdom, threaten its fortresses, and deface its noble houses figure not only as the signs of the king's extortionate taxes, but as the tokens of his dissolute nature written on the body of the state.

Sermons and other moralizing pamphlets of the period struggle urgently with questions of divine justice that depend, in turn, on a plague politics at-

---

30. Cf. Fracastoro on syphilis: "Unsightly sores broke out over all the body and made the face horrifyingly ugly, and disfigured the breast by their foul presence: the disease took on a new aspect: pustules with the shape of an acorn-cup and rotten with thick slime, which soon afterwards gaped wide open and flowed with a discharge like mucous and putrid blood. Moreover the disease gnawed deep and burrowed into the inmost parts, feeding on its victims' bodies with pitiable results: for on quite frequent occasions we ourselves have seen limbs stripped of their flesh and the bones rough with scales, and mouths eaten away yawn open in hideous gape while the throat produced feeble sounds" (*Syphilidis sive de Morbo Gallico*, 55–57). On the putrefying of knowledge, Bacon wrote: "Surely, like as many substances in nature which are solid do putrefy and corrupt into worms; so it is the property of good and sound knowledge to putrify and dissolve into a number of subtile, idle, unwholesome, and, as I may term them, vermiculate questions, which have indeed a kind of quickness and life of spirit, but no soundness of matter or goodness of quality" (*The Advancement of Learning*, in *Francis Bacon*, 140).

31. Bullein, *Bulleins Bulwarke of Defe[n]ce*, C2v. This tradition is described in Healy, *Fictions of Disease*, 23–24.

tempting to rationalize the vexed relationship between the individual sufferer and the suffering state as conceived under the aegis of a mysterious and angry providence. In this light, plague is seen as both a national and a personal event. In its assessments of guilt, seventeenth-century plague writing attempts to understand what is assumed to be a necessary, if typically inscrutable, connection between the afflicted political body (of the nation or the city), the body of the individual victim, and the will of providence. Was the nation afflicted because of the sins of its people, or were people dying because of some national sin? The question could be argued either way, but the fundamental issue is undecidable. The analogy has its own long history, of course—going back to the juxtaposition, in Thucydides' history, of Pericles' funeral oration on the endangered civic health of Athens with the outbreak of the plague a few months after.[32] Resting on the strength of such analogies, the connection must provide a way of rationalizing the otherwise impenetrable mystery, even the apparent quirkiness, of divine vengeance. The arrows of pestilence could not have been let fly at random. Individual victims may or may not be conspicuously sinful (children are always a problem in this equation), although it could be argued that contracting the disease is itself evident proof of the victim's moral vulnerability. Attempting to flee the plague, or remaining in London out of some vain assurance that one will be protected from it, or, alternatively, wavering in the faith that God has the power to extend his protection to those who remain—in these ways, the plague itself can provoke the very sins it punishes. But if some victims may (appear to) be "innocent," then from the most sweeping providential perspective, and in some way greater than the sum of its individual sinners, the nation itself must be guilty.

Reformation England appeals directly to the historical and monitory examples of biblical plagues, reading the significance of current outbreaks in the light of those that beset the Egyptians in Exodus and the Israelites in Numbers—with the effect that plague history becomes a mode of grafting sacred history onto the history of the nation. Had not all the Egyptians been made to suffer because Pharaoh hardened his heart, and were there not perhaps some "innocents" among the Egyptian herders whose cattle died of a murrain, or among the fathers whose firstborn were killed (not to mention the firstborn themselves), or among the legions of Egyptian cavalry drowned in the Red

---

32. For a history of this analogy, see Sennet, *Flesh and Stone.*

Sea? When the Israelites are more than once visited with plague in the desert, we are not always told how many of "the people" rose up against God, or murmured their dissatisfaction, or otherwise provoked the divine wrath; but each time, we are given mortality figures ranging into the tens of thousands with no specific assurance that only the rebellious had perished. The hinge between national and individual suffering, however, makes it possible to subsume the question of the individual under a more awesome conception of divine justice, arguing for what we would now call, in other circumstances, "national guilt."

In the frontispiece to *Britain's Remembrancer* (1628)—a text I will consider more fully in the next chapter—George Wither offers the vision of a "*dismall Cloud / Exceeding blacke, as from the* Sea *ascending, / And over all this* isle *it selfe extending*" (fig. 10, p. 101, below). The accompanying illustration shows a vast plague cloud hovering menacingly over a map of England, its blackness pierced by one merciful ray of light that will be extinguished if the nation remains impenitent. Even under such a cloud, the survival of the wicked could always be attributed to the wondrous working of divine mercy. The death of presumably innocent individuals—infants, godly ministers tending their flock—could be explained as collateral damage in a more broadly strategic and therapeutic assault on the body politic. The pestilential cloud will boil down on the nation only after the divine patience has been exhausted, but when it does, all must be engulfed. If the suffering of the guiltless could not be easily justified, it could at least be absorbed into a harsh but needful program of national purification. As Thomas Dekker tersely notes, "The altring of a State / Alters our Bodies, and our Fate" (90). Those who, like Shakespeare's Brutus, would undertake to alter the state could cast themselves as "purgers," not as murderers (*Julius Caesar*, 2.1.180), daring physicians willing to inflict a harsh cure for the sake of restoring the body of the state to health. It might also be argued in a Malthusian vein, as Dekker does in *A Dialogue betweene Warre, Famine and Pestilence* (1603), that plague brings with it a kindlier and quicker death than famine—as well as a more certain means of chastisement of sinners like the usurer, who is unlikely to take up a sword in war or to starve even in times of want (111).[33] By the same token, the guilt of the state could be accounted for by a long, conven-

---

33. Cf. Clapham, *An Epistle Discoursing vpon the Present Pestilence*, C2r: "Of all these three plagues, Sword, Famine, and Pestilence, I conclude the last to bring with it the most mercie," since "we die free of the other two plagues, and at the hands of a merciful Father."

tional list of its sinful members, chief among them vain courtiers, hypocritical churchmen, mendacious lawyers, and greedy merchants.

In the seventeenth century, it is still possible to believe that the plague is occasioned by malign astrological influence—a literal "disaster." Figure 15 (p. 115, below) shows the pestilence raining down on London in heavy drops from a miasmal cloud, which opens above to reveal a starry sky. That a calamity of such magnitude must affect the entire creation reinforces the conviction that the apocalyptic shock wave of God's anger will make itself felt at every level of human society, from top to bottom. Thus, says Dekker, "when Kingdomes breake, People dissolue, and (as with Thunder) Cities proud glories rent asunder" (90).

The analogy between people and cities can fuse into an image of the city itself as a corrupt pestilential body. In Jonson's "Famous Voyage," the sewers of London are imagined as the city's entrails, as a muddy "merd-vrinous" womb, or as a subterranean gut clotted with "stench, diseases, and old filth," the "least of which was to the plague a cosen."[34] So, too, in 1613 William Harvey compares the digestive tract to a long street winding "from Powles to Ledenhale."[35] If the fetid condition of London engendered disease, it was a short step to think of London as a diseased body, infecting its residents as they might infect each other and, in turn, thickening the miasmal contagion of the urban environment. The two plague years of 1603 and 1625 were particularly significant in that each heralded a moment of regime change—a potential political crisis echoing (as with thunder) the ominous lowering of the plague. The plague politics of 1603 will be considered in greater detail in chapter 3, in the context of Jonson's epigram on the plague death of his first son, and in a register that moves from the personal to the national. The central preoccupation in 1603 will be the "meaning" of the plague's arrival just in the brief interval between the death of Elizabeth and the (necessarily postponed) coronation of her successor. Here it might be observed that, as the counterpart to the father's sense of sin in Jonson's poem, Dekker reads the plague of 1603 as "[t]h'Inditement writ on Englands brest," God's punishment of the nation for a cumulative forty-five-year record of "high Treason" (86). In the lives it claims as a debt,

34. Jonson, "The Famous Voyage," in Ben Jonson, ed. Herford, Simpson, and Simpson, 8:85, l. 65; 86, l. 72. All subsequent citations of Jonson's works are from this work and will be given parenthetically in the text by volume, page, and (where needful) line number.

35. Quoted in Nicolson, God's Secretaries, 24.

the plague will repay the sins of the past and purify the city for James to enter into it (once the contagion has passed) like a bridegroom claiming his spotless bride: "For now the maiden Ile hath got, / A Roiall Husband (*heavenly Lott*)." Thus, when "*Faire Scotland* does *Faire England* wed," the plague will have played its role in the union of the kingdoms.

Unspeakable Suffering

Plague's implication in the early modern languages of theology, ethics, law, statecraft, and economics, as well as medicine and (for Bacon) the philosophy of knowledge—the ways in which, moreover, it connects these fields and facilitates the analogical machinery enabling a complex network of connections—leads to a more speculative assumption. I believe it will be productive to consider all literary texts written during plague times as plague texts. It would perhaps be prudent to qualify this assertion: all such texts may be seen to respond more or less directly to the constant threat of epidemic meltdown in which their authors lived. I prefer to let the claim stand in its stronger form, however, if only to test its limits. In other periods of literary study, analogous assumptions about the semantic pressure of the unspoken have yielded important insights. We have seen that the cultural tremors of the French Revolution and its aftermath echo everywhere in English writing after 1789, loudly in Wordsworth and Blake, and more softly, though with no less telling effect, in the novels of Jane Austen. Indeed, in *Emma*, the very absence of any awareness of the uneasy postrevolutionary English political climate on the part of the residents of Austen's provincial and self-satisfied Highbury helps us to appreciate both her affection for, and her ironic attitude toward, the little world she has created. For the Victorian period, scholars have traced the strands of Britain's preoccupation with empire not only in works such as Conrad's novels, where the theme figures explicitly, but in others where its partial concealment or even its attempted suppression is itself a crucial feature of the work's design. And what novel or poem written in the United States between, say, 1965 and 1980 can be understood apart from the war in Vietnam, or what postwar Jewish American or Israeli writing apart from the Holocaust?

To take such a claim seriously would be to find traces of plague writing where it does not overtly appear—a precarious method, to be sure. There are many things Renaissance texts may *not* be about, and it seems pointless to catalogue omissions. Yet I would argue for a significant difference between matters casually outside a work's field of immediate reference and matters whose omission is felt within the work—the cultural *parerga* that return us to the prior question of what can fall "within" or "without" a text. Boccaccio's tales hardly mention the plague, but their frame makes clear that they couldn't have been told without it. In Chaucer, only the Pardoner's Tale addresses the plague directly, but, as the masterpiece of a cunning storyteller who also happens to use his art to peddle quack remedies, the Pardoner's contribution offers a metacommentary on the entire pilgrimage, entwining the duplicities of his medical practice with the art of the practiced storyteller. Historians of Italian Renaissance art argue that during plague times, paintings of traditional motifs—lamentations, allegories of charity, *memento mori*—"inevitably acquired new plague-related resonances in the wake of the contagion."[36] In the period at hand, Shakespeare's plays are rich with the language of the plague, which makes itself felt both thematically and metaphorically—in *Coriolanus*, in *Troilus*, in *Measure for Measure*, in the "pestilence" poured into Othello's ear by Iago, or into the ear of old Hamlet by Claudius—even when the plague itself is not directly represented onstage.[37] In a gesture that points both to the air of the theater and to the polluted moral climate of Denmark, Hamlet sees his world as no other thing than "a foul and pestilent congregation of vapours" (2.2.302–3), and in his view everything else must be seen through that miasmal fog.[38] In both personal experience and cultural memory, plague clouds the early modern imagination, just as in its more immediate manifestations it was thought to hang in the air and cling unseen to buildings, fabrics, and coins. As I argue below, in Jonson's epigram on his first son I take the father's failure to specify the cause of young Ben's death from the plague as just such a significantly unspoken, and for Jonson unspeakable, omission.

In tandem with explicit plague narratives, other kinds of writing locate themselves as plague writing by omission—that is, by setting themselves against "contaminated" genres as plague-free zones. The venerable rhetorical tradition of refusing to speak characterizes such negative genres of plague

---

36. Mormando, introduction to Bailey et al., *Hope and Healing*, 2.

37. Munro's "The City and Its Double" offers a subtle reading of the "discursive" presence of plague in *Coriolanus* (256–60).

38. Neill emphasizes the plague atmospherics of English Renaissance tragedy in the introduction to *Issues of Death*, 15–33.

writing. It might be argued that apotropaic figures of demarcation or sequestration such as *occupatio* ("no man can tell," "I do not speak of") underlie distinctions within the generic system parallel to those rules of quarantine enforced by health authorities to separate the well from the sick. The conventions of genre will declare the "kind" of thing they represent by setting themselves apart from other kinds, defining themselves in terms of what they exclude. Plague offers an especially clear marker of that difference. Renaissance pastoral establishes its boundaries by just such acts of generic quarantine from the squalor and sophisticated corruption of city life (the province of satire). The "thousand fragrant posies" offered by Marlowe's passionate shepherd to his love will protect her from infection a thousandfold, enabling her to enjoy "all the pleasures" of her pastoral retreat and (by omission) none of the pain of a plague-ridden city.

Utopias (which tend to be salubrious places) are, as More's title suggests, "noplaces" that establish themselves as much by what they are determined not to be as by any positive constitution. Utopia came to be 1760 years ago when King Utopus cut the isthmus that had until then connected his realm with the mainland, and since then the well-being of the commonwealth has depended upon its isolation, as well as upon a list of stern prohibitions in the Utopian legal code. Utopia serves less as the blueprint of a possible society than as an antipathetic cure to the ills of England, prescribed by the narrator Raphael ("God heals") Hythloday. The *cordon sanitaire* that guarantees the health of this noplace has evidently failed on only two occasions in the history of the island, "both times as a result of a frightful plague" that obliged the Utopians to restore the population of their cities "by bringing people back from the colonies."[39] Bacon's *New Atlantis* adds the requirement that visitors to Bensalem must remain in quarantine until the authorities certify that they are free of disease.[40] Imagining the ideal country house as a blend of the utopian and the pastoral, Jonson begins his great country-house poem by emphasizing the power of such an exclusionary poetics: "Thou art *not*, Penshvrst built to enuious show" (8:93). The "walkes for health" (l. 9) open to the visitor in the gardens of Penshurst do not speak of the sewers of London. But Jon-

---

39. More, *Utopia*, 41.
40. On plague as a constitutive feature of utopias, see Totaro, *Suffering in Paradise*, especially chaps. 3 and 6.

son's mock-epic "The Famous Voyage," which should be read as its companion piece, does, taking us on an extended tour of the pestilential effluvia under the streets of the city.

In the same vein, Robinson Crusoe's island utopia, a little England reconstructed through the effort of an incredibly hardy, solitary survivor, should be read antiphonally against the blighted city of A Journal of the Plague Year. If Crusoe is about new beginnings (and itself marks the beginning of the "new" genre of the English novel), the Journal, to which I will return in chapter 6, marks off the diseased ground from which the novel departs. As it were the Inferno and the Paradiso of Defoe's imagination, these two works taken together as a kind of diptych also reenact Milton's double vision of Noah's flood—now, Crusoe's shipwreck—as the hinge between a "world destroy'd" and a "world restor'd." In the extreme version of my claim, all literary works produced in the plague times would implicitly assert a Jonsonian "Thou art not" as a condition of their being. To recur to Donne, the lovers of "The Canonization" will "die for love" and so, implicitly, not from the pestilence. Their story will be "fit for verse," and so not for the "plaguie Bill" that serves in the poem as an alternative text in which their names might have been inscribed. To write at all during plague times is not only to speak (or not speak) of it, but to tacitly offer the writing itself as proof against it, and as evidence that one has not fallen victim to it. Thus, I believe we can assume that an event of such destructive magnitude will be registered broadly, and by various means, in the writing of the host culture—surely in works where it conspicuously appears, and arguably in works where it apparently does not.

One venerable way of addressing the "unspeakable," an enormity so great that language is said to fail in the attempt, is to speak of not speaking of it. By their sheer magnitude, urban pandemics—claiming thousands of victims in days, if not hours, and bringing social disorder and psychic trauma in their wake—are said to exceed the limits of language. Like the Holocaust, or visions of the sublime, or, latterly, the "events of September 11," they can be described only in the rhetoric of indescribability—or in terms of other narratives to which they can be accommodated ("It was just like in the movies"). Speech grounded in ordinary experience or direct report cannot (it is said) encompass so extraordinary an event as an outbreak of plague. In A Journal of the Plague Year, even so meticulous a reporter as Defoe's H. F. will confess that at its height, the "Great Plague" of 1665 "rag'd for six or seven Weeks beyond all that I have express'd." The bills of mortality, which by the narrator's reckoning add up to 38,195 London dead for the period from August 22 to September 5 of that year, cannot account for the "Confusion among the People," which "was inexpressible." He wishes that he "could repeat the very sound of those groans and of those exclamations that I heard from some poor dying creatures," that he "could make him that reads this hear"; but he finds that not only the sight and magnitude of the epidemic but its horrifying soundscape are beyond his capacity to report.[41] Such gestures speak nonetheless—often at length, but always with the qualification that any account they offer will be at best fragmentary and inadequate, an impoverished synecdoche for a much greater whole.

Among such accounts of various cataclysms, the speechlessness of the plague, at one level a mere trope of rhetoric, seems all the more absolute in that, unlike victims of lingering disease (and unlike Holocaust survivors), those claimed by the plague cannot speak for themselves. Smallpox has at least one eminent English diarist, Lady Mary Wortley Montagu. Those suffering pain can describe their experience, if only in other words—there being, as Elaine Scarry has argued, no articulate language for pain itself.[42] To my knowledge, there are only two extant English first-person plague narratives written by survivors, both physicians. The first, "A Discourse of the Plague," remains unpublished in the Bodleian Library (MS Ash. 208) among the papers of the notorious "astrological" physician Simon Forman, one of the few to argue with unshakable conviction that the principal cause of the plague (when it was not inflicted immediately by God, or by the Devil) was a malign conjunction of the planets. Forman's claim to have cured himself of the disease in 1592, as well as his fortitude in remaining in London to treat his patients during the epidemic of 1603, greatly enhanced his reputation.[43] The second is by Dr. George Thomson (see chap. 2), who claims to have contracted, and recovered from, the disease after performing an autopsy on a victim of the plague of 1665. Even if other English survivors had left any written testimony, the delirium characteristic of the plague would have left them nothing of their own experience

41. Defoe, *Journal*, 190–91, 103.

42. Scarry, *The Body in Pain*, 3–4.

43. On Forman's plague writing, see Traister, *The Notorious Astrological Physician of London*, 44–47; and Kassell, *Medicine and Magic in Elizabethan London*, 100–122. Between 1603 and 1607, Forman wrote and revised a second plague manuscript (MS Ash. 1436), incorporating much of the material from the first.

to recollect. Plague can only be accounted for by those it spares. It can only be written from the outside. Plague writing can record only the anguish of the uninfected observer, and describe only the congeries of symptoms that rapidly transform the infected person into a suppurating corpse. The victim's body is marked by "tokens" that, for the Renaissance, are read as evidence of sin. But the language of the bubonic mark remains opaque and mysterious, neither clearly revealing the divine cause of which that mark is the effect nor translating the inner experience of the victim. If the imagination cannot comprehend the massive suffering of the social body, neither can it penetrate the inarticulate and inarticulable suffering of the individual victim, who becomes the "other" on whom one's own fears and fantasies are inscribed.[44] The London plague house may be taken as an architectural emblem of the speechlessness of the epidemic, a discourse in quarantine. It will be marked by a red cross or a sign reading "Lord Have Mercy" to warn the passerby away. From the inside, no voices will emerge, except for the cries of the dying.

In *Love's Labour's Lost*, plague provides Berowne with the material for an impromptu and hideously indecorous conceit on the love-sickness of the men of Navarre:

> Soft, let us see—
> Write "Lord have mercy on us" on those three:
> They are infected, in their hearts it lies;
> They have the plague, and caught it of your eyes.
> These lords are visited; you are not free,
> For the Lord's tokens on you do I see.
> (5.2.418–23)

Grotesquely, in this flight of Berowne's wit, the "Lord's tokens" are transformed from the painful buboes of those truly infected into the favors bestowed upon the ladies of France by their lords. The conceit bespeaks the plague only to suppress, and even mock, its terrifying reality by turning it into the figure of an amatory dalliance. Appropriately, Berowne's penance, imposed by Rosaline at the end of the play, will be to spend a year visiting "the speechless sick" and there to try with all the "fierce endeavor" of his "wit / To enforce the pained

---

44. On disease as the "other," see Sander Gilman, *Disease and Representation*, 1–17.

impotent to smile" (5.2.851–54). Berowne "must be purged, too," says Rosaline, of the "perjury" of his affected (and infected) language (5.2.818). Compelled to perform before an audience of "groaning wretches" in a pesthouse, Berowne will find in their agony the authentic "speechless" language of the plague. His command performance before those "Deaf'd with the clamors of their own dear groans" (5.2.864) will demonstrate the limits of Berowne's high-flown rhetoric to plumb the depths of pestilential suffering—as well as, perhaps, the limits of theater to stage, much less assuage, the obscenity of the plague. The inability to bespeak the plague, exceeding in these ways the conventional tropes of indescribability, leads us to consider speechlessness as a species of trauma, both individual and communal.

Trauma

In his 1997 review of Cathy Caruth and Dominick LaCapra—critics whose work represents the first wave of American trauma theory in the early 1990s—James Berger sees a traumatic "discourse of the unrepresentable" as the successor to earlier discourses of "the sublime, the sacred, the apocalyptic," and, more recently, of the "Other in all its guises."[45] Its advantage over these other modes—which it parallels, often claims to comprehend, and some- times seems to confuse—is that it offers a post-Freudian and post-Derridean model for correlating traumatic events, the emergence of such events into lan- guage, and the histories that both comprise. Arguably, its limitation for early modern studies is that the theory arises largely in response to the Holocaust, the defining modern event retrofitted onto historical catastrophes. Despite its impulse to historicize, and its subsequent engagement with diverse inci- dents of genocide or violence—Darfur, 9/11, domestic massacres at schools or fast-food restaurants, the war in Iraq with its psychological damage to service personnel—the theory remains rooted (traumatically) in that singular event. Nor is it clear, in such instances or indeed in the case of the Holocaust itself, that the traumatic process occurs—as its very specific delineation implies— in the same way, if at all, to every "victim." Recent work by Fritz Breithaupt on

---

45. Berger, "Trauma and Literary Theory," 573. The reference is to Caruth, *Unclaimed Experience*; and LaCapra, *Representing the Holocaust*. On trauma, the Holocaust, and history, see also Hartman, "On Traumatic Knowledge and Literary Studies"; and Lyotard, *The Differend*.

the pre-Freudian accounts of trauma in German Romanticism suggests that constructions of "trauma" themselves have a history, and may tell very different stories about the work of memory, repetition, and identity.[46] It would, therefore, be as much an interrogation as an application of trauma theory to confront it with the question of early modern plague. The project would be to see how an understanding of pandemic aftershock anticipates (or differs from) trauma theory, rather than to take these earlier events simply as precursors to be translated into our contemporary idiom.

Jean-Martin Charcot speaks of what we would call traumatic memory as a "parasite of the mind," an infestation feeding insatiably on the event it can neither represent nor erase.[47] Trauma for the individual is classically described as the need to repress the memory of an inassimilable kernel of experience—to consign it to a kind of psychic "black hole," in which, however, it cannot be contained. The theory, in Geoffrey Hartman's summary,

holds that the knowledge of trauma, or the knowledge which comes from that source, is composed of two contradictory elements. One is the traumatic event, registered rather than experienced. It seems to have bypassed perception and consciousness, and falls directly into the psyche. The other is a kind of memory of the event, in the form of a perpetual troping of it by the bypassed or severely split (dissociated) psyche. On the level of poetics, literal and figurative may correspond to these two types of cognition.[48]

Trauma cannot be "lived down," only relived; it cannot be addressed (or redressed) literally in the "real" of the victim's experience but continues, in Freud's "latent" state, to manifest itself otherwise, in "figurative" forms of expression—in dreams, hallucinations, neurotic physical or psychosomatic symptoms, obsessive behavior, and occasionally works of art. Freud himself, perhaps echoing his teacher Charcot, speaks of the time elapsed between the event and "the

46. Breithaupt, "The Invention of Trauma in German Romanticism." Breithaupt notes that September 11 is "traumatic" largely because the media found in trauma stories a "fitting narrative" in which the country becomes the "victim" (101 n. 47).

47. Quoted in van der Kolk, McFarlane, and Weisaeth, eds., *Traumatic Stress*, 9. Van der Kolk and McFarlane's first chapter, on traumatic memory, is entitled "The Black Hole of Trauma."

48. Hartman, "On Traumatic Knowledge," 537.

first appearance of the symptoms" as the "incubation period," a transparent allusion to the pathology of infectious disease.[49] In this passage from *Moses and Monotheism*, Freud's apparent hesitation at entirely rejecting the idea of an incubation period as only an allusion suggests that trauma might arise from a neurological disorder in which the mind is taken over in some pathogenic way akin to an infection of the brain. Although the remark seems to evoke an earlier impulse to regard psychological disorders as a form of brain fever, it also anticipates our own nascent understanding of the neurological bases of such disorders, an understanding that immediately troubles the distinction between "physical" and "mental" disease. Freud's example is a train collision, but his "incubation period" returns us at least figuratively to the scene of the plague—and to a connection, in the history of an epidemic, between those who succumb to the disease itself and those who, as survivors, nonetheless harbor the germ of a latent traumatic (re)infection. Plague's infectious process might then be most fully comprehended as an epidemic event that over time turns into, and returns as, its traumatic aftermath—Antonin Artaud's "psychic entity," and the endemic condition of Hartman's "perpetual troping."[50]

The same processes, it has been argued, hold true of communal trauma—a transference of individual psychopathology to the social body, and a fruitful area of post-Freudian study prompted by the Holocaust but ranging beyond an exclusive preoccupation with it to include trauma as an experience of individuals as victims of rape, car accidents, or child abuse. The sociologist Kai Erikson has investigated the Three Mile Island accident, as well as communities devastated by floods, underground gasoline leaks, and contaminated water supplies. His work has led him to two important conclusions that broaden the scope of trauma to include diverse urban or national populations leading "normal" lives, not just soldiers in war or prisoners in concentration camps. First, social trauma can result from a prolonged "period of severe attenuation and erosion as well as from a sudden flash of fear." This finding revises a narrower view in which, as Caruth puts it, "trauma describes an overwhelming experience of sudden or catastrophic events."[51] Second, "when the community is profoundly affected, one can speak of a damaged social organism in almost

49. Freud, *Moses and Monotheism*, 84.
50. See Artaud, *The Theater and Its Double*, 18.
51. Caruth, *Unclaimed Experience*, 181.

the same way that one would speak of a damaged body." Indeed, "in such circumstances, traumatic experiences work their way so thoroughly into the grain of the affected community that they come to supply its prevailing mood and temper, dominate its imagery and its sense of self, [and] govern the way its members relate to one another."[52]

London plague writing—medical, political, religious, literary—during and between the epidemic years of the seventeenth century responds to an epidemic catastrophe that left no person untouched. Meditations in an emergency, plague texts flood the presses as if to fill the void with explanation and consolation, confronting the brute fact of the city in a death grip. Plague orders are issued, published remedies abound, weekly bills offer a meticulous account of the dead parish by parish, and moralizing pamphlets wrestle with questions of divine justice. The vast and repetitive outpouring of plague sermons, jeremiads, and broadsheets characterizing each of the English epidemics may be read symptomatically as the psychosocial form of traumatic repetition—a collaborative, overdetermined, and never completely successful effort to write "out" the plague, in both senses of the word. But even in periods of intermission, when the volume of such overt material abates, the persistence of plague trauma (reflected as well, as we have seen, in survivors' memories and oral stories passed down) will lead us to expect other writing marked by a strong undercurrent of anxiety and propelled by the dual forces of memory and foreboding: memory because, although many victims of trauma report that they "remember nothing" of the event, they nonetheless (or for that very reason) live for years with its spectral and unexpected reappearances; and foreboding because Londoners had good reason to fear that yesterday's epidemic would be the precursor to the next. Theirs was an instance of pre- as well as post-traumatic stress, what Paul Saint-Amour has called, speaking of the anxieties of the nuclear age, "a proleptic traumatic symptom."[53]

What victims experience individually or corporately as memory may be described as the product of a Freudian Nachträglichkeit, as much the work

---

52. Erikson, "Notes on Trauma and Community," 185–90. Erikson here reflects on his findings in *Everything in Its Path: Destruction of Community in the Buffalo Creek Flood* (1976); and *A New Species of Trouble: Explorations in Disaster, Trauma, and Community* (1994).

53. Saint-Amour, "Bombing and the Symptom," 61.

of retrospective creation as simple retrieval. Indeed, Freud's insight suggests that traumatic accounts in their various guises are forms of fictional narrative that "make up" (for) the event that cannot be brought to light. *Nachträglichkeit* carries the usual meaning of "belatedness" or "retroactivity" in the standard translation; its range in Freud's German includes not only the neutral "supplement" or "postscript," but the more troubling resonances of a process that is "unforgiving," "resentful," or "vindictive" (*nachtragend*) as well. Plague writing after the fact will, in the most literal sense of the term, drag the past behind it—as the thing that cannot be forgiven or forgone, as the burden that cannot be put down, because it insistently supplies the very task it impedes. The inability to put the burden down marks the difference between mourning and melancholia. But in the anticipation, as well, of a recurrent plague that will have been, plague writing is also burdened with a traumatic future perfect that imagines in advance the horror into which one may be dragged—a kind of *Vorträglichkeit* that also marks our own premonition of pandemics to come. With all these nuances of the word in play, we can think of post-plague narratives as supplementary to the original event in a Derridean sense as well—a sense reflected in the slippage of the word "trauma." For the event gives rise to a traumatic reaction through which the event itself is retrospectively (and prospectively) constituted as traumatic. Just as the traumatic plague subject occupies a kind of temporal limbo, traumatic narrative functions as a ligature tying the event itself to the subsequent history of its (re)construction, and to the (pre)construction of its recurrence.

In their reconsideration of Freud's Wolf Man, Nicolas Abraham and Maria Torok designate the "crypt" as the site in which the experience giving rise to trauma is both buried and (in both senses of the word) encrypted. Their characterization of the crypt as an "intrapsychic tomb" makes it an eerily appropriate repository for the remains of the plague.[54] Throughout the sixteenth and seventeenth centuries, plague burials filled nearly every parish churchyard in London and its suburbs. As the need arose, larger purpose-built plague burial sites were established in the New Churchyard on the grounds of Bethlehem Hospital, and in Bunhill Fields. Then and thereafter, the specter of the plague pit haunted the London imaginary. Even today, as one historian reports, "one of the most popular elements in the mythology of London is the plague pit,

---

54. Abraham and Torok, *The Shell and the Kernel*, 130.

and especially the idea that many pits were dug in unconsecrated ground and afterwards forgotten. The site of any discovery of plentiful human remains in a location no longer used for burial tends to be identified as a plague pit, unless a more reliable history is quickly attached to it."[55] Whether in truth or in apprehension, Londoners could believe that the plague dead were interred just under their feet. Just as outbreaks were fueled by, it was supposed, noxious vapors seeping up from underground, plague memories might likewise emerge—as they do in Defoe's *Journal*—as a kind of exhumation of what lay buried in the pits, the dead whose bodies were already "encrypted" with the mysterious marks of their disease and with the memory of previous epidemics. The ghostly presence of plague death stalking the living would then figure in these still-potent remains.

Plague sermons engage in their own mode of theological decryption, unearthing the significance of the pestilence and playing out their own drama of forgetting and remembering. "*It is storied*," we are told by one divine, "that in a great battaile, many being slaine, and the bodies vnburied, there followed a great Plague; and this so infected men, that they forgat their fathers names, their children, their own names: I am sure our forgetfulnesse of God, and our *Idolatrie*, brought the last Plague among vs." And yet, the same preacher insists, forgetting can also be a salve: "There is a *remembrance* of iniuries, whereas the best remedy of an iniury is forgetting. And at *Athens* it was enacted a decree *obliuionis iniuriarum* . . . which the *Athenians call* the *Law of obliuion*." Thus, "the *remembrance* of our end by common mortality in *pestilence* or otherwise, still *toling* for the last gaspe, should *ring* out the death of malice, & *burie* all wrongs in the *graue of obliuion*, neuer to rise vp againe."[56] Another divine, also responding to the plague of 1625, preaches that the current outbreak is London's punishment for having too soon forgotten the last one: "This"—that is, both the plague of 1603 and the memory of it—"for some yeeres after, lay dead, and as buried in some perpetuall grave: therefore hath God opened our graues again, by killing with the Plague of Pestilence in that same Citie." The recurrence is thus a "reproofe of those who bury Gods benefits" in "Sepulchers of obliuion."[57] These tensions between burial and unearthing, oblivion

55. Harding, "Burial of the Plague Dead," 23–24.
56. Price, *Londons Remembrancer*, 16, 9.
57. Horne, *A Caueat to Preuent Future Iudgements*, 6, 7.

and recall—and, conflating these, between bodies and the memory of bodies—strongly suggest that the features of our own story of mass trauma are themselves the product of earlier plague times, stories encrypted but latent and ready to be repeated otherwise, in our time: after the Great War, after the Holocaust, after the (literal) unearthing of genocide from mass graves in Rwanda, and very likely again after the next great plague.

In the early modern period, the crypt suggests a psychological ground for the various modes of group denial or evasion—modes of partial or thwarted or resisted decryption—that are symptomatic of plague times and plague narratives from Boccaccio to Defoe: despair, neurasthenic shell-shock, desperate hilarity, carnivalesque eruption, or even a stoic determination to go on with the ordinary business of life (or storytelling) in the face of unutterable calamity. At the highest pitch of intense emotion, plague trauma manifests itself all over Europe, not only symbolically in the *Totentanz* but in outbreaks of "dancing mania," or tarantism—a phenomenon so widespread as to prompt a long discussion of it by Paracelsus as one among the "diseases that deprive man of his reason."[58] Trauma provokes, however, as the counterpart to (or the cost of) denial, a "repeated replaying of upsetting memories," the "persistence of obsessive and disturbing recollection."[59] We know that Jonson dreamed of his son's death the night before the news arrived. In the epigram itself, the child speaking from the grave reads eerily like the transcription of a recurrent dream.[60] As I shall argue in greater detail in chapter 4, Jonson's giving voice to the dead in the epigram replays the scene of the child's burial as an investment in the fantasy that the child is not really dead, or that the father is, while the "entombment" of traumatic memory likely accounts for the poem's omitting the cause of his son's plague death. Jonson will spend the rest of his career dragging the plague after him as an autobiographical narrative, reliving the part of the father to a succession of "sons of Ben," both in his verse and in the adoption of his literary tribe.

---

58. See Zinsser, *Rats, Lice and History*, 61–65. Paracelsus's treatise is translated in *Four Treatises of Theophrastus von Hohenheim, Called Paracelsus*, ed. Temkin.

59. Van der Kolk and van der Hart, "The Intrusive Past," 176.

60. Jonson's dream (1:139–40) presages Freud's account of the dream of the burning child, in which a bereaved father dreams "that *his child was standing beside his bed*" and spoke to him (*Standard Edition*, 5:509–10). In *The Interpretation of Dreams*, this case "links [Freud's] theory of dreams and wish-fulfillment to the question . . . of death, catastrophe, and loss" (Caruth, *Unclaimed Experience*, 93).

Because these motives are bound up with the stories people tell (and tell themselves) about surviving shipwrecks, floods, or terrorist attacks, trauma now, as in earlier periods, makes itself available to the investigator and the victim alike as narrative. I would argue that, as the record of a historical response to trauma, plague writing should be read as enacting—and, for Western modernity, producing—the complex of motives of post-traumatic expression as understood by clinicians today: commemoration; "bearing witness"; the attempt at healing; confronting belatedness; acknowledging (or refusing to acknowledge) "survivor's guilt"; groping for causes and effects that will suture a traumatic rupture into the fabric of the comprehensible; compulsive repetition of what cannot be absorbed or negotiated otherwise.[61] Trauma is the story of an unprecedented break in the order of things, a singularity that cannot be correlated to what came before or after. But from the fourteenth to the end of the seventeenth century in England, plague trauma unfolds in the historical narrative as the inexorable repetition of singular epidemics, each demanding of its survivors that they reproduce their own narratives in which the event can never be fully accommodated. As we have seen in the case of the oral history of plague vignettes, trauma narratives are bequeathed, in an attenuated but still potent form, as part of familial and national histories. Wars not only produce trauma but are fueled by traumatic memory: we "remember" the Alamo and the *Maine*, and we mark America's entry into World War II as a day that "will live" in infamy. Freud's narrative of the traumatized train-wreck survivor begins by imagining that "someone gets away, apparently unharmed from the spot where he has suffered a shocking accident," only to develop a series of disturbing symptoms later on.[62] That story fragment, itself part of the conventional trauma narrative of the "narrow escape," will be repeated not only by individuals actually involved in airplane crashes or rescued from burning buildings, but by those who claim that, but for a lost ticket or a sudden change in plans, they would have sailed on the *Titanic* or boarded one of the planes headed for the World Trade Center. A German psychotherapist who has studied the children and grandchildren of Holocaust survivors finds that the originary trauma is passed down the generations precisely because

---

61. See the various perspectives on traumatic recollection developed in Caruth, *Trauma*.
62. Freud, *Moses and Monotheism*, 84.

it cannot be resolved into ordinary experience.[63] Since one cannot "come to terms" with the death camps, the trauma manifests itself not only in individual symptoms (of guilt, anger, and so on) and dysfunctional family dynamics, or in bequeathed stories, but as often in the refusal to speak of the event at all—in an antinarrative or evacuation of narrative that the analyst takes as itself a kind of communication. Silence as well as speech, the symptom of speechlessness itself, can be the medium for transmitting Charcot's "parasite" to the next generation.

Trauma, as we have seen, has its own temporality as well. Or, more accurately, it has an atemporality that resists the narrative order that would fix the traumatic at a definite point at a manageable distance from the "now" of the victim. The clinical literature concurs that trauma "is in a sense, timeless." Although conventional stories such as those above are part of an intergenerational traumatic narrative, trauma itself cannot be "transformed into a story, placed in time, with a beginning, a middle and an end (which is characteristic for narrative memory). If it can be told at all, it is still a (re)experience."[64] In testimony by many Holocaust survivors, the event is never integrated into a sequential narrative ("This happened to me once") but persists in an eternal present ("This is still happening to me"). More precisely, it hovers between the past and the present in a time that neither can fully accommodate. As we shall see in chapter 6, Defoe's H. F. recalls the shrieks of a distraught mother who has just discovered the plague tokens on her daughter's thighs: "I remember, and while I am writing this story, I think I hear the very sound of it."[65] The scene of writing in such a passage intensifies the echo-chamber effect of traumatic recollection. Defoe writes that H. F. hears the shrieks as he, H. F., records (from the point of view of a contemporary adult observer) what Defoe himself could only have recalled as a childhood memory of shrieking, or of stories about victims shrieking that he may have heard from his uncle Henry Foe, the "real" H. F. Many critics of Defoe insist that A Journal of the Plague Year, published when its author was sixty-two, cannot be based on the personal experience of a boy of five. The persistence of traumatic memory puts this conclusion in doubt. Defoe's biographer James Sutherland notes that even

---

63. Gruenberg, "Transmission of Trauma of Nazi Persecution."
64. Van der Kolk and van der Hart, "The Intrusive Past," 176–77.
65. Defoe, Journal, 74.

if the young Defoe was shielded from the worst of it (he may, indeed, have removed from London with his family during the height of the infection), "what even the fondest parents would find it hard to conceal from a child in those terrible months was the constant shrieking of the dying and the bereaved and the lunatic." He continues, "It is surely not without significance that the cries of the wretched are insisted upon by Defoe all through the *Journal* to such an extent that the repetition becomes almost monotonous."[66] The narrative conflates the adult writer of 1722 with his fictional adult counterpart "writing" in 1665, the two of them bound by a memory of the incessant shrieking of the mother for her child.

Yet the same timelessness that would seem to exclude the traumatic from narrative can also be otherwise; L. L. Langer speaks of Holocaust testimony as if it were a Shakespearean sonnet: trauma "fixes the moment permanently in memory and imagination, immune to the vicissitudes of time." In this formal respect, writing can represent that moment, if not by direct access to its encrypted content, then at least by the creation of a document that re-places "it" from the mind to the page, making it available again and again in the experience of reading—creating a form, in other words, that mimes the need to "relive" the event, permitting the reader (and the writer) to return to the scene but from a safe distance. This constructive power of traumatic narrative should not be overlooked, insofar as it restores to the "victim" some measure of authority over the experience, some space for the assertion of agency that is lost if the person is thought to be (or thinks that he or she merely is) a prisoner of the past. Yet the form of trauma representation might be symbolized as the "empty circle" in a dream reported by the daughter of Holocaust survivors, a form that circumscribes but cannot contain the experience at its center.[67] Traumatic artworks—the post-Holocaust poetry of Paul Celan, the paintings of Anselm Kiefer, Art Spiegelman's *Maus*, or the genre of Holocaust anti-monuments most notably exemplified by Peter Eisenman's 2005 memorial to the murdered Jews in Berlin—can succeed only by indirection, where "meaning can arise from the empty spaces, silences and omissions within them."[68]

---

66. Sutherland, *Defoe*, 7.
67. Laub and Podell, "Art and Trauma," 991; the quotation by Langer is also cited here.
68. Ibid., 992. Laub and Podell note that "the aim is not to come to an 'objectively real' depiction of an event but to create a protected space wherein the remembrance of the traumatic experience can begin, if only haltingly, to occur" (994). Eisenman's memorial—a field of 2,711 concrete slabs of various heights—

A traumatic reading of plague texts in the broadest sense explains how—in Bacon, for example—plague does not emerge overtly in the philosophical writing. It does appear in *The New Atlantis*: visitors to Bensalem are held in quarantine until the authorities are satisfied that the ship's crew are free of any imported diseases that might contaminate the secluded commonwealth. Nonetheless, plague leaches out everywhere in Bacon's account of—one might almost say, his obsessive characterization of—the diseases and distempers of learning. His proposed remedy, the antidote to fruitless speculation, may be symbolized by the Bensalemite notary who boards the visitors' disease-ridden ship "holding in his hand a fruit of that country" whose fragrance serves him as "a preservative against infection."[69] The "empty circle" of the trauma dream also described Bacon's utopian fantasy, a noplace whose preservation depends upon the secret location of the island. But here, I believe, a further distinction comes into play, between the mechanisms of trauma as they may (or may not) drive individual behavior, and their discursive effects in plague times. Rather than the product of an "unspeakable" repression, Bacon's "diseased learning" (like the "plague" of sedition, in the language of seventeenth-century politics) may be seen as the plague's overflow, as it were, into adjacent areas of discourse. By its nature a thing so powerful and insidious as to frustrate all attempts at discursive quarantine or the repression of the directly unspeakable, plague will communicate itself to all precincts of language even as it spreads through every parish and across all boundaries of class and profession. Although plague produces a cornucopian medical literature full of cures and preservatives as useless as they are exotic, the failure to account for it in its own terms, as a natural phenomenon capable of being understood and treated, leads to its displacement onto the overlapping terrain of politics and theology—where rationalization and paranoia offer the explanations that medicine cannot supply.

The most intense explanatory pressure falls inevitably on plague theodicy, and it is in this realm that the traumatic crack appears most visibly. How could the death of a quarter of London's population in a few summer months

---

was described by Bundestag president Wolfgang Thierse at its opening as "a constructed symbol for the incomprehensibility of the crime" (Deutsche Welle, "Holocaust Monument Dedicated in Berlin," May 10, 2005, http://www.dw-world.de/dw/article/0,2144,1579615,00.html, accessed June 3, 2007).

69. Bacon, *The New Atlantis*, in Bacon, 459.

be the work of a just and merciful God? Despite an acknowledgment that there is, finally, something mysterious about the plague, theodicy can do no more than attempt to justify its operations—an unpromising task whose history goes back as far as St. Cyprian, who argued that the plague then ravaging third-century Carthage was a "holsome departynge" to the servants of God. In the words of Thomas Elyot's translation, the English could be assured that "there is no cause, that ye shoulde therfore thynke that deth is commune to good men with them that be yll. For good men be called to ioye: the yuell men be drawen into paine."[70] But how should one understand the multitude of victims being called to joy (or otherwise), and at regular intervals? The answer is that bodily affliction is spiritual physic: by "sicknesse," the faithful are asked to believe, "God exercises his *children*, and the *graces* which hee bestoweth vpon them."[71] In order to secure this benefit to the afflicted, God may use the Devil as the agent of second causes to foment epidemic disease, and God may even be pleased to "hide the right way of curing" from the physician.[72] The corollary to this special providence is that disease should be welcomed as evidence of grace, and therefore (in the words of Joseph Hall), "not to be afflicted is a sign of weakness."[73]

Looking back in 1625 to the previous epidemic of 1603, John Taylor finds an explanation in the divinely supervised conjunction of epidemics and politics. As each of these years saw the accession of a new monarch, it is possible to argue that God twice prepared the way by clearing the kingdom of sin, cutting down the "superfluous branches," and presenting James and Charles in turn with a "people purg'd and purifi'd." But since a second purgation was required just twenty-two years after the first, it is necessary to qualify the argument in a way that casts doubt on the efficiency, and perhaps even the justice, of the first: "Not that they then [in 1603] were of life bereft / Were greater sinners then the number left." Taking another tack allows Taylor to circumvent this problem, albeit in a manner that would not likely reflect the view of those plague victims who by the thousands followed the Virgin Queen to the grave:

---

70. Cyprian, *A Svvete and Deuoute Sermon*, c5v–6r.
71. Elton, *An Exposition of the Epistle of Saint Paul to the Colossians*, 71.
72. Sibbes, *The Soules Conflict with It Selfe*, 355.
73. Hall, *Meditations and Vowes*, 46. This and the passages quoted above are discussed in Harley, "Spiritual Physic, Providence and English Medicine."

And as *Elizabeth* when she went hence
Was wayted on, as did beseeme a Prince:
Of all degrees to tend her Maiestie
Nere forty thousand in that yeare did dye,
That as she was belou'd of hight and lowe:
So at her Death, their deaths their loues did show,
Whereby the world might note *Elizabeth*,
Was louingly attended after death.[74]

Robert Horne asks the same question: what could have caused "the finger of God, or rather whole hand" to inflict "so grieuous a Plague, or stroke vpon *London*" as that of 1625? His answer is stark: "Our Land was all ouer-runne with sin." Horne is certain, as he must be after the fact, that "in the whole Land there was a large confederacie and increase of sinfull men."[75] Plague theodicy can succeed in balancing the account only by discovering an enormous debt of accumulated guilt so widespread and offensive as to try even the divine patience; and when patience yields to righteous anger, the debt must be paid in an enormous toll of lives.

Yet the prior question remains unasked and unanswerable: whence this sudden and overwhelming efflorescence of sin, an outbreak evidently much worse than usual, yet not evident at all until a punishment has been inflicted for which a crime must be sought? Have those professionally adept at detecting sin among their flocks somehow not noticed the increase? Within the logic of the preachers' discourse, the scales will be balanced only if a weight of sin equal to that of the penalty can be put in the other pan. But these holy mathematics cannot bear the strain of producing arguments that must exculpate God of any possible injustice while holding the suffering guilty of all possible wrongdoing. The harsh retribution for all this excess guilt is apparent, but what is missing from this equation is its source.

As I believe my survey of this material in the following chapters will show, what is "unspeakable" in the many sermons and godly exhortations that pour forth in plague times is not the plague itself—with which these documents are overtly and obsessively preoccupied. The "unspeakable" lies elsewhere.

---

74. Taylor, *The Fearefull Sommer*, B2v.
75. Horne, *A Caueat to Preuent Future Iudgements*, 19, 20.

What cannot be thought, much less said, in this discourse is that the plague is in fact unjust and merciless, or a merely natural and casual event to which these attributes cannot be applied; or, worse, that it is the work of a God who has no interest in justice; or, worse yet, that the plague has no particular significance because there is no God. Plague cannot ask the question that Jonson only half-asks in "To Heaven": "O, being every-where, / How can I doubt to find thee euer, here?" Nor can it perform the thought experiment in the first line of the same poem: "can I not thinke of thee . . . ?" (8:122, ll. 15–16, 1). The unthinkable was, apparently, thought by others in the period—those "closet" atheists, in David Riggs's phrase, known chiefly through the attacks on them by their righteous (or politically motivated) enemies. The heresies of Giordano Bruno and the materialism of Epicurus and Lucretius were anathema to the devout. Richard Hooker, Thomas Nashe, Bacon, and a host of others (such as those out to get Christopher Marlowe) charged that "the School of Epicure, and the Atheists, is mightily increased in these days." Sir Walter Raleigh, in cahoots with the mathematician Thomas Hariot, was supposed to have set up a "school of atheism . . . wherein both Moses and our Saviour, the Old and New Testament are jested at, and the scholars taught among other things to spell God backward."[76] The fantasy of such a "school" reveals more about the allure of such thoughts to those who imagined that it exists than it does about the "scholars" who were supposed to offer instruction in the arts of atheism.

In a plague sermon of 1595, Richard Greenham warns against "those sins whereunto we are tempted, as when a man is noted to think blasphemouslie of God the Father, or to doubt whether there is a Christ or no, or to imagine groslie of the holy Ghost, or to deny God." These are "fearful & monstrous temptations": a man so tempted will feel "the Spirit, oft checking him for them," and yet "he feareth, lest then by long sute, he might fal into them." For "the Deuill will come sometimes to thee" and "vrge thee on in this manner: Surely, thou must do this sinne":

Thus, for feare of yielding of the one hand, and for shame of disclosing temptations on the other hand, many men haue pyned away, and

---

76. Quoted in Riggs, *The World of Christopher Marlowe*, 294–95. Riggs traces the history of late Elizabethan atheism more fully in "Marlowe's Quarrel with God."

almost haue bene overcome by them: If we should disclose this, saith these men, what woulde people say of vs? they would count vs Atheists, they would think we are the wickedest men in the world.[77]

"Many men" have been tempted so. Greenham does not say whether he himself had ever been so tempted, caught between fear and shame, hearing a voice that tells him what he "must do" but mortified at what people would say. Another contemporary preacher reports that Greenham was prone to memory lapses that seemed to stem from something like the paralysis of guilt that this passage suggests.[78] Yet the thought of atheism, even if not its acknowledged temptation, lurks behind the exhortation to avoid it—Greenham cannot *not* think it, however monstrous the thought—and the force of its repudiation is reflected in the urgency of the struggle described, in the need to deny the denial, and in the need to enlist the Spirit as the censor to keep the thought in "check." The urge "to think blasphemouslie of God" does not disappear but is submerged under the "shame of disclosing," an anguish so overwhelming that "many men haue pyned away"—that is, in the older sense of the word, they have not only been enfeebled as by a disease, but have been afflicted with an unendurable torment.

Greenham's case is unusual in the run of plague sermons for its acknowledgment of the specter of atheism, but I take it as the symptom of a traumatic process that makes sense of the surplus of guilt with which these texts are obsessed. Freud describes an instance of repression allied to psychosis in which "the ego rejects the incompatible idea together with its affect and behaves as if the idea had never occurred to the ego at all."[79] What is here concealed under the shame of the undisclosed is the thought otherwise *foreclosed* in this long and conventional plague sermon and, I would argue, in others of its kind. I use the Lacanian "foreclosure" as a stronger alternative to repression for two reasons. First, it enables us to imagine the unthinkable "[I] deny God" as a hole in the symbolic order of this discourse, not merely a negation or a thing

---

77. Greenham, A Fruitful and Godly Sermon, 67–69.

78. "It was a sanctified *remedie*, which reverend M. *Greenham* vsed, being often in his publick Ministery and priuate conference, troubled with a suddaine failing in his memorie: so as by no means he could recouer himselfe in those things he purposed to speak. *He would presently groane in his heart*, and humble his soule vnder the holy hand of God" (Price, *Londons Remembrancer*, 33).

79. Freud, "The Neuro-psychoses of Defence," in *Standard Edition*, 3:58.

rejected by the ego as an incompatible idea, but a thing beyond negation and compatibility entirely. The idea "occurs" to Greenham, but necessarily as an idea occurring to an "other" (indeed, the idea that even the "other" cannot disclose), and expressible only as the speech of the Devil.

Second, the idea is experienced not as a thing buried in the unconscious that can reappear from within, but as something entirely (r)ejected from it that seemingly returns from the outside. In his analysis of Daniel Paul Schreber, Freud was led to conclude that the patient's hallucinations were not the product of suppression and projection; rather, "what was abolished internally returns from without."[80] Lacan hones this into an aphorism: "Whatever is refused in the symbolic order . . . reappears in the real."[81] What returns from "without," in the Lacanian idiom, is precisely the Name-of-the-Father, Greenham's "God the Father," as the fundamental signifier of the discourse itself. The "empty circle" of the plague sermon contains (or cannot contain) the banished thought that no just God could kill innocents by the thousand. The blasphemy falls through the hole, as it were, only to reappear as that very ejected God wreaking the vengeance of the plague as the terrible price of that denial. By its own circular logic, the discourse thus allows for a cryptic recognition that faith in Jonson's "Good and great God" is severely tested, if not altogether shaken, by the plague, while at the same time it reaffirms the awful but reassuring reality of that God as evidenced by the pestilence itself as the instrument of his justice. This is not to suggest (necessarily) that the "many men" alluded to by Greenham—those tormented men who hear the voice of the Devil urging them from the "outside" to deny God—have been driven to a clinical psychosis of the sort whose cases lead both Freud and Lacan to the formulations I have borrowed for the occasion. I am suggesting, rather, that the crisis of the plague puts theodicy under the most intense pressure it can face (in a pre-nuclear and pre-Holocaust age), and that its one recourse, the only strategy by which it can preserve itself from collapse, is to adopt what these later analysts will call a psychotic structure. Rather than propose a retrospective diagnosis, I would regard this discourse—in all its emphasis on the unspeakable repudiation of the Father and his return in, and as, a disease—as

---

80. Freud, "Psycho-analytic Notes on an Autobiographical Account of a Case of Paranoia," in *Standard Edition*, 12:71.
81. Lacan, *The Psychoses*, 13.

an early modern discursive formation produced in plague times that power-fully exemplifies the structure that psychoanalysis will inherit and codify.

Faced with traumatic writing, critical reading in turn must reconceive itself in some measure as clinical interaction. The goal is not to master such nar-ratives (from a "safe" vantage point) but to engage them with an equal sense of vulnerability and therapeutic responsibility. This reading requires listen-ing with the third ear—paying attention to silences, refusals, omissions, and displacements as the necessary mode of access. Describing the therapeutic moment in language appropriate to plague testimony, A. Modell writes that "affects are communicative and contagious, so that the other person is in-volved in the affective repetition and will collude, either consciously or uncon-sciously, in confirming or disconfirming the subject's category of perception."[82] For Modell's purposes, "the other person" is the therapist; for the purposes of historical investigation, it is the reader of seventeenth-century plague texts. Despite the greater distance, the latter is also implicated in the traumatic process. If nothing else, reflection suggests that rereading plague texts "con-sciously or unconsciously" supplements the history of traumatic repetition. Recent trauma theory posits that history itself can—or must—be seen as traumatic, and our engagement with it as part of a continuing symptomol-ogy of "reliving" the event. Cathy Caruth interweaves the historical and the traumatic in her claim that "history, like trauma, is never simply one's own," that "history is precisely the way we are implicated in each other's traumas."[83] Accounts (such as this book, written in the shadow of the coming plague) necessarily produce what Saul Friedländer calls "splintered or constantly re-curring refractions of a traumatic past," not as a critical deficit (I hope) but as a necessary supplement to that history.[84] To understand our own age as a plague time—to write with no guarantee of immunity, even to write under the apprehension that finishing a book such as this is a race against the clock of the next pandemic—is to recognize our role as participants in, rather than observers detached from, the object of our study.

82. Quoted in van der Kolk and van der Hart, "The Intrusive Past," 177.
83. Caruth, *Unclaimed Experience*, 24.
84. Friedländer, "Trauma, Transference and Working-Through."

CHAPTER 2

The Plague and
the *Word*

The Word is God, and *God* hath spoke the word,
If we repent, he will put vp his sword.
JOHN TAYLOR, *The Fearefull Sommer*

It is a principal contention of this book that in the English Reformation, the infliction of plague is to be understood fundamentally as a language event foreshadowed by, and issuing from, the Word—an event, therefore, fundamentally discursive even before it becomes the subject of plague writing, an event that presents itself as a text to be read. The differences between English and Italian modes of plague representation help to illuminate this point, for in the world of Italian visual culture, not only the veneration of the plague saint but the ways in which the saint's mediation is understood as efficacious—and efficacious because it is *seen* to be so—provide a resource of comfort and explanation in the face of epidemic disease. Put simply, in the Italian tradition art relieves language of what would become, in England, the burden of accounting for the pestilence. With the Reformation and the consequent banishment of plague saints and the pictorial tradition in which their therapeutic advocacy is made visible and memorable, the English imagination conceives the plague not only as something to be written about, but as itself a form of writing. Scripture, rather than any intervening pictorial tradition, offers the proof text for an understanding of plague history, and scripture teaches that God uses the plague as a means of inscribing his judgment on the sinful.

The London preacher Sampson Price, exhorting his congregation not to forget the epidemic of 1625, connects the plague as a divine document with the origin of writing itself: "*Socrates* complained, that after the vse of letters, the Art of *memorie* decayed; for the care which before was had in heart and memorie, afterward was put in bookes; and that which was committed to the minde, was after put in trust in writing. O let that *flying rowle of Gods iudgement*, which lately hath gone ouer the face of the whole earth . . . euer be in our memorie."[1] The plague has become the "flying roll" of Zechariah's vision (Zechariah 5:1–4), now grown from its biblical dimensions of twenty cubits by ten cubits into a vast parchment blanketing the earth. Thus imagined as an enactment of God's judgment, plague inscribes itself as a memorial text by putting itself "in writing" as a prompt to its own recollection. As a legal document as well—the "roll," or legal record of its occurrence—plague puts itself "in trust" for future readers, who can consult it as the official register of that judgment. Indeed, as we shall see, a close etymological reading of the word discloses that in the Hebrew, "plague" is not only the consequence of

1. Price, *Londons Remembrancer*, 33–34.

the divine Word, but itself the word for "word." I am, finally, interested in the consequences of this linguistic turn for a number of related texts—medical, theological, and literary—that form and are formed by an engagement with the plague in early modern England.

Plague Saints

Along with its shadowy villains (the Jews, the "anointers"), Italian plague culture—a richly visual culture—has its heroes, preeminently among the ranks of the saints.[2] The catalogue of saints whose active career or posthumous reputation qualifies them as protectors against the plague numbers more than one hundred. Some, like Saints Adrian, Anthony, Francesca Romana, or the Sicilian Rosalia (who more than once freed Palermo of the plague, and was painted in this role by Van Dyck), have only a local or occasional celebrity, their fame secured in large part by the notable artworks depicting their intercession. In 1662, Luca Giordano painted St. Gennaro Freeing Naples from the Plague, and a century later Tiepolo produced several versions of St. Thecla performing the same office for Venice. Other saints are more widely invoked in a long tradition of ritual and representation. St. Gregory "the Great," consecrated as pontiff during the plague year of 590, ordered an image of the Blessed Mary carried in his inaugural procession. According to The Golden Legend, "The poisonous uncleanliness of the air yielded to the image as if fleeing from it and being unable to withstand its presence."[3] This image—the prototype of plague imagery—was supposed to have been painted by the artist-physician St. Luke himself, and it was afterward installed in the church of Santa Maria Maggiore in Rome. St. Nicholas, from whose preserved body a healing oil is said to flow, saved Florence in 1486, a miraculous intercession painted by Giovanni di Paolo. A Vasari altarpiece of 1536, now in Arezzo, shows God the Father, supplied with arrows by angels, thrusting himself forth from a dark plague cloud, while the Virgin and child enthroned in the center appease the divine wrath. The Virgin plays the same role in other paintings as the Madonna of Mercy to whom the saints make their appeal.

2. The most comprehensive recent account of this tradition is Bailey et al., Hope and Healing.
3. Jacobus de Voragine, The Golden Legend, 1:173–74.

The best-known figure associated with the plague in Catholic tradition is St. Sebastian. Martyred in the late third century by arrows that could be seen symbolically as the arrows of pestilence, he is venerated as an especially influential patron of plague sufferers (and continues his career to this day as the patron saint of those with AIDS). According to the earliest traditions, Sebastian was an officer in the imperial bodyguard. When he was discovered to be a Christian around AD 286, he faced a firing squad of Mauretanian archers, but survived to be healed of his wounds by the widowed St. Irene. He then had to be clubbed to death to get the job done. He is a familiar figure in Florence. In the 1370s, and very likely in the wake of the plague of 1374, an altarpiece of St. Sebastian commissioned for the Duomo was painted by Giovanni del Biondo (fig. 1). In del Biondo's composition, the botched execution appears in the middle, flanked by four scenes from the life of the saint. The narrative begins at the left with a scene of Sebastian preaching and continues through the central panel of his being skewered—so as to resemble a hedgehog, as the *Golden Legend* describes the effect of the barrage of arrows. To the right of the central panel, he is shown being beaten to death. Below that, the apparition of the saint indicates the location of his body to the Roman matron Lucina; in the same scene, we witness its subsequent retrieval from a Roman well. Finally, at the lower left, we find a plague scene, with townspeople petitioning the saint to come to their relief. Prayers for Sebastian's protection against the plague were answered in Rome in 680 and then, among other cities, in Milan in 1575 and Lisbon in 1599. During the Renaissance, he was painted by Raphael, Giovanni Bellini, El Greco, Holbein, Veronese, Guido Reni, Pollaiuolo, Mantegna, Perugino, and a host of lesser artists, often in altarpieces—such as that by Francesco Francia in Lucca in 1511—commissioned to commemorate his intercession on the city's behalf and to ward off future epidemics. Sebastian appears not only in panel painting and fresco, but in sculpture, miniatures, mosaics, and stained glass, and his image was carried through the streets in religious and civic processions during plague times.

Sebastian was not himself a plague victim, nor do the earliest accounts make mention of any special healing powers. Representations of him as a human target do not appear before the Renaissance, when in plague times the arrows could be seen symbolically as the missiles of a divinely inflicted pestilence, in a tradition going back to the plague visited on the Greeks by Apollo in the *Iliad*. The *Golden Legend* records that when "during the reign of King

FIGURE 1. Giovanni del Biondo, *Saint Sebastian Altarpiece*, Opera del Duomo, Florence (ca. 1379). Photograph: © Scala / Art Resource, New York.

Gumbert [in the eighth century] all Italy was stricken by a plague," it was divinely revealed "that the plague would never cease" until the saint's body was recovered from the well or sewer in which it had been dumped and an altar raised in his honor in Pavia. When this was done, "the pestilence ceased."[4] The retrieval of his body from a well echoes the well of living waters in the Gospel and Jacob's well in the Old Testament; and if the well fed into the sewers of Rome, the preservation of his body from the effluvial contamination often as-

---

4. Ibid., 1:100–101.

sociated with infectious disease would only have strengthened his authority as a plague saint. Sebastian's qualifications as an intercessor were also enhanced by his having survived a certain death, and to have done so conventionally, in most representations, while hanging Christ-like on a pole or a stake. Like St. Roche, who actually recovered from the plague, Sebastian is imagined as capable of conferring his own immunity on others by a kind of sympathetic magic. His survival after his ordeal on the pole resonates as an antitype of the Crucifixion and Resurrection, and more distantly of the brazen serpent in the book of Numbers, a common theme in plague art; for when the Israelites were afflicted with a plague of poisonous snakes for their habitual ingratitude, Moses was instructed to lift up a serpent of brass upon a pole, "and it shall come to pass, that every one that is bitten, when he looketh upon it, shall live" (Numbers 21:8).[5] Through this association, Sebastian's martyrdom also offers an antipathetic cure to those by whom he is invoked, much in the way that the afflicted Israelites were cured when they looked upon the image of their affliction.

Sebastian is often shown (as in fig. 2) in the company of his medieval counterpart St. Roche, a French noble born in Montpellier in 1295 who early developed a sympathy for the sick. While on pilgrimage to Rome, St. Roche (in Italy, San Rocco) stopped at Aquapendente and healed the plague-stricken with the sign of the cross. The same miraculous cures were repeated at Cesena, Mantua, Modena, Parma, and other cities across Italy. The legend has it that when Roche himself fell ill, he walked into the forest to die but recovered when he was tended by a friendly dog. Marked by the plague himself, he is to be identified by the bubo on his thigh prominently displayed in most representations. When in 1414 plague broke out in the city during the Council of Constance, the fathers of the council ordered public prayers and processions in honor of the saint, and immediately the plague abated. His relics were carried to Venice in 1485, where they are still venerated. In the 1560s Jacopo Tintoretto crowned the ceiling of the Sala dell'Albergo in the Scuola Grande di San Rocco in Venice, a confraternity dedicated to helping the poor and sick

---

5. The Gospel of John emphasizes the typological link between the brazen serpent in Numbers and the Crucifixion: "And as Moses lifted up the serpent in the wilderness, even so must the Son of Man be lifted up: that whosoever believeth in him should not perish but have eternal life" (3:14–15). All quotations from the Bible are from the King James Version.

FIGURE 2. Jacopo Tintoretto, St. Roche (2a, left) and St. Sebastian (2b, right), Scuola Grande di San Rocco, Venice (ca. 1578–81). Photographs: © Scala / Art Resource, New York.

in the name of their patron, with the *Glorification of St. Rocco*. Its counterpart on the ceiling of the Great Upper Hall above, Tintoretto's *Miracle of the Brazen Serpent* (fig. 3), underscores the connection between biblical and modern plagues. It also obliges the viewer, like the historical Israelites, to witness the miracle by looking up at the serpent on its pole—thus recalling a significant Mosaic instance of the therapeutic power of vision.

During the plague in Milan in 1576, Bishop Carlo Borromeo, third in the pantheon of major plague saints, gave himself up entirely to his people—visiting plague-stricken houses; comforting the afflicted in the hospital of St. Gregory, where the worst cases were sent; and persuading other, more reluctant clergy to assist him. In penance for his flock, he walked in procession barefoot, with a rope round his neck, at one time bearing in his hand the relic of the Holy Nail. With the Counter-Reformation, pictures of San Carlo filled the churches of Catholic Europe, emphasizing his active fight against the pestilence—and perhaps allegorically, against the rapidly spreading pestilence of the Reformation—through the power of the Eucharistic sacrament. He is shown leading processions, confirming adults during plague, adoring the plague cross, visiting a plague encampment to baptize an infant, and interceding to save the city of Milan (fig. 4).

These plague saints appeared in panel painting and fresco cycles, votive altarpieces and apotropaic images painted on city gates. Such prestigious works were commissioned by civic authorities, clergy, lay confraternities, and religious orders, as well as by individual donors. Images of plague saints were, however, also mass-produced in more ephemeral forms such as broadsheets and engravings. Depictions of San Carlo's plague miracles appeared in, among other forms, a set of engravings entitled *Vita, et Miracoli di San Carlo Borromeo*, issued in 1610, the year of the saint's canonization.[6] An anonymous Florentine engraving of Sebastian dating from the 1470s, of which there are several examples, includes the text of a recommended invocation to be recited by the purchaser. From the same period in Florence, another typical *ora pro nobis* engraving shows Sebastian surrounded by scenes from his life, including the crucial episode of the cessation of a plague in Rome only after the recovery of his body from the well (fig. 5). A print by the sixteenth-century German artist Erhard Schoen shows an assemblage struck from six wood blocks, intended to head a plague broadsheet and featuring images of St. Sebastian and St. Roche together with the text of a suggested prayer for succor. Such temporary images were also the staples of public processions over the centuries. In addition to *Pestblätter*—rough woodcuts or copperplate engravings providing devotional material for the individual, common in Germany and the Netherlands as well as in Italy during the fifteenth and sixteenth centuries—plague *gonfaloni*, banners of cloth decorated with the image of the saint, were carried in public processions and displayed in churches. I am emphasizing these fleeting examples as well as the more famous paintings on which they are sometimes based to suggest how widely such imagery was diffused, and also to suggest something of the popular devotional practices in which they were used. The devout, and no doubt apprehensive, purchaser of a *Pestblatt* would have an image of the plague saint and the text of an invocation.

---

6. See Jones, "San Carlo Borromeo and Plague Imagery," 72–73.

(*facing page*) FIGURE 3. Jacopo Tintoretto, *Miracle of the Brazen Serpent*, Scuola Grande di San Rocco, Venice (ca. 1575–76). Photograph: © Cameraphoto Arte, Venice / Art Resource, New York.

(*above*) FIGURE 4. Carlo Maratti, *Carlo Borromeo Saving Milan from the Plague* (1650). Engraving after a lost altarpiece for SS Ambrogio e Carlo al Corso, Rome.

FIGURE 5. Anonymous Florentine *ora pro nobis* engraving of St. Sebastian (ca. 1470–80).

Some examples offered the added reassurance that whoever carries the paper on his person will be protected from the disease.

These images serve to mediate, and ameliorate, the plague in three interconnected ways. First, as we have seen, the material image itself could function as a talisman and a prophylactic against the plague. Carrying it in a civic procession, mounting it over an altar, decorating it with flowers, or even keeping it in one's pocket (for insurance, along with a posy of fragrant herbs) could help in guarding against the infection. As the church was careful to insist, reverence should be shown to an image only insofar as it is the representation of a sacred personage. To overvalue it for the fineness of its execution or, worse, to invest it with miraculous properties was to fall into idolatry. But as the church's Reformation critics never tired of arguing, this scholastic distinction between the thing and the image of the thing was seldom observed in practice. Arguably, the object itself might be seen as having a special efficacy when it comes to the plague. If, as was commonly believed, the disease could be contracted by contagion—in its root sense, by physical contact with an afflicted person, with her bedclothes, or even with a coin she might have handled—why could it not be cured or even prevented by the same means? Ten years or so before Giovanni del Biondo painted his Sebastian for the Duomo in Florence, an earlier Sebastian altarpiece, now lost, was commissioned by the then Bishop of Florence, Filippo dell'Antella, in honor of a relic of the saint that he had brought back from Rome and donated to the cathedral. Able to effect miraculous cures on its own, the image of the plague saint becomes a relic no less potent than the actual relic displayed next to it, or the touch of the saint during his lifetime, or (in the case of St. Nicholas) the holy oil exuded from his remains. Its virtues in popular devotion are thus material before they are spiritual or symbolic.

Second, plague images properly used as a spur to devotion encourage the viewer to call upon the depicted saint, who will then perform his or her designated role as advocate and protector in a quasi-judicial proceeding. Often, a timely plea can ward off the plague altogether. The divine judgment having been rendered, however, by the appearance of the pestilence, the saint intercedes to beg for mercy for his convicted clients. Whether the court will entertain the plea is uncertain, but the saint has his own independent standing as one who bears a patron's responsibility to enter such a claim, and who can at his own discretion commute the sentence of individual petitioners, and perhaps even of his whole constituency. Given a favorable outcome, the beneficiary of the saint's efforts will endow a chapel, commission an altarpiece, or contribute a bolt of cloth as a votive offering, according to his means. As evidence of the community's repentance and gratitude, such *de voto* offerings will themselves mitigate the plague in the future. The legal issues, as it were, are thus construed as negotiable, rationalized into an appeals procedure, and personified in the saint as an influential representative of the convicted His torians remind us that this spiritual chain of petition, obligation, and gratitude also reflects, and is reinforced by, the relationship between patron and client in Italian Renaissance civic life.

Third, these images give an imaginative form to this process, and one in which, as I have emphasized in the examples above, the therapeutics of vision itself is key. Conventionally, in these altarpieces, the heavens above and the prostrate victims below are shown connected in a middle region filled with interceding saints and donors. The binary of heaven and earth is mediated by the presence of the saint in a scheme congruent with the view of pre-modern physics in which opposing elements (e.g., fire and water) are mediated by a third element (air) that shares the properties of both and so brings them into concord. In these examples (see, e.g., fig. 4), the vector of intercession is often represented by a great swooping S-curve opening an upward channel of communication that connects the world of suffering petitioners to the saint, and thence to the Virgin and Christ as the source of divine mercy. The figure of the petitioning saint is seen to implore the assistance of his superiors while he ministers to the afflicted and shields them with his body or, in one image of San Gennaro, with his billowing cloak.

In Giorgio Vasari's painting *The Virgin and Child Enthroned with Saints* (1536), Sebastian, in the lower right-hand corner, looks out at us in the manner of the interlocutory figure recommended to painters by Alberti as "someone who admonishes and points out to us what is happening there; or beckons with his hand to see" (fig. 6).[7] As also embodied in Italian Renaissance spectacle by the stock character of the *festaiuolo*, this figure both participates from the margins in the action of the drama and comments on its significance for the benefit of the spectator. Just as the saint joins heaven and earth, here his gaze (and ours in return) mediates the space between the painting and the viewer. The figure of Sebastian in Vasari's painting also elides the two roles of client and patron, since the petitioning saint occupies the same position (kneeling at the foot of the sacred personage) as that conventionally assigned in other sacred compositions to the patron of the work of art. Sebastian's gaze is one of acknowledgment, not only that of the patron

---

7. Alberti, *On Painting*, 78.

FIGURE 6. Giorgio Vasari, *The Virgin and Child Enthroned with Saints*, Museo Medievale e Moderno, Arezzo (1536). Photograph: © Scala / Art Resource, New York.

FIGURE 7. Camillo Landriani ("Il Duchino"), *Carlo Borromeo Administers the Sacraments to the Plague-Stricken*, cathedral, Milan (1602).

saint toward his earthly client, but of the saint who recognizes and wishes us to acknowledge his own position as a petitioner at the Virgin's throne. His gaze draws the viewer into the painting; it tells us that the saint sees our plight even as we see him, and it engages us as the first link in an unbroken visual chain of intercession. Similarly, in Camillo Landriani's *Carlo Borromeo Administers the Sacraments to the Plague-Stricken*, completed in 1602 for the Milan cathedral (fig. 7), a priest shown in the foreground of the painting holding the crucifix for the saint looks over his shoulder into the space of the cathedral on our side of the picture plane, and directly at the viewer. His gaze includes us in the company of plague sufferers surrounding the saint and, at the same time, "beseeches beholders in the cathedral to witness the administration of the sacraments."[8]

---

8. Jones, "San Carlo Borromeo and Plague Imagery," 66.

One remarkable example of the efficacy of the gaze is Francesco Solimena's painting *The Miracle of St. John of God*, the *modello* for an altarpiece in the Ospedale della Pace in Naples commissioned around the time of the saint's canonization in 1690 (fig. 8). The founder of an order devoted to ministering to the sick, St. John was personally credited with numerous miracles, among them the protection of the city of Naples, personified in Solimena's painting by the bedridden plague sufferer to whom he reveals himself. Sheila Barker argues that instead of an allegorized Naples, the young victim illustrates one of the two miracles adduced as proof for John's canonization, the "cure of 16-year-old Isabella Arcelli, a patient at the lazaretto on Tiber Island during the Roman plague of 1656 who . . . recovered overnight through the spiritual intervention of St. John of God, to whom she had prayed before going to sleep."[9] The painting represents the miraculous moment as occurring when the saint, gazing at his patient, displays his own portrait as the object of her gaze. This triangulation of the gaze (he looks at her, she looks at his image) inserts the portrait as the medium between the saint and his beneficiary; she comes to be healed by him (as we may hope to be) by looking at his picture. Oddly, Solimena's design even seems to suggest that the image of the saint—that is, the portrait of St. John within the painting—is not only a viable replica of the saint himself, but is somehow to be preferred in the treatment plan to his actual appearance. If indeed the painting records the visionary experience of an impressionable girl, her cure might be understood to proceed from the power of the image working in her—just as that same power, under other circumstances, might cause her to give birth to a hairy child if a portrait of John the Baptist hung over her bed.

A more highly elaborated theory of therapeutic vision underlies the most influential plague painting of the European seventeenth century, Nicolas Poussin's *The Plague of Ashdod*, completed at Rome in 1630–31 in the aftermath of Italy's worst outbreak since the Black Death (fig. 9). The subject is the biblical plague visited upon the Philistines after they seized the Ark of the Covenant (I Samuel 4–6). Scripture records that the Philistines (who had violated the *sanctum sanctorum* of the Hebrews) were punished, appropriately, with unspecified "tumors in secret places," but Poussin's rendering makes it starkly

---

9. Barker, "Plague Art in Early Modern Rome," 62 n. 49.

FIGURE 8. Francesco Solimena, *The Miracle of St. John of God* (ca. 1690). Williams College Museum of Art, Museum purchase, John B. Turner '24 Memorial Fund, Karl E. Weston Memorial Fund (93.6).

FIGURE 9. Nicolas Poussin, *The Plague of Ashdod* (1630–31). Photograph courtesy The Art Archive / Musée du Louvre Paris / Bagli Orti.

clear that we are witnessing a biblicized version of the current epidemic.[10] If, as it was commonly held, fear of the plague—an imagined foreboding of its terrors—could bring on its symptoms, or even the disease itself, might not so gruesome a depiction as *The Plague of Ashdod* actually fuel the epidemic? In the interest of the viewer's health, an Albertian interlocutor would have to have a menacing expression, "with an angry face and with flashing eyes, so that no one should come near."[11] However, as Barker argues at length in her analysis of the medical theories underlying the painting, Poussin's contemporaries would likely have understood—and experienced—the work as provoking an Aristotelian catharsis, relieving the mind of the malignant imaginings it brings to the fore, and so purging the viewer of both the fear of contagion and the

---

10. Poussin's motifs of an infant attempting to suckle its dead mother and a bystander reacting to the characteristic stink of the plague victim by holding his nose were widely admired and copied. See Mormando, introduction to Bailey et al., *Hope and Healing*, 20; and especially Barker, "Poussin, Plague, and Early Modern Medicine," to which the following discussion is indebted.

11. Alberti, *On Painting*, 78.

compassion that brings us empathetically "too close" to the contagious victims. Seen generically as tragedy rather than history, Poussin's *Plague* works—like other images of rotting corpses, imploring victims, and appalled survivors—as a "visual prophylactic" against the disease.[12] For Lodovico Castelvetro, the Renaissance authority on Aristotle's *Poetics*, the most "striking proof" of the tragic effect itself is to be seen "in epidemics, at the beginning of which, when three or four people have died, we are greatly moved by compassion and fear, but then once we have witnessed hundreds and then thousands die, these reactions of compassion and fear cease."[13] What may seem to us evidence of a self-protective neurasthenia figured instead as proof of a powerful homeopathic cure, and one all the more effective in that the image of the plague exposes the viewer only to an effective simulacrum of the plague—the painter's version of an inoculation—rather than to the thing itself.

The Saints Go Marching Out

In the artistic and ritual traditions surrounding Catholic plague saints, the visible thus fills a gap—material, juridical, representational—between the affliction and the afflicted, and in its appeal to the sight it does so with a therapeutic effect embedded in vision itself. It is not just that a painter might succeed in depicting the anguish of the plague, or the visible consolations available to the devout, more convincingly than the poet could describe them in words (although such a case might well be made by the proponents of *pictura* in their friendly rivalry with *poesia*). In Catholic culture, the image mediates inexplicable human calamity and its implacable divine origin. In his role as intercessor, the depicted saint pleads the case for mercy before the bar of divine justice, while his image, like his relics, can itself be therapeutic—whether displayed in grand altarpieces, carried in public procession for the benefit of the city, or employed in more modest forms as an aid to private devotion. Italian plague art fulfills the promise of the image of the brazen serpent: that whoever shall look upon it shall live. The Reformation, however, deprives the faithful of all these consolations and the representational means that made them possible. "Do not look for Christ with your eyes," Luther had warned, "but put your eyes in your

---

12. Barker, "Poussin, Plague, and Early Modern Medicine," 670.
13. Quoted in Barker, "Poussin, Plague, and Early Modern Medicine," 670.

ears." The brazen serpent, according to Andreas Karlstadt's 1522 tract *On the Abolition of Image*, was an "image" given by God as a special dispensation and for its particular moment in the history of the Jews—it was neither made by men, nor to be imitated by them. Debated at length as the scriptural crux of the Zurich disputation over images the following year, the brazen serpent was by consensus deprived of its visual potency. Reabsorbed into the text of the biblical narrative, it must be read as a sign (indexical, we would say, rather than iconic) pointing forward toward the Crucifixion, which in turn was to be worshipped "in the Spirit only," and not by any carnal, outward observance.[14] However strong the allure of Italian art for the English, and however tempered the iconophobia of the early reform in the later years of the Anglican middle way, these echoes persist. In sacred matters, especially those touching upon the proscribed cult of the saints (whose miracles were exposed as a blend of fraud and credulity), visual experience remains fraught with peril. The therapy of art, its comforts and harsh excoriations alike, becomes by default the task of the poet, the devotee of Apollo—who, as Thomas Dekker notes, is "both Poesies Soueraigne King, / And God of medicine" (100).

With the suppression of the old religion along with its saints, its images, its relics, and its penitential processions, the chain of intercession so powerfully forged by the "carnal" institutions of Catholic plague culture is thus broken. The reformers' injunction to worship "in the Spirit only" signals an inward turn toward an examination of conscience and behavior in the light of scripture, and away from such communal modes of expiation as the civic processions and flagellant societies of an earlier plague age in Italy. The same inward turn is reflected in a succession of plague orders banning public gatherings of all kinds and enforcing the isolation of victims (including restrictions on the numbers who could attend funerals). Quarantine becomes the emblem of an enforced privacy. In this effort to "banish from public view the victims of plague," Paul Slack finds the origin of a Foucauldian desire to render the diseased invisible while keeping them under forcible surveillance.[15] It also discourages the

---

14. For the context of these early debates as the crucible of a "poetics of Reformation iconoclasm," see Ernest B. Gilman, *Iconoclasm and Poetry in the English Reformation*, chap. 2, especially pp. 37–38. Karlstadt was to die of the plague at Basel in 1541. Whether his skepticism of the brazen serpent was a contributing factor is not recorded.

15. Slack, *Impact of Plague*, 308. In *Discipline and Punish* (198), Foucault begins his discussion of the Panopticon with the plague, seeing it as the "trial in the course of which one may ideally define the

English from looking beyond their own sins for others to blame, a difference from reactions on the Continent; in England, Slack notes, "there was no hysterical hunt for scapegoats, no terror of plague sowers, no rumour that plague had been caused by witches or other agents of the devil."[16]

The English seventeenth century, as we will see, produces its own plague imagery, albeit in the lowlier forms of woodcuts and engravings for printed material already embedded in the matrix of the word. Even in—indeed, especially in—these representations, nothing stands between the divine wrath and its object; there is no means of visualizing any traditional and authorized agency of appeal, mitigation, protection, or expiation. Writing in the time of the London epidemic of 1603, the preacher James Godskall scoffs at "the superstitious Papists, who in the time of plague runne to the house of the Spider to bee preserued, to stickes and stones, metals and papers." Of those "crying in the time of plague to their *Sebastian*," Godskall would ask, "If it lieth not in the power of mortall men that are liuing with vs to helpe, how much lesse can they that are dead? And farre lesse, one that perhaps hath neuer been?"[17] In the absence of the advocacy role played by the saint, the questions surrounding the justice of the plague become far more urgent. In this harsher version of plague theodicy, there is only the punishment to be borne for some unspecified but evidently massive sin, or for a long list of sins by which every Christian stands indicted, and only the hope (but never the assurance) that by prayer and repentance, divine mercy will lessen the severity of the judgment. If saints allow for revelation, their absence provokes interpretation. For the English, the question is not how plague can be shown but how (as itself a manifestation of the Word, legible both in scripture and as a sign written on the body of the afflicted) it can be read, written, spoken, and decoded. The sourcebook for studying the history of infectious disease would now be the Bible almost exclusively, and if the nature of current epidemics was to be parsed, their infliction had to be indexed to the cases there presented.

In a reformist spirit, English Paracelsians like Richard Bostocke rejected the Galenic tradition "proceeding from Idolaters, Ethnickes, and Heathens,"

---

exercise of disciplinary power," and the impetus for "the penetration of regulation into even the smallest details of everyday life."

16. Slack, *Impact of Plague*, 294.
17. Godskall, *The Arke of Noah*, E2r–v.

championing instead the "the auncient phisicke, first taught by the godly fore-fathers" and adumbrated in scripture. The alternative Paracelsian canon—including the fabled Hermes Trismegistus among the pristine theologians in the tradition of Egyptian mysteries—was true because, and insofar as, its teachings were conformable to the Word of God. Had not disease itself entered the world with the Fall, "[w]hereupon by the curse of God impure Seedes were mingled with the perfect seedes," joining "death to life, sicknesse to health, not onely in man, but also in all liuing creatures, Hearbes, Plants, Mynerals: and in the fruites of the firmament and ayer"?[18] Of the "propaga-tion of sinne, from the parents to the children," William Perkins insists, "[a]ll Adams posteritie is equally partaker of this corruption."[19] The biblical his-tory of disease thus teaches that disease is not only the consequence of sin but genetically identical to it, carried in the impure "seedes" transmitted from our first parents to all the generations of their descendants—and in each generation, from father to son.

In Jonson's "To Heaven," the poet in his grief (which, as we shall see, would include the grief of having lost his seven-year-old son to the plague) complains that there "scarce is ground" upon his "flesh t[o]'inflict another wound" (8:122, ll. 21–22). Struck down by melancholy and physical infirmity, he asks whether his state is to be "interpreted" (or misinterpreted) in him by the divine exegete as "disease"—the very *plaga*, or blow, that God himself, in his role as judge, has inflicted on the poet. If in the legal sense there "scarce is ground" for such an infliction, why must he be so ground down, so nearly consigned to the ground of which his own flesh is made, the ground to which he has already given his son in payment for his "sin"? Entering his own pleas, Jonson implores his God to be "[m]y iudge, my witnesse, and my aduocate" (8:122, l. 11). In the Italian tradition I have been surveying, these last two roles would be in the province of the saints, who, having witnessed the suffering of the petitioner and taken upon themselves the responsibility and authority of the advocate, will plead the case before the heavenly judge. In their absence, Jonson has no choice but to ask God to judge (himself). In Jonson's En-gland, the absence of any institutionalized mediation necessarily opens a gap

---

18. Bostocke, *The Difference betwene the Auncient Phisicke*, B4v.
19. Perkins, *A Golden Chaine*, 17.

between the divine utterance in all its mysterious power and the adequacy of any human response or redress.

The Plague as the Word

The fundamental connection between the plague and the Word stems from the etymology of the word *plague* in Greek, Latin, and Hebrew. I cite the eccentric divine Henoch Clapham for his especially detailed exposition of this point, but the substance of his remarks is to be found as commonplace material nearly everywhere in English plague writing, whether in medical treatises (as in George Thomson's *Loimotomia*, discussed below), in theological jeremiads, or in polemical pamphlets. I shall return to Clapham in chapter 3, where the context of his writing will be further developed; but for now, his foray into the multilingual history of the word is worth considering in itself and as a typical example of plague exegesis.

Clapham repeatedly emphasizes that pestilence is the Word of God—not only what scripture teaches about the infliction of disease, or what the plague itself might signify as an expression of the divine will, but, most interestingly for an investigation of plague writing, that the plague itself is to be understood and even experienced as a species of language. Like most preachers, Clapham offers two scriptural etymologies for *plague*. Through the Greek (πλαγά) and then the Latin (*plaga*), the word signifies "a blowe or stripe inflicted on mankind" by God. According to Clapham, many people "felt and heard the noise of a blow" at the moment they were struck, "and some of them have upon such a blow found the plain print of a blue hand left behind upon the flesh."[20] Such reports would offer experiential proof of the πλαγά as a "stroke," or a "wound." That the blow was also "heard" testifies to its resounding impact. At the same time as providence makes its "print" on the body with a stroke of the "hand," the force of the blow strikes the ear like the shock wave of a terrific utterance. The distinctive buboes, or "tokens," by which the sufferer is marked are to be read as inscriptions recording both the presence of the disease and the sin for which the afflicted person is brought low. Like the imprint left by the blow, they are, in effect, a form of evidence: as the law paints a red cross, also called a token, on the doors of plague houses, buboes are the sign by which

---

20. Clapham, *Epistle*, A2v, B1v.

God makes the Word of the plague evident as, and in, flesh. A story apparently circulating during the epidemic of 1625 tells of a woman who, having fled London, looks back rather like Lot's wife and cries, "Farewell London, farewell plague." Naturally she is struck down, and on her breast, along with the tokens, could be seen the words "It is in vain to fly from God, for He is everywhere."[21]

That the blow of the plague is also a form of inscription is confirmed, for Clapham, in the Hebrew derivation. The Hebrews "use the same letters (*Deber*) for *word* and *Pestilence*. And hereupon it is, that the Hebrues turne the word *Deber* by *Logos*, in *Psal. 91* so well as in other places, which in English is *word* or *speech*."[22] In another pamphlet, Clapham elaborates:

[B]y the *Septuagint* version of the word DEBER, it may be collected to haue bene the Church of *Israels* judgement. The word DEBER in proper English *The Pestilence*, they turne by the Greeke word *Logos* in English *The Word*; as if in the text it were not DEBER but DABAR, this indeed signifying a *Word*; and the very terme, that Saint *John* in his first chapter doth giue vnto the Son of God, by whom as by a *Word*, the Creature had his beginning and being. So that the 91. Psalm and third verse, they thus read, He *shall deliuer thee from the Word*, not the Pestilence. And why? Because that Pest (as the comon Creature at first) had the beginning and being solely by the word of God: and this Plague for contemning the blessed Covenant sealed vp in him that is *Logos the Word*. Afterwardes in the sixt verse of the same Psalme, the Hebrue-Greeks read, thou shalt not be affraide … *of the thing*, instead of pestilence. Why? Because it was such a RHEMA, such a PRAGMA, such a Thing, as they knew not properly how to terme it in the Greeke language.[23]

It appears that the translators of the Hebrew scripture into the Greek of the Septuagint mistook the one word for the other, since they rendered the word for plague as "*Logos* in English *The Word*; as if in the text it were not DEBER but DABAR." Their puzzlement seems to persist when they come to Psalm 91,

---

21. Cited in Wilson, *The Plague in Shakespeare's London*, 158.
22. Clapham, *Epistle*, B1r.
23. Clapham, *Henoch Clapham His Demaundes and Answeres*, B1r.

for there they translate the Hebrew "pestilence" simply as *the thing*," because "they knew not properly how to terme it in the Greeke language." Yet such an opaque translation, as Clapham goes on to speculate, may actually have been intentional. The Septuagint translators avoided common Greek words for epidemic disease, choosing instead the more mysterious "thing," whereby they "checked the Gentiles, as Ignorant of that plagues cause." A stumbling block to the Gentiles, DBR is a "miraculous Thing," at once a plague and a word, at once the Word and the Thing—that is, the substance of God's material creation that emanates from the Word, and from which the word cannot be separated. Thus, the Gentiles—frustrated by any attempt to comprehend the biblical plague in the usual (medical) sense—would be forced to leave "their great Naturians" and "come unto the written *Word* of God for better learning." And in so doing, "they shall finde that DEBER is indeed DABAR, which not only signifieth a *Word*, but also a *Thing*; Yes a *miraculous Thing*; as in Genes. 18. where *Sarah* thinking the word of promise impossible, the Angel thus checkes her; *shall any* DABAR *be heard* [i.e., "hard," but perhaps also "heard"] *to the Lord?* Where that miraculous thing was to be effected by the power of the word DABAR signifying both."[24]

Clapham's maze of biblical cross-references should not obscure the main point of his analysis, which centers on the wonderful coincidence, as it appeared to these divines, that the same three-letter Hebrew root DBR (דבר) can mean either "plague" or "word." The difference lies in the context, of course, and in the pronunciation ("deber," "dabar"), which is only visible in the post-biblical system of pointing Hebrew vowels. For Clapham, however, this Hebrew homonym signifies nothing less than a miracle. DBR was present at the creation when "as by a *Word*, the Creature had his beginning and being." As the Logos bespeaks the language of providential history, DBR is present again in Genesis 18, where the words of the angel fulfill the impossible promise (it-

---

24. Ibid. For Psalm 91:3, where the King James will have "noisome pestilence," Clapham follows the Vulgate (90:3, "verbo aspero") and then the Douay-Rheims version ("sharp word") for the rendering of the Hebrew "deber" or "dabar" (without points, the words have the identical root דבר [DBR]). In 91:6, "deber" is again "pestilence" in the King James, but Douay-Rheims ("business") follows the Vulgate ("negotio") and the Septuagint in understanding the Hebrew as "dabar." The Geneva Bible has "pestilence" in both 91:3 and 91:6. The note to 91:3 in the Geneva Bible reads, "Gods helpe is moste readie for vs, whether Satan assaile vs secretly, w[hich] he calleth a snare; or openly, which is here ment by the pestilence." This raises a possibility entertained by no other plague writing I have seen: that the pestilence is visited upon us by Satan.

self an anticipation of the new "beginning" of the Nativity) that Sarah should have a child. As identical with the Word, every Thing to the last syllable of recorded time reiterates the wonder-working of DBR in human affairs. DBR thus bespeaks the essential Augustinian conflation of words and things in the operation of the Logos, wherein "thing" is itself a word, and every "thing" (in the language of scripture) is also a sign (of another thing).[25] It also paradoxically conflates the double-talk of divine speech: judgment and mercy, the "blow" of pestilential death and the promise of renewed life. The example of the angel's announcement to Sarah suggests the redemptive sense in which this "thing" signified by DBR could be read as a blessing. Yet the conflation of the plague with the Logos, the Word itself, hints at a more disturbing implication that Clapham can't acknowledge—that God's Word is not only the agency of the pestilence, but pestilential in itself.

The connection between plagues and words recurs often in the writing of the time. In *The Wonderfull Yeare*, Dekker encourages his reader to *read* as a form of prophylaxis: "If you read, you may happilie laugh . . . because mirth is both *Phisicall*, and wholesome against the *Plague*"; but he also cautions that "this booke is . . . somewhat infected" with the same disease—playing on the fear that the book itself might be a source of contagion, "plague" harboring the plague (3). In *A Rod for Run-awaies*, Dekker imagines God's plague writing as a kind of bookkeeping, a figure that will recur in Jonson, Pepys, and Defoe— inevitably, insofar as the most tangible index of the plague is the body count: "For, God will not have his Strokes hidden: his markes must bee seene. . . . As his mercy will be exalted in our weekely Bills (when the totall summes fall) so will hee have his iustice and indignation exemplified, in the increasing of those Bills: and therefore let no man goe about to abate the number: His Arithmetick brookes no crossing" (151–52). In calculating these sums, God

---

25. Augustine writes, "All instruction is either about things or about signs; but things are learnt by means of signs. I now use the word "thing" in a strict sense, to signify that which is never employed as a sign of anything else: for example, wood, stone, cattle, and other things of that kind. Not, however, the wood which we read Moses cast into the bitter waters to make them sweet, nor the stone which Jacob used as a pillow, nor the ram which Abraham offered up instead of his son; for these, though they are things, are also signs of other things. There are signs of another kind, those which are never employed except as signs: for example, words. No one uses words except as signs of something else; and hence may be understood what I call signs: those things, to wit, which are used to indicate something else. Accordingly, every sign is also a thing; for what is not a thing is nothing at all" (*On Christian Doctrine*, 1.2.2–5, from http://ccat.sas.upenn.edu/jod/augustine.html).

has nothing to hide. As the evidence of his revealed will, the divine "strokes" reveal a set of books in perfect order. No man can "abate" (i.e., "cross" out, or cancel) the debt these books record. The lower the death toll, the greater the mercy; the higher the death toll, the greater the justice exacted by a cross God. Falling or rising, the numbers of plague deaths tabulated in the weekly bills of mortality strike a true balance between the two, and God alone is the keeper of the books. In these figures, the Word of the plague is marked on the body as with the "strokes" of God's pen, then retranscribed, in print, on the bills: bodies and bills are equally, and interchangeably, legible. God's "indignation" suggests that the genre of his plague writing is Juvenalian satire, an excoriation of evil.

Dekker's language also suggests that the plague body is a site of revelation, where at a time of apocalyptic suffering and the execution of justice on a mass scale, what is "hidden . . . must bee seene." Two things are hidden here, and revealed: the tokens of the individual's sin are plainly displayed on his body, while at the same time the marked body may be read as a page in the unfolding providential history "marking" the passage from the biblical plagues through the plague of 1603 and culminating in the end, when "there fell upon men a great hail out of heaven" and "the plague thereof was exceeding great" (Revelation 16:21). God's marks in scripture signify across time, as the Christian reader is instructed by George Herbert, and the destiny of the individual is implicated in this "motion":

> This verse marks that, and both do make a motion
> Unto a third, that ten leaves off doth lie:
> Then as dispersed herbs do watch a potion,
> These three make up some Christians destinie.[26]

The red crosses painted on the doorposts of plague houses in 1603 are prefigured in the blood painted "for a token" on the houses of the Israelites in Egypt, a sign both recalling the promise of Exodus 12:23—"when I see the blood, I will pass over you, and the plague shall not be upon you to destroy you, when I smite the land of Egypt"—and anticipating the final judgment, when the righteous will be saved even in the midst of universal calamity. Dekker's

---

26. Herbert, "Holy Scriptures II," ll. 5–8, in *Works*, 58.

God whose "Arithmetick" of justice and mercy "brookes no crossing" is both a cross God and the God who died on the cross. Like a *pharmakon*, the same Word inscribes the plague and prescribes its cure. Its "motion" is a "potion"; its verses, "dispersed herbs" waiting to be gathered up at the end into the posy of salvation. Herbert, who as a boy survived the plague summer of 1603 along with his schoolmates in the countryside, would write of the Word, "Thou art all health," health "thriving till it make / A full eternitie."[27]

In these formulations, DBR collapses the distinction between speech and writing, since this word, both recorded as a visible mark in scripture and expressed on the body of the plague victim, is the direct expression of God's living Word. It is felt as a kind of sonic boom to let the guilty know they have been "struck." In both formats (books and bodies), the Word is made visible, but the only thing to be seen is the "wonderful" evidence of the debt of sin, which the victim is now made to repay. The corollary to a theory of plague-as-speech holds that inflammatory speech itself is closely akin to plague, hardly less infectious than the tainted breath of the victim. In Italy, a Franciscan preacher regards the reformers as a scourge of the church, beginning when "the wicked Luther mounted his cathedral of pestilence" to spread his heretical doctrines among the masses.[28] Before accepting those heretical doctrines as his own, Henry VIII had castigated Luther's attempt to "enfect" the English "with the deedly corruption and contagious odour of his pestylent errours."[29] In his history of Richard III, More speaks of ambition and the desire of vainglory as a "pestilente serpente" spawning debate and dissension, a metaphor seemingly inevitable in both religious and political polemic.

In the emergency of 1603, Henoch Clapham's pamphlet would itself be regarded as a kind of contagion, infecting the vulnerable with its noxious opinions. From the beginning of the summer, the presses were spewing out dozens of plague pamphlets and broadsheets, sermons, medical tracts, ballads, and advertisements for quack cures.[30] Who could tell which of them, like Spenser's monstrous Errour vomiting books and papers, might spread panic, false hope, or disaffection? As with Dekker's "infected" book, the fear of

---

27. Herbert, "Holy Scriptures I," ll. 115–16, *Works*, 58.
28. Quoted in Mormando, introduction to Bailey et al., *Hope and Healing*, 19.
29. Quoted in Healy, "Discourses of the Plague in Early Modern London," 22.
30. On the connection between ballads and the plague, see Achinstein, "Plagues and Publication."

contagion (and the contagion of fear) attaches both to the pestilential speech proliferated by the published book and to the book itself as a material carrier of "contagion," like coins or bedclothes. To imply, as Clapham had in his book, that it was uncharitable for men of faith to refuse to minister to the sick might prompt ministers who left their flocks unattended to question their own motives. Worse, it might lead people to flout the law, questioning the efficacy of quarantine and, by doing so, aggravating the plague. What better remedy, then, for such a problem in "homeland security" than to quarantine the author of the *Epistle* behind bars?

Writing that same summer, Roger Fenton draws the connection between words and plagues tighter when he remarks that "[t]he word which commonly is vsed in Scripture of the pestilence, is deriued from a verbe that signifieth to speake, as some thinke, because, where it is, euery one speaketh of it, enquireth after it, how it encreaseth, what remedies there be for it." In reply to such idle chatter, and in the absence of a speedy atonement, God "will indeede speake with vs" in "a worde and a blow."[31] In his *Due Preparations for the Plague*, Defoe draws the same comparison in an attempt to describe the process of contagion: "The effluvia of infected bodies may, and must be indeed, conveyed from one to another by air; so words are conveyed from the mouth of the speaker to the ear of the hearer by the interposition and vibration of the air, and the like of all sounds."[32] In light of the suspicion that plague could indeed be communicated through the breath, or that the breath of the afflicted could thicken the poisonous miasma in which the pestilence lurked, metaphor slides easily into identity, suggesting that contaminated speech itself could not only provoke but disseminate the disease.

Case Studies

The three following graphic examples will illustrate the difference between the Italian plague imagery surveyed above and the English plague imaginary conceived by the light of the Word. They will lead to a consideration, in the following chapters, of Ben Jonson's epigram on the plague death of his first son, in which the "all father" has not only taken the poet's son, but—like a

31. Fenton, *A Perfume against the Noysome Pestilence*, A4v–5r.
32. Defoe, *Due Preparations for the Plague*, 12.

The meaning of the Title page.

Behold; and marke; and mind, ye British Nations,
this dreadfull Vision of my Contemplations.
Before the Throne of Heav'n, I saw, me thought,
This famous Island into question brought,
With better cares then those my Body beare,
I heard impartiall IVSTICE to declare
God's Benefits, our Thankelessesse, and what
Small heed, his Love, or Iudgements here begat,
I vew'd eternall MERCIE, how she strove
Gods just deserved Vengeance to remove.
That, so en reist our Sinnes, and cry'd so loud,
That, at the last, I saw a dismall Cloud
Exceeding blacke, as from the Sea ascending,
And over all this Isle it selfe extending:
With such thicke foggie Vapours, that their fleames
Send, for a while, to darken MERCIES beames,
Within this fearfull Cloud, I did behold
All Plagues and Punishments, that name I could.
And with a trembling heart, I fear'd each houre,
God would this Tempest on this Island poure.
Yet, better hopes appear'd: for, loe, the Rayes
Of MERCY pierc'd this Cloud, & made such waies
Quite through those Exhalations, that mine eye
De(s)his Inscription, thereupon espie;   ((said,
BRITAINES REMEMBRANCER: &, somewhat
These words (me thought) The Storm is, yet, delaid,
And if ye doe not penitence defer,
This CLOVD is only, a REMEMBRANCER.
But, if ye still affect impiety,
Expect, e're long, what this may signifie.
This having heard and seene, I thought, nor fit
Nor safe it were, for me to smother it:
And, therefor, both to others eyes, and mine,
Have off'red, here, what unto mine appeares.
Iudge as ye please, ye Readers, this, or me:
Truth will be Truth, how e'ere it censur'd be,
                                    GEO: WITHER.

FIGURE 10. George Wither, *Britain's Remembrancer*, title page (1628).

jealous rival poet himself—has spoken the word that will bury Jonson's flesh-made-word, his "best piece of *poetrie.*"

WITHER'S *Britain's Remembrancer*

As I noted in the previous chapter, the frontispiece to George Wither's *Britain's Remembrancer* (1628) offers the "*dreadfull* Vision" of the poet's "Contemplations": a "*dismall* Cloud / *Exceeding blacke, as from the* Sea *ascending,* / *And over all this* isle *it selfe extending*" (fig. 10). This is, apparently, a private vision, one "seen" only in the eye of the writer's mind. It is made visible in the accompanying illustration, but only as the transcription, as it were, of the mental image narrated in the accompanying verses, and not—as would be the case with the images we have seen above—as an image with its own uncontingent being. In the eight long cantos of invective, lamentation, and exhortation to follow, Wither will assume the role of the Old Testament prophet warning the nation of an impending pestilential calamity. At the top of the image, the cloud parts to reveal the name of God, the tetragrammaton that is at once the source of the threatened affliction and the only source of its relief. The divine is now represented by a word, effacing and replacing the human countenance no longer possible in an iconophobic theology. Nor are there any intermediate figures to cross the sharp dividing line in the image between the black cloud above and the white map of the kingdom below. Allegorical figures of Mercy and Justice preside over the scene to either side of the divine name. The cloud is full of archers, supine victims, cadaverous figures, and, to the left, an army on the march—a reminder that plague is one part of a triad of conventionally related afflictions also including famine and war.

From the distant perspective of Wither's cartographic image of England visible beneath the lowering cloud, it is clear that the nation, rather than (as in Italy) the town or the city, is endangered, its fate hanging in the balance. Indeed, in what follows, plague becomes the lens through which the nation itself comes into focus: Wither imagines it as a single diseased body with enfeebled sinews, poor digestion, and tainted blood, its corporate sins having already weakened its moral defenses.[33] In terms of the metaphor of the state-as-body, the new king is prudently exempt from any responsibility for the national malady, however, since "[w]e seldome see the *Bodies* torment bred / By aught which first arises from the head." Rather, "oftentimes we feele both head and eyes / Diseeas'd by fumes which from the *body* rise" (227). Perhaps coincidentally—or not, given Wither's increasingly pronounced Puritan leanings, and the further coincidence that the plague years of 1603 and 1625 mark the beginning and the end of James's reign—the cloud appears to descend from the north and at this moment hovers threateningly just above the Scottish border. On the causes of the pestilence, Wither acknowledges both sides of the question: it "partly *Metaphysicall* appears, / And partly *naturall*" (57). The sea surrounding that part of the island not yet covered by the roiling cloud is thronged with shipping, perhaps as a reminder of the commercial prosperity endangered by the plague, as well as of the maritime avenues of the plague's entry into Britain. The "*thicke foggie* Vapours" of the cloud suggest the "ascend-

---

33. Wither, *Britain's Remembrancer*, 226–27. Subsequent citations of this work are given parenthetically in the text.

ing" miasmal "Exhalations" of the plague, a further acknowledgment of what were thought to be its natural causes; but its descent from above certifies its divine origin. The cloud is pierced only by one merciful ray of light, which will, however, be extinguished if the nation remains impenitent.

The function of this shaft of light is to indicate, and illuminate, the language on the banner to which Wither draws our attention: BRITAIN'S RE-MEMBRANCER. Expounding the "meaning of the Title page," the poet takes heart from this "inscription," which he understands as signifying that his vision is only a warning, a reminder of what will descend on a sinful nation (yet once more, following the epidemic of 1625) if it remains obstinate. The relationship between inscription and image is here the reverse of what we saw in the Continental *Pestblätter*. There, the *ora pro nobis* provides a text that the viewer will address to the image. Here, the image serves to direct our attention to the inscription. As a "remembrancer," the image may be conceived, like the Protestant Communion wafer, as mnemonic rather than substantial. It asks us to remember past epidemics, and it recalls our attention to our own sins. Its function is thus indexical, the shaft of light directing the eye toward the words in which its "meaning" is revealed. The viewer, who appropriately holds a book in his hands—Wither's book—is given the role of a reader of language illuminated, like the language of scripture, by divine grace and explicated in the accompanying poem. Indeed, in this light, to take the image literally, as it were, would be a hermeneutic error, since the cloud is not "really" there but might only be there if the nation does not heed the call to repentance. Rather than representing any present reality—except for the psychological reality of the vision in the mind of the poet—it intends to move the viewer to recall his past sins in time or else to anticipate a disastrous future. Contemplation of the plague leads to a call for continuing the work of moral reformation. If Britain repents, the cloud and the image by which it is represented will evaporate, leaving the nation bathed in the unobstructed light of God's mercy. Nonetheless, as the occlusion of the divine in, and by, the image reminds us, God has his "hidden counsels," which we can only take on faith will not be inconsistent with his "disclosed purposes" (54).

Unfolding those purposes is the burden of the poet, here speaking not only as a latter-day Jeremiah but in the self-appointed capacity as Britain's "remembrancer." Unofficially a memoirist or diarist, a remembrancer is also an officer of the Exchequer, the Crown, or the City of London who acts as recording secretary, keeper of records (the official rolls), and administrative agent,[34] Years later, Wither notes that he had actually entertained some hopes of being appointed as City Remembrancer.[35] The would-be authorization thus combines the role of the prophet as one who speaks *against* the ills of the age with that of an official representative who speaks *for* the city or the court (here, for the entire nation), the one who records their proceedings and, in one of the remembrancer's historical capacities, collects their debts. In this judicial guise, even as he represents England in its appeal for mercy, Wither "taxes" the nation with its sins—or, as may be said, scourges it with a pro-phylactic dose of invective intended to avert a visitation more merciless in its collection of the lives God is owed. But the poet's prophetic zeal suggests that this is a joint appointment sanctioned by God as well as the state, as Wither seems willing to claim with only the hint of a scruple:

> And if by thee I was appointed, Lord,
> Thy *Iudgements* and thy *Mercies* to record,
> (As here I do) set thou thy mark on those,
> Who shall despightfully the same oppose?
>
> (283)

As Britain's remembrancer and God's, the medium of the divine warning and the mediator of an imperiled nation, the poet occupies the vacated role of the plague saint.

In explicating the frontispiece of his poem, Wither also speaks as the would-be emblematist, prospective author of *A Collection of Emblemes* (1635), the one work among the extraordinary number of his publications for which he is generally known today. Like the graphic "body" of an emblem, the fron-tispiece to the *Remembrancer* depends upon the "soul" of the accompanying poem to extract its meaning. Indeed, the 288 pages of verse following may be regarded as a vast exfoliation of the preceding image, a reading out into language of what the image implies. Although the emblematist juxtaposes text and picture as versions of one another, his practice, as W. J. T. Mitchell has noted, tips the scales in favor of language: poetry, the "speaking picture,"

---

34. *Oxford English Dictionary Online* (hereafter OED *Online*), s.v. "remembrancer."
35. Wither, *A Memorandum to London*, 28.

gives voice to the image's "mute poesy."[36] In Protestant emblematics, too, the pictorial body always carries a fleshly tinge, its function like that of the old law to point the reader (*as* a reader) toward the deeper significance explicated in the word. Geffrey Whitney precedes Wither in describing such a process of emblematic reading, in *A Choice of Emblemes* (1586). The reader who merely "gazeth" at a book "reapes but toile, and never gaineth fame: / First reade, then marke, then practice that is good, / . . . Then printe in minde, what wee in printe do reade."[37] Braden Cormack and Carla Mazzio read this passage in Whitney as recommending, in effect, a "vividly material" technology of fruitful reading, by which "remembering is a mental copying aligned with mechanical reproduction, so that reading-as-use essentially reprints the book, but this time in a form useful to a single individual."[38] The proper use of reading—a reading practice congenial to those accustomed to identifying the visible with the carnal, and with hearing scripture explained in terms of "doctrine" and "uses"—cannot stop at the superficial level of the gaze. It depends, finally, not upon any direct appropriation of the images in emblem books, but upon converting them, along with the text before one's eyes, into a kind of mental letterpress. The process is vivid, but what is copied into the mind is not the impression of an image (as it might be in a more Platonizing epistemology), but the impressed "mark" of the text that puts the image to use.

What indexes this emblematic procedure of reading to Wither's task as a plague writer is his use of the word "mark," the key term in the poet's contract, cited above, with the divine author. As the Lord's remembrancer, Wither will "record" God's judgments and mercies. His parenthetical "([a]s here I do)" calls attention not only to his book as proof that he is fulfilling his duties by inscribing his "mark" on the wicked, but also to the specific moment and activity of writing this very line. With the marks that appear on the page, the poet's muse sets "her markes on those / Who *Vertue* in her honest cause oppose" (6). God's part, in turn, will be to set his "mark" on all who oppose his own judgments and mercies, and as well—or so the blurry syntax of the passage seems to say—on those opposed to the poet's record. Co-authors of Britain's destiny, God and Wither both set their mark on a spiteful nation. In this context, it is not for

---

36. Mitchell, *Iconology*; see especially pt. 2, "Image versus Text: Figures of the Difference," 47ff.
37. Whitney, *A Choice of Emblemes*, 171.
38. Cormack and Mazzio, *Book Use, Book Theory*, 2.

the sake of mere rhetorical emphasis that the poet begins by thrice exhorting the nation to "[b]ehold; *and* marke *and* mind" the "meaning of the Title page." In addition to its more recent meanings (to "look," "regard," or "note well"), the verb *mark* for Wither still means, in its older senses, to "record," "inscribe," or "annotate"—that is, literally to mark the text.[39] This a diligent Renaissance reader would likely do in any event as an aid to memory, perhaps by underlining or by putting an asterisk, a pointing hand, or a marginal remark next to the key passages that Wither himself emphasizes by use of the word.

The three terms of Wither's exhortation also work as a sequence: one beholds the image (or the text as an image, what one sees on the page at first glance) and then commits it to mind (thereby minding its injunctions) by the more attentive, intermediate process of putting his own mark on it. The reader thus becomes, as an accomplice of the author, a writer in the act of reading, pen in hand. Again and again in the course of the following poem, the author cautions his readers to "marke" his words so that they themselves may be marked, for good or ill—either with "[t]hose markes, that Seales of thy free pardon are" (25), or with the pestilence that once "could mark / Their eldest-born" of Egypt (22).[40] If the pestilence should come again, armed with its characteristic bubonic signs, the disease—itself a plague-writer on human flesh—will choose its victims by a judicious (and judicial) reading of the marks with which they are already inscribed, as if it were poring over volumes in a bookstall:

> It is a rationall *Disease*, which can
> Pick, with discretion, here and there a man;
> And passe o're those, who either marked are
> For *Mercy*; or, a greater *Plague* to beare.
>
> (57–58)

---

39. OED *Online*, s.v. "mark." Cf. definition 9, "to annotate," as in the example given from John Wycliffe's *English Works*: "Grete clerkis merken vp-on þis worde of þe gospelle."

40. In the same vein, evil men are "markt for Vengeance" (224), plague victims are "markt for Death" (107), and Jews bear the "mark of *Caine*" (167); but God "doth know / And Marke" the nature of the faithful man (61; cf. 101). Even illiterate peasants "[w]ho for their *Names* will make their *Sheepmarks* stand" will not escape being marked, since they "can play the subtile cheating knaves" as well as their betters (213).

Leaving it perhaps intentionally unclear by whom men are to be "marked," the passage explains (away) the vexed problem of a plague theodicy by providing a reason why some are spared and others not, although it would doubtless be cold comfort to lucky ones to know—or, rather, to fear, since individuals cannot read the marks of their own salvation—that they may be passed over only because a "greater *Plague*" lies in store.

God will be particularly provoked if any should dare to "burne this *Rowle*, in which recorded are / Thy just *Inditements*." If you think to consign Wither's book to the fire, "it shall written be / With new additions" and reissued by the plague in an expanded version that will add the sin of biblioclasm to your list. It will be "deeply stampt on thee / With such *Characters*, that no time shall race / Their fatall image, from thy scarred face" (255). Thus, if you fail to keep the *Remembrancer* in mind, you will wear it on your face.

In Wither's final apocalyptic vision, an unrepentant nation will be laid waste wholesale, though by a still-rational disease that acts with due "proportion":

Yea throughout all this *Iland*, it will rage
And lay it wast before another age.
For, not our *cities* onely tainted are
With sinnes contagion; but ev'n ev'ry where
This *Land* is so diseas'd, that many doubt
(Before it mend) some blood must issue out.
There is not any Towneship, Village, Borrough,
Or petty Hamlet, all this Kingdome thorough,
But merits (in proportion) as much blame,
As any City of the greatest fame.

(213)

In this account of Britain's destruction, plague is seen (and its Author vindicated) as the agent of the cure for a land already "so diseas'd" as to require the most drastic measures. The prescribed therapy, however, goes far beyond a course of Galenic bloodletting, exceeding in the poet's inspired vision of it any measure of proportion or rationality by which the disease is supposed to be governed. Instead, the poet imagines a proto-nuclear scene of a devastated and depopulated nation:

Thy *Villages*, where goodly dwellings are,
Shall stand as if they unfrequented were.
Thy *Cities*, and thy *Palaces*, wherein
Most neatnesse and magnificence hath bin,
Shall heaps of rubbish be; and (as in those
Demolisht *Abbies*, wherein Dawes, and Crowes,
Now make their nests) the bramble, and the nettle,
Shall in their halls, and parlours, root, and settle.
Thy Princes houses, and thy wealthy Ports,
Now fill'd with men of all degrees and sorts,
Shall no inhabitants in them retaine,
But some poore Fisherman, or country Swaine,
Who of thy glories, when the marks they see,
Shall wonder what those mighty ruines be;
As now they doe, who old foundations find,
Of Townes and Cities, perisht out of mind.
The places where much people meetings had,
Shall vermine holes, and dens for beasts be made.

(256)

These and other such remarkably exultant passages foresee the plague com-
pleting the work of the Reformation with a vengeance. Where the Henrician
reformers had left "Demolisht *Abbies*" in their wake, the plague will reduce
whole villages, cities, and courts to "heaps of rubbish." Wither's muse has now
taken flight, affording him the same bird's-eye view of the nation as that of the
map of England on the title page, and transporting him into a (near) future
when the very features of that map ("wealthy Ports," "Townes and Cities") will
have been effaced. He has now also gone far beyond any recognizable account
of even the most widespread epidemic, imagining the nation as a universal ruin
from which all human presence has also been wiped away—save for that of a
solitary "Fisherman, or country Swaine." This post-apocalyptic survivor, whose
only companions are the birds, the beasts, and the vermin, seems to inhabit
some even more remote future when the cities and their people will not only
have perished but "perisht out of mind," and he alone will be left to "wonder,"
as he gazes, "what those mighty ruines be." What he sees in its final stage is the
unwriting of a Vitruvian history of civilization wherein human builders learn

from the birds and beasts, constructing their first rude, and then more elaborate, shelters and forming human communities. This undoing of the nation is the dark vision that haunts the discourse of national identity. It here enlists the memory of the early Reformation as a founding event of Wither's England, but in the service of a nightmare of not only the nation's demise but the world's decreation. As a link in the history of catastrophic upheaval, Wither's book suggests as well the connection between the imaginary of the bubonic plague as an instrument of the divine wrath—an unsparing root-and-branch reformer whose work will not be finished until the world is destroyed—and the apocalyptic religious and political visions of the mid-seventeenth century.

Worse yet (though it seems no literate person will be left to care), the fishermen and swains who apparently make up the tiny remnant of Britain's people will no longer be able to read the "marks" represented by the "mighty ruines" before them. With no memory of what caused the destruction they survey, the plague itself will have been effaced from the record: they are left merely to "wonder," for—like degraded stone fragments on which some dead language is inscribed—the ruins will now be illegible, even though they record the DBR of God's glory. When Britain will have crumbled into one of the dead civilizations buried beneath its own ruins, not only the cities and the plague but remembrance itself will have disappeared. The process seems inevitable, despite the poet's exhortations to repentance, a consummation devoutly to be wished as the fulfillment of his own prophecy. When Wither asserts that "God (with a *writers inke horne*) one hath sent, / To set a *marke* on them that shall repent" (278), there can be little doubt as to the identity of the co-author to whom this dire commission has been entrusted. The inkhorn recalls us to the immediate scene of Wither's writing, to the ink that marks the letters of his dark predictions, and to the "*dismall* Cloud / *Exceeding blacke*" that spills down the map of England. When the Black Death has covered all the white space on the page, the plague writer's work will be done.

PLAGUE BROADSHEETS

Wither's inkhorn reminds us as well that in the absence of any extant plague painting, English plague imagery is graphic, largely in the form of woodcuts. In Wither's *Remembrancer*, in Thomas Dekker's *A Rod for Run-awaies* (1625; fig. 11), and in Henry Petowe's *The Country Ague* (1625; fig. 12), these are already embedded in a book, and so share the black-and-white format and the

FIGURE 11. Thomas Dekker, *A Rod for Run-awaies*, frontispiece (1625).

reproductive technology of the printed word. When the plague strikes, England produces and reproduces its own humbler repertoire of occasional plague imagery: broadsheets depicting the ravages of a London outbreak (figs. 13–16). These appeared weekly or monthly during plague seasons. They disseminated weekly mortality statistics taken from the official bills, and they featured pious exhortations, the text of sermons, comparative figures for other plague years going back in most cases to 1592, "remedies," and other bits of plague "news." Sheets would be reprinted—in some cases, from plague to plague—with the same illustrations and hortatory material, but flanked by the latest mortality figures.[41] Very likely, anxious Londoners would get their updates from such sheets. Many copies of such ephemera have not survived, but according to Walter George Bell, others were kept and treasured, perhaps as a record of the past epidemic or as admonitory reading material for the next.[42] The broadsheet illustrations, like Dekker's

---

41. *Londons Lord Have Mercy*, shown in examples from 1665 (figs. 13–15), also exists in a version published in 1637 (STC [2nd ed.] / 4273, in the British Library), which contains mortality statistics up to the most recent outbreak of 1636.

42. Bell, *The Great Plague*, 125.

FIGURE 12. Henry Petowe, *The Country Ague*, title page, detail (1625).

earlier title-page image, all follow the same basic design, with slight variations. Justice with her sword and flail may be seen in the angry cloud hanging over the city, pestilential arrows fall from the sky, the afflicted cry out for mercy, and death brandishes his dart and hourglass or his arrows in triumph. Weak and dispirited people are shown attempting to flee the afflicted city. Those with the means ride; others walk, or stagger, or fall to their knees, whether in prayer or in exhaustion. Mothers cradle dead infants; infants attempt to suckle dead mothers. Coffins are scattered here and there, while the uncoffined dead lie splayed on the open ground or abandoned in their winding-sheets. It is a "picture," says Dekker, "not drawne to the life, but to the death" (138).

The scene tends to be set in a kind of no-man's-land, a liminal space outside the city walls but not yet in view of any refuge in the country. The few scattered human figures visible in what is supposed to be a broad plain seem to foreshadow Wither's prophecy of a land bereft of people. Petowe's *The Country Ague* (1625; fig. 12) shows Mother London prepared to welcome back those of her children who have "made your peace with God"; to judge from the woodcut, they will return to a wasteland. Between the numbers of those who die and those who flee, laments Dekker, "the most populous City of Great Brittaine is almost desolate" (147). And yet Dekker also sees the plague as a necessity, not only because it is "the Purge to clense a Cittie" of sin, but because it enforces a grim yet ultimately charitable, proto-Malthusian solution to the problem of urban overpopulation and the consequent threat of famine: "Of Euils, tis the lighter broode, / A dearth of people then of foode" (102). In these illustrations, an armed watch guards the city gates, for no one can leave the city (officially) without a certificate of health from his parish, or return in obvious ill health. The broadside illustrations emphasize the reception runaway Londoners will face on the other side, even if they manage to get past security at the city gates. In Dekker's words, "the Countrey-people stand there, with Halberds and Pitchforkes to keepe them out" (149). With all gates barred, the solid barrier of the city wall at the runaways' back, and an alarmed peasantry blocking their path, what we see in effect is a killing field with no exit—and with a barrage of arrows raining down on those who pray and those who flee alike.

The verses below the woodcut in two 1665 versions of *Londons Lord Have Mercy upon Us* (figs. 13 and 15) appeal to the "Reader," reminding him of all the earlier outbreaks in the century and urging him to repent—through the act of doing what he is already doing, namely, reading:

> Let all infected Houses be thy *Text*,
> And make this *Use*, that thine may be the next.
> The *Red Crosse* still is us'd, as it hath bin,
> To shew they Christians are that are within:
> And *Lord have mercy on us* on the door,
> Puts thee in mind, to pray for them therefore.
> The *Watchman* that attends the house of sorrow,
> He may attend upon thy house to morrow.

The reader's eye is directed from the poem to the woodcut of the houses, and from there to "all infected Houses" in London, which are also to be regarded as a "*Text*." Those houses will have "*Lord have mercy on us*" inscribed on the door (just as the broadsheet does at the top), as well as the red cross as a sign of a plague house. The sign, the inscription, and the house are all to be read (like the broadsheet itself) as a composite text—in fact, as the kind of scriptural text on which a plain-style sermon might be composed, with its emphasis on the doctrine and the "uses," or such applications to the individual

LONDONS
LORD HAVE MERCY UPON US.

A true Relation of Seven modern *Plagues* or *Visitations* in *London*, with the number of those that were Buried of all Diseases; *Viz* The first in the year of Queen ELIZABETH, *Anno* 1592. The second in the year 1603 the third in (that never to be forgotten year) 1625. The fourth in *Anno* 1630. The fift in the year 1636. The sixt in the year 1637. and 1638. The seventh this present year, 1665.

An exact and true relation of the number of those that were buried in *London* and the Liberties of all Diseases, from the 17 of March 1592. to the 22 of December, 1592.

	totall.	Pl.
March 17	311	31
March 24	219	29
March 31	297	27
April 7	203	23
April 14	290	37
April 21	310	41
April 28	350	29
May 5	339	38
May 11	300	42
May 15	410	58
May 26	410	62
June 1	441	81
June 9	399	99
June 11	401	108
June 23	850	118
June 30	1440	927
July 7	1510	893
July 14	1491	258
July 21	1507	852
July 28	1503	988
August 4	1550	797
August 11	1532	615
August 18	1508	449
August 25	1490	507
September 1	1210	563
September 8	621	451
September 15	629	349
September 22	450	130
September 29	408	317
October 6	421	323
October 13	330	308
October 20	320	301
October 27	310	301
November 3	309	209
November 10	301	12
November 17	321	93
November 24	349	94
December 1	231	86
December 8	229	71
December 15	386	39

Baptized 5817
The totall 18884
Of the Plague 11503

1603.
| | totall. | Pl. |

Certain approved Medicines for the Plague, both to prevent that contagion, and to expel it after it be taken; as have been Approved in Anno 1625. as also in this present Visitation, 1665.

TAke a pint of new Milk, and cut two cloves of Garlick very small, put it in the milk, and drink it mornings fasting, and it preserveth from infection.

READER, what ever thou art, rich or poor, Rowse up thy self, for Death stands at the door...

A cheap Medicine to keep from infection.

1636.
Buried in *London* and the Liberties, of all diseases, the number as followeth, totall. Pl.

		Pl.
April 7	199	2
April 14	205	4

This Week was added to the City parishes.
S. Marg. Westminster. Lambeth.
S. Mary Newington.
Redriffe Parish.
S. Mary Islington.
Stepney parish.
Hackney parish.

		Pl.
April 21	289	14
April 28	253	17
May 5	232	10
May 11	308	55
May 19	299	35
May 26	330	62
June 2	359	62
June 9	345	87
June 16	381	102
June 23	304	79
June 30	352	104
July 7	115	81
July 14	373	104
July 21	371	99
July 28	422	151
August 4	461	206
August 11	538	285
August 18	638	331
August 25	789	459
September 1	1011	638
September 8	1069	650
September 15	1306	865
September 22	1493	924
September 29	1403	993
October 6	1401	991
October 13	1001	555
October 20	1300	838
October 27	1104	733
November 10	959	673
November 17	857	476
November 24	459	167
December 1	393	115
December 15	381	
December 29		

The totall of all the Burials this year, 27413
of the plague, 11011.

1638.
Buried in London & the Liberties this year of all diseases, 11661
of the plague, 508

1646.
Buried in London, and the Liberties, this year of all Diseases,
Of the Plague, 2436

1647.
Buried in London, and the Liberties, this year of all Diseases, 14652
Of the Plague, 4385

1648.
Buried in London, and the Liberties, this year of all Diseases, 11509
Of the Plague, 693

1665.
Buried in London & the Liberties, of all diseases, the number as followeth.
	totall.	Pl.
April 25	398	2
May 2	388	0
May 9	347	3
May 16	353	9
May 23	385	14
May 30	399	17
June 6	405	43
June 13	558	112

1637.
	totall.	Pl
January 5	281	116
January 12	214	123
January 19	168	59
January 26	289	67
February 2	151	103
February 16	28	78
February 23	154	44
March 1	161	69
March 9	332	100
March 16	307	88
March 23	303	50
March 31	343	113
April 7	301	98
April 14	289	79
April 21	300	109
May 11	300	100
May 18	185	74
May 25	314	83
June 1	290	54
June 8	272	72
June 15	266	116
June 22	304	105
June 29	371	156
July 6	361	163
July 13	331	130
July 20	335	17
August 3	300	99
August 10	375	74
August 17	309	30
September 7	227	36
September 14	300	31
September 21	189	18
September 28	166	11
October 5	174	13

The total of the Burials this year,
of the plague, 5603

In the Out-Parishes this Week of the Plague,
S. Andrews Holborn 91
S. Bartholomew great 5
S. Bartholomew Less 0
S. Brides parish 8
Bridewel Precinct 0
S. Botolph Aldersgate 0
S. Botolph Algate 14
S. Dunstans Stepney 39
S. Dunstans West 3
S. Giles Cripplegate 114
S. Olaves Southwark 0
S. Saviours Southwark 1
S. Sepulchres parish 100
S. Thomas Southwark 8
Trinity Minories 1
At the Pesthouse 8
S. James Clerkenwel 5
S. Katharine Tower 0
Lambeth Parish 0
S. Magdalen Bermond 40
S. Mary Newington 4
S. Mary Islington 14
S. Mary Whitechappel 16
Redriff Parish 1
Stepney Parish 33
S. Clement Danes 24
S. Paul Covent Garden 14
S. Martins in the Fields 113
S. Mary Savoy 1
S. Margarets Westminster 56

Buried in the 97 Parishes within the Walls, from July 11 to the 18, of the Plague, ——56

1625.
Buried in *London* and the Liberties of all diseases, Anno 1625. the number here following.

	totall.	Pl.
September 1	3897	3344
September 8	3157	2550
September 15	2148	1672
September 22	1994	1551
September 29	1236	852

1630.
	totall.	Pl.
June 24	301	13
July 1	306	43
July 8	311	41
July 15	226	50
July 22	275	77
July 29	256	65
August 12	242	66
August 19	251	51

A Posset Drink to remove the Plague from the Heart.

AN Ale Posset-Drink with Pimpernel seethed in it, till it tastes strong of it, drunk often, removes the Infection, though it hath got to the very Heart.

An approved Remedy against the Plague.

TAke a sprig of *Rue*, alias, herb-of-grace, and shred it, and put it in a Figg or two, and eat it every morning fasting, it keeps the Body from Infection, and purifieth the blood.

Buried this week of all Diseases, 1761. Of the Plague, 9. Increased in the Burials, 459.
Parishes clear of the Plague, 76. Parishes Infected, 54.

London, Printed for Francis Coles, Thomas Vere, and John Wright.

FIGURE 14. *Londons Lord Have Mercy upon Us*, detail (1665).

as the preacher may draw out of the text for the day. As in the frontispiece
from Wither, the image has no "meaning" except in the use to which it is put.
Its value (as "thy *Text*") resides not in what one invests in the image, but in
what one draws out of it. The only human figure "visible," as it were, in this
text is the "Watchman," who watches us. Arguably, the saint's role as one who
watches over the afflicted has here been reduced to a surveillance function
performed by the officer of the parish deputed to ensure that no one leaves a
house under official quarantine.

The most obvious difference between Catholic plague imagery and the
Reformation plague art considered above lies in content and affect—in the
bleak portrayal of a killing ground rather than the more hopeful depiction of
a saintly intervention. These black-and-white woodcuts appearing in broadsheets or pamphlets have been "bleached" of color and detail, and depleted of
visual interest. Although they remain objects of vision no less than the grand-
est panel painting, they may also be described as more "linguistic" than iconic
in form, for two reasons. Absorbed into the format of the printed page, they
often contain texts and are themselves surrounded by texts that they illustrate,

LORD H VE MERCY UP)N US.

A true Relation of seven mod.. .lagues or *Visitations* in LONDON, wit. ne number of those that were Buried of all Diseases : *Viz.* The first in the Year of Queen *Elizabeth*, Anno 1592. The second, in the Year 1603. The third, in (that never to be forgotten Year) 1625. The fourth, in *Anno* 1630. The fifth, in the Year 1636. The sixth in the Year 1637. and 1638. The seventh in this present Year, 1665.

Certain approved Medicines the Plague, both to pre-at that contagion, and to well it after it be taken; have been Approved in no 1625. as also in this sent Visitation, 1665.

A cheap Medicine to keep from Infection.

Ake a pint of new Milk, and put two cloves of click very small, put it the Milk, and drink it mings fasting, and it pre-reth from infection.

A Posset Drink to remove the Plague from the Heart.

AN Ale Posset-Drink with Pimpernel seethed in it, till it tastes strong of it, drunk often, removes the Infection, though it hath got to the very Heart.

An approved Remedy against the Plague.

TAke a sprig of Rue, alias, herb of grace, and three it, and put it in a Figg or two and eat it every morning fasting, it keeps the Body from Infection, and purisi eth the bloud.

Reader, what ever thou art, rich or poor,
Rowse up thy self, for Death stands at the
If God sayes strike, he must, & will come in, (door;
For death we know is the reward of sin.
His very breath is so infectious grown,
He poysons every one he breathes upon ;
He is the Rich-mans terrour, makes him flye,
And bear away his baggs, as loath to die.
What shall the Poor do that behind do stay?
Death makes them rich, by taking them away.
But what shall Poor men do, that here do live,
'Tis surely fit the Rich should comfort give,
... Means unto them still afford ;
... such Rich men speak the rich in the Lord ;
Death ... all, but as ...
A Plague, which if ou mayst do if thou repent.
Doth make them fearful of ... punishment
Due unto sin, for time that ... vil spent.
Oh why was this not thoug.. m long ago !
When God expected our R entance to ?
Seventeen years since, a ltle ... Plague God sent,
He shook his Rod to move u.. to repent :
Not long before that time , a dearth of Corn
Was sent to us to see if we would turn :
And after that , there's no e deny it can ;
The Beasts did suffer for the sin of man :
Grasse was so short and small, that it was told,
Hay for four pound a Load was daily sold.
These Judgements God hath sent even to cite us
Unto Repentance, and from sin to fright us.
Oh stubborn *England* ! childish and unwise ,
So heavy laden with iniquities.

Return, return, unto thy loving Father,
Return I say with speed, so much the rather,
Because his Son thy Saviour pleads thy cause,
Though thou hast broken all his holy Lawes :
Say to thy self, My sins are cause of all
Gods Judgements that upon this Land do fall,
And sin's the cause that each one doth complain,
They have too much, sometimes to little rain :
Say to thy self, this Plague may be removed,
If I repent , as plainly may be proved
By *Niniveh* , that City great and large,
For God hath given unto his Angels Charge ;
To strike and to forbear as he sees fit ;
If it be so, then learn thou so much wit,
To use thy self endeavour to prevent
A Plague, which if ou mayst do if thou repent.
Let all infected Houses be thy Text ,
And make this *Use*, that thine may be the next.
The *Red Crosse* still is us'd, as it hath bin,
To shew they Christians are, that are within :
And *Lord have mercy on us*, on the Door,
Puts thee in mind , to pray for them therefore.
The *Watchman* that attends the House of sorrow,
He may attend upon thy House to morrow.
Oh where's the vowes we to our God have made!
When death and sickness came with Axe & Spade,
And hurl'd our Brethren up in heaps apace,
Even forty thousand in a little space :
The Plague was now is not yet removed,
Because that sin of us is still beloved,
Each spectacle of Death and Funeral ,
Puts thee and I in mind , We must die all.

FIGURE 15. *Londons Lord Have Mercy upon Us*, version 2 (1665).

Londons Loud Cryes to the Lord by Prayer:

Made by a Reverend Divine, and Approved of by many others: Most fit to be Used by every Master of a Family, both in City and Country. With an Account of Several modern Plagues, or Visitations in *London*, With the Number of those that then Dyed, as well of all Diseases, as of the *Plague*; Continued down to this present Day *August*, 8th. 1665.

O Mnipotent Lord, thou sin-revenging
God, who for disobedience diddest
Deut. 28. threaten thine own people of Israel *to smite*
35. *them in the knees, and in the legs with a sore*
Botch that could not be healed, from the sole of
the foot unto the top of the head: to smite them
vers 27. *with the botch of Egypt, whereof they could not*
be healed: Thou who by the mouth of thine
onely Son diddest fore-tell to the Jews that
Nation should rise against Nation, Kingdome
against Kingdom, and that there should be Fa-
Mat.24.7 *mines and Pestilences in diverse places:* Be
pleased, ô thou great, offended Lord, in the
bowells of thy compassion *to let thine anger*
Psal.85.4 *cease,* and to bow down thine eare to us
miserable sinners. O our God, thou seest
how we groan under the burthen of thy
wrathful indignation, bemoaning the generall sufferances for our more general sins.
Our sins, our sins doe far exceed the transgressions of Israel: yea they are greater
then those of the Jews against the true Mes-
sias; for thine own Apostle beareth them
witnesse, that *Had they known it, they would*
1Cor.2.8 *not have crucified the Lord of Glory:* but we
alas, both have known, and doe know him;
& yet we *crucifie to our selves the son of thee*
Heb. 6. 6 *our God afresh; and daily put him to an open*
shame. For these our offences thou hast begun thy Revenge, yea, and most justly too;
for thou art deer, though man should judge
thee. Under this thy heavy wrath we groan
O Lord, we cry, we howle; for *sicknesse* in-
creaseth, *death* approacheth: yea such a
sicknesse, and such a *death*, as maketh us
feare both our selves, and our neighbours;
because we have not *feared* thee the Lord of
hosts. Thou seest, ô Lord, our afflictions;
even that our *houses* are made our *prisons*, &
our *sores* our *companions.* Our *streets* are turned into *pastures*, our *towns* into *wildernesses*
and for our backwardness in our devotions,
our very doores instruct us to addresse our
selves unto thee, and to beseech thee *Lord* to
have mercy upon us. Our *days* are consumed
in sorrows, and languishing; and our *nights*
in weeping, and mourning. Thou woun-
dest us, and we cry; thou smitest us, and
we roare, thou plaguest us, and we are
troubled, we are dismayed. Our *Golgothaes*
are surfeited with the dead, and our habitations *infected* with the living. We fly from
place to place, from Country to Country;
and yet wee fly not from thy presence, wee
avoid not thy judgments. What shall wee
Jer.8.22. do, What shall we do? *Is there no balm,* O
Lord, *in Gilead? Is there no Physitian there?*
Why then is not the health of the daughter of
thy people recovered? Thy Son, thy mercifull Son, thy sweet Son Jesus was *sent*
to binde up the broken hearted, and to open the
Isa.66.1. *prisons to them that were bound, and to com-*
v.2. *fort them that mourn:* and he was not backward in the performance of this for which
he was sent; for *he healed all manner of sick-*
nesse, and all manner of diseases among the
Mat.4.23 *people.* At thy feet therefore, ô *Jesus* thou best
c.15.30. Physitian, we *cast our selves down. A mul-*
titude we are that ly at thy feet: Cure us, ô
Christ, heal us, ô Jesus, as thou diddest the
multitude. *A whole multitude once did seek*
to touch thee; for there went virtue out of thee;
Luk.6.19 *and thou healedst them all.* Thou wert *moved*
Mat. 14. *with compassion*, and didst *heal their sick.* Ma-
14. ny didst thou cure of their infirmities, and
plagues. Behold thy hand is not shortned that
Luk.7.21 *it cannot save; neither is thine ear heavy that*
thou canst not hear. The number of petitio-
Isa.59.1. ners cannot deter thee; the multitude of
[illegible]
Mat.3.10 *healed many:* therefore, with the multitude
in the Gospel, we presse upon thee, that we
may but *touch* thee; for thou hast virtue in
thee; thou hast power to heal. O Lord hear,
ô Lord forgive, ô Lord *heal* us of our grievous *wounds.* In the depth of thy fury when
thou didst resolve to be revenged of a Re-
Ezek. 12. bellious people, it was yet thy promise that
16. thou wouldest *leave a few from the Sword,*
and from the Famine, and from the Pestilence,
that they might declare all their abominations
among the people where they should come; that
they might know that thou art the Lord. As
thou hast *Plagued,* us thou hast *punished,* so
sorely, so grievously, that but few of us are
left: yet ô Lord, now at last look in mercy
upon us: ô Lord let this remnant finde thy
compassion. O cure us, ô heal us, ô help us
for thy mercy's sake. When thou wert angry
with *Egypt*, thou didst threaten to *smite it;*
but, even at that very *instant*, thou didst like Isa.19.22
wise promise to *heal it; and* that they should
return unto thee their Lord, and that thou
wouldest be intreated of them. Thou diddest Jer. 33 6
proclaim unto *Judah* that thou *wouldst bring*
it health, and cure; and wouldest *cure them,*
and reveale unto them abundance of peace &
truth. Thou didst promise unto Zion, that
thou wouldest *restore health unto her, and heal* cap.30.17
her of her wounds, because she was called an
out-cast by the people, *saying,* [illegible]
whom no man seeketh after. These were thy
promises even in the midst of thy threat-
nings, and wilt thou be worse unto us then
thou wert unto *Egypt*, or *Judah*, or *Zion?*
True it is that thou expectest our conversion; thou commandest us to *turn unto thee* Joel 2.12
with all our hearts, and with fasting, and with
weeping, and with mourning. To thee therefore, ô God (though formerly we have not,
yet now) do we turn. Wee turn unto thee
both our weeping *Eyes*, and our dejected
Countenances, and our wringing *Hands*, and
our bended *Knees*, and our mourning *voyces*,
and our groaning *hearts.* Merciful God, behold our *Tears*, and view our countenances,
and look upon our hands, strengthen our
knees, and hearken to our voyces, and comfort our hearts. *The Priests*, ô Lord, even
thine own *Ministers* doe *weep between the* vers.17.
Porch and the Altar, as they say, Spare thy
people, ô Lord, and give not thine heritage to
reproach. Our *Ezra's pray, and confesse and* Ezra.10.1
weep, and cast themselves down before thine
house; and the people assemble themselves un-
to them, both our men and our women, and our
children; for we all weep very sore. We weep
as the Israelites did *before the doore of the* Num. 2.
tabernacle of the congregation, when twenty 56.
and four thousand of them dyed of the *Pe-*
stilence. Thus we mourn; thus we weep;
our Eys, our Hearts, our very souls do weep:
ô let us tast of thy love; let us feel thy compassion. Make us to boast of thy praise, as
thy servant *David* did; when he *cryed unto*
thee, and thou didst heal him. Thou hast been Psal.30.2
wroth with us, as thou wert with the Jews
for their *covetousnesse;* and thou hast *smit-* Isa.57.17
ten us: thou hast *hid thy self, and hast been*
angry; yet we have gone on *frowardly in the*
wayes of our hearts. But O our God, do thou
make us as penitent as those Jews, and then
say unto us as thou didst unto thy Judah,
I have seen thy wayes, and I will heale thee: v.18.
I will lead thee also, and restore comforts unto
thee and to thy mourners. Alas, we mourn, and
yet we are punished: we grieve, and yet we
are *Plagued;* and all because *our iniquities*
do testifie against us: But for thy name's sake, Jer.14.7.
O Lord, be pleased to spare us. *O the hope*
of Israel, the Saviour thereof in the time of vers.8.
trouble, why shouldest thou be as a stra
the land; and as a way-faring man that tur-
neth aside to tarry but a night? Why shouldest
thou be as a man astonished; as a mighty man vers. 9.
that cannot save? Thou, O Lord, art still in
the midst of us, and we are called by thy name;
therefore, we pray thee, *leave us not.* O here
is a *Pestilence in our land;* and we *make our* 1 King 8.
prayers and supplications, and *stretch forth our* 37.
[illegible] vers. 38.
heaven thy dwelling place, and forgive; that v. 39.
we may *fear thee,* and walk in thy wayes all v. 40.
the dayes of our lives. Or if the sins of us
thy people cause thee to stop thine ears at
our prayers, O hear thou our *Hezekiah's*
praying for us, who have not cleansed our 2 Chr. 30
selves. Stay the *Plague* from us thine Israel, 18.
as thou didst from thy people, when thy servant *Phinehas executed judgment.* Cause our Psal. 106.
Aarons to take their Censers, and to put fire 30.
in them from off the Altar, and to put on in- Num. 16.
cense: O let them come quickly to our 46.
congregations, and make an attonement for
us. Let them *stand between the dead and* v. 48.
the living, and let the Plague be stayed. Thine
Angel stretcheth forth his hand upon our Je- 2 Sam.24
rusalem to destroy it: O do thou as in the 16.
time of King David; *Repent thee of the evill*
and say unto the destroying Angel, It is enough;
stay now thy hand. Hear us, O Lord, for the
distressed *People* in this *City* and *Nation;* and
hear *them* for *us*, and hear thy *Christ* for us
all: That to *Him*, and *Thee*, and thy *bles-*
sed Spirit, we may render (as is most due)
all Praise, and Glory, and Thanksgiving,
and Obedience, from this time forth for
ever more, *Amen.* Saying as Christ himself hath taught us, *Our Father, &c.*

An exact and true relation of the number of those that were buried in *London*, and the Liberties of all Diseases, from the 17 of *March* 1591; to the 22. of *December* 1592.

		total.	Pl.
March	17	351	31
March	24	219	29
March	31	307	27
April	7	203	33
April	14	290	37
April	21	310	41
April	28	350	29
May	5	339	38
May	12	300	42
May	19	450	58
May	26	410	62
June	2	441	81
June	9	399	99
June	16	401	108
June	23	850	118
June	30	1440	927
July	7	1510	893
July	14	1491	258
July	21	1507	852
July	28	1503	983
August	4	1550	797
August	11	1532	651
August	18	1508	449
August	25	1490	507
Septem.	1	1210	563
Septem.	8	621	451
Septem.	15	629	349
Septem.	22	450	130
Septem.	29	408	327
Octob.	6	422	323
Octob.	13	330	308
Octob.	20	320	302
Octob.	27	310	301
Novem.	3	309	209
Novem.	10	301	107
Novem.	17	321	93
Novem.	24	349	94
Decem.	1	331	86
Decem.	8	329	71
Decem.	25	386	39

Baptized 5827
The total. 25886
Of the Plague, 11503

1603.

		total.	Pl.
March	17	108	3
March	24	60	2
March	31	78	6
April	7	66	4
April	14	79	4
April	21	98	8
April	28	109	10
May	5	90	11
May	12	112	18
May	19	122	22
May	26	122	32
June	2	114	30
June	9	131	43
June	16	144	59
June	23	182	72
June	30	267	158
July	7	445	263
July	14	612	424
The Out-Parishes this Week were joyned with the City.			
July	21	1186	917
July	28	1728	1392
August	4	2256	1925
August	11	2077	1743
August	18	3054	2719
August	25	2853	2535
Septem.	1	3385	3034
Septem.	8	3078	2728
Sept.	15	3129	2815
Sept.	22	2456	2192
Sept.	29	1961	1731
Octob.	6	1831	1649
Octob.	13	1312	1142
Octob.	20	648	852
Octob.	27	625	504
Novem.	3	737	592
Nov.	10	585	441
Nov.	17	384	255
Nove.	24	198	102
Decem.	1	223	105
Decem.	8	163	55
Dece.	15	200	66
Dece.	22	168	74

The total of the Burials this whole year, 38250
Of the Plague, 30553.

1625.

Buried in *London* and the Liberties of all diseases, Anno 1625. the number here following.

		total.	Pl.
March	17	262	4
March	24	226	8
March	30	243	11
April	7	239	10
April	14	256	24
April	21	230	25
April	28	305	16
May	5	292	30
May	12	332	45
May	19	379	71
May	26	401	78
June	2	395	69
June	9	434	91
June	16	510	165
June	23	640	239
June	30	942	390
July	7	1222	593
July	14	1781	1004
July	21	2850	1819
July	28	3583	2471
August	4	4517	3659
August	11	4855	4115
August	18	5205	4463
August	25	4841	4218
Septem.	1	3897	3344
Septem.	8	3157	2550
Septem.	15	2148	1672
Septem.	22	1993	1551
Septem.	29	1236	852
Octob.	6	833	538
Octob.	13	815	511
Octob.	20	651	331
Octob.	27	375	134
Novemb.	3	357	89
Novem	10	319	92
Novem.	17	274	48
Nov.	24	231	27
Decemb.	1	190	15
Decemb.	8	181	15
Decem.	15	168	6
Decem.	22	157	1

The total of all the Burials this Year, 54082
Of the Plague 3542

1630.

		total.	Pl.
June	24	205	19
July	1	209	25
July	8	217	43
July	15	250	50
July	22	229	40
July	29	279	77
August	5	250	56
August	12	246	65
August	19	269	54
August	26	270	67
Septemb.	2	230	66
Septemb.	9	259	63
Sept.	16	264	68
Sept.	23	274	57
Sept.	30	269	56
Octob.	7	236	66
Octob.	14	261	73
Octob.	21	248	60
Octob.	28	214	34
Novemb.	4	142	29
Novem.	11	215	29
Novem.	18	200	18
Nov.	25	226	7
Decemb.	2	221	20
Decem.	9	198	29
Decem.	16	217	5

The total of the Burials this whol year 10554
Of the Plague, 1317

Against the Plague.

Take leaves of Sage Wormwood, of each an ounce & half, Rue six ounces and half, wash them in Spring water, cut & beat them let the juice run from them, & put it in an Earthen Pot with half a pint of strong white wine Vinegar, cover it close for 24. houres, strain it and add an ounce of Turbith finely powdered, cover all close 24. hours more, afterwards strain it, & then use it.

1636.

		total.	Pl.
April	7	219	2
April	14	205	4
This week was added to the Bill these Parishes, St. Marg. Westminster. Lambeth. St. Mary Newington Redriff Parish St. Mary Islington Stepney Parish Hackney Parish			
April	21	285	14
April	28	259	17
May	5	251	10
May	12	308	55
May	19	299	35
May	26	330	62
June	2	339	67
June	9	345	87
June	16	381	103
June	23	304	79
June	30	352	104
July	7	215	81
July	14	372	104
July	21	395	120
July	28	423	151
August	4	461	206
August	11	538	283
August	18	638	[illegible]
August	25	787	429
Septemb.	1	1011	638
Sept.	8	1069	650
Sept.	15	1306	865
Sept.	22	1229	775
Sept.	29	1403	928
Octob.	6	1405	921
Octob.	13	1302	792
Octob.	20	1002	555
Octob.	27	900	458
Novemb.	3	1300	138
Nov.	10	1104	715
Nov.	17	950	573
Nov.	24	857	476
Decemb.	1	614	12
Dec.	8	459	167
Dec.	15	383	89
Dec.	22	316	76
Dec.	29	283	125

The total of the Burials this whole year 27415
Of the Plague [illegible]

1637.

		total.	Pl
January	5	318	126
Janu.	12	314	73
Jan.	19	268	59
Jan.	26	289	72
February	2	351	103
Feb.	9	315	104
Feb.	16	285	78
Feb.	23	254	44
March	2	262	69
March	9	332	100
March	16	303	80
March	23	260	65
March	30	343	115
April	7	301	98
April	14	288	79
April	21	300	90
April	28	319	107
May	4	292	81
May	11	300	105
May	18	285	74
May	25	314	83
June	1	269	72
June	8	273	74
June	15	268	110
June	22	304	106
June	29	371	159
July	6	362	163
July	13	325	133
July	20	321	140
July	27	335	117
August	3	300	89
August	10	275	74
August	17	228	53
August	24	225	43
August	31	209	30
Septemb.	7	227	36
Sept.	14	200	21
Sept.	21	184	21
Sept.	28	197	27
October	5	166	15
Octob.	12	198	17
Octob.	19	174	13

The total of all Burials this year, 14270
Of the Plague, 3603

1638. Buried 16621
Of the Plague 508

1646 Buried
Of the Plague 2436

1647. Buried 16452
Of the Plague 5285

1648. Buried 11509
Of the Plague, 693

1665.

Buried in *London* and the Liberties of all diseases the number followeth;

		total.	Pl.
April	25	398	2
May	2	388	0
May	9	347	9
May	16	353	3
May	23	385	14
May	30	399	17
June	6	405	43
June	13	558	112
June	20	611	168
June	27	684	267
July	4	1006	470
July	11	1268	725
July	18	1761	1089
July	25	2785	1843
August	1	3014	2010
August	8	4030	2817
August	15		
August	22		
August	29		
Septem.	5		

Buried in the 97 Parishes within *London*, from *August* 1st. to the 8th. 341
And of the Plague 208

In the Out-Parishes this Week, of the Plague 2609

S. Andrews Holborn	183	*Hackney Parish*	6
S. Bartholmew great	17	*S. James Clerkenwel*	136
S. Bartholmew lesse	6	*S. Katharine Tower*	12
S. Brides Parish	66	*Lambeth Parish*	1
Bridwel Precinct	5	*S. Leonar. Shoreditch*	228
S. Botolph Aldersga.	46	*S. Magda. Bermonds.*	7
S. Botolph Algate	81	*S. Mary Newington*	16
S. Botolph Bishopsgate	133	*S. Mary Islington*	14
S. Dunstans West	20	*S. Mary Whitechappel*	158
S. George Southwark	39	*Redriff Parish*	2
S. Giles Cripplegate	356	*Stepney Parish*	136
S. Olives Southwark	64	*S. Clement Danes*	42
S. Saviors Southwark	41	*S. Paul Coven garden*	16
S. Sepulchers Parish	205	*S. Martins ith' fields*	213
S. Thom. Southwark	8	*S. Mary Savoy*	6
Trinity Minories		*S. Margaret Westm.*	173
At the Pest-house	10	*At Pest-house.*	39
S. Giles in the Fields	259		

Buried in *London* this week of all Diseases	4030
Of the Plague	2817
Increased in the Burials this week	1016
Parishes Cleare of the Plague	44
Parishes Infected	86

[illegible] by J. Mabb, for R. Burton, [illegible] Gilbertson. 90

FIGURE 16. *Londons Loud Cryes to the Lord by Prayer* (1665).

or that in turn explain their meaning. Thus, they take on an emblematic significance as the "body" dependent for their meaning upon the verbal "soul" of the
accompanying description. Furthermore, their proper "use" as adjuncts to the
text requires that the viewer/reader see past the page to the inner significance
indicated by the graphic marks. These illustrations, then, have a linguistic
transparency, and they ask for a mode of apprehension closer to the explica-
tion of a text than to the observation (much less the veneration) of a pictorial
image. As a form of visual language, they support a "reading" congruent with
the plague itself as the visible mark of God's Word.

THE PEST ANATOMIZED

My last example faces the title page of George Thomson's *Loimotomia: or The
Pest Anatomized* (1666; fig. 17). This illustration of an anatomy tightens the
focus from Wither's Britain and the broadsheets' London to the individual
body as the scene of the plague's devastation. Thomson, a physician and tire-
less polemicist, achieved some small fame in 1651 when he performed the first
successful splenectomy, on a dog. Unlike the dog in Swift's academy of pro-
jectors, Thomson's survived, and the experiment brought him to the attention of William Harvey and Robert Boyle.[43] Before publishing his anatomy
of a plague victim, as well as an accompanying volume of "consolatory advice"
entitled *Loimologia*, Thomson was already in the fray of current medical debate as a proponent of chemical medicine and an uncompromising enemy of
the "Galenical gang."[44] Thomson's attitude toward the Galenists is clear from
the running title of his *Galeno-pale*, published in 1665: "A chymical trial of
the Galenists, that their dross in physick may be discovered with the grand
abuses and disrepute they have brought upon the whole art of physick and
chirurgery." The Galenic doctors, he charges, would fraudulently persuade a
gullible and terrified public "that they are able to do something extraordinary
for the Prevention and Cure of this present Infection." Having not abandoned
his own patients in London during the Great Plague, Thomson reserves particular scorn for those cowardly Galenists whose philosophy left them "no
longer willing to breathe in this unsanctified impure air" of the city, and who,

---

43. Clericuzio, "Thomson, George," in *Oxford Dictionary of National Biography Online*.
44. Thomson, *Loimologia*, 4. Subsequent citations of this work are given parenthetically in the
text.

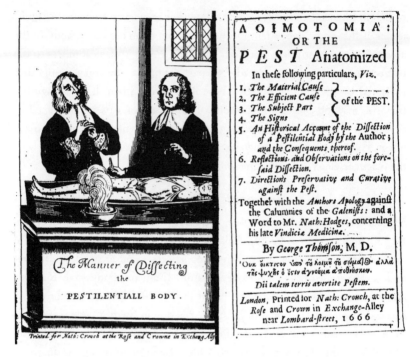

Λ O I M O T O M I A :
OR THE
P E S T Anatomized

In these following particulars, *Viz.*
1. The *Material Cause* ⎫
2. The *Efficient Cause* ⎬ of the PEST.
3. The *Subject Part*   ⎭
4. The *Signs*
5. *An Historical Account of the Dissection of a Pestilential Body by the Author; and the Consequents thereof.*
6. *Reflections and Observations on the foresaid Dissection.*
7. *Directions Preservative and Curative against the Pest.*

Together with the *Authors Apology against* the Calumnies of the *Galenists:* and a Word to Mr. *Nath: Hodges*, concerning his late *Vindiciæ Medicinæ.*

By *George Thomson*, M. D.

Ουκ οικτισον ὑπὸ τῷ λοιμῷ τῷ σώμα]Θ· ἀλλὰ τῆς ψυχῆς ὁ ἐστιν ἀγνοῦμα ἀποθνήσκειν.

Dii talem terris avertite Pestem.

London, Printed for *Nath: Crouch*, at the *Rose* and *Crown* in *Exchange-Alley* near *Lombard-street*, 1 6 6 6

The Manner of Dissecting the

PESTILENTIALL BODY.

Printed for Nath: Crouch at the Rose and Crowne in Exchang Ally

FIGURE 17. George Thomson, *Loimotomia: or The Pest Anatomized*, frontispiece (1666).

in the face of the epidemic and in violation of their professional calling, are "vanished and gone I know not whither in a trice" (12). In a passage of Spenserian extravagance, Thomson credits his own polemical fortitude with having "ripped up, and sufficiently anatomized, *usque ad Sceleton*, (so far as a short Treatise would permit) the huge deformed bulk of the monstrous, mutilated Galenical body," as it "was high time for such an unweildy, lazie, cumbersom, good-for-little, voracious, *animal Sarcophagum*, *Cruorem consumere natum*, a devourer of more then *Bel* and the *Dragon*, having surfeited himself with bloud and humours, should now expire or breathe out his last, and become food for the birds of darkness." Although he sees yet "some of the Spawn or Issue of this *Polyphemous* Gyant left in the land," (12), Thomson has slain the monster of Galenist error that gave them birth.

In the *Loimotomia*, Thomson turns from his dissection of the grotesque body of his professional rivals to the anatomy he performed on the body of a plague victim, the fifteen-year-old male servant of one of his patients. Thomson's is, to my knowledge, the first such procedure in the English record, and one fraught with no small peril to the heroic anatomist. The title page shows the subject of the anatomy, the body marked with the characteristic "tokens" of the plague, laid out in an open coffin. The physician—on the right, holding a scalpel—has made his first incision. The subject's skin and its underlying layer of muscle are already peeled back from breastbone to groin, and the anatomist seems to pause meditatively before taking the next fateful step of opening the body cavity. The table on which the body rests resembles a Communion table—an association reinforced by its also displaying, as a kind of censer, a pot of smoking herbs to sweeten the air, as well as by the half-prayerful, half-apprehensive attitude of the physician's assistant on the left. In another tradition, these remains might be mistaken for a sacred relic, but here it's just a corpse, the object of investigation rather than veneration.

The face of the table bears a caption duplicating in its format the same spatial relationships as in the image, with those doing the "*Dissecting*" above and the "PESTILENTIALL BODY" below. To an eye schooled in the imagery of plague saints, the lower register looks as if it might otherwise have displayed the scene of a saint's martyrdom. In Italy, Sebastian was frequently the subject of predella decorations on the front face of the altar, and other saints might be visible under the altar, whether preserved in part or whole, or in effigy. Such spectral presences as lurk behind Thomson's "PESTILENTIALL BODY" are familiar in the English Reformation, most notably in the ghost of the Virgin inhabiting the political theology of the Virgin Queen, or on church walls where sacred imagery was whitewashed and overwritten (as Luther had urged) by the language of scripture. Elizabeth Mazzola has called such residual forms the Reformation's "sacred remains," an apt phrase in this context.[45] On Thomson's title page, the effacement of such a virtual image and its replacement by the name of the thing reconfigures the design of the page into an emblem, a composite of picture and motto (the "body" and "soul" of the emblem) where the identification of the image rests upon its verbal support.

In its turn as the pictorial version of the caption below, the "pestilential body" about to yield up its inmost nature must be read by the anatomist as significant, its visible symptoms the elements of a sign system that makes up

---

45. Mazzola, *The Pathology of the English Renaissance.*

the corporal discourse of the disease. Like the plague houses of the broadsheet, the plague body must be made legible, put to verbal "use" through the intervention of reading. In this respect, Thomson's experiment owes as much to post-Reformation theology as to the tradition of Vesalian anatomy or to the theories of chemical medicine. It is indebted as well to Bacon's example of scientific inquiry, itself heralding a reformation of learning. *The Advancement of Learning* (1605) had exposed the "diseases" and "peccant humors" festering in the body of knowledge, and Bacon had assumed the role of the physician dedicated to restoring natural philosophy to health. His cure involved, in the first instance, a purging of the language of natural philosophy. For all his insistence on the direct observation of nature, there is in Bacon more than a remnant of the reformers' distrust of the evidence of the visual imagination—it was Calvin who said that the "eye is the Devil's doorway." Thomson himself, following the chemical theory of Jan Baptist van Helmont but speaking as Bacon might of the power of the "idols" to seize upon the imagination, believes that "none was ever infected by the Pest, but either from an *Idea* or Image of Hatred, Terrour and Diffidence in the phantasie of the individual Person, or in the *Archeus*, the Innate Spirit of every part of the body, as *Helmont* hath proved" (2). But unlike Castelvetro, the Italian critic of Aristotle who sees in this power the cathartic possibilities of tragedy as a form of psychic cleansing, Thomson sees the terrifying images engendered by the plague (like the image of the Galenist monster that feeds on the terror of plague victims) as posing a mortal danger:

Did not the vital Spirit at first running away, afterward entertain treacherously, as it were, into its privy Chamber, shaking hands, and hugging in its bosom that which is virulent, poysonous and deletery, and thereby appropriate the same to it self, entering into a firm league with that which is *Tristissima mortis Imago*, the lurid and dismal Picture of pestiferous dissolution, conspiring and co-operating with an irreconcilable Enemy to mans health; neither the venom of any Mineral, Vegetable or Animal, nor the Heteroclite poyson of the Pest could injure us, or any way damnifie us. But as the Case stands, *Perditio nostra à nobis*; and that which was in the beginning ordained for a sole preservative to us, doth often become our bane and destruction. And *Spiritus ille vitalis qui Actiones sanas etiam morbosas edit*: That Archeus which is the instrument of Sanity, is likewise the Author of Maladies. (34)

Just as Donne's "Holy Sonnet 14" finds the reason "weake or untrue," all too vulnerable in its fallen state to resist being "captiv'd" by the "enemy" (328, l. 8), so Thomson's Archeus, "the instrument of Sanity," conspires with a "lurid and dismal Picture" to betray its responsibility as our "sole preservative" and throw open the gates of the body to the plague. We fall ill, then, when in the "privy Chamber" of our being we are terrified into practicing a kind of psychosomatic idolatry. In the dry light of a Baconian therapeutics, the false images of things must be dispelled, while the *visibilia* of raw observation—the marks on, and in, the plaguey body on the dissecting table—become a means of understanding (rather than contracting) the plague only when their significance is drawn out into verbal observations and principles.

Thomson begins his report by assuming his reader to be a "curious linguist" who will first of all expect a proper "Nomenclature of the Pest in various terms" as the framework for everything that follows (7). He then notes the customary etymology of the plague—"The Hebrews call it דבר ... *quod sit res à Deo edicta vel decreta*"—though with an irony that suggests his anatomy will delve deeper into the matter than just the expected nomenclature, in order to disclose the *res* beneath the "various terms" by which the plague is superficially denominated. In language that interconnects the physician's Helmontian physiology with his probing of the cadaver before him (and that seems as well to harness the apocalyptic, revelatory power of the plague), Thomson claims that "the pest cannot withstand that subtile all-searching Spagyrick [i.e., alchemical] power, which like Lightning, penetrates to the Center of things, dissolving them into their first Principles, destroying what is superfluous in them, and extraneous, keeping entire and untouched that which is pure and defaecate" (5). But when he comes to the heart (or the stomach) of the matter, he discovers a world of signs, the body's own nomenclature, that returns us to the scene of writing and reading. Thomson follows van Helmont in his conviction that disease is seated in the "*Archeus*, the Innate Spirit of every part of the body" (2). Observing the "Cutaneous spots" on the body, he understands that "they always signify an endeavor in the Archeus to extrude that which is noxious" (111–12). At the same time, the anatomist also carefully monitors his own vulnerability to the disease-ridden corpse: "For my own part, I can avouch by several Signs, being very curious and exact in the consideration of my own state, that I often received the Scent or Tincture of the Pest, but quickly washed it off by some Balsamical odour, causing a profluence of a kindly Sweat" (139). Opening the stomach, he finds that "a black matter like Ink did shew it self, to the quantity (as nigh as I could guess) of a wine pint," and he concludes that "[w]hen the Natural ferment of the Stomack in the Pest is so far lost, that instead of white, a black juice is engendered, it is a certain sign of the abolition of the final spirit, and consequently of approaching Death" (73, 112–13).

The body itself is well on its way to corruption, even though the victim has been dead less than twelve hours. As Donne notes in his anatomy of the world,

> But as in cutting up a man that's dead,
> The body will not last out to have read
> On euery part, and therefore men direct
> Their speech to parts, that are of most effect.
> ("The First Anniversary," 244, ll. 435–38)

Donne's quibble turns such "parts" into parts of speech, the parts that speak to the anatomist even out of the belly of the dead. Thomson reads the most significant "part," the stomach whose contents indicate by a "certain sign" that the boy's condition was mortal. In dissecting the stomach, the anatomist performs a quasi-sacramental ritual. By a kind of reverse transubstantiation—"wine" to "black juice"—the anatomy has revealed the "pure" first principle of the plague, its innermost substance, to be a corrupt liquid. But this body will be preserved not as the relic of a saint, but "entire" in the pages of the book, having engendered the very "Ink" that will supply the "matter" of Thomson's anatomy (what the doctor holds in his right hand may be a pen as well as a scalpel, poised as if the anatomist were prepared to write on, rather than cut into, the body). In this example, as well as in those of Wither's frontispiece and the broadsheet illustrations above, plague turns bodies and cities into texts, and it turns those enveloped in the uncertainties of the plague cloud, or terrified by the baneful images its terror engenders in the fantasy, into readers of signs for their own good.

Of course, the plague that strikes the Catholic Continent is the same as that inflicted on England. Wherever it strikes, it causes the same pandemic devastation and the same massive social trauma, and it raises the same urgent questions by which it must be rationalized. The difference I have been trying to suggest is one between an iconic tradition that domesticates the plague within a matrix of intervention, advocacy, commiseration, protection, and justification, and an iconoclastic tradition in which all such comforts are stripped away. The English plague reader confronts a disease that presents itself as a lethal and enigmatic text. Although there is great contention about the second causes through which the plague is brought to bear, its overt meaning—the fundamental meaning that subsumes all the others—is that it must be a punishment for some unspecified and unrepented personal or national sin. Thomson, even in 1666, is exceptional in that he makes no assumptions about the spiritual state of the boy on the table. The anatomist finds no signs of divine edicts or decrees: no black sin, no matter for theological speculation, only the "black matter" of an inky putrefaction. As I hope to show in the case of Ben Jonson, the plague's covert meaning—that in fact it has no "meaning" at all, that it is a signifier with no transcendental signified—perhaps rises closer to the surface of consciousness in a culture driven to questioning than in one where the ultimate questions are deflected, even if not answered, by the therapeutic intercession of the saints. As I have noted, the figure on the left in Thomson's frontispiece—the anatomist's assistant, presumably—seems to be absorbed in prayer or meditation. As a kind of residual petitioner, a visitor from the lost world of plague-saint iconography, he seems particularly forlorn. His upturned face directs us toward nothing except an opaque, leaded-glass window in the upper right corner. Thomson himself appears as the more authoritative figure, his left hand poised over the pestilential body in a gesture that seems to hover ambiguously between reluctance and benediction. His right hand holds the scalpel he has just used to separate the outer layers of skin and muscle and which he will employ again, in a moment, to make the deeper incision opening the chest wall and the suppurating abdominal cavity to view, thus providing the only form of revelation this image has to offer.

The anatomy concludes with the physician himself contracting his subject's disease:

Having finished the Dissection of this loathsom Body, I presently found some little sensible alteration tending to a stiffness and numness in my hand, which had been soaking and dabling in the Bowels and Entrals then warm, though it was Ten or Twelve hours after the Youth expired; whereupon having cleansed away that foulness it was besmeared with,

I held it for some time over a dish of burning Brimstone, and so received the Gas thereof, but in vain. *Seriùs ejicitur, quam non admittitur;* I might better (had I foreseen what I do now) kept it out, than thrust it out; for those slie, insinuating, venemous Atoms, excited by the heat of the body, opening the pores of my skin, had quickly free ingress; the Archeus, the Porter of my hand, that should have better guarded it, forthwith tergiversating, and taking its flight, being extreamly terrified at the Alarum of so fierce and potent an Enemy, and afterward in an abject manner conducted it to the principal place of the Souls residence, the Stomack; where after this lately entered poyson had dressed and habited it self with that spirit that had the perfect Idea and Image of this sickness, it was to act a Tragical part (the Archeus being obliged to be Executioner to bring to pass its own Ruine) and now do I carry about me the very Pest, closely spreading like a Gangrene, diffusing its malignity into all my members, covered over for some short space as it were in the ashes of silence, while I in the mean time visited, visit others visited, administring that help to them, which I (then more perplexed at my Neighbours Calamity, than sollicitous for my own) suffer my self to want, relating with joy what an Inquest I had made into that Subject which had made a Conquest of me. (77–78)

The account enacts a microdrama whose elements Thomson might see writ large on the streets of London as he made his rounds—or onstage, as the anatomy theater sets the opening scene for the theatrical plot of the doctor's downfall. Like infected outsiders infiltrating the city through an unguarded gate, or stealthy housebreakers on the prowl through a stricken neighborhood, the "slie, insinuating" atoms of infection find "free ingress" through the pores of the physician's hand. The terrified Archeus has abandoned its post as the doorkeeper and, now in thrall to the "Idea and Image of this sickness," has no choice but to take on the "Tragical part" of its own executioner. The Archeus's first impulse, like that of many a terrified Londoner, is to flee. But evidently realizing there is no escape, it turns traitor ("tergiversating" is the act of an apostate or renegade) and conducts the intruder into the stomach, "the principal place of the Souls residence." From this strategic seat, the usurping pest threatens to produce the play's last act by "diffusing its malignity into all my members," just as in a residence similarly breached, the plague will spread to all members of the household. If carried to its dire conclusion, the play would be a revenge tragedy—a "Conquest" for an "Inquest," an invasion of the anatomist as retribution for his invasion of the plague's dead boy. The outcome would likely have been fatal, had the doctor not been able to cure himself with megadoses of his own medicine, including a "large Toad" dried and hung about his neck to draw the pestilential poison into its desiccated body (86).

In the end, Thomson emphasizes his devotion to his calling despite the betrayal of his fugitive Archeus and his own ripening illness. More perplexed at his patients' suffering than solicitous for his own, he visits the visited, administering the care to his fellow victims that he denies himself, and even "relating with joy" the tale of his landmark autopsy (though we are not told with what pleasure those on the lip of the grave might have received these glad tidings). His book, like the passage cited above, moves from a clinical report to a self-fashioned legend and a testament to the author's professional vocation. The final role in the drama, then, turns the heroic monster-slayer (Christian name, George) into a secular, iconoclastic saint—one who contracts the plague but manages to survive it by mustering all his skill and resolve against the baneful power of the "Image of this sickness," and who continues to minister to his flock heedless of his own safety (and protected by the dried toad, if not by the Holy Nail).

With the movement of the plague from Italy to England, there was, I have suggested, a corresponding shift in the way the culture represented and responded to the devastation wreaked by the disease. To be sure, the plague experience of medieval and Renaissance Italy, like that of England, extends for more than three hundred years, from the disease's first foothold in western Europe in the 1340s until almost the end of the seventeenth century. My aim has not been to cover that history—a task that has been undertaken by many others in both countries—but, by way of a few paradigmatic examples, to mark a set of crucial differences disclosed when the plague crosses the frontier of the Reformation. Over those centuries in Italy, there is, of course, a vast body of plague writing that I have not taken into my purview. In particular, England is indebted to the Italian experience in medicine and public health policy (most notably the institution of quarantine). I have chosen instead to stress the differences stemming from the absence in England of the palette of religious, social, and artistic practices that supplement the written tradition in Italy with a rich and varied visual plague culture. With this loss—of the saints and the efficacy of their representations and relics, of the pageantry of the plague procession, of the altarpieces and banners and panel paintings that mitigate the horror of the pestilence, not least through the pleasures of the eye—plague writing takes on a correspondingly heavier burden in England, finding both its material and its consolations exclusively in the Word.

In *The Wonderfull Yeare*, Dekker imagines what a man might encounter as he walks through the streets of London during the plague, "in the dead houre of gloomy midnight" (28–29). He would hear "the loude grones of rauing sick men" and "Seruants crying out for maisters wiues for husbands, parents for children, children for their mothers." Amid this "dismall consort," punctuated by the "Bells heauily tolling," there is little to be seen except for "some frantickly running to knock vp Sextons" and others (desperate to avoid having their houses placed under quarantine) "fear-fully sweating with Coffins, to steele forth dead bodies, least the fatall hand-writing of death should seale vp their doores." The "fatall hand-writing of death" refers ambiguously to the plague itself and to the sign of its presence inscribed on the doors of the plague house—the red cross and the words "Lord Have Mercy." But insofar as the parish officers charged with marking plague houses only transcribe what has already been written there by the plague, the distinction disappears. Such scenes of visual deprivation cast the plague into a kind of representational darkness that makes it all the more horrifying, all the less accommodated, and far more mysterious in the questions it raises. It becomes the thing heard in the shrieks of the afflicted, and the thing written thrice over—in scripture, on the bodies of the afflicted, and on the doors of the houses—and again, in the work of plague writers. Language is thus the only, and the only appropriate, instrument by which it can be probed.

[CHAPTER 3]

Jonson, Regime Change, and the Plague of 1603

Heaven is our heritage.
Earth but a player's stage
Mount we unto the sky.
I am sick, I must die.
    Lord, have mercy on me.
THOMAS NASH, "A Litany in
Time of Plague" (1600)

The Alchemist has always figured as the richest imaginative document of the Jacobean plague years. Plague sets the scene of Jonson's comedy, and plague holds the mirror up to the nature of London—and the London theater—under epidemic siege. As Cheryl Lynn Ross has shown, "the world of Ben Jonson's *Alchemist*—its setting, its rogues and their victims, the structure of the play, and the moral judgments inherent in the text and on its margins—is the world of London during a plague."[1] Beginning with the plague world of *The Alchemist*, and as a prelude to Jonson's poetry in the next chapter, I will argue that 1603 plague theology and politics also establish a context for understanding Jonson's nondramatic verse, especially the epigram "On my first Sonne."

Seven-year-old Benjamin Jonson died of the plague, we know, during the epidemic of 1603; and we know, too, that by design or happenstance the elder Jonson managed to evade a similar fate. Like *The Alchemist*'s Lovewit, he had quit the city and was staying at Robert Cotton's country house in Huntingdonshire at the height of the epidemic. Jonson's Oxford editors—and, following them, nearly all scholars who have commented on the poem since—call attention to the account by Drummond of Hawthornden of the father's uncanny premonition of his son's death. The night before the fatal news arrived from London, Jonson dreamed that the boy appeared to him with the "Marke of a bloodie crosse on his forehead" (1:138–40)—a mark like the "red Crosses set vpon dores" of plague houses by the municipal authorities.[2] Yet most readings of the epigram tend to overlook the "unspoken" but specific cause of the boy's death, or else to regard it as incidental information. Despite the attention paid to Jonson as a plague playwright, no one has fully considered the meaning of this poem in relation to the lived experience of the pestilence in the early seventeenth century—to the ways in which the successive waves of bubonic plague were endured and imagined by the survivors and the bereaved, and represented in contemporary accounts.

Plays and Plagues

The sheer numbers, as we have seen, tell the tale. According to the official bills of mortality, there were at least 225,000 deaths from the bubonic plague in

---

1. Ross, "The Plague of *The Alchemist*," 439.
2. Dekker, *Plague Pamphlets*, 76.

London and its environs between 1570 and 1670 (the figure for England as a whole is around 750,000). In 1593, more than 15,000 people died—one out of every eight Londoners, given a total estimated population of 123,000. Jonson, recently returned to London unscathed from his military service in the Netherlands, was doubly fortunate in avoiding the arrows of the pestilence. In 1603 at least 25,000 (according to the bills), and probably thousands more whose deaths went unrecorded, succumbed to the plague in London and the liberties: one in every five persons, young Benjamin Jonson among them. Thomas Dekker, Jonson's rival playwright and an indefatigable chronicler of the pestilence in London, gives an exact figure of 30,578 for that year and notes that in its worst week, the plague claimed 3,035 individuals (143). A like number died in 1625, followed by at least 50,000 during the Great Plague of 1665.[3] Seventeenth-century mortality tables for London can thus be graphed as a series of sharp spikes indicating the number of plague deaths during these epidemic years of 1593, 1603, 1625, and 1665. In the dormant periods between these peaks, however, the plague never really disappeared, nor did the constant fear of its return. Overall, the population of London, like that of most other European cities, more than doubled during these years. The demographic pattern is made up of gradual recoveries and sudden decimations. In the course of the century's long plague cycle, new births and in-migration from the country quickly replenished London's population numbers once an epidemic subsided. But the numbers plunged once more when weather conditions and the ecology of rats and fleas made another outbreak possible, and the density of a renewed and non-immune urban population made it all but inevitable. In plague times, the image of London life changed from one of pestering multitudes to deserted streets. Plague historian Paul Slack observes that "even if we ignore years in which less than 100 casualties were notified, plague was present [in London] in twenty-eight of sixty-four years between 1603 and 1666." Overall, he concludes, "at least a fifth of all deaths from 1603 to 1665 can be attributed to it."[4] In the plague of 1603, Jonson's home parish of St. Giles, Cripplegate, was one of the hardest hit in London, with nearly three thousand plague deaths in a population of less than five thousand.[5]

---

3. Mullett, *The Bubonic Plague and England*, 86; Slack, *Impact of Plague*, 146.
4. Slack, *Impact of Plague*, 147.
5. Phillips, "'Fleshes Rage,'" 19; Slack, *Impact of Plague*, 155.

In its production history as well as its plot, *The Alchemist* reflects the disruption of city life brought on by visitations of this dread disease. For most of Jonson's career as a dramatist, plague, or the threat of it, closed the theaters for longer or shorter periods of time. In 1583 the Court of Aldermen, grappling with the "terrible occasion of God's wrath and heavy striking with plagues," warned against

> the assembly of people to plays, bearbaiting, fencers and profane spectacles at the *Theatre* and *Curtain* and other like places to which do resort great multitudes of the basest sort of people and many infected with sores running on them being out of our jurisdiction . . . beside the withdrawing from God's service, the peril of ruins of so weak buildings, and the advancement of incontinency and most ungodly confederacies.[6]

Under the heading of "profane spectacles" are jumbled weak buildings, ungodly conspiracies, poor church attendance, and the "many infected"—all as occasioning God's wrath, with the implication that those afflicted must also be weak, ungodly, and profane. These threats seem to be regarded as all the more ominous because those infected with running sores are "out of our jurisdiction" and so ("running") beyond the reach of the law. The court seems to hover between regarding "the assembly of people" as a means of spreading the plague, and such assemblies as evils in themselves inviting the plague.

If Jonson returned from the army in 1592 with the ambition of becoming an actor, it was not possible for him to embark on this career until the theaters reopened in 1594. *Volpone*, produced in 1606, is obsessed with diseases real and feigned, including Sir Politic Would-Be's crackbrained project for identifying merchant ships carrying the plague.[7] During the late summer of 1610, with "the sicknesse" once more "hot" (5:293, l. 1) in London, as in the setting of Jonson's new play, the King's Men were forced to withdraw to Oxford, taking *The Alchemist* with them.[8] Audiences who were warned by the authorities that they risked infection by crowding into public playhouses might see their own vulnerability reflected in Jonson's "Argument" to *The Alchemist*. The master

---

6. Wilson, *The Plague in Shakespeare's London*, 52–53.
7. See Harris, *Sick Economies*, chap. 5, "Plague and Transmigration."
8. Riggs, *Ben Jonson*, 170.

having "quit" the city "for feare" (and, significantly, because he could afford to), the little world of Lovewit's house is turned upside down by the charlatans to whom he has abandoned his authority (5:293, l. 1).[9] For the course of the play, the audience finds itself crowded together in quarantine, the playhouse having become a virtual (and perhaps a real) pesthouse.

Meanwhile, the greater world outside the playhouse might be transformed at any moment into a carnivalesque theater of death. The "Plague doth rage," wrote John Davies during the epidemic of 1603, "[m]aking our Troy-nouant a tragicke Stage / Whereon to shew Death's power, with slaughter sore."[10] Plague-season London, as we have heard, echoed to "the loude grones of rauing sicke men" careening through the streets in their final agony, and to the voices of wives crying out "for husbands, parents for children" (Dekker, 27), while Jonsonian mountebanks hawked their posies and elixirs to the desperate. Corpses were thrown into carts as householders responded to the cry, "Bring out your dead!" At day's end, the harvest was hauled to the burial pits. For Dekker, the dramatist turned plague pamphleteer when the theaters closed in 1603, England itself had become a vast plague playhouse, offering him the opportunity to expand his horizon as a playwright to a national scale:

> These are the Tragedies, whose sight
> With teares blot all the lynes we write,
> The Stage wheron the Scenes are plaide
> Is a whole Kingdome.
>
> (96)

Indeed, Dekker's account of the "Wonderfull Yeare" is plotted in detail as a tragedy. The queen's funeral in the spring of 1603 "was but the dumb shew, the Tragicall Act hath bin playing ever since" (13). With the plague threatening soon after, "Death" is cast as a "Spanish Leagar, or rather like stalking

---

9. See Barroll, *Politics, Plague, and Shakespeare's Theater*, especially chap. 3, "Pestilence and the Players"; Ross, "The Plague of *The Alchemist*"; and Neill, *Issues of Death*, 22–29. Neill writes that the action of *The Alchemist* "implicitly equates the pestilence raging outside Lovewit's usurped house with the moral disease rampant within it. The Alchemist's den is not merely a microcosm of the city, of course; it is also presented as a type of fraudulent theatre—to the point where Face's epilogue actually identifies his ill-gotten pelf with the takings of the playhouse itself" (24).

10. Davies, *Humours Heau'n on Earth*, 245.

Tamburlaine" poised for the attack at the head of a besieging army, a scourge who "hath pitcht his tents . . . in the sinfully-polluted Suburbs" (31). Having breached the walls of the city, this marauder is imagined as having marched through the "capitall streets of *Troynouant*," where he mercilessly "plaide the tyrant . . . making hauock of all" (33). It is as if Dekker is plying his old trade, cobbling together familiar bits, channeling Marlowe, and perhaps Hamlet ordering up the scene of Priam's slaughter. We are given a glimpse of the dramatist hard at work when Dekker reflects on the difficulties of scripting, as much as recording, the critical scene of Elizabeth's death and James's succession: "Oh it were able to fill a hundred paire of writing tables with notes, but to see the parts plaid in the compasse of one houre on this stage of the new-found world" (21). To see the plague as a tragedy "plaid" out as a gruesome form of street theater is to offer a mordant comment on the closing of the playhouses: deprived of one form of entertainment, London audiences could be part of an even more impressive show, and for free. For Dekker, tragedy is also the appropriate genre, not only because a sudden coming to grief is its burden and death its outcome, but because, as John Twyning notes, the tragic drama of the period deals with dislocations, with the loss of place, the loss of traditional certainties, and the loss of self—a drama, in short, of traumatic "dispossession" that holds the mirror up to the London of 1603.[11]

Contemporary opinion as to the causes of the plague—the vexed questions of sin and judgment impinging directly on Jonson's poem—will be considered below. But if evidence of sinfulness was to be sought, the theater was a conspicuous target, not least because—as Davies's and Dekker's vision of the city as itself a tragic stage suggests—the merely fictive slaughter of the playhouses seemed to have spilled out into the streets, with Death as an all too real revenger. Emphasizing the connection between plays and plagues, antitheatrical writers such as "I. H." were quick to charge that the licentiousness of the theater itself had brought down the wrath of God upon London, and so to conclude that his "pestilential arrows, which fly among us by day, & lethally wound us by night," will not be "quivered up, till these menstruous rags be torn off (by the hand of authority) from the city's skirts."[12]

---

11. Twyning, *London Dispossessed*, 6.
12. I. H., *This VVorlds Folly*, B3. Neill comments on this passage: "In its blurring of moral distinctions, its counterfeitings, its violations of vestimentary order, its breaking of the accepted boundaries

That "I. H." perceives the "city's skirts"—Dekker's sinfully polluted suburbs—to be both the source of the plague and the locale of the theaters is echoed within *The Alchemist*, as Ross notes, by Subtle's having come from the liberties, and by the invasion of Lovewit's house (and Jonson's stage) by the same fetid alchemist, who is himself a kind of vagrant infection.[13] Years later, Jonson will return to this theme in the Caroline masque *Love's Triumph through Callipolis* (1631). In the antimasque, the god of Love cannot enter the city for fear of an infection in "the suburbs, or skirtes" caused by "certaine Sectaries or deprau'd lovers"—a diseased race, corrupt, sordid, and brutish, mere cattle and not men, an envious mass, the symptom of whose overheated frenzy is a continual vertigo beyond all order or measure (7:736, ll. 22–24). These tainted sub-urban lovers represent a foreign threat to boot, since they are costumed in the outlandish habits of the four principal nations of Europe, a feverish confederacy of Hollanders, Frenchmen, Spaniards, and Italians threatening the city with contamination at its very gates. These are comical foreigners, but they recall the "Spanish Leagar" of Dekker's plague tragedy, itself a distant reminder that, but for the grace of God, London might have found a Spanish army at its gates in 1588. Had the tribulations narrowly avoided by the defeat of the armada only been postponed until now? Underlying this conceit is the connection, real or imagined, between plague as an imported disease and the growing numbers of foreigners pressing in on the walls of the ancient city as London finds itself transformed in these very years from a regional capital to a cosmopolitan center. If only in the ideal world of the masque's Callipolis, the Queen—as the paragon of beauty and goodness—has the power to dispel the infection: the depraved are "vapor'd hence" (7:738, l. 94), and Love can now safely enter the city to initiate the revels.

The language of "skirtes" and "outskirts" imagines the city's unregulated environs as contaminated by female impurities. In Jonson's antimasque for *Love's Triumph*, a "Mistress," the tainted counterpart of the Queen who will ultimately fumigate these diseased minions away, leads the depraved lovers in their "anticke gesticulation" (7:736, l. 30). The mistress "herself"—a male

---

of hierarchy and gender—and perhaps even in its promiscuous creation of a mass audience, heaped together in a pit—playing constituted, in fact, a kind of metaphoric plague for which the actual disease was the proper and inevitable retributive substitute" (*Issues of Death*, 25, 26).

13. Ross, "The Plague of *The Alchemist*," 442.

actor in skirts—would embody the moral pollution "she" portrayed. "Menstruous rags" recalls Thomas Lodge's recommendation that if the body is to purge itself of the plague, "no accustomed euacuations either by fluxe of *Hemeroides*, or of the belly, old vlcers, menstruall blood, itches, or such like should be restrained."[14] Ridding London of her theaters (already marked by their lack of moral restraint) would then be a form of civic medicine, purging the social body of its pestilent contamination—a view shared, among many, even by Dekker: "A Plague's the Purge to clense a Cittie" (102). The poet and plague pamphleteer Henry Petowe regards it as a particular mercy that the plague of 1603 should have first broken out "on the Skirts which we terme the Subburbs of the City":

> The reason why it pleased God to strike the exteriour members, before the interiour parts: I meane the Subburbs before the body of the City, may demonstrate vnto vs, that the Lord would yet looke downe in mercy on the body, if that the perishing of some loose members may cause repentance. For as in a faire and costly garment, after it is framed by the labor of the workeman, and through his negligence, or mistaking, it chance to bee made somewhat vnfit, or with some other fault, and therefore dooth displease the owner, yet if it may bee mended by altering the skirts, or extremest parts, without taking asunder of the whole, he will be drawn to a better liking of it: So the Lord, that euer taketh delight in sparing and shewing pitty, and doth seeke to recall manie into the way, by the punishment of fewe, in the first breaking forth of his wrath, began to punish the skirts and subburbs of the City, that the City it selfe seeing the rod so neere, should feare betimes.[15]

Petowe's analogy might well seem thoughtlessly cruel to all but those who could afford "a faire and costly garment." Those not fortunate enough to have the Lord as their tailor—those occupying London's theatrical margin—are stigmatized as "exteriour," "vnfit," and "extreme" (as well as female and foreign). Petowe's example indicts the "workeman" as the cause of the plague, not the

---

14. Lodge, *A Treatise of the Plague*, D1r. Subsequent citations of this work are given parenthetically in the text.

15. Petowe, *Londoners their Entertainment in the Countrie*, A4r–v.

"owner" for whom the garment has been made. In a classic instance of the distinction drawn by Mary Douglas, those "few" impoverished victims on the outskirts are set off from the "interiour parts" of the city occupied by London's elites. A sermon of 1577 had more succinctly argued the same point in a compelling (though logically questionable) syllogism: "[T]he issue of plagues is sin, if you look to it well; and the cause of sin are plays: therefore the cause of plagues are plays."[16]

Physicians and Divines: A "Just" Plague?

In Jonson's day (and long after), the welter of conflicting medical opinion about the nature and cause, or causes, of the plague created more confusion than it dispelled. Lodge noted that "any increase of such creatures as are engendred by putrefaction" (worms, flies, serpents) is a sign that the plague is near (c2v). But in a time when natural history still held to the Plinian view that such creatures sprang up spontaneously from the warm springtime mud, the exact role of rats and fleas, let alone of the bacterium *Y. pestis* and the complex vectors of its transmission, were inconceivable. The mysteries of the plague—its origins, its modalities, the selection of its victims, and ultimately its "purpose"—were perforce referred to theology. But in these sacred precincts, too, the insistence that plague was the scourge of sin led to another set of vexed and ultimately impenetrable questions about (in the language of Jonson's poem) "[m]y sinne" and the "iust day."[17] What sin? How just? A strictly naturalist explanation would, in theory, dispense with all such questions as it sought for causes by whatever lights were available to it: a man fell ill because he had the ill luck to be exposed to putrefied air or to come in contact with some source of contagion. The state of his soul could have nothing to do with it. A strictly supernatural explanation would similarly dispel all the quandaries arising from experience by asserting that God, as his punishment for sin, might strike down or save whom he pleased without always making his reasons apparent, although they could often be discerned by strenuous rationalization. It would not be beyond his prerogative to make use of corruption to fight corruption, but too curious an inquiry into which natural means

---

16. White, *A Sermo[n] Preached at Pawles Crosse*, 47.
17. For the text of Jonson's poem, see the beginning of chapter 4.

he may choose, and how they operate, would only be a distraction from the need for repentance. In practice, there were few strict positions on either side, with the result that, according to their emphasis, both the medical literature and the spiritual are involved with negotiating the even more perplexing issues of first and second causes.

A sampling of plague treatises published in London during and immediately after the epidemic of 1603 allows us to briefly survey the current state of medical knowledge. The most notable of all these plague publications from a literary point of view are two pamphlets by Dekker, *The Wonderfull Yeare* (1603) *and Newes from Graues-ende* (1604), along with the later *A Rod for Run-awaies* (1625), which looks back at the earlier outbreak and treats the crucial question of flight, to which we shall return. Some few, like Henoch Clapham, seemed unpersuaded that the disease was contagious. Only "Atheists, mere Naturians and other ignorant persons," Clapham wrote, "do hold it to be a natural disease, proceeding from natural causes only: as from corruption of ayre, caused by vnseasonable Planetes aboue, or else from carrionly stinking smelles here belowe."[18] To believe that infection could be spread by (merely) natural causes seemed to limit, or even deny, God's purposeful choice of victims. It discouraged the fearful from performing their Christian duties to others, and it encouraged the ungodly to think that they could escape the plague by fleeing to the countryside, when in fact there could be no limit to the reach of divine vengeance. "This opinion of infection," some were said to argue, "doeth vtterly ouerthrow charitie towards the visited by the plague . . . so that it is a very countermaund to Christ his iudgement concerning visitation of the sick."[19] Besides, if the disease can be spread by one person breathing on another, then, asks Thomas Dekker, "who breath'd vpon the first?" (84). But even most preachers conceded that it would be mistaken to conclude that the disease is not contagious, even if one believes, as one must, that "[n]one can die of the plague but such as are specially appointed thereunto."[20] And if it be objected that the Bible—otherwise the only authoritative source of historical epidemiology—nowhere specifically asserts that plagues are infectious, it would be "against all reason, to make the Bible a booke of phisicke,"

18. Clapham, *Epistle*, A3v.
19. Balmford, *A Short Dialogue concerning the Plagues Infection*, 41.
20. Ibid., 60.

just as it would be to doubt from like omissions in scripture that "the French disease commeth by whoredom."[21] Almost all physicians, seconded by civic authorities concerned to justify the necessity of quarantine, also insisted that the pestilence was undoubtedly "infectious" or "contagious."

Both terms meant that it was communicable (as indeed the plague is, in its pneumonic form), but not in our modern sense. "Infection" was somehow (or, rather, *something*) spread through a miasmal corruption of the air or water, through the stench of unburied bodies, or, as Lodge adds in his *Treatise of the Plague*, through "euill vapours that issue from the earth, or certaine Caves," or from "divers sorts of Plantes, and venomous beastes" (c2v). As late as the Great Plague and the advent of the Royal Society, Robert Hooke and Thomas Sydenham agreed with Boyle's neo-Galenic theory that epidemics were caused by effluvia seeping up from deposits in the earth's crust.[22] Lodge notes that in the warm weather, "Rats, Moules, and other creatures, (accustomed to liue vnder ground) forsake their holes and habitations," but he sees this phenomenon as a "token of corruption" of the soil itself (c2v). What we take to be a discrete process of transmission among individuals exposed to an infectious agent was, in Jonson's day, an enveloping ecological soup of poisonous gases, putrid oozes, befouled water, noxious smells, and—as some, but not Lodge, believed—malign astral influences (the Italian *influenza*), which all combined to contaminate the air. As a noxious environmental contamination, "infection" might thus be warded off by the use of handkerchiefs soaked in vinegar or nosegays of fragrant herbs. "Contagion" was frequently interchangeable with "infection," or regarded as a consequence of infection: thus Portia's surprise that Brutus should "steal out of his wholesome bed / To dare the vile contagion of the night" (*Julius Caesar*, 2.1.264–65). Strictly speaking, however, *contagion* remained closer to its root sense of "contact," implying that the disease lurked in bedclothes and on coins, clung to walls, and could be spread by touch. On this theory, it was common in plague times for merchants to keep a bowl of vinegar handy on the counter to purify the coins that might pass into their hands. Thus, Lodge defines contagion as "an euill qualitie in a body, communicated unto an other by touch, engendering one and the same disposition in him to whom it is communicated" (B2v). A "contagion" could be a poison; Hamlet so names the

---

21. Ibid., 78.
22. Dewhurst, *Dr. Thomas Sydenham*, 66.

ointment with which he will "touch" his point (4.7.48), and the symptoms of poisoning (as we see in the demise of the elder Hamlet) are often represented as those of a pustulant disease. As such, "contagion" functions symbolically as the lethal opposite of the "King's touch"—by which, on one occasion in 1633, Charles I "healed" one hundred people in Holyrood Chapel.

At one extreme, an emphasis on the manifold and baneful sources of environmental infection could lead to the view expressed by Lodge that the plague "violently rauisheth all men for the most part to death, without respect or exception of age, sexe, complexion, gouernment in life, or particular condition whatsoeuer" (B1v). At the other extreme, a classically Hippocratic emphasis on "aptitude," "complexion," and "government" could lead to the more hopeful conclusion that a well-balanced individual could, with proper diet and exercise and a certain equanimity of temper, enjoy a virtual immunity from external assault. This last might be empirically verified by observing that not everyone fell ill and that, indeed, some who came into close contact with plague victims remained unaffected. The environmentalist explanation was no respecter of persons: it leveled all orders of men and imagined a plague that struck with blind indifference to any moral, or other, discrimination. The older Greek explanation preserved a greater sense of individual autonomy, but while it recognized the virtue of moderate self-government as a defense against infection, it left little room for sin and repentance to enter the equation. Neither explanation provided a role for the "government" of magistrates or monarch or for the ministrations of the clergy: it was out of their jurisdiction. The compromise position tended to juxtapose these equally problematic alternatives rather than to resolve their differences. Thus, the physician James Manning is concerned to leave nothing out of the account, even if the result reads like a jumble: "The Pestilant feuer is taken not only by infection in the ayre, infused by celestiall orbes, and from putrified places, in and vpon the earth; but also by bad humours about the heart and ill affected spirits in the heart, whose aptitude doth entertaine the said infection, yet not alike in all, for all then should die alike, but according to the complection."[23]

---

23. Manning, A New Booke, Intituled, I Am for You All, 6. As Wilson notes (The Plague in Shakespeare's London, 5), Shakespeare combines all these senses—the astrological, the providential, the miasmal, and the poisonous—when Timon would have Alcibiades "[b]e as a planetary plague, when Jove / Will o'er some high-vic'd city hang his poison / In the sick air" (Timon, 4.3.116–18).

Unsurprisingly, given the range of English medical practitioners—from licensed and unlicensed physicians of whatever persuasion, to barber surgeons, apothecaries, quacks, and charlatans—the list of herbs, metals, poisons, amulets, and potions all guaranteed to either cure or prevent the disease was as bizarre as it was lengthy. In addition to George Thomson's desiccated toad, it included, among other things, the smoke of fragrant woods, vinegar air fresheners, floral pomanders worn about the neck, various pills and purges, unguents and poultices, and concoctions of roots, seeds, leaves, spices, chestnuts, and much else, steeped in water or wine (with sugar and lemon juice). Lodge recommends cakes of arsenic applied to the armpits, along with the following purgatives, listed by the "complexion" of the patient:

Those that are chollerique, ought to be purged with an infusion of *Rubarb*; if they be wealthy: and if poore, with the Electuary of the iuice of *Roses*, by taking three Drammes, or halfe an ounce thereof in *Sorrell*, *Endiue*, or *Purslane* water, or else by *Diacatholium*, *Diaprunis*, *Laxatiue*, the sirope of *Roses*, *Cassia*, or the pilles of *Rubarb*, *Femetorie*, or those that for their gentle working are called (by the Phisitians) *Aureae*. The Flegmatique, ought to be purged with *Agaric*, *Diaphenicon*, *Diacarthami*, the pils *Aggregatine*, *Cochiae*, according to the strength of their bodyes, the qualitie of the humor which are offensiue at the discreton of the learned & experienced Phisitians, by whose directions and prescriptions such medecines are to be ministred, & not according to the custome of this time, by foolish Idiotes and ignorant Emperiques. Such as are melancholy should be purged with the infusion of *Sena* and *Epithemum* with a little *Anice seede*, and *Diacathelicon*, with the *Confection*, *Hamech*, *Diasene*, *Solutiue*, the pilles of *Femitory*, and *Aureae*. I forbeare to call the pils, *De lape Armeno*, and *Lasuli* into vse, because they are too violent, and scarcely well prepared. Such as are weake and delicate persons (As woman with childe, children, and aged people,) it shall suffice to purge them with an ounce of *Cassia*, extracted with halfe or a whole dramme of *Rubarb*, or two ounces of *Manna*, or three ounces of sirope of *Roses*, or with the sirope of *Sucery* with *Rubarb*, but with this Prouiso alwayes, that the direction be taken from a learned and diligent Phisitian, and not according to the fancie of foolish chare women, and ignorant practizers. (DIV)

This extraordinary pharmacopoeia further distinguishes between treatments affordable by the rich or by the poor. In a pointed reminder of the social and professional divisions within the medical community, as well as of the conflicting theoretical and therapeutic claims of the Galenists and the Paracelsians, Lodge warns that none of these remedies should be administered by ignorant practitioners, including idiots, "Emperiques" (i.e., adherents of Paracelsian chemical medicine), and women.[24] Working from a very different set of assumptions based in an empiric pharmacopoeia of salts and metals and an occult fascination with "spiritual seeds," alchemical and Neoplatonic mysteries, sympathetic powers, astral influences, and baneful particles wafting upward from the souls of the sinful, all of which both evince and provoke heavenly anger, the advocates of the chemical medicine—as we saw in the later case of the militant Thomson—would dismiss the Galenists as adherents of a discredited (and pagan) orthodoxy. And of course, for every proponent of amulets or arsenic or toads, there was likely to be a rival prescriber ready to denounce all these in favor of a sovereign remedy of his own, or one of which he had heard on good authority from a Spaniard who had treated Philip ii, or from a famous Tuscan apothecary recommended by a certain noble lady.

From the perspective of those moralists and godly ministers whose contributions to the plague literature of 1603 were no less numerous, and even more heated, than those of the medical men, speculation about the immediate causes of the epidemic was, finally, beside the point, as was the debate about methods of treatment. Subterranean effluvia, corrupted vapors (such as those arising from graves like Ben's), the effect of drought, or the influence of the stars were matters of concern to mere "naturians." The Christian understood that these were all the second causes of an affliction whose first cause was sin, and whose only remedy was repentance. In the course of

---

24. Lodge himself was learned and experienced, but in 1603 he was still an unlicensed physician: "In 1597 Lodge left England for France where he received a medical degree from the University of Avignon in 1598. In 1602 his medical degree was recognized by Oxford, though his application for a licence from the College of Physicians was denied. Between 1598 and 1610 Lodge practised medicine, at times in London and at times in the Low Countries and France.... Lodge's shifting between the continent and England during this period, together with his marriage to a known Catholic, leads biographers to assume that his intermittent exile and the denial of a licence to practise from the College of Physicians resulted from his Catholicism and possible participation in Counter-Reformation activities" (Halasz, "Lodge, Thomas," in *Oxford Dictionary of National Biography Online*). On women as medical dispensers, see Katritzky, *Women, Medicine and Theatre*.

these debates, scripture was scoured for plague references that might unlock the mysteries of wholesale human suffering.[25] But explaining the plague as a providential event only raised an even more urgent concern with the justness of its infliction. Although the physician Lodge had acknowledged that we are "now vnder the fatherly correction of Almightie God, and punished for our misdeeds by his heauy hand" (B1v), his incontestable observation that the plague's heavy hand appears to be general and indiscriminate in its effects— it "violently rauisheth all men"—could only with difficulty be reconciled to the actions of a just God. The implication of his remark that the signs of the plague are what "the common people" (but perhaps not learned physicians?) "call Gods tokens" (B2v) could not go unchallenged.

Quite evidently, not all exposed to infection or contagion fell ill with the same disease, or fell ill to the same extent or with the same symptoms as their neighbor. How to understand that the plague seemed at once a universal and a selective affliction? Dekker addresses the question by asking why, if "the Ayre does (round about) / In flakes of poyson drop on all," are not all alike struck down—and why, in that case, do we not see nature herself infected, so that the animals and birds would all fall ill as well, and the "Fish swim to shore full of disease" from their polluted rivers (83–84)? Others thought that corrupt and rotten humors in the bodies of some individuals made them more apt than others to receive the effects of the venomous air. This appeal to the disposition of the individual, as we have seen, invokes the perspective of the Galenic tradition, mediated through Italian medical theory, which tended to focus more on the endogenous processes of disease than on its external causes. Whatever might be in the air, individuals fell ill because of some humoral imbalance to which their own nature or improper diet made them prone, and their buboes could be read as evidence of the body's trying to right itself by expelling some noxious substance.[26] Dekker, however, sees what the

---

25. Scriptural passages repeatedly cited include Lev. 26, Num. 14:11–12, Deut. 28:21–22, 1 Sam. 5–9, 2 Sam. 24:12–13, and Ps. 106:29–30, showing that all bodily sickness proceeds from God, as punishment for transgression of his commandments; 2 Sam., chronicling the plague visited on David for numbering the people (as London did, by posting bills of mortality); Jer. 16:4, showing that those dead of pestilence "shall be as dung vpon the earth" (Davies, *Humours Heau'n on Earth*, 237); and, in the New Testament, John 9:23 and Luke 13:12, instructing us, somewhat troublingly, that "those which are afflicted, are not alwayes greater sinners than others."

26. Carmichael, "Contagion Theory and Contagion Practice in Fifteenth-Century Milan," especially 223–24.

physician might regard as the variable complexion of the individual as a specifically, and exclusively, spiritual condition from which no person is immune. In his view, the plague "[s]ucks virid poison from our soule," rather than from the air or the ground, for "euery man within him feedes / A worme which this contagion breedes" (85). Yet the equally incontestable observation that some remained unscathed demanded to be explained. The answer could only be that God's arrows—directed by his hidden will, to be sure—were aimed only at those he wished to chastise. As the birds and fish could not be held morally responsible, they could not be targeted. But why, on that "iust day"—a day that in the providential history of justice recapitulates the era of biblical chastisements and anticipates the Last Judgment—were children and godly preachers struck down, and the wicked often as not spared? By what measure of "fatherly correction" could the plague leave a father to mourn a seven-year-old son? Why were some parishes or households visited with "slaughter sore" and others barely touched?

James Balmford, rector of St. Olave's, Southwark—an outlying parish on the city's "skirts"—addresses these matters with no less ingenuity than conviction in his *Short Dialogue concerning the Plagues Infection*, intended for the comfort of his parishioners. Those unaffected by the plague, though they sleep in the same bed with a victim, may be protected by God's "special providence," since he "preserueth those that trust in him."[27] Nor will God take any "hence before they haue done all that seruice, which in his counsel was appointed" (52). The anti-contagionists err in thinking that only the faithless are stricken. To be sure, those who in their pride imagine themselves safe because of a high opinion of their own righteousness are in the greatest peril of being struck down. Yet the wicked might remain untouched, as Henoch Clapham argues, either because God chooses to be merciful even to them, or because even in their (wickedly) "bragging of their faith in God, touching deliuerance from pestilence," their deliverance itself showed that in that particular faith, at least, they were sincere.[28] Godly men may, however, be taken if they "faile in faith," if not in faith of their ultimate salvation, then "touching the particular promise of preseruation from the plague" (*Short Dialogue*, 57)—which is as

27. Balmford, *A Short Dialogue*, 45. Subsequent citations of this work are given parenthetically in the text.
28. Clapham, *Epistle*, B4r. Subsequent citations of this work are given parenthetically in the text.

much as to say that whoever doubts the power of heaven to protect him, thinking perhaps that he is not deserving of protection because of his sins, cannot complain of injustice if he contracts the disease. Clapham insists that there must have been among "Believers so dying, a want of faith for apprehending this particular deliuerance, this temporary mercy"—that is, a lack of faith that God could, or would, deliver them from the plague at that moment. Thus, though they "haue not lacked faith for their eternall iustification & finall saluation," their temporary and particular doubt caused them to die when they might otherwise have recovered or been spared altogether (*Epistle*, B3v). A sign of such "temporary" faltering is that men may be overly fearful of infection, in which case God may "iustly take hold of their feare" (*Short Dialogue*, 58). In case one does fall ill, Lodge finds support in Avicenna for a similar medical argument about the debilitating effect of fear: "They that are manly, and confidently beare out their sicknesse without any showe of feare, they are those which for the most part escape" (c3v).

Balmford's parishioners must understand in any event that "by the death of the faithfull, God glorifieth his iustice and wisedome":

> His iustice amongst the wicked, in giuing them cause to say, If God spare not the greene tree, what will become of the drie? His wisedom amongst the godly, least they should say, For our righteousnesse we are deliuered. As for the good of the belieuer, I marvell that you should forget that which is so often taught in funeral sermons, that as the wicked are reserued for a further mischiefe, So the righteous is taken away from the euill to come; besides, that he resteth in glorie from more and greater labors, then the wicked are commonly subiect unto. (59)

The evil to come from which the righteous victim is spared would surely include, "if no other miserie, yet age"—the one shred of consolation Jonson can find in the death of his son. When the death of the believer, redounding to the glory of God, can be so complacently rationalized as both just and beneficial, even to—especially to—the "greene tree," expert and searching analysis of the divine intention yields a plague theodicy that explains everything—and therefore nothing. Caught on the dilemma of natural processes and divine origins, Clapham insists that although the plague may be communicated from person to person by means of what we would call a secondary infection, in respect of its divine origin it cannot be contagious; it is, rather, "to bee numbered amongest *Supernaturalls*, and so not infectious, seeing the partie so smitten, could not by all the corruption in his nature sende out such a *Word*, such a *Thing*, begetting the same effect in another" (B1r). Clapham's distinction between a supernatural (and therefore *un*contagious) pestilence as a blow struck against individuals for sin, and the same pestilence transmitted from one person to another (as contagion) in its subsequent natural form, represents his bold but unconvincing attempt to accommodate the two realms in which plague was seen to operate. Here he has, in effect, pressed the argument to the point where the only thing revealed by its implosion is the strain of the attempt, making it tortuous, and ultimately impossible, to reconcile the conflicting views of the plague as a moral and as an infectious agent. Taken together, the apologetics of 1603 prove by scripture and reason that the plague may claim the wicked or spare them, as it may also spare the righteous or claim them, all with equal justice. The question of its possible injustice—the unspeakable possibility that all are taken unjustly—leads to the inevitable conclusion that the plague cannot be unjust no matter what it does or does not do. The logical corollary—that if the plague can always be proven just, it can never be proven not unjust, as the distinction itself disappears—is unthinkable. Racking the dilemma of justice to the breaking point, theodicy cannot admit its failure, nor can it easily entertain the possibility that, in Luther's words, "sometimes Satan so preuaileth, and hath such successe in that he goeth aboute, that by sudden plagues he bringeth men to horrible destruction." At the point of its inadmissible failure, theodicy can only fall back on Luther's argument that as long as there is no higher standard of justice against which the divine conduct can be measured, "[w]hat God wills . . . must be right because He so wills it." To ask why he does it is to seek access to that part of the divine mind hidden from our view.[29]

Plague's meaning can be parsed at length, but finally "this disease hath in it," as Francis Herring concludes, "*Diuinum quid*, a secret and hidden nature, so that we may iustly with the inchanters of Egypt acknowledge it the finger of God."[30] That Pharaoh's magicians are here brought in as witnesses seems an odd (though defensibly scriptural) note, suggesting unspeakably that our

---

29. Luther, *On the Bondage of the Will*, 40, 177, 191–92.
30. Herring, *A Modest Defence*, "To the Reader."

knowledge of God, "secret and hidden" from us, is itself a kind of enchantment, and the actions attributed to him a kind of legerdemain. The plague's fingerprints are everywhere. It speaks from the Word, and through "such a Word" as inscribes the tokens of its infliction as a terrible blow, a blow of the "heavy hand" of "fatherly correction." The meaning of the Word is hidden; only its pain is palpable. A father who had benefited from that correction by losing a son might wish to "loose all father, now."

Andrewes and Clapham at the Extremes

The two political poles of 1603 plague theology—and its attendant politics—are clearly exemplified in the contrasting figures of Lancelot Andrewes and Henoch Clapham. In 1603 Andrewes was dean of Westminster Abbey, master of Pembroke College, Cambridge, and a chaplain of the Chapel Royal in Whitehall. He would go on to hold the bishoprics of Chichester, Ely, and Winchester in succession; he became a privy councillor in 1609; and he was the leading figure among the translators of the King James Bible. If Donne would be London's most dazzling preacher, Andrewes was already its most influential. In that plague summer he was also a "runaway," to Chiswick. In this pleasant retreat along the Thames, he had charge of the boys of Westminster School, the eleven-year-old George Herbert among them, evacuated for their safety.[31] Meanwhile, his own parish of St. Giles, Cripplegate, recorded 2,879 burials, most of them plague victims.

Surely aware that his flight would be unfavorably compared with the steadfastness of other vicars who remained with their flock, Andrewes preached a remarkable plague sermon at Chiswick on August 21. The plague works through natural means—but these are to be grounded in the authority of scripture, which also endorses flight. The Law, he contends, itself gives evidence of the air having been infected when pestilence descended upon Egypt. It also cautions against exposing oneself to contagion, in the restrictions it places on contact with lepers. Andrewes's own (mis)reading of Proverbs 14:16 has Solomon asserting that "[a] wise man feareth the Plague [literally, "evil"] and departeth

---

31. Nicolson, *God's Secretaries*, 28–29; Welsby, *Lancelot Andrewes*, 78–79.

from it."[32] Furthermore, if (in 1 Chronicles 21, 30) "King David himself durst not go to the altar of God at Gibeon" because "he was to pass through infected places" to get there, then would it not be foolish for any man to run such a risk (5:225–26)? According to Andrewes, the true cause of the plague must be diagnosed by the preacher rather than the physician. Andrewes's text for the day is Psalms 106:29–30, in his own translation: "Thus they provoked Him to anger with their inventions, and the Plague broke in upon them. Then stood up Phinehas and executed judgment, and the plague was stayed" (5:223).[33] From this, Andrewes draws out the two main threads of his sermon. First, the cause of the plague: the "inventions" that had provoked God's anger included not only "new meats in diet" and "new fashions in apparel" but, crucially, "new tricks, opinions and fashions" in divine worship, innovations our "fathers never knew of" (5:229). Clearly enough, this indictment is meant to cover Separatists, Anabaptists, Familists, Legatine-Arians, and Presbyterians of all stripes, here incongruously allied with followers of fashion and gourmands as whoring after novelty. By implication, it extends to Catholics as well, since in Andrewes's reading of Matthew 16:22, "invention" was precisely "St. Peter's fault, when he persuaded Christ from His passion, and found out a better way as he thought than Christ could devise" (5:229). It turns out that the Roman church, anticipated in Peter's errant notion that he knew better than Christ, was guilty of "invention" from the very beginning. As Andrewes argued afterward in his *Responsio ad Bellarminum*, such Romish doctrines as transubstantiation were no part of the primitive church but, rather, novelties concocted by papal councils more than a thousand years later (8:261). "Our appeal is to antiquity," he insists. "We do not innovate; it may be we renovate what was customary with those same ancients, but with you has disappeared in novelties."[34]

---

32. Andrewes, *A Sermon of the Pestilence*, 5:225. Subsequent citations of this work are given parenthetically in the text. The thing to be feared in other versions of Proverbs 14:16 is "evil": *malum* in the Vulgate, κακόσ in the Septuagint, all translating the Hebrew רע, which means "evil" or "harm" in a very general sense but has nothing specifically to do with plague. Restoring the literal sense behind Andrewes's tweaking of the proverb raises one of the several dilemmas Andrewes needs to evade. How can the plague be an evil when it is to be understood as the instrument of God's righteous anger?

33. The KJV and Douay-Rheims version have "inventions," following the Vulgate *adinventionibus*. Hebrew has מַעַלְלֵיהֶם, "with their doings."

34. Quoted in Nicolson, *God's Secretaries*, 189.

For the sectaries and separatists, Andrewes's argument contains a further historical irony. Their "inventions" are nothing new, merely the re-invention of the oldest kind of error, that committed by the founder of the Roman church at the moment when he thought it might be better if Christ were not to go to Jerusalem to be killed. Indeed, Andrewes is eager to trace the history of "invention" even farther back, to the Fall—the origin of all subsequent temptations to be "witty, and to find out things ourselves to make to ourselves, to be authors and inventors of somewhat, that so we may seem to be as wise as God, if not wiser" (5:228–29). This, says Andrewes, is "the old disease of our father Adam" (5:228): the world's first invention is the original and endemic infection of pride. From this point of view, with the new plague of 1603, the duty to chasten "invention" (by a therapeutic "renovation") must be understood as a kind of antipathetic remedy for the plague, going back to the very root of the disease.

As Andrewes develops his theme, Psalm 26 instructs us in the cure as well as the cause of the disease. The cure must be "twofold," stemming from the two meanings of the word *palal* that Andrewes finds [in the form וַיְפַלֵּל] in the Hebrew text: "'Phinehas prayed,' some read it: 'Phinehas executed judgment,' some other; and the word bears both" (5:224). Since "[o]ne contrary is ever cured by another" (5:224), God's anger will first of all be appeased by the sweetness of prayer: "For as the air is infected with noisome scents or smells, so the infection is removed by sweet odours or incense; which Aaron did in the Plague. . . . Now there is a fit resemblance between incense and prayers"; as the Psalmist says, "Let my prayer come before Thy presence as the incense" (5:230). But prayer is not enough, for the plague to which the Psalmist refers (in Numbers 25:7–8) was visited upon the Israelites when a man brought a Midianite woman into the very heart of the congregation. It did not abate until prayer was supplemented with an execution of judgment forceful enough to counter the double threat of the stranger and the woman. And a memorable execution it was: "Phinehas took his javelin, wherewith in the very act of fornication 'he thrust them both through,' Zimri and his woman, 'and then the Plague was stayed from the children of Israel'" (5:232).

The cure, it must be emphasized, does not depend solely on the combination of prayer and punishment, both implied in a single word. Its effectiveness depends on the dual remedies of prayer and the punishment alike issuing from the single authority of Phinehas: "There were two persons. Both of them were in Phinehas. For as he was a priest, so he was a prince of his tribe. So then both these must join together, as well the devotion of the priest in prayer, which is his office, as the zeal of the magistrate in executing judgment, which is his" (5:232–33). As one who enforces the law, Phinehas stands in "blessed conjunction" (5:233) with Moses; and as one who offers prayer, he fulfills his priestly duty as the grandson of Aaron. Indeed, in recognition of Phinehas's zeal, God bestows upon the seed of Aaron a covenant of everlasting priesthood (Numbers 25:13), thus authorizing the priestly succession that leads from Aaron and Phinehas to Andrewes himself. As "two persons" in one, Phinehas foreshadows the dual nature of Christ and ultimately, for Andrewes, the dual nature of godly authority. Andrewes means that the clergy and the civil arm must work in concert, each in its own province, whether appealing for mercy or administering justice, but to a joint end. He also means that the two are, finally, the same—whether the power of each is jointly vested in the other, or whether the same person exercises both.

Although Andrewes is careful to balance the two therapeutic functions of priest and prince, the force of his language falls much more heavily on the execution of judgment. The image of prayer wafting upward like a cloud of sweet incense allows him to suggest that prayer is truly medicinal, like the incense thought to disperse the contagion in the air. Against Puritan suspicions, this remedy also allows him to defend the use of incense as a spiritual practice, an adjunct to divine service not unlike prayer: "Sennacherib's Plague, it is plain, came from Rabshakeh's blasphemy; blasphemy able to infect the air, it was so foul. In which regard Aaron's act might be justified, in putting odours into his censor to purify the air from such corruption" (5:229). But the incense quickly evaporates as Andrewes presents us with the scene of judgment: Phinehas took his javelin and skewered Zimri and his Midianite woman "in the very act of fornication." By a strangely appropriate logic, the two fornicators joined as one in their coupling are killed by the one man who is "two persons," while the penetrating "thrust" of Phinehas's judgment doubles that of the fornicating Zimri. In the Authorized Version of the book of Numbers (as it would be translated by the First Westminster Company, directed by Andrewes), Phinehas "thrust both of them through ... and the woman through her belly" (25:8). The violence of this scene is partially subdued into allegory when Andrewes admonishes every man, in the absence of a Phinehas, to "be Phinehas to himself" and "so judge himself" (5:233). But the thrust of his passion, and the threat behind it, leave no doubt that the public health is better served when malefactors responsible for the plague are subject to the same harsh judgments as were imposed on the Israelites in the desert when they disobeyed the "magistrate" Moses and set off after strange gods and strange women.

During the epidemic of 1603, the weight of the law fell heavily on Andrewes's adversary in the arena of plague political theology, the preacher Henoch Clapham, whose contentious views have been quoted above. Following the appearance of his *Epistle Discoursing vpon the Present Pestilence* in 1603, Clapham faced two related allegations investigated by the bishop of London and referred, in turn, to Lancelot Andrewes—who in executing judgment was to play the role of Phinehas to Clapham's Zimri. It was charged, first, that Clapham's pamphlet had spread discontent by denying that the plague was contagious, the basic assumption on which government policy was based. Royal orders issued that summer prohibited the publication of any "opinions . . . that it is a vain thing to forbeare to resort to the Infected, or that it is not charitable to forbid the same, pretending that no person shall die but at their time prefixed."[35] If "Ecclesiasticall," any such offenders were to be forbidden to preach, but Clapham was imprisoned—likely on the strength of the second allegation, that he was supposed to believe that the afflicted died from a lack of faith. In the same pamphlet, he had not helped his case by sharply attacking ministers who (like Andrewes) abandoned their parishes: such "Fleers are left of God to belie scripture, and to abuse their brethren, which is a worse plague then that they flie from" (c3r). While serving more than three years in the Clink, he published two additional pamphlets in his own defense, *Henoch Clapham his Demaundes and Answeres touching the Pestilence* (1604) and *Doctor Andros his Prosopopeia answered* (1605), the latter explicitly taking up the points of controversy in his interrogation by Andrewes. Here Clapham attempts to argue that there were really two plagues, that caused immediately by God, and that issuing from the natural processes by which it was inflicted. The first was not infectious; the second was.

Clapham had not denied that the plague was infectious, but he had left himself vulnerable to the allegation by the harshness of his opinion. In his

---

35. *Orders, Thought Meete by His Maiestie . . . to Be Executed throughout the Counties of This Realme . . .*, order 16, B2v.

view, only an atheist or an ignorant person could be so deluded as to believe that the pestilence arises only from natural causes. Neither providentialist nor naturalist arguments could be proven or refuted. Belief in astrological influence was on the wane, but comets might still be taken as portents of disaster, even if their passage was no longer thought to infect the air. No medical writer in the period would go so far (in print) as to attribute outbreaks of epidemic disease to nature alone, and no divine could explain how God's arrows found their target except through natural means. If neither first nor second causes could be ignored, how were they to be accommodated? The question resolves itself in turn into that of contagion, on which, to his regret, Clapham took an extreme position.

If the pestilence were not "contagious" or "infectious"—these concepts were themselves inevitably unclear in an age when the actual vectors of infectious disease could not even be imagined—then, from a Christian perspective, every individual afflicted must have been singled out to receive the divine stroke. This would explain why even in the same household, some fell ill while others were spared. It could not easily explain why the "innocent" suffered, nor (except, perhaps, to Andrewes) would it reveal the exact sins, individual or national, that had provoked such terrible retribution. If the plague were not "contagious," it would be more difficult (but not impossible on biblical grounds) to justify flight or to insist on the need for quarantine. For Clapham to denounce "Fleers" nonetheless called attention to the wretchedness of the great mass of people left behind, "the sick and needie" forcibly confined by watchmen and deprived even of those "workes of mercie" that were their only succor (c3r).

From prison, Clapham complained that, according to the second charge trumped up against him, he was supposed to have written that "[a]ll that dyed of the plague were damned, as dying without faith."[36] Refuting this libel drew him into the tangle of theological debate forced upon those who refused to believe that "nature" (whether through the apparent operation of chance, or the susceptibility of individual constitutions, or the contamination of bedclothes) was not guided by a divine purpose in the selection of those afflicted. In the emergency of 1603, Clapham's pamphlet might itself have been regarded by the authorities as a kind of contagion, infecting the vulnerable with

---

36. Clapham, *Demaundes*, A2v.

its noxious opinions. Clapham was regarded as a loose cannon, as wayward in his ecclesiastical career as he was prolific and unpredictable in his writing. In the 1590s he had led a Separatist congregation in Amsterdam, where he quarreled with other splinter groups of religious refugees, "[s]ometimes haled by this faction, sometimes pulled by that faction."[37] By the end of the decade, he had returned to the fold and set himself to composing dialogues exposing the errors of those to the "right" and to the "left" of the middle way. (The character in the dialogues who represents Clapham's former error in decamping for Amsterdam is called "Flyer.") By 1603 Clapham had made his peace with the church of Lancelot Andrewes, in time for his pamphlet to be seen as a threat from within rather than an attack from without. His insistence in the *Epistle* on the providential origin of the plague, together with his implicit critique of official policy and his charge that those who sought for explanations in nature were no better than atheists, puts Clapham in the company of those Puritan ministers who spoke for the "meaner sort of people"[38] and (either openly or by insinuation) against the government's plague orders in force that year. The requirement of a rigid quarantine could have no justification if the blow was struck by God's chastising hand and not by some mysterious contagion. Furthermore, the loophole of flight allowed the better sort, including public officials and divines, to abandon their responsibilities, leaving the great mass of Londoners to their fate—and all in the vain hope that they might so far remove themselves as to be out of the divine reach.

As we have seen, against the word of Jacobean law Clapham insistently and repeatedly emphasizes the Word of God—not only what scripture teaches about the infliction of pestilence, or what the plague might signify as an expression of the divine will, but that the plague itself is to be understood as identical with the Word. It would be increasingly difficult, and ultimately impossible, for most people to reconcile logically or theologically the conflicting views of the plague as a moral and an infectious agent. But if Christian thought cannot provide an unambiguous theodicy to explain, and thereby justify, the perplexing and horrifying experience of pestilence, it can offer an imaginatively powerful association between the language of plague and plague

---

37. Clapham, *Antidoton*, 6.
38. Clapham, *Demaundes*, 3–4.

as a form of language. For the purpose of understanding the assumptions behind plague writing more generally, Clapham's excursion into the tangles of biblical etymology reveals a fundamental identification of pestilence with the "word" and the "logos," the "thing" and the "deed."

Andrewes's Phinehas, understood by a single performative word to be saying and doing, praying and executing justice, brings the plague to an end when he combines the offices of priest and magistrate. So for Clapham, in its origin the plague issues from a single divine word ("plague") that is also a deed and a thing (the plague), immediately spoken and enacted. But the identification of the plague with the word—an utterance delivered with immediate and powerful force, and one to be understood by direct reference to scripture—makes Clapham's etymological exercise far more radical in its implications than anything Andrewes might countenance. For when every man equally and directly hears the "word" and feels the "blow" on his flesh, there can be no exclusive warrant for Andrewes's priesthood. The world can no longer be divided between the "everlasting priesthood" conferred on Phinehas in Numbers 25:13 and the mass of sinful sufferers to be punished by his descendents. Luther's universal priesthood has now, implicitly, been reconceived as a universal priesthood of the plague-ridden. Plague is registered in the authenticity of suffering more indelibly than in the reason for its infliction. To the extent that the plague is, in Clapham's view, exclusively God's to inflict or remove according to his own hidden will, then to that same extent Andrewes's priestly "javelin" seems less the instrument of divine justice than the weapon of a vengeful ecclesiastical power—and a power wielded from a safe distance at that. The consequences of this can be seen in Jonson's insistence in "To Heaven" that "I know my state," and "I feele my griefes too" (8:122, l. 21). The knowledge and feeling of suffering form the "ground" (to use Jonson's word) of the individual's authority. They may also be seen in Defoe's plague world of 1665, where there are no priests in evidence, where plague is written in the characters of individuals struck by it, and where such authority as there may be to ameliorate its effects (rather than punish its victims) is vested not in the court and the preachers who have fled for their own safety, but in the lord mayor and aldermen of the city—both because they have resisted the temptation to flee, and because they are willing to risk sharing the suffering of those to whom they conscientiously minister.

The Nation's Plague

In the plague writing of 1603, the sins that had evidently provoked God's wrath may stem either from individuals (whether singly or as members of suspect groups, such as mendacious lawyers, players, or malcontents) or from the state. Indeed, in the year of Jonson's epigram, the nation itself comes into focus, for better or worse, as teeming with excess population, as a cosmopolitan hub, and as in need of renewal after the death of its aged queen—all themes refracted in the nation's response to the worst plague epidemic in living memory. These two sources of sin, the individual and the national, provide moralists concerned with diagnosing the cause of the pestilence with convenient alternatives, for when the one seemed insufficient—for example, in justifying the death of the "innocent"—the other could come conveniently into play. Sin writ large on an urban or national scale required divine retribution to be seconded by official vigilance. The call by "I. H." for the "hand of authority" to take strong action against the corruptions of the theater reminds us that, for Jonson's age, plays were not only corrupt (and corrupting) in themselves; they also represented the potential for—even if they did not actually result in—the kind of civil disorder reported in accounts of urban epidemics going back to Thucydides and Boccaccio. As readers of Thomas Lodge's 1603 *Treatise of the Plague* would understand, Jonson's Subtle is one of those "vagabond, masterlesse men, and of a seruile and base condition," whose entry into the city should be barred by the magistrates (F2v). In the response of the court and the city, a Foucauldian plague politics is unveiled, one driven as much by panic on the part of London's elites as by a considered plan to contain the epidemic and relieve the stricken. Benign measures for improving sanitation, removing the dead, appointing "searchers" and watchmen, appropriating parish and crown funds to meet the emergency, and compiling bills of mortality went hand in hand with more repressive policies for increasing surveillance, quarantining infected houses under guard (for six weeks, by long-standing orders of the Privy Council), restricting travel and commerce, harrying undesirables out of the city, and banning public assemblies, as well as closing theaters once the number of recorded plague deaths rose to a certain threshold.[39]

---

39. For an account of the increasingly oppressive regime put in place from the 1590s through the early Jacobean years, see Healy, *Fictions of Disease*, 89–95.

In England as in Italy, contagionist assumptions lay behind such public health measures. Those who doubted that the plague could be communicated directly from one person to another—and these doubters could, like Henoch Clapham, be imprisoned for preaching such doctrine in opposition to official policy—located the source of the pestilence in fetid air and urban filth, and argued that fear of "contagion" should not dissuade Christians from ministering to the sick. Mistaken though they were, they were led by their error to advocate sanitation reforms that would result, inadvertently, in cleaning out the habitats of rats and fleas. Official policies, however harsh, arguably had some effect in containing the epidemic (just as, today, most would probably agree that the closing of airports and the enforced quarantine of passengers or even of cities would not be imprudent if we were faced with a pandemic threat). Penalties for violating plague orders, though difficult to enforce, were even harsher, responding as they must have to the widespread evasion of quarantine regulations—and to the specter of crazed victims stumbling through the streets, some of them bent on infecting others before they died. Throughout the summer of 1603, as in other plague times, funds were disbursed through the poorest parishes for the relief of the needy.[40] Nevertheless, Jacobean policies could be—and were—seen as repressive insofar as the restrictions favored those with the means to leave and places to go, while virtually imprisoning the hapless poor in the center of the epidemic. Those provisioners and shopkeepers who could flee did; food was short, compounding plague with the threat of famine. The mood on the street was a kaleidoscope of despair, anger, hysteria, and neurasthenic denial. London ministers and physicians who (like Clapham or Lodge) remained at their post were the exceptions.

London orders prohibiting the sale of used bedding or enjoining householders to sweep the street in front of their door also mandated that vagrants and masterless men should not be allowed to roam freely, and that infected persons who strayed from their parish were to be pursued and brought back for punishment. One royal proclamation of 1603 called for pulling down the ramshackle housing that had sprung up in parishes near the city walls and its environs—like Jonson's St. Giles to the north, as well as those on the south side of the river—because "the great confluence and accesse of excessiue

---

40. Wilson, *The Plague in Shakespeare's London*, 70–74, 89, 91, 105.

numbers of idle, indigent, dissolute and dangerous persons, And the pestering of many of them in small and strait roomes and habitations in the Citie of *London*, and in and about the Suburbes of the same, haue bene one of the chiefest occasions of the great Plague." The wording of the proclamation leaves it unclear whether those "pestering" together in squalid tenements are the victims or the cause of the pestilence, while it suggests that the danger lies as much in their "idle" and "dissolute" nature as in the conditions of their dwellings. The same year, another proclamation emphasized the urgency of enforcing the existing statute "against Rogues, Vagabonds, Idle, and dissolute persons" and recommended banishment overseas for the incorrigible.[41] These edicts reflect an anxiety about the rapid growth, during the last decades of the sixteenth century, in the numbers and density of the population in the poorer parishes—a threatening "confluence" of uprooted country dwellers, disbanded soldiers, and immigrants perceived as a plague in themselves. Writing in 1583, John Hawkins was certain that of all the world's cities, "*Rome* nor *Athens* nor the rest were neuer pestered so, / As *England* where no roome remaines."[42] Barbara Freedman's research has shown that in the 1590s, the threat of food riots, workers' protests, and other unlawful assemblies repeatedly led to the closing of the theaters under the pretext of plague.[43] The occupation of Lovewit's house (abetted by the "corrupted" servant Face) enacts in miniature the prospect of London's throwing open her doors to the influx of an unmastered, "pestering" crowd.

Regime Change

In 1603, when the finger of God could be seen moving over England as it had over Egypt in the time of the biblical plagues, its indications were of particular moment because of the arrival of the pestilence only weeks after the death of Elizabeth. In the recollection of his conversations with Jonson, Drummond

---

41. *By the King a Proclamation against Inmates and Multitudes of Dwellers in Strait Roomes and Places in and about the Cities of London, and for the Rasing and Pulling Downe of Certaine New Erected Buildings*; and *By the King a Proclamation for the Due and Speedy Execution of the Statute against Rogues, Vagabonds, Idle, and Dissolute Persons.*

42. Hawkins writes as an advocate of relocating England's surplus population to Virginia; see Ernest B. Gilman, "Sycorax's 'Thing,'" especially p. 112. See also Slack, *Impact of Plague*, 159–60.

43. Freedman, "Elizabethan Protest, Plague, and Plays."

of Hawthornden notes that Jonson was at Robert Cotton's country house "[w]hen the King came jn England, at that tyme the Pest was jn London" (*Ben Jonson,* 1:138–40). Elizabeth having died on March 24, 1603, her successor literally "came in England" on April 6, when he crossed the Scottish border, but his arrival at London at the beginning of May coincided with the outbreak of the disease. The new monarch was crowned in Westminster on July 25. With the plague growing hot, however, his triumphal entry into the city was postponed until the following March. For the rest of the summer and the autumn of 1603, James "from place to place, to saue himself did flie," until the epidemic burned itself out.[44] Drummond's linking of the new king with the pestilence is more than coincidental, since their simultaneous arrival inevitably raised the question of such an apparently ominous conjunction. How is Dekker's "Tragicall Act," following so soon upon the "dumb shew" of Elizabeth's funeral, to be understood in the context of a plague politics—not as an isolated visitation but, as it had been for the Israelites at the Exodus, the unfolding of a providential drama?

The one inadmissible reading was that insinuated by Catholic propagandists, who charged that James's accession had in itself called down the divine wrath on the kingdom. On the contrary, the plague could be read as a Malthusian mercy destined to solve the problem of a burgeoning urban population that would otherwise pose an immediate problem for the new king. Roger Fenton (recalling 2 Samuel 24, in which David's taking a census brings down a plague on the people) wonders "whether our ouer-much confidence . . . make vs to number the people as *David* did, and secure our selues in the strength thereof; which causeth God by this kind of iudgement to subtract (as fast as we multiplie)."[45] Perhaps London's own very remarkable growth, "numbered" in the parish registers and noticeable particularly in its "pestering" liberties, had provoked a God concerned with keeping all his accounts in balance to begin moving large numbers of people into the minus column. Clapham recalls that at the time of the outbreak, "[f]amine was threatned vpon the death of our late souveraigne Elizabeth." Sent as a blessing in disguise to solve the problem of an impending food shortage (and with it a repetition of the bread riots of the previous decade), the plague kills quickly under the blow of "a

---

44. Davies, *Humours Heau'n on Earth,* 233.
45. Fenton, *A Perfume against the Noysome Pestilence,* n.p.

mercifull Father," thus "leauing us not to lingring Deaths, whereby we might be more pained" (B3r). Nonetheless, the pestilence could not be interpreted merely as a form of population control, but as a sign of God's more inveterate anger with the nation.

The reasons for that anger could only be surmised. For William Ward, it is because of those who "do not with great feare & reuerence use his dreadful name" that "this present iudgment of God by plague and pestilence is iustly fallen vpon our English nation."[46] For others, the guilt lies with those who plague the state. Francis Herring, a physician intent on proving that the disease is infectious, notes that Cicero often calls "*Cataline, and other such like factious firebrands, Pestes patriae*, the plagues of their country: because as the plague spreadeth his poison vpon the bodies of men: so they infected the mindes of such Citizens as conuersed with them, with poisonfull and seditious thoughts and inclinations."[47] Similarly, Thomas Diggs published an "antidote against the pestilent treatises of secular priests,"[48] and James Balmford notes that in Acts 24:5, St. Paul is called by his enemies "a Pestilent fellow" because his teachings were thought to spread "sedition and heresie" (80). In the same language, preachers could inveigh against "the contagion of sin," against "that pestilent and most infectious canker, idlenesse," or against a "contagious broode of Scismatickes." Fenton warned that God "will indeede speake with vs" through the plague, a warning issued in a sermon on the rebellion of Korah (Numbers 16:41), when the "children of Israel murmured against Moses and against Aaron."[49] We may regard such expressions of an insidious threat to the body politic as figurative, but in their historical context, the distinction often seems blurred.

The politics of contamination also reveals the class differences between men like Andrewes, who regard themselves as priests and magistrates, and those like the onetime Separatist and unpredictable pamphleteer Clapham, whose doubts about quarantine led him to speak for the "meaner sort of people" and (either openly or by implication) against the government's plague orders in force that year. If "plague" was a form of speech, then speech could

---

46. Ward, *Gods Arrovves*, 10.
47. Herring, *A Modest Defence*, A3r.
48. Diggs, *Humble Motives for Association to Maintaine Religion Established.*
49. Fenton, *A Perfume against the Noysome Pestilence*, n.p.

be an agent of the plague. Analogies between the pestilence and infectious speech reinforce the supposition that not only open rebellion and heresy, but faction, inflammatory rhetoric, murmuring, the "lewd, lousey language" of canting thieves and beggars,[50] and even seditious thoughts—which spread from one person to the next, especially when susceptible persons congregated in groups—may well provoke God's anger against the nation. Taken together with the usual condemnations of sin on the part of individuals, these more sweeping indictments suggest a bottom-up view of national guilt. Discontent bubbles up like the fetid exhalation of gases that thicken the air. The nation as a whole therefore suffers once the sum total of its subjects' evildoing has tipped the balance between justice and mercy. For Henry Petowe, even as the arrows of justice were being prepared, God's mercy was extended to "the diuine *Eliza*" in the timing of her death, for just before the pestilence struck, she "departed from this *Chaos* of iniquitie, as one too worthy the gouernment of so wicked a people."[51]

Dekker, however, proposes an alternative, top-down explanation, since in his view, the crime deserving of such a terrible and widespread judgment as the plague must be found in the highest councils of state: "Sure tis some Capitall offence," Dekker insists: "Some high, high Treason doth incense / Th'Eternall King, that we are / Arraign'd at Deaths most dreadfull barre." Reading "[t]h'Inditement writ on Englands brest" in descending order, he looks to find "[p]rinces Errors, / Or the faults of Peeres," or "[t]he Courtiers pride, lust, and excesse, / The Church-mans painted holiness; / The Lawyers grinding of the poore," and so on down a list of vices that seep from the heights to infect the entire kingdom (86). "Whether one sin alone, or whether / This Maine Battalion ioyned together / Do dare these plagues," Dekker admits, "we cannot tell" (87). Although the "high" traitors cannot be named, or the "Princes Errors" specified (these are "husht" crimes, duly repaid by an affliction issuing from the hidden will of God), Dekker's sweeping judgment makes it clear that under Elizabeth, the kingdom has accumulated an enormous debt of sin—as the divine Bookkeeper has only just calculated as he closes the books, as it were, on the dead queen's long reign:

50. Harman, "Caveat for Common Cursitors," 113.
51. Petowe, *Londoners Their Entertainment in the Countrie*, A3r–v.

Or, it may be, *Iehouah* looks
But now vpon those Audit-Bookes
Of 45 years husht account,
For houres misspent, (whose summes surmount
The Price of ransomd Kings) and there
Finding our grieuous debts, doth cleere
And crosse them vnder his own hand,
Being paid with *Liues*, through all the land.

(88)

The implication of Dekker's conceit is scandalous, since the Auditor—finally attending to his duties after a forty-five-year lapse of attention—has discovered a second set of books, a "husht account," where all the misspent hours of the previous monarchy have been furtively recorded; but the debt is now repaid with lives, perhaps Elizabeth's among them. The "summes" of accrued debt will be balanced out in the tabulation of the bills of mortality. Far from being the harbinger of the pestilence, however, James is its beneficiary, espousing a realm with a "cleere" moral slate: for since God's "Maiden-Seruant's gone, / And his new Vizeroy fills the Throne, / Heauen meanes to giue him (as his bride) / A Nation new, and purified" (88).

As now "the maiden Ile hath got, / A roiall Husband" (88), this settling up of accounts insinuates that Elizabeth's failure to marry and produce an heir may have been among the prince's errors charged to her reign. The same reflection on the queen is implied in Dekker's elaborate conceit on Elizabeth's death, beginning with the account of a tempest:

The Element (taking the Destinies part, who indeed set abroach this mischiefe) scowled on the earth, and filling her hie forehead full of blacke wrinkles, tumbling long vp and downe, (like a great belleyed wife) her sighes being whirlewindes, and her grones thunder, at length she fell into labour, and was deliuered of a pale, meagre, weake childe named *Sicknesse*, whom Death (with a pestilence) would needes take vpon him to nurse, and did so. This starueling being come to his full growth, had an office giuen him for nothing (and that's a wonder in this age) Death made him his Herauld: attired him like a Courtier, and (in the name) charged him to goe into the Priuie Chamber of the English Queene, to summon her to appeare in the Star-chamber of heauen. (11)

Here the "earth" produces a child, as if in ironic recompense for the Virgin Queen's failure to produce one herself—a child named "*Sicknesse*" delivered out of its groaning mother as, in the medical theory of the day, the pestilence billows out of crevices in the ground. The conceit implies that Elizabeth herself, her own "forehead full of blacke wrinkles," is far too old to endure such "labour." Having, as it were, given over her long-preserved virginity to the courtier Death, she dies in childbirth, giving birth not only to her own death but also, by her failure to conceive before, to the plague that is about to ravage the kingdom. That this low-born "starueling" should have been preferred at court glances at the unseemly jockeying for place while the succession remained uncertain. It was known to everyone that Elizabeth did not die of the plague, but Dekker's account elides that fact, allowing us at least to imagine that she was in some sense its victim, and that its entry into her "Priuie Chamber" to deliver its baleful "summons" virtually indicts her with the crime of bringing the epidemic down on her realm. The succession, however, will now be assured by the marriage of Scotland to "faire *England*"—a nation restored, as it were, by the plague to an Elizabethan virginity, just as it was forty-five years ago when the previous reign began and England seemed ripe for a royal wedding.

Elizabeth, then, would have paid with her life, having "left vs," as Henry Chettle notes in his elegy for the departed queen, "in her death, more secure, by committing vs to our lawful Prince, matcht to a royal fruitful Lady, that hath borne him such hopeful issue."[52] Her death, though not caused by the plague, is thus written into the script as its prelude, both a punishment and a self-sacrifice by which she bequeaths her maidenhood to the nation. No longer the husband of the Virgin Queen, by this renovation England has become the virgin bride, a symbol writ large of the "royal fruitful Lady" James brings with him from Scotland. All this is engendered by the divine Dramatist, a merciful father whose plot is geared toward the production of a "hopeful issue"—a

---

52. Chettle, *Englandes Mourning Garment*, B4v.

son. Medical opinion held that the plague was borne on "Southerly windes."[53] James is himself a "Sunne," as Petowe notes when he celebrates the "wholesome *North* from forth whose wombe did spring / The blessed Sunne of our felicitie": James's "bright beames" will both dispel the miasma of the plague and "guild our posterities."[54] In the long view of British history, Chettle sees the new king as heir to the "godly *Constantine*" who "[p]urgde this Iles aire from Idoll-hated sinne" when "[b]lacke Pagan clouds darkned this goodly Clime."[55] In his epigram "To King James," Jonson himself praises the new monarch in the same terms, for having "purg'd" the realm: "First thou preserued wert, our king to bee, / And since, the whole land was preseru'd for thee" (8:38, ll. 5, 9–10). Elizabeth's long-preserved virginity has preserved the kingdom for her successor, who in turn—after the therapeutic purge of the plague, and after his own providential preservation—restores the kingdom to health. Given England as his bride, James thus transforms the drama of the succession into a marriage comedy, albeit one still recovering from Dekker's "Tragicall Act," which has left the stage littered with twenty-five thousand bodies.

My purpose in this chapter has been to follow the interwoven threads of medicine, theology, and politics that informed the body of plague writing when Jonson wrote. The next chapter sees his verse as part of that fabric.

---

53. Ibid., c2v.
54. Petowe, *Englands Caesar*, c1r.
55. Chettle, *Englandes Mourning Garment*, f4v.

[CHAPTER 4]

Here Lies *Ben Jonson*

When the King came jn England, at that tyme the Pest was jn London, [Jonson] being jn the Country at Sr Robert Cottons house with old Cambden, he saw jn a vision his eldest sone (yn a child and at London) appear to him wt ye Marke of a bloodie crosse on his forehead as if it had been cutted wt a suord, at which amazed he prayed unto God, and jn ye morning he came to Mr. Cambdens chamber to tell him, who persuaded him it was but ane appreehension of his fantasie at which he should not be desjected[.] jn ye mean tyme comes yr letters from his wife of ye death of yt Boy jn ye plague. He appeared to him he said of a Manlie shape & of yt Grouth that he thinks he shall be at the resurrection.
WILLIAM DRUMMOND of Hawthornden

EPIGRAM XLV: ON MY FIRST SONNE
Farewell, thou child of my right hand, and ioy;
    My sinne was too much hope of thee, lou'd boy,
Seuen yeeres tho'wert lent to me, and I thee pay,
    Exacted by thy fate, on the iust day.
O, could I loose all father, now. For why
    Will man lament the state he should enuie?
To haue so soone scap'd worlds, and fleshes rage,
    And, if no other miserie, yet age?
Rest in soft peace, and ask'd, say here doth lye
    BEN. IONSON his best piece of *poetrie*.
For whose sake, hence-forth, all his vowes be such,
    As what he loues may neuer like too much.
BEN JONSON

In 1603–4, twenty-eight books dealing with the plague were published in London, many of which were reprinted during the century's later outbreaks.[1] As we have seen, they include works by writers otherwise well-known, and known to Jonson—John Davies of Hereford, Thomas Lodge, Thomas Dekker—as well as by a host of more obscure physicians and divines. An out-pouring of sermons and jeremiads filled the bookstalls of London, along with an equal number of tracts offering cures and preservatives against the plague. It would be impossible to prove that Jonson read any of this, but unlikely to suppose that he read none of it, or that his own experience was untouched by it. These documents allow us to recover a sense of the shared social trauma and the common language resonating through Jonson's very private griefs.

Reduced to its bare-bones plot, the plague drama of 1603 as scripted by Thomas Dekker, Henry Chettle, Henry Petowe, and others casts England's new king in a recognizably Jonsonian role, as the blessed son of a heavenly Father, and the father of a son. In an epigram, Jonson would praise James as the "best of kings" and the "best of poets." He would reinvoke this implicit royal connection in "To Penshurst," where he imagines the king and his son attracted by the hospitality of the estate where Jonson, the best of poets, already presides in the seat of honor. But any resemblance Jonson may have seen between accounts of the royal succession and his own unfortunate lot in 1603 would have been shadowed by the harshest irony. Petowe is comforted that "in the selfe same houre of [Elizabeth's] departure, did our almightie Father not leaue vs destitute," but gave us a "royall king."[2] But in that selfsame hour, Jonson was left destitute. James Balmford believes that "kings should (out of a fatherly care) preserue their subiects from destruction, by infection, as well as by the sword" (6), but for Jonson's son, who lacked the care of his father, the fatherly care of the monarch made little difference. In the elegies and panegyrics of the plague year, furthermore, London is typically personi-fied (as in fig. 12) as the grieving "mother of cities" awaiting the arrival of her absent spouse, mourning those who have died and desolate in her abandon-ment by those who have fled: "How can a Mother choose, but euer weep, / When as her children loath their natiue bed?"[3] In William Muggins's *Londons*

---

1. Slack, *Impact of Plague*, 23–24.
2. Petowe, *Londoners Their Entertainment in the Countrie*, A3r–v.
3. Ibid., A4r–v; Petowe, *Englands Caesar*, D1r–v.

Mourning Garment (B3r), the city similarly bewails her own forlorn parent-hood in language that mirrors Jonson's epigram as it imagines a bereaved father burdened with "too much . . . loue" for a dead son:

Art thou a Father, or a Mother deare?
Hadst thou a Sonne, or Daughter of thy side:
Were not their voice, sweete musicke in thy Eare,
Or from their smiles, could'st thou thy countnance hide.
Nay, were they not, the glories of thy pride?
I doubt too much, thy loue on them were set,
That whilst thou liuest, thou canst not them forget.

For his part of London's official pageantry welcoming the king—an event postponed until the following June because of the plague—Jonson designed an inscribed frame "couered with a curtaine of silke, painted like a thicke cloude, and at the approach of the K[ing] was instantly to bee drawne. The Allegory being, that those cloudes were gathered vpon the face of the Citty, through their long want of his most wished sight: but now, as at the rising of the Sunne, all mistes were dispersed and fled."[4] For Jonson, who fled only to receive the news of his son's death among those noxious London mists, the only consolation afforded at the time was the vision of young Benjamin's ulti-mate rising, as "he shall be at the resurrection."

In the spring and summer of 1603, the new reign and the possibilities for patronage it offered were very much on Jonson's mind. David Riggs speculates that, aside from wishing to escape the plague, Jonson may have made the jour-ney to Huntingdonshire in order to "join forces with Cotton, who was inti-mately involved in the plans for the Jacobean succession."[5] Near the time of his son's death, Jonson would have been preparing his *Particular Entertainment* for Queen Anne and Prince Henry, an outdoor pageant performed on June 25 when the royal mother and son stopped at Robert Spencer's estate at Althorp on their way down from Scotland. Jonson's published script acknowledges the absence of the royal father on that occasion ("O that now a wish could

---

4. B. *Ion: His Part of King Iames His Royall and Magnificent Entertainement through His Honorable Cittie of London, Thurseday the 15. of March. 1603* [i.e., 1604], B2r.
5. Riggs, *Ben Jonson*, 93.

bring, / The God-like person of a king") and then turns to Prince Henry in the momentary apprehension that the royal son has been "neglected":

> But loe, where
> His kingly image doth appeare,
> And is all this while neglected:
> Pardon (lord) you are respected
> Deepe as is the Keepers hart,
> And as deere in euery part.
> See, for instance where he sends
> His sonne, his heire; who humbly bends
> Lowe, as is his Fathers earth,
> To the wombe that gaue you birth.
> (7:127, ll. 187–88; 191–200)

To turn "neglect" into "respect," the speaker—here, a Satyr who pops out of the woods to do homage—cues Spencer's "eldest sonne" (as Jonson identifies him in a marginal note). The twelve-year-old William Spencer will stand in for his father Sir Robert, who has no role in these festivities. Offering obeisance "to the wombe" of the royal mother in the humble gesture of his low bow, Spencer's son bends to "his Fathers earth." Refracted through Jonson's private griefs, this scene—with its doubling of two first sons as the images of their two absent fathers; its commissioning the one as the father's emissary to humble himself before the mother and imagining the other as "all this while neglected," but then repairing that neglect by making him "appeare" and reassuring him that he is "deere"; its beginning with the vain hope that a "wish could bring" the absent father, and ending with the rhyme of "earth" and "birth" that closes the circle of life and death—all reads very like a dream. Riggs rightly dismisses the *Entertainment* as artistically negligible, a slight woodland fantasy far from Jonson's best piece of poetry.[6] But as a complex, overdetermined reworking of the theme of fathers and sons, it may stand as the festive counterpart to Jonson's vision at Cotton's house, and as a prelude to the epigram deprived of "too much hope."

---

6. Ibid., 98.

Jonson's "Roman Frame of Mind"

Given the inescapably stark realities of life and death in Jonson's London, it might seem surprising that the plague and its contemporary accounts have not figured more importantly in readings of Jonson's nondramatic poetry. One groundbreaking exception is the work of Patrick Phillips, who shows that the shadow of the plague haunts Jonson's writing career, from the epigrams to his epitaphs for John Roe, through *The Alchemist* to the Cary-Morison ode—all documents in the history of the poet's bereavement.[7] Such an overview goes far toward probing the sources of Jonson's deep-seated melancholy, his continuing traumatic need to rewrite the death of his "best piece of *poetrie*," his returning to the scene of a young man dead of infectious disease and mourned by the older poet, and the motivation behind his paternal sponsorship of a younger generation of the "Sons of Ben." Yet little has been written on the plague origins of this project in the valediction for his "lou'd boy," for three reasons, as it seems to me. First, only in the past thirty years have historians begun the task of reassessing the systemic impact of infectious disease on a global scale in the early modern period, and in such fields as migration, colonization, and urban history.[8] In this endeavor, as I have noted, literary historians—with the exception of those medievalists who have written extensively on the literature and art of the Black Death of the fourteenth century—have for the most part lagged behind their colleagues in the social sciences. Second, the cause of the boy's death is not alluded to in the poem—a significant omission, but one that does not seem to compel immediate attention if the reader does not have this very history of the plague in view.

---

7. See Phillips, "'Fleshes Rage': Ben Jonson and the Plague," for a broader reading of Jonson's recurrent engagement with the plague in his other verse.

8. The title of Laurie Garrett's *The Coming Plague: Newly Emerging Diseases in a World out of Balance* reflects the shift from an older, pre-AIDS narrative that assumed that all infectious disease would soon fall before the weapons of medical research to a narrative that at its most nightmarish sees the inevitable breakout of Ebola, Lassa fever, and an untold number of future biohorrors (including smallpox, once thought eradicated) as an imminent threat to the existence of humankind. Her reportage is greeted by AIDS activist and playwright Larry Kramer as a "magnificent attempt to make people realize that the future health of the world is in great danger" (in Garrett, ii). One reviewer finds in it a moral lesson very much in the spirit of seventeenth-century plague jeremiads: sexual carelessness, the "widespread misuse of antibiotics," and the "destruction of the rainforest" have planted "the seeds of the next plague in humanity's hubris" (iii).

Third is a reason peculiar to Jonson studies: the critical tendency to contextualize the poem within what Katharine Maus has called the poet's "Roman frame of mind." This influential appeal to Jonson's Roman temper—with its effect of distancing the epigram from its immediate occasion and casting it in a mold of classical restraint—has seemed sufficient to explain the grave and understated tone admired as the poem's distinctive excellence. Thus Maus observes that the Roman moralists "regard with awe those who can accept the death of a child with relative equanimity," and that Tacitus, as Jonson would have known, "cites Agricola's restraint upon the death of his son as a proof of his sound character."[9] Jonson's paradoxical resolve at the end of the poem, that "hence-forth, all his vowes be such, / As what he loues may neuer like too much," directly renders the final line of Martial's epigram 6.19, on the death of a boy "worthy of his master's true love": "quidquid ames, cupias non placuisse nimis." The comment by Martial's Loeb translator—that "excessive excellence or good fortune, and the praise of it, was supposed to rouse the jealousy of the gods"—may plausibly be taken to explain both the Latin sentiment and, in the English version, the father's "too much hope" for the son.[10] Reading Jonson's verb "to like" in "the active seventeenth-century sense of 'to please,'" Wesley Trimpi concludes, in a similar vein: "It is precisely because a child should not delight us as a pastime but rather be loved as a human being," with the tempered fatherly affection recommended by Aristotle, that "Jonson borrows Martial's caution that what he loves should never please him too much."[11] Similarly, Maus sees the father's obscure wish, in line 5, to "loose all father now" as adumbrating the "Roman idea" of a necessary detachment of feeling from the son to whom, in death, Jonson begins to grant "some separate identity."[12] Stephen Booth's more recent view that the poet's play on the etymology of his son's name reflects a "slick determinedly detached intellectuality" gives us the same imperturbable Jonson in a less sympathetic light, a Jonson "detached" from, if not incapable of, heartfelt grief.[13] Yet if Drummond's memory is to be trusted, Jonson's frame of mind at the news of his son's death had little in it of the Roman father's tempered and

9. Maus, *Ben Jonson and the Roman Frame of Mind*, 119.
10. Martial, *Epigrams*, 2:374–75.
11. Trimpi, "'BEN. JONSON his best piece of poetrie,'" 147, 149.
12. Maus, *Ben Jonson and the Roman Frame of Mind*, 122.
13. Booth, *Precious Nonsense*, 77.

decorous restraint—which, as it appears in the finished poem, may strike us less as a stoic victory over the passions than as a failure of those same venerable gestures in the face of an inconsolable loss. We need in any case to be mindful that the Roman Jonson is a critical construct—one that Jonson himself helps to fashion, to be sure, and one that, partly by his fashioning, reflects the neo-Roman style of the Jacobean monarchy. It served Jonson as a mode of poetic restraint—a sublimation and rationalization of the poem's encrypted content, imposing the *ratio* of a measured response upon a chasm of unmeasurable grief. It has served Jonson criticism as an instrument of balance, a counterpoise to the roistering, unrestrained, morose Jonson, that fat bagful of appetites, ambitions, and resentments.

The epitaph on his son demands a subtler reading of its author and of the moment of its composition. Here emotion is recollected, but not in tranquility. In light of the terrible events of 1603, the poem as a document in the history of human mourning is better understood as a Roman reframing of the father's very English, peculiarly tangled feelings of grief, anger, and guilt as a plague survivor.[14] If the cause of the child's death is not mentioned in Jonson's poem, neither is that of the boy in Martial's original. But the poem's omission, or suppression, of the plague does not remove its influence on Jonson's language and emotion. Indeed, trauma theory would lead us to regard this central but unspoken fact—in Dekker's language, the "husht account" of Jonson's poem—as a traumatic kernel, the empty circle around which the poem takes shape. To measure more fully the implication of Jonson's epigram in the plague discourse of the moment, we have reviewed the chief concerns of that discourse and its characteristic modes of expression. It should now be possible to locate the epigram within two plague frames: the outbreak of 1603 read as a moment of national crisis marked by the death of Elizabeth and the concurrent entry into the kingdom of her successor and the pestilence; and—indexed to these broader events—the death of young Benjamin as a more intimate crisis for his poet-father.

---

14. Dennis Flynn, seeing Donne as "a 'survivor' of the Elizabethan persecution" of Catholics, cites Bruno Bettelheim's insight that the threat of being killed, and the knowledge that one's "closest friends and relatives are being killed," raises the "unsolvable riddle of 'Why was I spared,'" and also with completely irrational guilt about having been spared" (Flynn, "John Donne: Survivor," 17, 24; quoting from Bettelheim, "Trauma and Reintegration," 26).

Jonson's Sin

I have quoted at some length from the plague texts of 1603 not only to suggest the larger epidemiological, theological, and political framework of Jonson's poem, but also to reveal the smaller textures of the common language and even the particular phrases it evokes and transforms: the groaning of parents for children, the flight of London's "evil sons," the plague "justly fallen" on the sinful, the afflicted fallen "at thy right hand," the "heavy hand" of God's vengeance, the "hand of authority," the crossing out of sin "under his own hand," a debt "paid with lives," plague deaths as God's "subtraction," the reading of plague as an "indictment," the arraignment of the sinful "at death's most dreadful bar," God's "fatherly correction" of the afflicted, the righteous justly struck down to spare them from the "evil to come," the importance of "fatherly care," the acts of a "merciful father," the "hopeful issue" of the royal father, the admonition to parents bereft of their children that "too much, thy love on them were set." These are all the ways in which God would "speak with us" through the plague.

Dekker's "Audit-Bookes" and the persistent language elsewhere of accounts, multiplication and subtraction, and grievous payments underwrite the rueful debtor's language of Jonson's poem: "Seuen yeeres tho'wert lent to me, and I thee pay, / Exacted by thy fate, on the iust day." There can be no doubt that the day of his son's death is "just" in the sense that God is a scrupulous accountant, calling in his loans exactly when they are due. Nor can there be any authorized doubt that the transaction is otherwise "just"; the pestilence as an indictment for sin is there to be read out of scripture by every preacher in the land. Is not every man called to account, in anticipation of "the generall daie of accoumpte and audite to bee made at the throne of God"?[15] But for what particular "sinne" of the father must the death of the son be "exacted" from him—required, demanded, even extorted from him—in recompense? What debt was crossed out by the same divine hand that, in Jonson's dream, had marked the forehead of his son with a "bloodie crosse"—the sign of the cancelled debt, the sign of the plague by which that debt was paid, and (if it be not too much to hope) the sign of the son's resurrection through God's mercy? In the dark comedy of *The Alchemist*, plague foments an outbreak of unrestrained mendacity and moral corruption, but are these sins (as evidence

---

15. Udall, *The First Tome or Volume of the Paraphrase of Erasmus upon the Newe Testament*, preface, 14.

of the human condition, or as especially "hot" just at this moment) also to be taken as the just cause of an epidemic that claims the life of a seven-year-old child? Apart from the burden of some accumulated national debt, plague writers point to other individual sins—hours misspent in drunkenness, gluttony, or even, as Dekker notes, the "Schollers enuy" (86)—"sins" that, though unacknowledged in the poem, may have struck closer to home in Jonson's case. Yet in the casting up of accounts, none seems to balance the death of a son. The death of the child of a sinful parent might, in the view of a moralist like "T. C.," be of benefit to a child, for "[i]f yong children dye from wicked fathers and mothers, then be the children deliuered, and the fathers and mothers punished."[16] But doubts arise. How does one justify the sum when the sins of the fathers are to be repaid by the innocent? And how is that death to be understood except as a poignant exception to the Jacobean drama, partly of Jonson's own authorship, of a providential purgation—with its celebration of the new king's "hopeful issue" as the proof of recovered national health? Is the poet who had composed an entertainment honoring the sons and heirs of the new reign to be repaid with the loss of his own? In these lines—or, rather, in the controlled anger of their tone—Jonson comes closer than any plague writer of 1603 to acknowledging what in his great poem "To Heaven" he poses as a question that carries its own answer: "How can I doubt to finde thee euer, here?" (8:122, l. 16).

In the context of the plague theodicies of 1603, Jonson's self-diagnosed, puzzling "sinne" of "too much hope"—the only one to which he admits—has a more specifically Christian than Roman resonance. It may be foolhardy to tempt the gods, as Niobe did, by immoderate pride in one's children, but it was Augustine who taught that we should regard all earthly possessions, even those most dear to us, as only on temporary loan. Preaching after the plague of 1625, Sampson Price lists among the causes of the pestilence that parents have "gloried in the number of their children, and set too much their hearts vpon them."[17] It would also suggest a failure of faith to admit the fear that must give rise to hope, the presumption to think that perhaps God did not have it in his power to preserve the child (if he had a mind to). One cannot "hope" that the will of God will not be carried out. Thus, Jonson vows that what he loves, he

---

16. T. C., *A Godly and Learned Sermon*, c5r.
17. Price, *Londons Remembrancer*, 17.

may never "like too much" in the sense of being too much attached to one who belongs to God, one whose innocence may not protect him from a judgment after all, and whose loss would otherwise break a father's heart. (That he *will* continue despite all—as the final emphasis of the line implies—to like such a boy as Ben *too much* for his own good hints at the futility of "all his vowes.") Such resolve, however difficult to sustain, made hard practical sense in a year when plague deaths (on top of the alarming rate of child mortality that characterizes the early modern period) rendered it unlikely that any child would live to attain the "Manlie shape" Jonson imagined for young Ben in his dream. Jonson's "too much hope," then, may have been to hope too much—as what father would not?—that his son would simply survive.

Flight

The one sin unspoken in the poem but evident from the circumstance of Jonson's dream—"he being jn the Country at Sr Robert Cottons house"—is that of fleeing the city in an attempt to protect himself from the plague. Of this sin Jonson is de facto guilty, whether or not it was his intention to evade an impending epidemic when he left London sometime in the spring of 1603. In contemporary plague writing, the centrality of the moral debate about flight could not be ignored. Luther and Calvin had each pondered the question, and, as we have seen, English divines from the mid-sixteenth century onward carried the contention into Jonson's time.[18] In favor of flight, it might be argued prudentially that nowhere does scripture deny the right of self-preservation— although a recognition that most Londoners had no means of travel and nowhere to go made it difficult to argue that the titled and the wealthy should be able to ride out to their country houses with a clear conscience. Thus, "I. H." declares that "*Lots* sonnes [were] worthily consumed, because they would not forsake *Sodome*,"[19] and Balmford assures his parishioners that flight is permissible so long as one's servants left behind "[m]ay be well gouerned while they be in health, and well prouided for, if they fall sicke" (71–72). In any event, were not God's people enjoined to flee from evildoing as from flood and fire, or from the pestilence which, in Egypt, had claimed the lives of so many first sons? The

---

18. Slack, *Impact of Plague*, 40–44.
19. I. H., *This VVorlds Folly*, A3r.

dilemma of flight was underscored in the case of Lancelot Andrewes, for his decision to safeguard the children of the Westminster School, Jonson's alma mater, and to personally supervise their relocation to the country obliged him to abandon his own devastated parish—Jonson's parish—of St. Giles, Cripplegate, of which he had held the living since 1588. The 2,879 souls recorded as dead of the plague in St. Giles before the autumn were left untended by their minister.

Yet surely the fond hope, or the arrogant conviction, that flight would guarantee one's safety—no less than the hope (Jonson's "hope"?) that those one left behind would somehow remain untouched—flew in the face of providence. Surely it was a blasphemy to limit the power of God to smite or protect whomever he pleased without regard to geography. On this there is nearly unanimous opinion in the plague writing of 1603, and Jonson could hardly have been unaware of the judgment it cast on him. "T. C." insists that the Word of God teaches us "not to flye euill and infected places," but to "leave off from sinne."[20] Henoch Clapham cautions against the abuse of Proverbs 22:3 and 27:12 ("A *prudent* man seeth the plague and hideth himself"); safety is assured only "to him that coucheth vnder the Lords wings," not to him who attempts to run from danger: "If thou were with *Ionah* vnder the hatches, and after with the Whale in the bottome of the Sea, he will finde thee out" (*Epistle*, A4v–B1r). Nor should the righteous fear to remain in the city, for (as Psalm 91:7, adduced by "T. C.", assures us) "[t]hough a thousand fall at thy side, and ten thousand at thy right hand, yet shall it not come nye thee."[21] Christians, says Roger Fenton, should "carefully auoid that faithlesse and Paganish fearefulnesse, whereby we are made to break all the bonds of Religion, Consanguinitie, Alliance, friendship and pollicie," and he particularly singles out "the husband forsaking and abandoning his deare wife" and "the parents leauing their children to sinke or swimme."[22] Henry Petowe rises to the height of his eloquence in driving home the same point:

How many thousand Citizens, or rather euill sonnes, as I may rightly tearme them, fled from their mother *London*.... [T]o fly from the

---

20. T. C., *A Godly and Learned Sermon*, A7r.
21. Ibid., A2v–3r.
22. Fenton, *A Perfume against the Noysome Pestilence*, B2r.

performance of their charitable duties, shewes a distrustfull flying from God, flying from God do I say? Oh whither could they flie? Into what countrey? What towne? What Citie? To liue secure, and to hide themselues from him that is all almighty, Flyest thou to the vtmost bownds of *Europe*, nay to any priuate angle of the world, why there *Iehouah* is.[23]

In *The Alchemist*, Lovewit's departure must be measured by this standard; he betrays his own insensitivity on this point (and perhaps that of his playwright) when he speaks blandly of his "knowne auersion / From any air o' the towne, while there was sicknesse" (5:403, ll. 34–35). Jonson's absence from the "mother"—both Mother London and the mother of his children—casts him in the role of an "evil son" for whose flight the innocent son was to pay.

In 1625, another plague year (and another year of royal transition fraught with the same anxieties about the divine intention at such a climacteric moment), Dekker published *A Rod for Run-awaies*. Here he speaks scornfully to those who are "merry" in their "Country houses" and warns that "Gods arme, like a Girdle, going round about the world" has no limit to its reach (145, 169–70). Whatever the subtleties of the debate, the strong consensus in 1603, as in all plague years, is that flight is always sinful on the part of magistrates, ministers, and the fathers of families, who thereby betray their obligations to those under their care. In his pamphlet of 1604, *Newes from Graues-ende*, Dekker bluntly admonishes those who abandon such vital responsibilities: "you do erre / In flying from your charge so far . . . so Lambes do perish, / So you kill those, y'are bound to cherish" (96). Seen from this unforgiving vantage point, the absentee father's unspoken "sinne" is the sin of murder. One may feel that Lovewit's reappearance in London at the end of *The Alchemist*—with his relief at finding his household healthy and fortunate, his forgiveness of all their childish truancies while he was away, and the unexpected rewards the play has in store for him, including a rich widow and a cellar full of loot—fulfills a Jonsonian fantasy: the return of the prodigal father.

In another passage, Dekker imagines a far darker scene, of a father fleeing into the country with his son under the illusion that he has put a safe distance between himself and the plague:

---

23. Petowe, *Londoners Their Entertainment in the Countrie*, BIr–v.

Now is thy soule iocund, and thy sences merry. But open thine eyes thou Foole! And behold that darling of thine eye, (thy sonne) turnde suddeinly into a lumpe of clay; the hand of pestilence hath smote him euen under thy wing: Now doest thou rent thine haire, blaspheme thy Creator, cursest thy creation, and basely descendest thou into bruitish & unmanly passions, threatning in despite of death & his Plague, to maintaine the memory of thy childe, in the euerlasting brest of Marble. (*Wonderfull Yeare*, 30)

It might have offered some small, though ironic, solace for Jonson to reflect, on the evidence of such an anecdote, that Benjamin (dead, in London, under the Lord's wing) would not have been safe even under his father's wing in Huntingdonshire. But knowing that he had, though inadvertently, left him behind and in harm's way—along with his wife and another son, three-year-old Joseph, whose fate is unknown—could only have sharpened his remorse.[24] Dekker's passage may serve as a kind of ur-text for Jonson's poem. Here we see in raw form the anger, the self-reproach, the open blasphemy, the unconstrained passion, and the desire to cling to the memory of the child—to turn the "lumpe of clay" into marble—that will be (incompletely) subdued by the Roman decorum of Jonson's polished epigram.

The Voice of the Dead

That the child is said to be Jonson's "best piece of *poetrie*"—the father's masterpiece—evokes the Greek sense of the poet as a "maker" and thus, as Riggs notes, "links the vocations of fatherhood and art."[25] It will now be the work of this grieving father to turn his own lump of clay into a durable "piece" of verse that will keep the memory of the child alive: "And there he lives with memorie; and *Ben*," as Jonson will write in the ode to Cary and Morison (8:246, l. 84), although the result (like the Roman copy of a Greek original) can only be second-best. The making of an epigram requires the stoneworker's arts of

---

24. In the case of the toddler confined in a plague house, Riggs finds "no evidence to suggest that Joseph survived the year 1603. Jonson, who entered the world as a fatherless child, in all likelihood was now a childless father" (*Ben Jonson*, 97).

25. Ibid., 96.

concision and excision. Of all the genres of poetry, this sparse and disciplined form depends most on what is cut away. But just as the space surrounding a monument is nonetheless an invisible part of its total articulation, so Jonson's epigram is shaped by its unspoken surround: no mention of the plague, no mention of the father's flight. These absences bespeak Jonson's loss. Indeed, the poem is marked by the wish to cut away even more: "O, could I loose all father, now"—all thoughts of fatherhood, as the line is usually read, but also thoughts of the royal father and God the Father, all the just and merciful fathers who, if they did not cause his misery, cannot assuage it. Like the writing, the reading of the poem will be a work of manual labor akin to the bricklayer's trade of Jonson's stepfather. Jonson wants the reader to feel the heft (as well as the fragility) of his *Epigrammes:* "Pray thee, take care, that tak'st my book in hand" (8:27). This is the product of handiwork: not of the heavy hand of God's justice, or of the hand of royal authority, but of the poet's "right hand," as both the subject of the epigram and the writing hand, the instrument of commemoration. The preacher says, "[t]he *Plague* is Gods hand, *Iad Iehouah*, because the might and power of God is more manifested in this then in other punishments. O let not this *hand* be out of our sight, but as that hand that wrote at *Balshazars* feast; and thereupon his countenance was changed, his thoughts troubled, the *ioynts* of his lyns were loosed, and his knees smote one against another."[26] The poem opposes Jonson's hand to God's. As Jonson's "right hand," the dead child is invoked as the poet's collaborator, empowered through the father's hand to speak his own piece. In the course of the child's speech, it appears momentarily that it is the *father* who lies in the grave (students always "misread" the line "here doth lye / BEN. IONSON"). Such confusion of the dead and the living suggests other links to the plague writing of 1603.

The dead, Dekker tells us, pile up so quickly that they can only be shoveled indistinguishably into pits where "twentie shall but haue one roome." There "friend, and foe, and yong and old, / The freezing coward, and the bold" find a common end (94); whole families are buried together, "husbands, wiues & children, being lead as ordinarily to one graue, as if they had gone to one bed" (33–34). One (in the) grave, one (in) bed: not so far in apprehension from Jonson's bed in Huntingdonshire, the churchyards of London resound with

26. Price, *Londons Remembrancer*, 33.

an antiphonal chorus of wailing. "Here cry the parents for their childrens death," writes John Davies; "[t]here howle the children for their parents losse." Davies's *Picture of the Plague* takes us to the graveyard and asks us to look "there" and "here" at a woeful procession of fathers and sons in each other's roles, acting out a "like desire":

> There wends the fainting Son with his dead Sire
> On his sole shoulders borne, him to interre;
> Here goes a father with the like desire
> And to the graue alone, his Sonne doth beare.

With an evident taste for chiasmus, Death dispatches his messengers "to fetch both one and the other out of life": "the Sire doth fetch the Sonne, the Sonne the Sire."[27] The biblical Benjamin—literally, in the Hebrew, the child of his father's right hand—received a blessing from his dying father Jacob; but in time of the plague, warns Dekker, the "Father dares not come neere the infected Son, nor the Son come to take a blessing from the Father, lest hee bee poysoned by it" (144). If the errant father kills the child in effect by his absence, the child in turn has the power to kill the parent in fact if he comes too close: "The trembling father is vndone, / Being once but breath'd on by his sonne" (92). Often as not, the one will follow the other into the same grave.

Less often, people thought to be dead speak from the grave. In what is probably an urban legend, Dekker tells of the drunkard who topples into a pit of plague victims one night and whose oaths in the morning terrify the sexton who disturbs his sleep: the sexton "beleeued verily, some of the coarses spake to him, vpon which, feeling himselfe in a cold sweat, tooke to his heeles" (53). With London's churchyards and plague pits brimming over with the newly dead, its streets populated by the fresh corpses of those just now alive, it would not be difficult to imagine (in terror, or in hope) that their voices might not yet be stilled. In effect, Jonson's epigram revisits the graveside to perform an act somewhere between a commemoration and an exhumation. In his study of such early modern poetic "archaeologies," Philip Schwyzer notes that "in their encounters with ghosts, both Hamlet and Macbeth do not immediately assume that they are beholding spirits, but rather the actual bodies of the

---

27. Davies, *Humours Heau'n on Earth*, 230, 237.

dead, vomited forth from the grave."[28] Of the beings so encountered, as of
the Derridean specter, "On ne sait pas si c'est vivant ou si c'est mort."[29] When
Jonson's ghostly child rises to "say" who "doth lye" here, the chilling shadow of
this *danse macabre* of the living and the dead on the lip of the grave falls over
the poem.

When young Ben says "here doth lye / BEN. IONSON," we hear the voice
of the dead, and in our experience of this compact yet complex line, we think
first of the father as the occupant of the grave, as in the due succession of
families he should be. Father and son have changed places: the mourner becomes the mourned. It is an uncanny moment, intimately familiar but impossible: *unheimlich* in the literal sense that it both reflects and attempts to
recoup the moment when Jonson was not "at home." Ben's apostrophe to his
son implies, in the root sense of this figure, a "turning away," an aversion: an
aversio from the person addressed by the speaker in order to turn to another,
absent, person, who (in a prosopopoeia) is given the power to speak. This
turning away, as Jonson did when he abandoned his family in London, and
his return to the graveside in the fantasy of the poem, is reinscribed in the figure. "Here doth lye / BEN. IONSON" is also an ethopoeia, the figure by which
one puts oneself in the place of another, feeling what that person feels and
speaking as he would. Speaking of the ambiguous "position of the plague witness," Elana Gomel describes fictional chroniclers such as Defoe's H. F. and
Mary Shelley's Last Man as "suspended between life and death."[30] The BEN.
IONSON of the epigram occupies just such a liminal position. Jonson's line
discloses what Paul de Man calls, in another context (that of Wordsworth's
Essays upon Epitaphs), "the latent threat that inhabits prosopopeia": by making the dead speak, "the symmetrical structure of the trope implies, by the
same token, that the living are struck dumb, frozen in their own death."[31] The
son's words evoke both the ancient mysteries of vatic utterance and demonic
possession and their descendent in modern ventriloquism, for the voice both

---

28. Schwyzer, *Archaeologies of English Renaissance Literature*, 121–22.

29. Derrida, *Spectres de Marx*, 26.

30. Gomel, "The Plague of Utopias," 411. In this context, Gomel cites Primo Levi's insistence (in
The Drowned and the Saved) that, in her words, "the only authentic witnesses of the atrocity [of the
Holocaust] are the dead themselves," so that "bearing witness necessitates speaking *for* and *as* the dead"
(430 n. 5).

31. Paul de Man, "Autobiography as De-facement."

proceeds from the dead child and is "thrown" there by the father, who cannot be shown moving his lips.[32] In this state, the poet's "own death" hangs between the poles of fear and desire. A dream gave the father his first premonition of young Ben's death but also envisaged the child as a grown man, not dead after all (in both senses) but as he would appear at the resurrection. The vision of the son suddenly grown to a manly shape resonates eerily against Dekker's allegorical figure of the infant "Sicknesse" as a "starueling being" in an instant "come to his full growth" (11): both images reflect a sense of the sudden change brought on by the pestilence and, in Jonson's case, an impossible glimpse of the man the child would never become. As the dream's ultimate counterpart (or, as I would argue, the ultimate product of this remarkable experience), the epigram invokes a dreamlike graveside scene that allows us to momentarily imagine—in Freud's phrase, from his analysis of the dream of the "burning child"—that the "dead child behaves as though alive." "Here lyes" names an unalterable permanence but is spoken in the present tense: the tense, as Freud notes, in which wishes are represented as being fulfilled.

Just as the dream moves between the present and a spectral future of the child in the manly shape of the father, in the poem the "presence" of the speaking child is itself suspended between two different moments in time. It occupies the present moment when the voice of the poet invokes and joins with that of the son to declare in unison that "Ben Jonson" is dead; and "at the same time" it also anticipates some impossible future when the child will be "ask'd," presumably by a curious passerby, who lies in the grave, and he will reply with (and in) his father's name. Yet the father must have lost all moral right to that title when he abandoned his family; as a runaway, he became one of Petowe's "euill sonnes" of Mother London, and it is he, rather than the son, who in a just accounting should incur the penalty. When the child seems to speak, it is as if he has lost "all father, now"—a father lost when Jonson fled, and lost again in the poem's fantasy that the father, not the son, is dead. But it is the father who has revived the son—paying, as he willingly would, the price of his own life in the exchange. And it is the child, his voice restored as at the resurrection, who relieves the father of the painful burden of saying the words "here doth lye"—in effect, since the son can speak, giving the "lye" to those

---

32. The brief history sketched here is elaborated in Connor, *Dumbstruck: A Cultural History of Ventriloquism.*

very words. The "soft peace" denied to Jonson in his grief is granted him in an apprehension of his fantasy: an anticipation of his own death as commemorated by his "best piece" of poetry. Yet as the epigram resurrects the son, its notional graveside scene also recalls the more gruesome symbolism of Jonson's dream. Lodge had offered his assurance as a physician that those who "are manly . . . for the most part escape" (c3v). Jonson had escaped, but in doing so had given up all claim to be manly. His "Manlie shape" is instead conferred in the dream on his son—the "Marke of a bloodie crosse on his forehead as if it had been cutted wt a suord" proposing to himself that he, rather than young Ben, deserved that violent stroke. The overriding sense of loss in the poem, starting with Jonson's absence from the deathbed and compensated for in the poem's fantasy of a reunion of father and son in which they nevertheless can never really be present to each other, recalls Lacan's punning on the traumatic as the "troumatique"—a "missed encounter."

As the presiding deity of plague poetry, Dekker declares, Apollo has a double role as "both Poesies Soueraigne King, / And God of medicine" (100). The Apollo Medicus is also, for the Greeks, the god who unleashes the arrows of the plague, a *pharmakon* who harms and heals, or whose harming heals. When Dekker's Apollo "bids vs sing" of the pestilence, the poet both speaks of the dead as their "Soueraigne King"—speaks for the dead, for the sovereignty of death, on behalf of the dead, and so makes them speak through his sovereign power. As the priest of Apollo, the poet's plague speech is at once life-giving and lethal, like the breath of the diseased father who would pronounce a poisonous blessing on his son. "The language of God & Adam in the old Testament, doth terme" the pestilence "Deber," of "Dabar to speake, whether it be a speech of life or death."[33] To bespeak the plague is to evoke a contaminating language, to inflict its blow symbolically and epidemiologically. "If you read," says Dekker in the preface to *The Wonderfull Yeare*, "you may happilie laugh; tis my desire you should, because mirth is both *Phisicall*, and wholesome against the *Plague*, with which sicknes, (to tell the truth) this booke is, (though not sorely) yet somewhat infected" (3). Just as for Robert Burton writing is both a cause of and a cure for melancholy, the plague text has the same double nature. Taking the role of "all father" on himself, Jonson utters the speech of death, "Farewell, thou child"—but in remaining silent

---

33. Clapham, *Epistle*, A4r.

about the pestilence, he refrains from speaking the killing word itself. Instead, he puts the "speech of life" into the mouth of his son, reviving him briefly as a kind of prelude to the vision Jonson saw in his dream of Ben as he would appear "at the resurrection." It is then given to the undead son to bespeak the father's death in his own concise epitaph on BEN. IONSON

Old Camden, Young Ben

EPIGRAM XIII: TO WILLIAM CAMDEN

CAMDEN, most reuerend head, to whom I owe
    All that I am in arts, all that I know,
(How nothing's that?) to whom my countrey owes
    The great renowne, and name wherewith shee goes.
Then thee the age sees not that thing more graue,
    More high, more holy, that shee more would craue.
What name, what skill, what faith hast thou in things!
    What sight in searching the most antique springs!
What weight, and what authoritie in thy speech!
    Man scarce can make that doubt, but thou canst teach.
Pardon free truth, and let thy modestie,
    Which conquers all, be once ouer-come by thee.
Many of thine this better could, then I,
    But for their powers, accept my pietie.

BEN JONSON

Jonson's dream about his young son takes us back to the role of the poet's teacher "old Cambden"—William Camden, who was with Jonson at Robert Cotton's country house and who, according to Drummond, reassured the poet that his foreboding was "but ane appreehension of his fantasie at which he should not be disjected." In the *Epigrammes*, "On my First Sonne" is quite naturally paired with "On My First Davghter," a sweet and less complex poem on the death of six-month-old Mary that clearly provides the armature on which Jonson builds the epigram on his son. However, the strongest and most intimate bond in Jonson's poetry is the "liuing line" connecting fathers and sons—the phrase, from Jonson's poem on Shakespeare, hovers between poetry and paternity (8:392, l. 59). When he comes to write of the death of a son and a father's grief, the mother drops out. Camden, too, had retired to the country to escape the plague, rejoining Cotton—his former student, fellow member of the Society of Antiquaries, and the companion of his chorological expedition to Carlysle three years before. As I have noted, Camden, Cotton, and Jonson were presumably among those laying the groundwork for James's accession, with Cotton (who adopted the middle name "Bruce") rushing to complete a defense of the Scottish claim even as Jonson was planning his welcoming entertainments. Cotton, for his part (and doubtless with Camden's assistance), was engaged in the exercise of establishing paternities, tracing his own descent from Robert the Bruce, and that of James through Henry VII and all the way back to the Saxons.[34] The three could hardly have avoided some discussion of an impending epidemic and its likely impact on the royal entry into London—including, one might speculate, some concern for the safety of the prince (who came separately into England with his mother) as well as that of the new king. In 1601, Jonson had presented Camden with a copy of *Cynthia's Revels* inscribed to the master with his own name and the dedication "Alumnus olim, aeternum Amicus"—from your erstwhile pupil (or foster son) and eternal friend (8:662). Camden's presence at the creation of the "fantasie" that would issue in the poem (with its own fantasy that young Ben can speak from the grave—that he lives after all, just as Camden had said) suggests a powerful affiliation between "On my First Sonne" and the epigram "To William Camden" (8:31).

In 1603, William Camden was "all" the "father" Jonson had—not the clergyman father, who died before Jonson's birth, or his bricklayer stepfather (whose calling Jonson rejected, or perhaps rather transformed into poetry). It is to this surrogate father and former master at Westminster School that Jonson owes "[a]ll that I am in arts, all that I know." This obligation is repaid by a poem to Camden; in the plague year, Jonson's debt to his heavenly Father is repaid by a son, his best piece of poetry. The poet's wish to "loose all father, now" may include an unspoken desire to loosen his bond to Camden, whose voice carried all the weight of a father's authority for Jonson, and who had only given him false hope by dismissing Jonson's ominous dream. It is nonetheless from the "authoritie" of Camden's "speech" that Jonson inherits his own voice as an author, and it is that gift of speech that he lends to the son, making him, however briefly and posthumously, a poet.

---

34. Sharpe, *Sir Robert Cotton*, 114–15.

Camden, in the terms of Jonson's praise, has the Adamic power of conferring names: it is to his magisterial book, the *Britannia*, first published during
Jonson's years at Westminster, that "my countrey owes / The great renowne,
and name wherewith shee goes." The hallmark of Jonson's poetic authority
in the *Epigrammes*, and the source of the renown he hopes to achieve by the
publication of that volume, lies in his own power to honor the names of the
virtuous—including Camden himself, the "most reuerend head" whose name
heads the epigram—and to deprive the vicious of their names by renaming
them according to their moral nature—as "My Lord Ignorant" or "Person
Gviltie." I would argue that in the context of the plague, it cannot be by accident that, in the order of the 1616 folio, Jonson places his scornful epigram
"To Doctor Empirick" just before the poem to Camden:

> When men a dangerous disease did scape,
>   Of old, they gaue a cock to AESCVLAPE;
> Let me give two: that double am got free,
>   From my diseases danger, and from thee.
> (8:31)

Having "got free" of his diseases and the doctor's clutches, Jonson can speak
the "free truth" about Camden, praising him for the "skill" the empiric clearly
lacks. The "great renowne" merited by the one is opposed to the obscurity to
which Jonson's verse would consign the other. As the mark of Jonson's gratitude to Camden, the poem itself repays in other terms the debt of a cock to
Aesculapius traditionally owed by the patient grateful for his recovery. Such
juxtapositions are typical of Jonson's arrangement of the *Epigrammes*. Here,
the contrast with the death-dealing doctor implies that Camden is not only
the influential scholar but the good physician, commanding the speech of
life—able by the gift of literacy to make the poet "all that I am," and by the
very word "Britannia" not only to proclaim the country's fame, but to call it
into being. That power is in turn conferred upon the son, who names the
occupant(s) of his own grave.

Still, the knowledge that young Ben can only speak through his father's
lines, that young Ben can no longer utter a living line, or stand in his father's
line as a first son—most of all, that the dead son will never be able to offer

his own father the "pietie" that Jonson offers Camden—underscores the poignancy of the comparison. Jonson's *pietas* is Virgilian. With Camden figured as Jonson's "reuerend head" (perhaps transposed, in the dream, into the "forehead" on which the bloody mark of the Father is inscribed) and the son as the "child of my right hand," it is as if the three are part of the same body. As the plague writers emphasize, the afflictions of individuals are bound up with the destiny of the body politic, now repaying a massive national debt with lives. The very survival of "our Troy-nouant" is imperiled by a pestilence that threatens to bring to a tragic end the epic project of civilization-building fathered by Aeneas and, in the case of Britannia, celebrated by the "English Virgil," Camden. More intimately, the filial line connecting Camden, Jonson, and—until the summer of 1603—young Ben ultimately runs back to Anchises, Aeneas, and young Ascanius. Represented everywhere in antiquity (and long before Virgil) on coins, pottery, medals, and wall decoration, the trio embodies the key emblem of Roman identity, both in its present greatness and in its origin as the inheritor of the Trojan imperium. Roman images show Aeneas as the linchpin of history and the guarantor of its continuity. In the Virgilian vision of patrilineal responsibility, a burden both personal and political, it is the fate (and the burden) of Aeneas to lead the past into the future by shouldering his aged father while leading his son by the hand out of the burning city. But Jonson's "right hand" is severed, buried in the city. In the underworld of the *Aeneid*, the father rises from the grave to speak to the son. With the encounter of the living and the dead in Jonson's poem, the Virgilian roles are sadly reversed.

Furthermore, the Latin sources of Jonson's poem on "old Cambden" reveal a preoccupation with the "miserie" of age—the very grief (so Jonson would console himself) that young Ben had "so soone scap'd." In 1603 Camden was fifty-two, a man at least in his late middle age by early modern standards. He would live another twenty years, but his health was never robust:

During his four years as headmaster Camden's health, always frail, began to deteriorate and travel was increasingly difficult. In 1592 he was beset by a quartan ague and passed blood; his health remained poor for a long time. In his "Memorabilia" or autobiographical notes . . . he records being freed of the ague only in 1594. In 1597, after his travel to

Salisbury and Oxford, he was afflicted by "a most dangerous sickness" and taken into the house of one Cuthbert Line, whose wife was able to cure him. From about this time for the remainder of his life Camden was plagued by intermittent but severe illnesses.[35]

If Jonson's reader (instructed by the example of Camden's scholarship) searches "the most antique springs," the language of the poem will yield up a wealth of misery. Jonson's Latinate praise of Camden's gravity—"Then thee the age sees not that thing more graue, / More high, more holy, that shee more would craue"—renders a line from a letter by the younger Pliny (4.17.4) in which the Roman writer speaks of his late mentor, Corellius Rufus. Pliny here recalls that Corellius "displayed the vigour of youth, despite his failing health and advancing age," and that as Corellius lay dying he spoke of his close friendship with his younger colleague.[36] Contrasting youth and age and emphasizing the warmth of Corellius/Camden's friendship with the younger Pliny/Jonson, the letter also deepens the sense of the old scholar's gravity by casting it in the shadow of the "grave." In another letter (1.12), Pliny meditates on Corellius's long years of suffering from the gout, which spread from his feet through all his limbs: "He bore up through sheer strength of mind, even when cruelly tortured by unbelievable agony" ("eum quiden incredibiles cruciatus et indignissima tormenta pateretur"; 36–37). In the end, having "suffered so long from such painful affliction that his reasons for dying outweighed everything that life could give him," Corellius did the one thing for which Jonson, in "To Heaven," dare not wish: he committed suicide. Pliny's reflection on Corellius's end poses the Jonsonian dilemma of cutting short a life of suffering: "When we see men die of disease," Pliny writes, "at least we can find consolation in the knowledge that it is inevitable, but when their end is self-sought, our grief is inconsolable because we feel that their lives could have been long" (34–37).

Pliny also supplies Jonson with the "authoritie" of Camden's "speech" and with the latter's "faith . . . in things" ("Iam quanta sermonibus eius fides, quanta

35. Herendeen, "Camden, William," in *Oxford Dictionary of National Biography Online*.

36. "Observatur oculis ille vir quo neminem aetas nostra graviorem sanctiorem subtiliorem tulit." All quotations from Pliny and their English translations are from the Loeb edition of the letters and panegyrics, *Pliny the Younger*, translated by Betty Radice; the quotation here is from pp. 292–95. Subsequent citations are given parenthetically in the text.

auctoritas, quam pressa et decora eunctatio"), as well as with the beautiful line "Man scarse can make that doubt, but thou canst teach" ("Nihil est quod discere velis quod ille docere non possit"), this time from a letter (1.12.2–3) in which Pliny lets his correspondent know that he is "exceedingly worried about Titius Aristo, a man I particularly love and admire, who has been seriously ill for some time" (68–69). Unlike Corellius Rufus, Titius Aristo—a noted jurist and mentor of Pliny in the law—resists the temptation of suicide, despite his almost unbearable suffering: "His patience throughout this illness, if you could only see it, would fill you with admiration; he fights against pain, resists thirst, and endures the unbelievable heat of his fever without moving or throwing off his covers" (70–71).[37]

Of these prolonged agonies there is no hint in the language Jonson culls from Pliny's letters. And yet it is surely significant that, of all the classical sources Jonson might have consulted for descriptions of learned and generous men, the ones he chose focus precisely and at length on the "miserie" of age. Corellius Rufus and Titius Aristo provide the pattern for William Camden, and Pliny's tone the decorum of Jonson's reverence for his teacher. But the suffering of these Roman progenitors is written out of Jonson's account—just as, in the poem on his first son, the horror of a bubonic death (on which other plague writers dwell in gruesome detail) is never acknowledged. These miseries will return in Jonson's "To Heaven," a poem burdened with "feare," "horror," "griefs," and "sinne," in which Jonson—as if he were caught between the tenacious clinging to life of Titius and the suicide of Corellius—dare not "wish for death" (8:122). The poem to Camden conceals a substrate only hinted at in Jonson's crucial rhyme of "graue" and "craue" in lines 5 and 6—a craving for the grave heard both in the buried reference to the Roman fathers' weariness of life and in the ambiguous epitaph put into the mouth of the English son. Jonson's poetry here, as elsewhere, calls for a kind of critical archaeology akin to Camden's unearthing the antiquities of Britain. In these poems especially, his grave language conceals but echoes an encrypted literary predecessor. Jonson's own skill draws upon a bilingual register—something beyond the capability of his "mere English" reader—to

---

37. In the ode to Cary and Morison, Jonson's "Brave Infant of *Saguntum*" represents the opposite of these long-suffering Romans: foreseeing "lifes miseries" from the womb, this "Wise child" took his own life by refusing to be born (8:242–43, ll. 1, 19, 7).

create the impression of a Latin original, a text written in the language of the father, beneath its English surface. On this level—a "Roman" subsurface marked not by decorous restraint but by the themes of disease, of the affection and broken ties between fathers and sons, of early death and long suffering, of suicide and endurance—the poems on Camden and on his first son find their common ground.

CHAPTER 5

John Donne
Translating
the Plague

Who will beleeve mee, if I sweare
That I have had the plague a yeare?
JOHN DONNE, "The Broken Heart"

In 1625 the plague struck again, and with even more terrible force. "This was the year," John Evelyn's *Diary* records, "in which the pestilence was so epidemical, that there died in London 5000 a-week."[1] One pamphleteer puts the perennial question into the mouth of the personified nation: "But what haue I done (sayth *England*) that such things as these should befall mee?" The answer then, as in 1603, was that England had "requited the Lord evill for good." The "good" could be tallied up as the account of God's particular care for the English. Had he not "dispelled the mists and clouds of Popery and superstition" and given his favored nation "many great and glorious deliverances, the like never heard of, especially those of the *Gunpower-Treason* and *Eighty-eight*"? And under James, had the country not enjoyed a long reign of "peace and quietnesse," during which "no noise of Warre hath been heard in thy streetes"?[2] The intervening period of calm made the recurrence seem all the worse, and all the more difficult to read out of (or into) God's providential plan. Compared with the outbreak of 1625, "all former Plagues"—according to another pamphleteer, the anonymous author of *Londons Lamentations and Teares*—"were but pettie ones": "This to future Ages and Historiographers must needs bee Kalendred the Great Plague"—as indeed it would be, until an even greater one struck in 1665.[3] It was, in all, a "Yeere full of fatall and memorable Accidents; the ending of a mightie and prudent King, the beginning of a mightie and prodigious Plague, (besides the marriage of a mightie King, and the setting forth of a mightie Nauy) such an one, as no Age, no Record, no Chronicle ever mentioned the like, within this our faery Land, in this our famous Citie."[4] The king died on March 27, and although there was no question of the succession, as there had been in 1603, the coronation of Charles I was immediately darkened, as his father's had been, by the pestilence. Even the good news—of the new king's marriage (putting to rest the controversy over the Spanish match) and the "setting forth of a mightie Nauy" (headed, as it turned out, for an inglorious defeat at Cádiz)—was demoted by the plague

---

1. Evelyn, *Diary and Correspondence*, 1:5.

2. S. P., *Two Precious and Divine Antidotes*, 3.

3. *Lachrymae Londinenses*, "Epistle Dedicatorie." Things might have been even worse if the lord mayor and aldermen of London, to whom the *Lamentations* is dedicated, had not been vigilant, for then "wee had been in danger to haue had a further Plague added; our Throats cut and to be bee despoiled of our Goods, by a certeine Rout of Rascals that continually lie lurking and hunkering about the City."

4. Ibid.

to a parenthesis. The England that was Spenser's "faery Land" seemed a faded vision. It was a year that, like 1603, saw an outpouring of plague sermons, official orders, medical pamphlets, and plague broadsheets (the Short Title Catalog lists more than forty plague publications for the year 1625), including Thomas Dekker's *A Rod for Run-awaies*.

My purpose in this chapter is to set Donne as a plague writer into the context of this fatal and memorable year and, by doing so, to correlate the epidemic crisis in London with a transformative personal crisis for Donne, occasioned by his own near-fatal illness two years before. My central texts include three works not usually taken together but, as I shall argue, all part of Donne's engagement with disease—his own, London's, and the world's. The *Devotions upon Emergent Occasions*, published the year before the plague as a meditation on his recent illness, would (by coincidence or, likely, by the design of the printer) be in the bookstalls during the plague year, along with the 1625 edition of the "Anniversaries." These earlier poems, with their pro-longed lament for a "sicke World" (232, l. 23), would now likely be reread in the light of the plague, and in the context of Donne's writing, as a prelude to the *Devotions*.[5] The third text is Donne's one plague sermon—arguably the finest of that dismal genre—preached at St. Dunstan's, January 15, 1626, on Exodus 12:30: "For there was not a house where there was not one dead." In its emphasis on the resurrection, the sermon echoes Donne's conviction in the *Devotions* that God calls "Lazarus out of his tomb, and me out of my bed" (138).[6] In both texts, Donne will understand God's plague writing as a process of "translation." It is this last figure that I want to explore most fully below.

At Death's Door

In November and early December of 1623, Donne was among those London-ers fallen dangerously ill with what physicians today would diagnose, on the basis of his reported symptoms, as "relapsing fever"—a louse- or tick-borne in-fection called "the spotted fever" or "the spotted death" in seventeenth-century

---

5. All quotations from Donne's poetry are, unless otherwise noted, from *The Poems of John Donne*, ed. Grierson, vol. 1, and are cited parenthetically in the text by page and line number.

6. All quotations from the *Devotions* refer to *Devotions upon Emergent Occasions* (University of Michigan Press, 1959) and are cited parenthetically in the text.

accounts.[7] If the bubonic plague invariably struck during the summer, spotted fever was its winter counterpart. This precursor epidemic, with a mortality rate of 30 to 70 percent in a pre-antibiotic age, serves as a reminder that plague, though the more devastating, was only one of a suite of unchecked infectious diseases that early modern flesh was heir to. The *Devotions*, written during Donne's convalescence, was published in January 1624. R. C. Bald dates Donne's two hymns—the "Hymne to God, My God, in my Sicknesse" and "A Hymne to God the Father"—to the same months (not, as Izaak Walton thought, to Donne's last days). In a letter to Robert Ker, Donne says he is out of bed, putting his meditations into order, but hasn't been able to leave his bedside: "I sit there still" as "a Prisoner discharged, sits at the Prison doore."[8] In the "Hymne to God the Father," the poet asks to be forgiven of "that sinne which I have wonne / Others to sinne? and, made my sinne their dore" (369). In the "Hymne to God the Father," death's door becomes the portal to the heavenly choir room where Donne awaits his entrance, "here at the dore," tuning his "Instrument" (369).

With the new year of 1624, Donne emerged through the door of this nearly fatal illness into a period of reinvigorated work in the church. The dean of St. Paul's since 1621, he came into the additional living of St. Dunstan's-in-the-Field in March 1624. On Easter day 1624, he preached at St. Paul's on the resurrection. The theme of this sermon, the first since his illness, struck a personal chord as well as one appropriate to the occasion. In the *Devotions*, he sees "this bodily rising" from his own sickbed as "an earnest of a second resurrection from sin, and of a third, to everlasting glory" (144). The same sequence of resurrections is repeated almost verbatim in the Easter sermon at St. Paul's, when Donne speaks of "a Resurrection from sin, by grace" and "a Resurrection from temptation to sin, by way of death, to the glory of heaven" (6:664).[9] On March 27, 1625, the king died. On April 3 (and on one day's notice), Donne had the honor of preaching to the new monarch at St. James's—an invitation that signaled the royal favor he would enjoy as the successor to the aging and

---

7. Biographical information for this period of Donne's life is taken from Bald, *John Donne*, 450–90. For the term "spotted fever," see the OED. In the *Annus Mirabilis*, Dryden speaks of the Great Plague of 1665 as a time when "spotted deaths ran arm'd through every street, / With poison'd darts" (68).

8. Quoted in Bald, *John Donne*, 450–51.

9. Unless otherwise noted, all quotations from Donne's sermons are from *The Sermons of John Donne*, ed. Simpson and Potter, and are cited parenthetically in the text by volume and page number.

infirm Lancelot Andrewes. This *First Sermon Preached to King Charles* was in the bookstalls in at least two editions that same year.[10]

By late spring, however, Donne fell ill again, whether with a "relapse" of his earlier fever or some other illness we cannot be sure. After his sermon on Whitsunday, June 5, Donne would not preach again in London until Christmas. In a letter of June 21, 1625, to Sir Nicholas Carey, he announced his intention of "changinge my prison" by going into the country with "some few of my family" to recuperate at the Chelsea estate of Sir John Danvers and Lady Danvers (the mother of the poet George Herbert).[11] With the plague already spreading in London, it was prudent for him to take advantage of the hospitality at Chelsea for a prolonged period. He remained through the summer and autumn, occupying himself by writing out a number of his sermons from the notes he had kept. In a commemorative sermon delivered after Lady Danvers's death in 1627, Donne would recall his hostess's charity in relieving the sick at a time when, even in the country, "every doore was shut up" lest "*Death* should enter into the house" (8:90).

Donne returned to London only toward the end of December 1625, in time to preach the Christmas sermon at St. Paul's. This was followed on January 15, 1626, by a plague sermon, his "First Sermon after Our Dispersion, by the Sickness" at St. Dunstan's, and then by his Second Prebend sermon at St. Paul's on January 29. Just before his return, Donne assured Sir Henry Goodyer in a letter from Chelsea that "the report of my death" had been much exaggerated, but it "hath thus much of truth in it, that though I be not dead, yet I am buried within a few weeks after I immured my self in this house, the infection strook into the town, into so many houses, as that it became ill manners, to make any visits."[12] Donne was now back in his own house, a body resurrected, a prisoner liberated, and the instrument of his preaching once again in full tune. He would remain in relatively good health until his final illness in 1631. In the course of his last decade, however, the two years beginning with his illness at the end of 1623 and culminating in the St. Dunstan's plague sermon at the beginning of 1626 mark the penultimate crisis of Donne's life. At the height of his professional eminence,

10. *The First Sermon Preached to King Charles*; and *Foure Sermons vpon Speciall Occasions*.
11. Quoted in Bald, *John Donne*, 472.
12. Donne, *Letters to Severall Persons of Honour*, 233–34.

he was laid low by diseases that he would understand in the bowels of his suffering as the harbinger of his own mortality. Not himself a victim of the plague, he nonetheless found himself at death's door in a year when many thousands in London (including more than six hundred in his own parish of St. Dunstan's) passed through it, and when his own "rising" coincided with the recovery of the city. His letters in this period have not lost their touch of wit, but their recurrent language of imprisonment, burial, and death houses suggests how deeply Donne is "immured" in the moment of the plague. With "so many houses" struck by the pestilence, and so many doors marked with the red cross, the text upon which the St. Dunstan's sermon is based (Exodus 12:30) must have struck Donne as God-given: "For there was not a house where there was not one dead" (6:349).

The Anniversaries: "Thinke that thy body rots"

It would hardly be possible to omit the "Anniversaries" from any discussion of Donne's plague writing. To be sure, no cause is given for the death of Elizabeth Drury in December 1610, just short of her fifteenth birthday. There were relatively few cases of plague that year, although the memory of the 1603 epidemic was fresh in mind, and 1610 fell at the end of a four-year period during which plague "was responsible for more than 10 per cent of recorded burials every year."[13] For Donne, who admits that he never saw her, it was sufficient for the occasion to know simply that she was dead. "The First Anniversary," referring to the first anniversary of the girl's death and titled "An Anatomie of the World," appeared in 1611, followed in 1612 by the sequel, which included both "The First Anniversary" and the new "Second Anniversary," titled "The Progresse of the Soule." Reissued in the plague year of 1625, however, a work that promises on its title page to represent the "frailty and the decay of this whole world" in the "untimely death" of a young girl—and one that in its opening sequence offers the hope that "[t]his new world may be safer, being told / The dangers and diseases of the old" (234, ll. 88–89)—would doubtless be understood to speak to the present crisis.

We cannot know precisely when during the year the 1625 edition of the "Anniversaries" appeared. As is the case for all editions of the poems, including

---

13. Slack, *Impact of Plague*, 145.

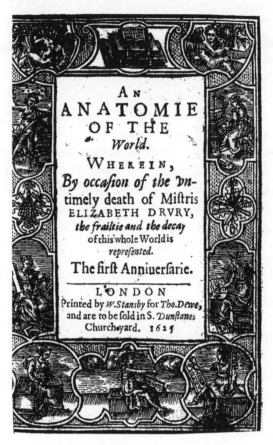

FIGURE 18. John Donne, *An Anatomie of the World*, title page (1625 ed.).

those of 1611 and 1612, there is no entry for this edition in the Stationers' Register.[14] A 1621 edition had been printed by Augustine Mathewes for Thomas Dewe. The 1625 edition was printed by William Stansby, also for Thomas Dewe, to be sold in Dewe's shop in St. Dunstan's churchyard (fig. 18). Having had, one may assume, some success with the title in 1621, the same bookseller would have welcomed a fresh supply once the author had become vicar in the very parish where his shop was located. But Donne's appointment to St.

---

14. After the initial publication of the first poem in 1611, it appeared together with the second in 1612, and then in subsequent editions of 1621, 1625, 1635, 1649, 1650, and 1669.

Dunstan's had come early the previous year. Why would Dewe have waited? It is possible that the publication of a number of Donne's sermons in the three years since his elevation to St. Paul's, followed now by that of the *Devotions* in 1624 and his prestigious *First Sermon Preached to King Charles* in 1625—both printed by Mathewes—created a renewed interest in Donne's earlier work. Stansby, the printer of the 1625 edition of the "Anniversaries," had also produced the first edition of the "Anatomie of the World" in 1611. With no new material at hand, might Stansby not have thought to make his bid for the Donne market with a reissue of the "Anniversaries"? The publication date of 1625, however, makes it just as likely that the volume was brought out to take advantage of a boomlet for plague texts (of which the Stationers' Register lists eight between May and December of 1625, among the far larger number of extant sermons, orders and proclamations, "receipts," dialogues, bills of mortality, lamentations, and poems published during the same period).[15] Arguably, too, in 1625 Stansby's own interest in plague materials may have been as strong as his interest in Donne, since in that year he is also listed as the printer of a plague tract entitled *Londons Lamentation for Her Sinnes*, as well as a year-end *Generall or Great Bill* tabulating all the plague deaths in London and its environs for the past twelve months.[16]

These conjectures are strengthened by the design of the 1625 title page (fig. 18), which, unlike that of 1621 or the editions of 1611 and 1612, is framed by a decorative border representing the seven liberal arts. Herbert J. C. Grierson notes that this is "probably" the theme of the border (2:186)—in fact, there can be no doubt—but he does not comment on its possible significance. The seven liberal arts, assuming the design was not randomly chosen from Stansby's stock of title-page woodcuts, have their pertinence to the "Anniversaries" insofar as Donne's meditations range over the sun and the planets (astronomy), the deformities of the earth (geometry), the loss of proportion and harmony (arithmetic), and the heavenly choir (music), and they do so with a relentless pyrotechnic energy that displays the poet's mastery of the verbal arts of logic, grammar, and rhetoric. (That the knowledge gleaned from these arts is regarded in the poems with the deepest skepticism casts the iconography of the

---

15. Arber, ed., *Transcript of the Register of the Company of Stationers of London, 1554–1640*, 4:103–16.

16. William Crashaw, *Londons Lamentation for Her Sinnes and Complaint to the Lord Her God; A Generall or Great Bill for This Yeare.*

title page in a retrospectively ironic light.) At the same time, two of its details echo the plague iconography with which we are already familiar. The figure of rhetoric in the central panel at the bottom is represented unconventionally as a seated woman holding a pair of scales (not a book, or else, in the allegorical mode stemming from medieval tradition, a sword and a lily, to indicate the power and beauty of her art). As such, she might be an image of forensic rhetoric specifically; but, posed as she is against a background of a boiling, lowering cloud—the telltale convention of plague illustration—she would much more likely be seen in the plague year as the figure of Justice weighing the nation's fate in the balance (cf. fig. 10). Similarly, the two contrasting vignettes at the top left and top right of the frame have a more immediate connection with plague imagery than with the motif of the seven liberal arts. In the context of 1625, the reclining figure on the left holding a cornucopia would suggest all the "good" that had poured down upon an undeserving nation. On the right, at first glance, a person appears to cradle a dead or languishing child in his (or her) arms: a parent lamenting an "untimely death," whether the death of Elizabeth Drury or the death of a plague victim. On closer inspection, this tiny vignette resolves itself, rather, into the image of the child as an angel rising from her deathbed and holding a heavenly plant. Between these two vignettes, an open book, presumably the Bible, rests on a lectern; it serves visually as a kind of fulcrum on which the images to either side are evenly balanced. In terms of a plague theodicy, the justice of an epidemic would thus be reflected in this framing motif—on the one hand, all God's foison, and on the other a death representing the judgment visited upon the nation for having "requited the Lord evil for good," and a resurrection as the emblem of the reward that awaits the faithful soul.

None of this is meant to imply that Donne had a hand in the publication of the 1625 "Anniversaries" or in the choice of a title-page design. There is no evidence that at the time he was even aware of the book's appearance, especially as he was in the country from June through most of December. The carelessness of the 1625 text, evidently a rush job, further suggests that he could have had nothing to do with it. Frank Manley finds that neither the 1621 nor the 1625 edition "has any authority. The first of these was printed from the 1612 edition and the second directly from 1621."[17] These two latter editions,

---

17. Manley, in *John Donne: The Anniversaries*, 86–87.

according to Donne's variorum editors, fail to incorporate the errata from the edition of 1612 and so "progressively corrupt the text."[18] My ideal reader of Donne as a plague writer is not, however, the modern editor (or Donne himself), but a parishioner at St. Dunstan's in 1625. This reader has heard, and perhaps also purchased, the vicar's sermons. Having come across the "Anniversaries" while browsing in Thomas Dewe's bookstall in the churchyard, he will find nothing on the title page to suggest that this publication of "1625" is not a current work but deals with a death fifteen years in the past. To such a reader during the plague year, Donne's poems would serve (to borrow a title from Frank O'Hara) as "meditations in an emergency."

In 1625, the name "Mistris Elizabeth Drury" would have meant even less than it did to Donne's readers in 1611. As a kind of saint manquée, the dead girl—or, rather, "Shee"—functions in the poem above all as a symbol of loss, including (as critics have noted) the loss of her royal namesake, whose death had ushered in the epidemic of 1603. The "Anniversaries" hover at the far portal of mortality, where "Death must usher, and unlocke the doore" (255, l. 156). "The Second Anniversary" offers a strenuous meditation geared toward allowing the reader to think his way toward the "essential joy" (264, l. 443) of which Elizabeth Drury's soul now partakes. The example Elizabeth Drury offers is not one of a pious life or of miracles performed, but of her death, the sole entryway to her otherwise unattainable present bliss, and one from which the earthbound reader is debarred. When only "mis-devotion frames / A thousand Prayers to Saints" (266, ll. 511–12), her death can be mourned (and finally celebrated), but she cannot be invoked. A pale afterimage of the St. Sebastians and St. Roches of the Catholic tradition and perceptible only in "the twilight of her memory" (233, l. 74), Elizabeth Drury's ghost inhabits the poem in plague times as a reminder and a remainder of the possibility of saintly intercession, but she can offer none of the consolations of the old religion. Absorbed as she is in the unity of the godhead, detached as she now is from all earthly concerns, it is impossible to imagine her appealing on behalf of those left behind—or of our being able to appeal to her, since the world is "speechlesse growne" since her death (232, l. 29). Her perfection serves only as the occasion for the reader to reflect on the world's ruin. In the midst of an epidemic and in its aftermath, moreover, the "frailty and the decay of this

18. *Variorum Edition*, 6:38.

whole world" might well be taken as observable fact rather than as the fancy of a hyperbolical imagination, and the malady of "sicke World" (232, l. 23) as a literal diagnosis. Regarding these poems, especially the opening 250 lines of "The First Anniversary," through the lens (or amid the thicket) of contemporary plague writing, such a reader would find Donne's meditations on disease remarkable in two ways.

First, there is no reason in Donne to suppose, as most plague writers do, that epidemic disease is an extraordinary event demanding the discovery of some extraordinary efflorescence of sin in order to explain and justify its occurrence. If, as the poem declares, "[t]here is no health" (234, l. 91)—and if we enjoy, at best, a precarious "neutralitie" between the opposed humors of the body—then disease must be understood as our ordinary state, and even epidemic disease as the general breakdown of an already unstable system: we are "borne ruinous" (234, l. 95). Our ruin is, of course, the fruit of our first parents' disobedience in the garden—a point Andrewes, Bostocke, and Perkins had made earlier in tracing the origin of the plague back to the Fall, but not with Donne's mordant insistence on its consequences. The Fall can be taken as the moment when the death gene, as it were, is inserted into the human program, for we begin to die the moment we are born. To ask why we are ill is to labor under the delusion that we should be, or indeed ever are, well. Donne would concur with Montaigne that we do not die because we are sick; we die because we are alive. The question, then, would not be to determine why a particular plague had been called down, but to understand that the ultimate justification for all human misery had been written into the divine plan at the moment of Adam's lapse. An affliction, to be sure, disease must nonetheless be understood (as Donne does in the *Devotions*) as an "occasion" for the spiritually healthful exercise of the *ars moriendi*. Thus Donne, in the St. Dunstan's sermon: "The next thing that we are to practice after we are born, is to die" (6:356).

Second, even so violent an epidemic as that raging in 1625 must be regarded, in the long view, as the local and predictable symptom of what the poet imagines, now in the vein of a "naturian," to have been a general decline in the vigor of the human race since the beginning. Diminished in stature and abbreviated in years, we are "scarce our Fathers shadowes cast at noone" (235, l. 143). Ague and lethargy, the loss of the "intrinsique balme" believed by the Paracelsians to protect the body against the putrefaction, the drawing out of its "vitall spirits" (231, l. 13): these are the symptoms not only of the individual inflicted in body and spirit, but of the whole creation in its death throes. The "frailty" and "decay" of the world appear in the poem as the reflection of Donne's traditional *contemptus mundi*, but the diagnosis also comports with the ecology of the plague as understood by natural philosophers and physicians: for them as well, the origin of the disease in rotten exhalations, ill winds, and miasmal clouds pointed to the same "sicke World." For Donne, the depletion of human health is the symptom (and perhaps the cause) of a universal corruption that reaches as far as the heavens themselves, as the telescopic diagnosis of a now disordered Ptolemaic cosmos confirms.

The St. Dunstan's Sermon

As the anatomist of a moribund world—a world rotting away so utterly that it may not even "last" until the completion of the autopsy—the poet of the "Anniversaries" urges the reader to flee, not to the countryside but to the safer haven to which we are directed by the progress of Elizabeth Drury's soul. The world itself might serve only to be dissected for the evidence of its corruption. In contrast to the fresh perception of nature's beauties, to the sense of wonder found in George Herbert or Thomas Traherne, Donne's writing reflects what John Carey calls the poet's "almost total deadness to the world's beauty, abundance and animation."[19] Here as elsewhere, and as the concomitant to his deep *contemptus mundi*, Donne's writing enacts an agoraphobic desire for sanctuary (in some "little roome," in the "living walls" of the flea, in the eye of the beloved), or else for some avenue of escape: "Wee can dye it, by it, if not live by love" ("The Canonization," 15, l. 28). In the love poetry, his alternatives to being inscribed in the "plaguey bill" are the two open to those who would seek to avoid the world's infection: quarantine or flight. In 1611, the death of Elizabeth Drury had provided the occasion for a meditation that, however intense its energy, functioned for the reader as a kind of abstract thought experiment: "Thinke that thy body rots." The one body in question, that of Elizabeth Drury, never assumes a fleshly substance but is, rather, easily resolved into the "Idea" of a woman, and "not as she was" (1:133). But as Carey also notes, beginning in 1620—after the preacher had lost his wife, a son, and a daughter—Donne's sermons begin to dwell with a gruesome imaginative ferocity on the decay of

---

19. Carey, *John Donne*, 132.

the body, and equally on the hope of a glorious resurrection in the flesh.[20] In the aftermath of his personal losses, of his own illness, and now of the mass die-off of 1625, both sides of this equation are given added weight. The death of the world, however much Donne may have believed that time was actually ticking down through its eleventh hour, had functioned in "The Anniversaries" as a witty hyperbole. The plague made that prospect seem all too real, and its antidote—the re-incarnation of all that rotted flesh—all the more to be desired.

Calling their attention to the church in which they are assembled, Donne reminds his parishioners at St. Dunstan's that "in this lamentable calamity, the dead were buried, and thrown up again before they were resolved into dust, to make room for more." In church, all the ground beneath their feet "is made of the bodies of Christians," and so murky has the very air become from these hasty burials and reburials that "[e]very puff of wind within these walls, may blow the father into the sons eys, or the wife into her husbands, or his into hers, or both into their childrens, or their childrens into both." But that the plague dead were "thrown up again" should also recall the moment of Christ's resurrection, when "some of the dead arose out of their graves, that were buried again." These instances of the dead refusing to stay buried lead inevitably to the preacher's question: "But are all these dead?" Donne's final, and characteristic, rhapsody on the resurrection insists that "all these dead bodies shall be restored by the power, and are kept alive in the purpose of Almighty God"; that they shall "renew, or rather continue their being"; that their state in the grave is "not annihilation." Thus, "[a]s between two men of equal age, if one sleep, and the other wake all night, yet they rise both of an equal age in the morning; so they who shall have slept out a long night of many ages in the grave, and they who shall be caught up in the clouds, to meet the Lord Jesus in the aire, at the last day, shall enter all at once in their bodies into Heaven" (6:362). The more Donne's imagination dwells on corpses, the greater the need for assurance that the repentant will be re-incorporated in Christ.

The mode of that re-incorporation is suggested in Donne's further assurance that "the body of man is wrapt up in the Contract, and in the eternal Decree of the Resurrection." For, Donne continues, "[a]s soon shall God tear a leaf out of the Book of Life, and cast so many of the elect into Hell fire, as leave

---

20. Ibid., 227.

the body of any of his Saints in corruption for ever" (6:363). The biblical history of the plague is what we deduce from "this Text" in Exodus. The ultimate chapter of that history, its redemptive finale, will see the plague body "wrapt up" (in both senses of the word), into another text: God's eternal decree. In this conclusion, the distinction between the body of the saints and the book that guarantees their resurrection in the body is collapsed. The conflation of the body and the book harks back to "The Exstasie": "Loves mysteries in soules do growe, / But yet the body is his booke" (53, ll. 71–72). "[P]ure lovers soules" must "descend / T'affections, and to faculties," or else a "great Prince"—the body itself—"in prison lies" (53, ll. 65–68). When Donne now imagines the resurrection, the process is reversed. The great prince must be freed from his captivity; bodies must ascend into the realm of purity, intact and uncorrupted, to be incorporated (as bodies) into the Book of Life. Between the living body and its ultimate reconstitution, death itself is elided. Death is no more than a sleep from which the sleeper will awaken refreshed in the morning, and evidently with no memory of the intervening time and no trace of the body's decay. In the end, there will be no difference between those who have "slept out a long night of many ages" and those who will never suffer death because they will be alive on the last day, to be rapt directly into heaven.[21]

Arguably, Donne's emphasis upon the resurrection of the body—complete, repaired, unmarked by death—is the obverse of a deeper fear of the body's corruption. The resurrection is both comforting and necessary also because he cannot accept the kind of arguments we have seen employed by other divines to justify the ways of the plague to men. Thus, in the sermon "Preached to the King's Majesty at Whitehall" of February 24, 1626, in the month following the plague sermon at St. Dunstan's, Donne insists that "God can call up *Damps*, and *Vapors* from below, and powre down putride *defluxions* from above, and bid them meet and condense into a *plague*, a *plague* that shall not be onely uncureable, uncontrollable, unexorable, but undisputable, unexaminable, unquestionable; A *plague* that shall not onely not admit a *remedy*, when it is come, but not give a *reason* how it did come" (7:81). Although it is clear from the St. Dunstan's sermon that God rained down terrible plagues upon the Egyptians because of Pharaoh's perversity and rebellion, any attempt to hold God accountable by examining, let alone questioning, his judgments must

---

21. See Carey's fine discussion of the resurrection of the body in *John Donne*, 219–30.

run up against the unpenetrability (to coin a Donnean word) of the divine intention. One might argue, as Donne does, that the judgment upon the Egyptians was at the same time a mercy to the children of Israel, since "God hath a Treasury of both, *Mercy* and *Justice*"; but as part of this reassurance, Donne considers the disturbing possibility that for his own reasons, God might just as easily have "changed the persons, and made the *Egyptians* the object of his *Mercies*, and us of his *Justice* (6:353). The very examples that God provides even in, or especially in, his harshest judgments also serve as a mercy to those who can profit by them. However, the ultimate mercy is guaranteed by the "contract" by which—at least for God's saints—not only will the ravages of a plague death be repaired in the resurrected body, but death itself will have been annulled. All questions raised in plague time will have become irrelevant when "we shall all be in a place that reckons not by minutes" (6:363).

The St. Dunstan's sermon is organized as a survey of the four "houses" Donne draws out of his text from Exodus 12:30, "For there was not a house where there was not one dead": the houses of the Egyptians, our own houses, the "house" of the human body, and the church as the house of God. For one who had himself been recently housebound by illness, the device is no mere trope of rhetoric. It allows him to contract the expanse of providential history and the differences in scale among these "houses" into the span of his sermon. It also allows him to regard these not only as his own "examples," but as an exemplary series of texts instituted by God himself—a "manifold Catechism" ordered so as to "imprint" the Word (6:353) over and over again by a kind of informational redundancy:

> [B]y that Text which we have read to you here, and by that Text which we have left at home, our house and family, and by that Text, which we have brought hither, our selves, and by that Text which we find here, where we stand, and sit, and kneel upon the bodies of some of our dead friends or neighbors, he gives to us, he repeats to us, in full, a various, a multiform, a manifold Catechism, and Institution, to teach us that . . . *there is not a house in which there is not one dead*. (6:351)

Just as (echoing the "Anniversaries") human life today is "abridged and contracted" to "threescore and ten" (6:349), so the divine author also abridges epic events into the smaller volume(s) of our own experience—but with no loss of the essential meaning of the text in the contraction. Thus, scripture and history present us with many "Catechisms" of mass destruction "written in Red Ink"—the plagues upon the Egyptians, or (as Donne claims) the death of "Two hundred Millions" slain by the Roman church in its attempt to stamp out the Reformation. But in our own experience, God "presents his lesser *Catechisms,* The several Funerals of our particular Friends in the congregation; or he abridges this *Catechism* of the Congregation to a less volume then that, to the consideration of every particular piece of our own Family at home: *For so, there is not a house in which there is not one dead*" (6:355). These are all, alike, "so many places of Infection, so many temporal or spiritual Pesthouses," as though we could reckon all human experience as a recurrent disease that can be described in—or, rather, contracted to—the single phrase from Exodus that provides Donne with the text of his sermon.

Devotions

Donne's textualizing of houses and bodies—his imagining them all as leaves within the book of God's creation, each a version of the other—has its roots in the "Word made flesh" and in the long tradition of God's "two books." The same tradition will lead, later, to Henry Vaughan's beautiful poem "The Book," in which the speaker asks to be given "amongst thy works a place" when all the scattered material of the world, including the physical materials that have gone into the making of the book itself, will be restored.[22] I would argue, though, that Donne's language in the sermon rests more immediately on the figure of "translation" elaborated two years before in an oft-cited passage from the *Devotions*:

> And when [the church] buries a man, that action concerns me; all mankind is of one author, and is one volume; when one man dies, one chapter is not torn out of the book, but translated into a better language; and every chapter must be so translated; God employs several translators; some pieces are translated by age, some by sickness, some by war, some by justice; but God's hand is in every translation, and his hand

22. Vaughan, *Silex Scintillans*, 81.

shall bind up all our scattered leaves again for that library where every
book shall lie open to one another. (108)

It seems clear that Donne has this idea in mind when he notes at the beginning of the St. Dunstan's sermon that God "employs what person he will, and
executes by what instrument it pleases him to chuse, age or sickness, or justice,
or malice or (in our apprehension) fortune" (6:349). The conceit recalls the
great project of translating scripture anew begun in 1604 and resulting in the
publication in 1611 of what has come to be called the King James Bible—the
Authorized Version from which Donne draws the text of his 1626 sermon.
Several committees of translators were employed at Westminster, Cambridge,
and Oxford, and at the end of the process the scattered leaves produced by
these working groups were bound together at London's Stationer's Hall by a
final select committee from whose hand the final publication issued. In Donne's conceit, the members of the committee appointed by God are not the
kingdom's most eminent divines, but "sickness," "war," and "justice"—together,
a committee well qualified to translate even the most recalcitrant subjects.

"Translation" proves to be an especially rich and subtle figure for Donne,
one of which, as a crucial tool in understanding scripture, he always makes his
congregation aware as he develops a sermon. In an undated sermon preached
at a christening, for example, he adjudicates among a number of conflicting
translations of his text from 1 John 5:7–8 (into the Syriac, the Greek and Latin
Fathers, the Vulgate, and even Luther's German) in defense of his text as it appears in the Authorized Version, in which the Trinity is named as "The Father,
the Word [rather than "the Son," "who is always present in it"] and the Holy
Ghost" (5:139). That the Son is always present in the Word—that every "word"
finds its common denominator in the "Word" and is thus conjoined to every
other word—grounds the process of translation, just as the "Word" itself can
stand in for the "Son" in the enumeration of the Trinity. Later in the same sermon, Donne comments on Isaiah 9:8 ("The Lord sent a word unto Iacob, and
it lighted upon Israel"), invoking the etymological connection in the Hebrew
between the "word" and the plague: "[T]here the word is a judgement, and an
execution of the Judgement: for that word, that signifies, a *word* there, in the
same letters exactly signifies, a *pestilence*, a Calamity; It is a word and a blow;
but the word here [i.e., in the verse from 1 John 5:7–8], is *verbum caro*, that
Word which for our sakes was made ourselves" (5:141). Donne's thought moves

through three languages: the Hebrew DBR in Isaiah (signifying, as nearly all exegetes note, both "word" and "pestilence"), the Greek "logos" in the verse from 1 John, and the Latin gloss rendering "logos" as the "Word made flesh" (and also, now, through the Latin, as the "Word made *dear*"): *verbum caro*. As the Old Testament "word" is carried over into the New—in all the senses of "translation" I discuss below—the "same letters" take on a new, metaphorical significance, or, rather, they more fully reveal their spiritual significance (paradoxically, by taking on flesh). Thus fleshed out in the Son, the "word" (as the plague) must be understood not as the word of our infliction but as the Word of our salvation, and a promise of the resurrection (in the flesh).

In this light, the three sections of each of Donne's devotions—the "meditation," "expostulation," and "prayer" issuing from each stage of his illness and recovery—may be read not only as the conventional divisions of the meditative form invoking the senses, the reason, and the will, but as an exercise in triple translation, with each successive draft rendered into a "better language." Once each of these translations has reached its third draft, Donne more fully understands the particular "chapters" of his illness, all of which are bound up together as the book of his near death and his "preternatural birth, in returning to life, from this sickness" (dedication to Prince Charles). In moving from the account of his physical symptoms to an analysis of their spiritual significance and then to prayer, he hears, in the tolling of the bell, "that I was mortal and approaching to death"; but "[i]f that be thy language in this voice, how infinitely am I bound to thy Heavenly Majesty for speaking so plainly unto me . . . not [with] the voice of a judge that speaks by way of condemnation, but of a physician that presents health in that" (120). What he had first taken to be an unmitigated death sentence handed down by a "judge" is, in translation, a binding certificate of health presented by a "physician" greater than those who attend his bedside. His temporary recovery will point toward the ultimate healing that will be his when "death" is properly translated as eternal life, and he is himself translated into the divine library. In this sense, the *Devotions* participates in a collaborative exercise in translation, its author translating and being translated, with "God's hand" in "every translation."

The mutual "translation" of bodies and texts—in effect, a version of the school exercise of double translation, and in Donne's "practice" a qualifying exercise toward his own final translation at death—is facilitated by the greater range of the word in Donne's English than in our own. In its older

senses, the word *translation* has both literal and figurative or spiritual meanings beyond the rendering of a text from one language to another. From the
Latin *translatio imperii*, capital cities, empires, or the idea of empire itself
could be "translated" elsewhere. Persons may be "translated"—conveyed, carried across, promoted—from one place or condition to another (a bishop
to another see, the relics of a saint to a different resting place). Since "[b]y
faith Enoch was translated that he should not see death" (Hebrews 11:5), the
word serves as a type of the resurrection for those who do not (or hope not
to) die before their entry directly into heaven. According to Richard Hooker,
the Savior's own "Ascension into heauen" was "a plain locall translation of
Christ according to his manhood."[23] For Sir Thomas Browne, the word can
indicate a change of heart or an act of moral regeneration such as might
prepare one for that final ascension: "Time, Experience, self Reflexions, and
God's mercies, make in some well-temper'd minds a kind of translation before Death."[24]

Two other of the word's former uses also inflect Donne's "translations."
The rhetorical handbooks employ the word as a synonym for *metaphor*, as
signifying the transference or "carrying-across" of meaning, "a translation of
woordes frome their proper signification."[25] In this sense, the "metaphorical
God" of the *Devotions* works as a translator in the realm of sacred history
even before he binds up all the scattered leaves in heaven (124). Donne's divine translator is a figurative God not in his "words only," but in his "works
too." In the concatenation of his temporal works, "circumcision carried a figure of baptism, and baptism carries a figure of that purity which we shall
have in perfection in the new Jerusalem" (125). Like those "ancient servants,
whose delight it was to write after thy copy"—and the servants of King
James who worked on the translation Donne holds in his hands—Donne is
"pleased to speak to thee in such a language as thou wast pleased to speak to
them, in a figurative, in a metaphorical language" (125, 126). The way Donne
speaks metaphorically in this passage is to "call the comfort" he receives in
the "indication of the concoction and maturity" of his disease "a discovery

---

23. Hooker, *Laws*, 5.55.8.

24. Browne, *Christian Morals* 2:6, in *The Prose of Sir Thomas Browne*, 393.

25. Elyot, *Bibliotheca Eliotae*, s.v. "metaphora." See also Wilson, *Arte of Rhetorike*, 174: "Men vse
translation of wordes (called Tropes) for neede sake, when thei can not finde other." Bacon's *Advancement of Learning*, 1.7.17 (in *Francis Bacon*), refers to an "excellent use of a metaphor or translation."

of land after a long and tempestuous voyage" (126). Just as each subsequent and "better" translation of God's historical works (circumcision, baptism, the New Jerusalem) reveals a meaning of greater "purity," so Donne's translation of his latest symptom reveals more clearly in the figure of the voyage of discovery what this "indication" truly indicates. It is perhaps not coincidental that the figure of the "voyage" here employed translates Donne's recovery (as a prevision of the New Jerusalem, a passage in the voyage toward that destination) by means of a metaphor for translation itself, the conveyance of meaning into a new domain. In this light, the task of translating scripture into vernacular languages, and the like procedure of individual Christians "translating" their own experience according to the paradigms set forth in scripture, both participate in and are ultimately completed as part of God's larger project. As the fruit of a long process of translation, the library of the New Jerusalem will have finally acquired the world's definitive collection of "works"—those of God's own authorship, those written after his copy, and the copyists themselves, who, like Donne, have contributed to the project in book and body alike.

The second meaning of *translation*, now almost entirely lost from the language but worth resurrecting as a gloss on Donne's plague writing, more closely conjoins rhetoric and medicine. In the humoral vocabulary of the time, the word can specify the movement of corrupted humors into the brain (causing madness) or, more generally, the transference for better or worse of a disease, or of the "morbific matter" that causes disease, from one part of the body to another. One later medical dictionary refers back to this "translation" as a change in the "seat" of the disease.[26] The movement of such matter around the body could be characterized, in turn, as a "metastasis," a term already found in Hippocratic discourse but also as a rhetorical term in Quintilian. In this latter sense, George Puttenham calls "Metastasis" the "flitting figure, or the Remoue," and notes that "discretion" sometimes obliges us to "flit from one matter to another, as a thing meete to be forsaken, and another entred vpon"; and Angel Day says that "*Metastasis* or *Transitio*" is employed as a tactic for

---

26. The OED *Online* (s.v. "metastasis," 2) cites Robley Dunglison's *Dictionary of Medicine* (1857): a "translation" or a "change in the seat of a disease; attributed, by the Humorists, to the translation of the morbific matter to a part different from that which it had previously occupied. Earlier citations are from Robert Boyle ("Madness ... by the translation of the Humours into the Brain") and John Arbuthnot ("Translations of Morbific Matter in Acute Distempers").

abruptly shifting one's ground, as "when in briefe wordes we passe from one thing to another."[27]

These connections supply a context in which we can read Donne's "book . . . translated into a better language." *Translation* in its several early modern senses (metaphorical, medical, and rhetorical) taps into a mutually defining root system of metaphors from which Donne's plague language emerges. In the therapeutic sequence of translations that make up sacred history, the Egyptians were consumed by a plague, but in the end, God speaks not with "the voice of a judge . . . by way of condemnation, but of a physician that presents health." The divine Physician (as Donne imagines in another, undated sermon from the same period) runs the same risk of infection from his patients during plague times as does the earthly physician:

> Depart from me, O Lord, for I am sinful enough to infect thee: As I may persecute thee in thy children, so I may infect thee in thine ordinances; depart, in withdrawing thy word from me, for I am corrupt enough even to make thy saving Gospel, the savour of death unto death. . . . And if I be too foul for God himself to come near me, for his ordinances to work upon me, I am no companion for myself, I must not be alone with myself; for I am apt to take, as to give infection; I am a reciprocal plague; passively and actively contagious; I breathe corruption, and breathe it upon myself. . . . [I am not worthy] That thy Spirit should ever speak to my spirit, (which was the form of words, in which every communicant received the Sacrament, in the primitive Church, *Lord I am not worthy that thou shouldest enter under my roof*). (9:310–11)

If "plague" translates as the "word," and if it is inflicted by the Word of God, then it seems possible that those sinners it infects are so contagious as to contaminate the Gospel itself, and even to endanger God if he should approach too close. The corrupt sinner can, reciprocally, "corrupt" the word by misconstruing the *saving* Gospel as the *savour* of death. God can correct the error by restoring these words to their original meaning—not without the attendant

---

27. Puttenham, *The Arte of English Poesie*, 194. The OED *Online* (s.v. "metastasis," 1) cites the 1599 edition of Angel Day's *English Secretorie* (1586).

reciprocal irony that it is by the "savour of death," a prospect to be savored in the end, that the "saving" promise of the Gospel is to be fulfilled.

Just as the rhetoric of the St. Dunstan's sermon moves (metastatically) from "house" to "house," translating the text of Exodus from its application to the Egyptians to its significance for our families, for our bodies, and for the church, so the plague can be imagined as moving through the body of history as "morbific matter" that passes from one thing to another, but which will finally be expelled as the bodies that populate history are restored to health in the resurrection: a *metastasis* that will in the end come to rest in the *stasis* of eternity. In the St. Dunstan's sermon, Donne performs a number of small acts of translation to make this process clear. That "God might have changed the persons, and made the *Egyptians* the object of his *Mercies*, and us of his *Justice*," suggests not that God is capricious in his actions, but that his two great attributes proceed from the same Word, of which in any particular instance both "justice" and "mercy" are accurate renditions. Thus, "the death of Jesus Christ is the Physick of mankinde" (6:357), God's "tempest" is "refreshing" (6:360), and "putrefaction a perfume." The sermon's final transition requires the congregation to revise its translation of the text with which the preacher began: "For there was not a house in which there was not one dead." "But are they all dead? *They were*, says the text. . . . *They were dead*, but they are not" (6:362, 363). Some, to be sure, always will be dead: the Egyptians, and those in plague times today who are given over to their "lusts and wantonness" (6:359). But for the rest, the promise of the resurrection in the flesh—the translation of putrefaction into perfume—requires us to understand that in the heavenly library where every book shall lie open, there is "not one dead."

The Translation of Trauma

The trajectory of Donne's recovery from his illness of 1623 to the pulpit of St. Dunstan's two years later takes him from the "house" of his confinement to the "house" of God where the sermon is delivered. That he has regained his health—that, in his own house, there was *not* one dead, that he feels like a "Prisoner discharged," though still sitting at "the Prison dore"—he regards as an instance and a promise of the resurrection. The scheme of the sermon, moving from Pharaoh's "house" to the church where "[t]he Master of the house" is "Christ Jesus" (6:357), charts the same course across the broader expanse of scriptural history, since (as the famous conceit of the "beheaded man" at the beginning of "The Second Anniversary" illustrates [252, l. 9]) the Israelites' release from their Egyptian bondage and their safe passage to freedom prefigure the joyful translation of the soul over the red sea of death. In the house of the church, not only is there not one *dead*, but there is one *born*, for the "religious love of God, is the first-born of Religion, and this is Zeal. . . . [T]hat which makes me a Father, and gives me an off-spring, a first born, that's Zeal; By Religion I am an *Adam, but by Zeal I am an* Abel produced out of that Adam" (6:361). For the Christian, the death of the firstborn translates over time into the birth of the firstborn—a resurrection by which, remarkably, the preacher is the "Father" who gives birth to himself.

The ability of Donne's rhetoric to produce life out of death—to read both his own disease and the ensuing epidemic that provides the occasion of his preaching as ultimately therapeutic events—offers the key, I would argue, to his negotiation of the trauma of the plague. Not that Donne is unmindful that in 1625 "the hand of God fell upon thousands in this deadly infection" (6:259). As he tells his congregants, the savor of death hung in the streets, and even at that moment they might be breathing in the dust of their friends and relatives. But his specific list of those who were cut off by the plague is restricted to men who took advantage of it for (and to) their own sinful ends, "in their robberies, in half-empty houses; and in their drunkenness in voluptuous and riotous houses; and in their lusts and wantonness in licentious houses" (6:359). With no pause to imagine that the plague might drive people to desperate acts, the indictment also includes those who "broke into houses, and seeking the Wardrobes of others, found their own winding-sheet, in the infection of that house where they stole their own death" (6:359). These voluptuaries and housebreakers were not more "affected" by the plague than "those *Egyptians,*" and so it was their punishment to be infected, and to die a death from which they will never be revived (6:359). For Donne, in the historical translation of Egypt to London, the world seems to be divided into latter-day Egyptians "soaked in sin" (6:359) and condemned forever, and zealous Israelites for whom death will be the doorway to resurrection, with no moral grey area in between.

This moral certainty, framed within a rigid typological scaffold, allows Donne to remain untroubled by any doubts about the justice of a mass extermination such as would preoccupy other plague preachers and push the fundamental questions of theodicy to the point of collapse. For Donne, as we have seen, the door to such direct interrogation of the divine purpose is firmly barred in the face of a calamity not only "uncureable, uncontrollable, unexorable, but undisputable, unexaminable, unquestionable." But Donne's deeply skeptical refusal to engage directly in the questions of theodicy (plague does "not give a *reason* how it did come") only leads to another door that circumvents the issue entirely by "translating" plague into its opposite, and more perfect, meaning as an agent of redemption. Such perplexing questions as arise from the death of innocents and the immunity of the wicked are not to be adjudicated on a local scale. Donne is not concerned with the cases of individuals, or even of nations beset by the pestilence because of some accumulation of sin in recent years. For him, the plague is to be read in, and translated across, the widest sweep of sacred history. Just as the disease moves from house to house in the London of 1625, it has moved from the houses of Egypt to those of this city—which "we may call, *The Holy City*, as Christ called *Jerusalem*, though she had multiplied transgressions . . . she had not cast away his Law" (6:359)—each time translated into a better language, until finally it ushers the blessed "*into the Kingdom, prepared for you, from the beginning*" (6:366). Though we are born ruinous, the very debilitating consequences of our fall from the perfect health enjoyed in the garden fortunately provide for our salvation.

Donne's brilliance in elaborating this perspective stands as proof against the kinds of traumatic traces we have seen in other plague writing of the period. It represents, I would claim, the last "successful" accommodation of the plague to theology in the English seventeenth century. Its success is founded on its ability, within the set of assumptions driving it, to overcome the one crucial feature that marks an experience as traumatic in the first place: its resistance to being translated into other words. In Donne's view, any one outbreak forms one more link in a legible sequence of epidemics, each representing and represented in the others, and all of them under the supervision of a divine Physician pledged to restore his patients to health. The scheme incorporates the structure of traumatic repetition, but it disinfects it, as it were, by incorporating repetition within a coherent narrative design. Rather than experiencing repetition as an unsuccessful or blocked attempt to fit the traumatic event into the order of things, Donne's theology sees repetition as the very key to the integrity of that order. It is a vision that only a preacher of Donne's conviction and rhetorical skill could sustain.

CHAPTER 6

Writing the "*Great Plague*"

Pepys and Defoe

The "Great" Fire of 1666 marks a significant moment in the narrative of a newly "Great" Britain, one appropriately celebrated in the heroic verse of Dryden's *Annus Mirabilis*. As Erik Bond argues, the construction of the fire as epic anticipates and gives imaginative form to the epic project of reconstructing London itself.[1] The same is true of the "Great" Plague of the year before. During the Cromwell years, Andrew Marvell's *Upon Appleton House* had envisaged the nation as a "Table rase and pure," a blank canvas scoured of the incrustations of the past and ready to receive the image of a new order of things.[2] This had been achieved, in the end, not by the violence of the civil war, but by the two calamities of fire and pestilence, which had more ruthlessly cleared the land of buildings and their inhabitants than could any marauding army. The "houses" of London, to recur to the central allegory of Donne's St. Dunstan's sermon after the epidemic of 1625, had been turned into charnel houses by plague and fire. The city's dwellings and churches now had to be rebuilt physically and—for Donne's godly successors among the plague pamphleteers of 1665—spiritually, on the basis of tribulation and repentance. Along with the Dutch wars of the same decade, these two "great," if cataclysmic, events tested and purified a nation about to rise from its own sickbed and its own ashes. At this Miltonic moment between a world destroyed and a world restored, the center of England's social and economic gravity shifts even more decisively from the country houses earlier celebrated by Jonson and Marvell to the city that would, due in no small measure to the power of Samuel Pepys's Royal Navy, soon transform itself into the engine of empire. Together, all the great events of the latter seventeenth century—the Restoration, the fire and the plague, and the Glorious Revolution of 1688— precipitate a discursive shift in the worlds of politics, religion, literature, and (what will come to be called) science, after which, in retrospect, England will be seen to have emerged from the "early" modern period. In what follows, I want to read Pepys and Defoe on the plague as reflecting, each in his way, a transitional aspect of that emergence: an engagement with infectious disease that hovers between the providential and the quotidian.

Bond finds that Pepys's diary accommodates the fire—and, I would add, the plague—by collating its otherwise unaccountable horror with the ordinary

---

1. Bond, *Reading London*, xiii, xxi–xxii.
2. Marvell, *Poems and Letters*, 1:76, 1446.

events of a life that goes on, rather than by subsuming his individual experience to some great design. Closer to picaresque than to epic, the *Diary* offers a microhistory suited less to grand narrative than to local observation and chance encounters. Pepys tracks events at street level, notes the fluctuations in the death toll as published in the bills of mortality, and produces a record of the plague indexed to the daily activities of the writer. In this way, Pepys's diary entries for the plague year of 1665 are of a piece with the day-to-day accounts of H. F. in Daniel Defoe's *Journal of the Plague Year*, written in 1722, although with crucial differences in social perspective as well as in the proximity of the two narratives to the event itself. In the parlous years of the second Anglo-Dutch war, Pepys was pleased to be regarded as "the right hand of the Navy," the man responsible for provisioning the fleet, tallying the accounts of a complex and not incorruptible system of supply, and much else (89).[3] He was also a man on the make in every sense of the word, improving his estate even as he rationalized, and profited from, the business of the Naval Office. He was the table companion of such notable figures as the Duke of Albemarle, the Earl of Sandwich, and Commissioner of the Navy Sir William Penn, as well as the fondler and occasional bed companion of more than a few women, whose liaisons with the diarist are dutifully recorded.

Defoe's H. F., in contrast, is a small tradesman, a pious saddler given to worrying about his stock no less than the state of his soul. He roams the streets of London alone, reporting anecdotes, offering opinions, and recording the local details of the plague along with its aggregate tally. His view of the city is taken from, and focused on, a much humbler vantage point than Pepys's, although both are "walkers in the city" rather than observers from on high. Pepys prefers to travel by coach or by water. His observations of the plague are for the most part noted en route among his many important engagements. H. F. wanders on foot, lingering over and meditating at length on what he sees—since, with his saddlery shut down, he has nothing better to do. That the *Diary*, moreover, stands as a "living" record of the Great Plague only counterpoints the evident problem of authenticity in Defoe, whose part-documentary, part-fictive, narrative "recalls" the event almost six decades later. These accounts thus reflect two very different strategies of writing and two

---

3. *The Diary of Samuel Pepys*, ed. Latham and Matthews, 6:89. All quotations from Pepys's plague-year entries are from this volume and are cited parenthetically in the text.

different imaginative engagements with the plague of 1665. In comparison with the providentialist impulse by which most pamphleteers and divines had understood the plague, and by which many would continue to interpret (or, rather, reiterate the same arguments about) its theological "meaning" well into the following century, the *Diary* and the *Journal* presage an increasingly secular engagement with the same event—an engagement deprived of high theological drama, no longer exhaustively legible according to the biblical script of justice and mercy, but an engagement shadowed nonetheless by the remainder (and the reminder) of that depleted vision.

The Case of Pepys: Dallying and Tallying

In what follows, I read Pepys on the plague as reflecting an emergent response to infectious disease that hovers between the providential and the quotidian. I focus, first, on a *Diary* entry at the height of the Great Plague in which Pepys muses on an erotic dream that brings him "great pleasure." Second, I track an uncanny liaison in the entries for that plague summer between Pepys's running account of the weekly plague deaths, as posted in the bills, and the tallying up of his own increasing financial fortune—the latter an exercise that also brings him "great joy." In Pepys's text, these two pleasures together constitute allied forms of compensation, erotic and economic, for the terrors of the epidemic.

On August 15, 1665, after an early-morning visit to one of his naval suppliers, the hemp merchant George Cocke, Pepys records a "plague time" dream of the night before:

> Up by 4 a-clock and walked to Greenwich, where called at Captain Cockes and to his chamber, he being in bed—where something put my last night's dream into my head, which I think is the best that ever was dreamed—which was, that I had my Lady Castlemayne in my armes and was admitted to use all the dalliance I desired with her, and then dreamed that this could not be a wake but that it was only a dream. But that since it was a dream and that I took so much real pleasure in it, what a happy thing it would be, if when we are in our graves (as Shakespeare resembles it), we could dream and dream but such dreams as this—that then we should not need to be so fearful of death as we are this plague time. (191)

In its immediate content, this is not a plague dream. Its vision of unimpeded desire seems all the more powerful—indeed, possible at all—because all thought of danger seems banished from this midsummer night's dream. The connection to "this plague time" occurs as an afterthought; it is not clear whether Pepys's brief meditation on death might have formed part of the dream, if only as its subconscious basis, or whether it emerged in response to it, either at the time of the visit to Captain Cocke or, more likely, that evening, when the diary entry was set down. In any event, the fear of death casts its retrospective shadow on, and intensifies the erotic pleasure of, the remembered dream—which is itself bracketed in Pepys's entry between the "bed" and the "grave."

But what "something" put the dream into Pepys's head that morning? Was it the sight of Captain Cocke in bed, as Pepys had been just a few hours before when he had the dream? Or was it the thought that the "cock" awakens dreamers from their dreams, making them first aware that they were dreaming? Was it the apprehension that Cocke (whom Pepys evidently expected to find awake and ready to do business even at that early hour) might harbor the plague, in which case Pepys might be returned to his own bed, not perchance to dream but to fall into a pestilent delirium? Or was it perhaps the flickering thought of Pepys himself "in bed" with the king's notorious mistress Lady Castlemaine—where one might, perhaps, catch a disease passed on by a monarch Pepys elsewhere characterizes as "governed by his lust, and women"? If the latter, then the name "Cocke" may have played its role as a prompt, since if he were to enjoy free dalliance with Lady Castlemaine—for Pepys, the object of a fascination bordering on prurient obsession—he might justly regard himself as a "Captain [of] Cocke." Mingling erotic desire with infectious disease, the force of the dream's recollection is thus a potent blend of pleasure and fear compounded on different ways of lying: in one's bed, in the king's bed (a venture risking the royal displeasure, or even much worse), on one's deathbed, and (hence) "in our graves." The dream itself is experienced, or recalled, *as* a dream within the dream, doubly illusionary—this could not be happening—and yet, as the source of "real" pleasure just because it isn't happening, very likely an intense physical experience for the dreamer, *un petit mort*.

The fear of death, overt in "this plague time," also lurks in the allusion to Shakespeare. For Pepys—who had seen and admired Thomas Betterton in the role of Hamlet no fewer than three times in the previous five years[4]—the fantasy of dallying with my Lady Castlemaine might, in the Prince's words, be "a consummation / Devoutly to be wish'd" (3.1.8–9). But under cover of this "happy thing" imagined by Pepys is a partial, and repressed, memory of Hamlet's suicide soliloquy. An apprehension of what dreams may come, if it were possible to dream in the "sleep of death," should give Pepys pause if he were following Hamlet more closely. Reversing Hamlet's logic, Pepys allows himself to imagine that death itself might be a happy thing if it did not extinguish one's erotic dream-life—the wish, as it were, for a postmortem resurrection of the flesh. Unacknowledged in this allusion to *Hamlet* is the thought that bedding the king's mistress (with Lady Castlemaine in the role of a lascivious Gertrude) and coming into a man's bedchamber in plague time might be alternative forms of suicide. But Pepys prefers to dally with the notion that the "real pleasure" of his erotic fantasies might persist even after death, and with the hope that such posthumous satisfaction might mitigate the terrors of the grave. Pepys's Shakespearean moment faintly echoes the staging of the plague as tragedy. But in its overt form it fires his erotic imagination, restaging the scene as a comedy. The confusion between waking and dreaming in Pepys's account seems to transform Lady Castlemaine into a fairy queen, and the dreamer himself into a Bottom at the moment of his awakening—two central characters in a comedy Pepys had also seen, and one all the more erotically charged for being played out now under the shadow of death.[5] Like a play within a play, the encryption of Hamlet's grave soliloquy within the narrative of the recollected sex dream is of a piece with the *Diary* itself as the (literal shorthand) encryption of Pepys's imaginative life as a lover in plague time.[6]

---

4. Tomalin, *Samuel Pepys*, 136, 412 n. 7.

5. On September 29, 1662—soon after the theaters had reopened—the *Diary* notes that Pepys "saw 'Midsummer Night's Dream'" and found it "ridiculous" save for "some good dancing and some handsome women, which was all my pleasure." What Pepys may have seen, however, was a performance of *The Merry Conceited Humours of Bottom the Weaver* (1661).

6. Francis Barker uses a later but very similar moment in the *Diary* (Pepys's entry for February 9, 1668) as the keynote to his discussion of the "tremulous private body." In this entry, bracketed by reference at the beginning and end to a salacious book called *L'eschelle des filles*, which Pepys reads in the privacy of his chamber, is a memorandum that "Pegg Pen" was "brought to bed yesterday of a girl" and, in the same sentence, that people were only just getting back on the street after a particularly vicious two-month siege of smallpox. Pepys, according to Claire Tomalin, had earlier made "sexual advances" to the girl who was Sir William Penn's daughter, apparently as an act of spite against her father (*Samuel Pepys*, 143). Barker's Pepys is a much more tangled and guilty creature than mine, but significantly, at

The *Diary* records some of the most vivid—that is, most morbid—vignettes on record of the Great Plague of 1665. Some, like the dream of "my" Lady Castlemaine, commingle desire and death. In one, an amorous young man pokes his head into a passing coach, "believing there might be some lady in it that would not be seen," and there sees "somebody look very ill, and in a sick dress and stunk mightily" (181). In others, plague intrudes unexpectedly into Pepys's daily round, as when his hackney coachman slows down, informing his passenger that he was "suddenly stroke very sick and almost blind" (130–31). In June the diarist comes upon a harbinger of the fomenting epidemic: houses in Drury Lane marked with the red cross and the words "Lord have mercy on us" (120). In August, Pepys reports that the pestilence has claimed his physician, Dr. Burnett (203). In October he encounters searchers with their rods in hand coming out of the same Captain Cocke's house after having determined that the death of the captain's black servant was not due to the plague (283). Pepys wonders at "the madness of the people of the town, who will (because they are forbid) come in Crowds along with the dead Corps to see them buried" (211). Forced to walk home one dark night with a lantern, he is "in great fear of meeting some dead corses carrying to be buried" (199). But like the amorous young man in the plague vignette (and like Defoe's H. F.), he can also find himself drawn to forbidden sights. In the same turn of phrase that suggests the dead might still be animate, the entry for August 30 notes that Pepys himself, following a sudden impulse, "walked toward Moorefields to see (God forgive my presumption) whether I could see any dead Corps going to the grave; but as god would have it"—is he relieved or disappointed?—"did not" (207). He reports "an odd story," likely an urban legend passed infectiously from mouth to mouth, of an alderman "stumbling over a dead Corps in the street; and going home and telling his wife, she at the fright, being with child, falls sick and died of the plague" (187). The *Diary* is full of such notations, especially during the high plague months of August and September—of corpses in the street, of fears that so-and-so has fallen ill, of a distraught father spiriting his one remaining child out of a plague house in hopes of preserving him (202), of the awful tolling of the bells, and of the "sadder and sadder news" of the plague's increase as tracked by the numbers

the center of the "Pegg Pen" entry, as of the "Captain Cocke" entry, are the figures of furtive desire and epidemic infection conjoined in the same "bed." See Barker, *The Tremulous Private Body*, 3–14.

in the bills (208). Having heard that there were three thousand plague deaths during the first week of August, on the ninth Pepys decides to redraw his will, "the town growing so unhealthy that a man cannot depend upon living two days to an end" (187).

Yet the *Diary* suggests that during this very period, Pepys conducts himself as if he depended upon living forever, pursuing his Navy Board business, paying calls, shopping and wenching, all with a ferocious energy that belies (and, as he might have imagined, even wards off) the devastation around him.[7] Against the terror of death, the balance tips toward real pleasure. On Sunday, September 3, he writes, "I put on my coulour silk suit, very fine, and my new periwigg"; but "what," he wonders, "will be the fashion after the plague is done as to periwigs, for nobody will dare to buy any haire for fear of the infection—that it had been cut off the heads of people dead of the plague" (210). Intertwined with such grim musings about the perils of a future shopping trip is Pepys's running tally of his own financial good fortune. It emerges especially in the late summer months that profit, or the pleasure to be had from profit, is as effective against the plague as the dreamy pleasures of Lady Castlemaine. On August 13 he has set his affairs in order so as to be in a "much better state of soul" if "it should please the Lord to call me away this sickly time"; then, having done the math, he is delighted to find that he is worth "the sum of 2164£—for which the Lord be praised" (189–90). On the sixteenth, the day after his visit to Captain Cocke, he finds, to his "great joy," that he has "got home 500£ more of the money due" to him (193). On the thirtieth of August—having taken his walk toward Moorefields to see "any dead Corps going to the grave"—he sits up late to put his private accounts in order, and he discovers, again to his "great joy," that he is now worth £2,180, not counting plate and goods, which he values at another £250 (207). Toward the end of September, he reflects that even "in this sad time of plague, everything else hath conspired to my happiness and pleasure, more for these last three months then in all my life before in so little time" (240).

---

7. Tomalin cites a letter from Pepys to Lady Carteret in which Pepys seems to attribute his "perfect state of health" equally to "God's blessing and the good humours begot" by his active social life. Given the number of his reported contacts with corpses and infected individuals, Pepys may well have been immune to the plague. He once noted—without, of course, being able to realize the possible connection to the plague—that when he shared a bed with a friend, "all the fleas came to him and not to me." See Tomalin, *Samuel Pepys*, 175, 168.

Pepys's biographer wonders what to make of this "most noticeable fact" about her subject's plague year: "that it was one of the happiest of his life," a year in which he "worked long hours, profited by every opportunity to make money, and quadrupled his fortune." His days filled with energetic bustling, Pepys rolls along, she says, as if on an "adrenalin high" like that of "men and women at war or under bombardment." Whether measured by the space in the *Diary* devoted to his many cheerful pursuits, or by the emphasis he places on his many successes even in such dark times, the plague is "largely relegated to the background."[8] It is true that, preoccupied as he always was with business or pleasure, Pepys may have become inured to what loomed in the "background" of his excursions through the afflicted city. On the evening of August 15, the day that had begun with his early-morning visit to Captain Cocke, he "met a dead Corps, of the plague" being carried off—one of the many he was to encounter that season—but he is grateful to admit that he "was not much disturbed by it" (192). After all, he had just come from a very full social evening brimming with his "pleasure" in "getting some bills signed by Sir G. Carteret, and promise of present payment from Mr. Fenn [the Navy paymaster]; which doth rejoice my heart" (191–92). The combination of adrenaline and a dulled sense of horror, even if the "relegation" of the plague may be said to exemplify the traumatic suppression of that horror, cannot fully account for the balancing act performed by the *Diary* between the human debit recorded in the bills of mortality and the bills of payment credited to his account that same summer.

On Wednesday, August 2—"it being a public fast . . . for the plague"— Pepys spent the day indoors working on his "month's accounts" (179). The order for this fast (to be held on the first Wednesday of every month) exhorted the faithful to prayer and urged that "[t]he wealthier sort are earnestly moved to bestow the price of the Meal forborn, upon the poor."[9] But for Pepys, it was another day in a string that brought him "great joy"—a day for tallying up rather than dispensing his money, as he finds himself "really worth 1900£—for which the great God of heaven and earth be praised" (179–80). In the context of the *Diary*, this calculation comes two days after Pepys notes

---

8. Ibid., 170.

9. *A Form of Common Prayer, Together with an Order of Fasting, for the Averting of Gods Heavy Visitation upon Many Places of This Realm*, A2v.

(on July 31) that the plague toll for the previous week was "about 1700 or 1800," sad news "after the greatest glut of content that ever I had" (178). It also comes the day before he hears (on August 3) that the current bill numbers the dead at "2010 of the plague" (180). Given these two running totals—the misery of rising plague deaths on the one side of the ledger, the joy of Pepys's rising fortunes on the other—and given, too, Pepys's characteristic habit of cross-indexing the two lists, it is tempting to read the underlying logic of these journal entries as a kind of magical accounting procedure. The tallying of accounts—Pepys's public occupation—becomes his holiday task on this Wednesday, and something of a holy task as well, issuing in an exclamation of praise. It is as if there were a proper equation in Pepys's mind between the "great God" whose bounty has yielded Pepys his £1,900 and the "great joy" he feels as the worthy recipient of such largesse, the outward sign of his salvation. Perhaps coincidentally—but what a "great" coincidence it would be—the sum he arrives at for his own fortune is almost exactly the average of the two figures for plague deaths entered before and after he does his books. It is as if the £1,900 on the plus side of his personal ledger somehow balances out and compensates for the number of plague deaths entered in the bills of mortality—God's ledger, as it were. For Pepys, then, plague can be factored into (or out of) a system of sacred economics that also resolves, in its way, the question of divine justice, since God would appear to redeposit with Pepys what he withdraws from the accounts of others less fortunate, like the stricken hackney driver and the stinking woman in the coach.

On Sunday, November 5, late in the season but with the plague still increasing "much at Lambeth, St. Martin's and Westminster," and so raising the "fear it will [spread] all over the city," Pepys "heard the Duke of Albemarle's chaplin make a simple sermon: among other things, reproaching the imperfection of humane learning, he cried: 'All our physicians cannot tell what an ague is, and all our arithmetique is not able to number the days of a man;' which, God knows, is not the fault of arithmetique, but that our understandings reach not the thing" (289). While the chaplain's point recalls Donne's skepticism about the reach of our knowledge, Pepys's gloss reflects a proto-Newtonian assurance of an underlying mathematical, and hence moral, order in the world. Our understanding may be limited, but the "arithmetique" remains perfect, faultless, and just—a divine instrument, something "God knows" even if we don't, as Pepys is able to calculate for himself in the running balance of the *Diary*.

As a professional man of numbers, Pepys seems particularly interested in recording this sermon, one of the few to find its way into the pages of the *Diary*. There are, then, two sets of books by which a scrupulous accountant can rely on human learning to "number the days": the public tally of the Navy Office finances, and the private tally of Pepys's own fortunes. The sums of the one, insofar as they concern his own income, are factored into the other. There, however, they are transmuted into a kind of spiritual capital—not only as the evidence of God's favor, but as a transcription, however imperfect, of God's own faultless accounting procedures, and a kind of arithmetic proof of the justness of things. Like Crusoe weighing the "Evil" against the "Good" of his own condition—tabulating his "comforts" against his "miseries" very "impartially, like debtor and creditor"—Pepys adapts the form of the balance sheet to his own private account.[10] A diary in code, in effect a secret ledger, thus allows Pepys to "tell" (his days, his fortunes, his adulteries) without "telling."

It is tempting to make much of the encryption of the *Diary*, as if Pepys's shorthand were not only the means of recording his (ill-concealed) amours but their writerly analogue, forms of secrecy in word and deed. Clearly, Pepys did not expect his diary to fall into other hands (neither did he burn it in the end), but if it had done so in his own day, it would likely not have been regarded as deeply mysterious. Although his shorthand manuscript was not deciphered by scholars until the nineteenth century, Pepys employed a well-known system first published in Thomas Shelton's *Short Writing* in 1626 and, under the titles *Tachygraphy* or *A Tutor to Tachygraphy*, reissued in at least thirteen editions during the diarist's lifetime.[11] Even Pepys's habit of alluding

---

10. Defoe, *The Life and Adventures of Robinson Crusoe*, 83.

11. The edition I have consulted is Thomas Shelton, *Short Writing the Most Exact Methode* (1630). One of the ironies of Pepys scholarship is that Victorian scholars labored painstakingly over the diary without realizing that the key to its cipher, Pepys's own copy of Shelton, was among the collection of his own books preserved in Magdalene College (Tomalin, *Samuel Pepys*, 383–85). Pepys's one recorded comment on secret writing is contained in his reply to a letter received in 1682 from one Nathaniel Vincent, a fellow of Clare Hall, asking his opinion about the usefulness of a vanishing ink of Vincent's own invention for preserving the secrecy of diplomatic correspondence. Pepys answers—politely, if tongue in cheek—that the point of such correspondence is not to vanish but to be preserved for the record. Furthermore, if the recipient of such a letter did not know the secret of the disappearing ink, how could he reply in kind? And if he did, then the method would be secret no longer (*Letters and the Second Diary of Samuel Pepys*, 145–46). Shelton's system itself was preceded by earlier ones, frequently republished, that were first devised by Timothy Bright (*Characterie: An Arte of Shorte, Swifte and Secrete Writing by Character*, 1588); John Willis (*The Art of Stenography*, 1603); and Edmond Willis (*An Abbreviation of Writing by Character*, 1618).

to the fondling of maidservants in pidgin French or Spanish is transparent, while his close friends (not to mention his long-suffering wife, Elizabeth) had no need of the *Diary* as evidence of his philandering. However much the *Diary* has acquired, for us, an aura as the repository of a buried life, its author would have been among "those many hundreds" who, as Shelton claims, were already practicing his shorthand, who had become proficient in it "with few houres paynes," and who could thus have easily deciphered Pepys's text if they had happened to stumble across it.[12] Arguably, at the end of a long and full day, Pepys may have found the system congenial as much for its convenience as for its apparent secrecy. Nonetheless, the *Diary* might be described in other terms as the site of Pepys's private meditations, a text in which the details of his public life are reproduced but in a form excluded from public view, as an *aide-mémoire*—one of the uses of the shorthand system—and as the material for his own intimate reflection. Its mode is both stenographic, in being a personal daybook not unlike the public accounts for which Pepys was responsible in the Naval Office, and confessional. In its tally of his daily joys and sorrows, it served its author as the secular equivalent of a spiritual autobiography.

For the advantage of Shelton's system, as its deviser intended, was its facility as a means of recording sacred matters. In this, Shelton followed the lead of his predecessors in the art of stenography. For example, the ninth edition of John Willis's *Art of Stenography* (1628) ends with a long list of exemplary sentences to be transcribed into shorthand for practice. These are compiled for the most part from biblical passages, moral proverbs, and other homiletic material such as the student might actually encounter in church. Shelton's system was commonly used, likely by Pepys himself, for taking notes on sermons.[13] A table at the beginning of *Short Writing* lists a number of symbols for whole words (*angel, Christ, congregation, covenant, devil*, and so on through the alphabet) indispensable for such a purpose. According to Shelton, his method has in this regard "already declared it selfe vsefull in the service of the Church."[14] His one reference to the secrecy of his shorthand script, in a preface titled "To the Christian Reader," implies that it will be a secret only to

---

12. Shelton, *Short Writing*, A3v–4r.
13. Tomalin, *Samuel Pepys*, 40, 396 n. 9.
14. Shelton, *Short Writing*, A1v.

non-Christians, since it affords "the great priviledge that many Marchants and others in forraine parts inioy, having to my knowledge whole Testaments and Bibles written by this Art, who vse them without feare or danger of bloudie Inquisiters."[15] The appeal to merchants and travelers to foreign parts may suggest why Pepys was made aware of the system in the first place.

Pepys thus appropriates Shelton's technique, but the *Diary*'s relation to the original purposes of Shelton's script is more complex. On the one hand— perhaps like other diaries of the period so kept, and now lost—Pepys's *Diary* represents a moment in a history of the secularization of shorthand. Systems originally intended to facilitate note-taking at sermons would come to be employed by parliamentary journalists, court reporters, and eventually by secretaries in business offices. In the context of the *Diary*'s main business, Pepys's occasional pious phrases ("I thank God I was not much disturbed by it"), albeit more frequent during the plague months than in other periods, seem less heartfelt than merely conventional. His engagement is with the ordinary rather than the extraordinary. There seem to be no other dimensions to his world, however colorful and populous, than those bounded by the Navy Office, the court, and the cityscape traversed in the course of his appointments, official and recreational. For a man in a hurry, shorthand offers the most practical and expeditious form of writing. On the other hand, in 1665 Pepys seems no less concerned than Clapham, Jonson, Dekker, and the host of plague preachers to work out the logic of God's justice at a time when he seems to require an appalling number of lives to balance the divine books. The scriptural economics of these writers—calculations of the debts to be repaid in lives, the necessity of repentance to balance the ledger of sinfulness—now reemerges in Pepys but as economics per se, inscribed in a cipher that, according to Shelton, others had used to keep their copies of scripture away from inquisitive eyes. The divine account book of the earlier writers has become literal and material for Pepys. Rather than in (and as) the Word, for Pepys the plague is justified arithmetically.

The *Diary* thus indexes the plague to the erotic and the economic, the two most potent forces in the writer's life, and the two sources of his greatest pleasure. Between these two poles, the plague's terror is suspended, the divine tragedy rewritten as the human comedy. With death on every side of him,

---

15. Ibid., A4r.

Pepys regards his own prosperity if not as the sign of his election, then surely as the mark of God's favor and, moreover, as itself the source of his deepest "joy." Though he himself does not take a wider view of the matter, his personal (good) fortune is linked to the prosperity of the maritime power he is helping to create, and thus to a narrative of imperial expansion foreseen by the plague writers of 1603 in their conviction that the pestilence had wiped the slate clean and prepared the way for the nation's future greatness. Equally, Pepys's pleasure in plague time stems from his amatory prosperity (whether real or "real"), tallied in the number of kisses stolen and bosoms furtively caressed. The only theological speculation about an afterlife to be glimpsed in his entries for the plague year is the diarist's wish that you could take it with you after all, if only as the posthumous dream of a liaison with Lady Castlemaine.

The Case of Defoe: Rehearsing the Plague

Most of the critical questions provoked by Defoe's *Journal* stem directly or indirectly from the problem of the author's relation to his own account, published in 1722, some fifty-seven years after the Great Plague. Both Pepys and Defoe record the same mortality figures—whether freshly posted, in the case of the *Diary*, or retrieved much later by Defoe, who bolstered his history by including the texts of official proclamations and by carefully tabulating mortality statistics from the published bills. As testimony to the long shelf life of plague anecdotes, both also report the kinds of stories circulating since Elizabethan times: of apparently healthy people suddenly stricken, or falling down dead upon hearing the news that a loved one has died, of the horror and allure of mass graves. Pepys's *Diary* for 1665 may well be unique in the history of plague writing for its unexpected cheerfulness in the face of disaster. Nonetheless, it bears the stamp of a straightforward and unquestioned authenticity as the stenographic transcript of observations set down daily and within hours of the event. As a matter of biographical and generic concern alike, the diagnosis of Defoe's case seems far more difficult. Where is Defoe in this anonymously personal, distantly immediate work, and what kind of work is it: history, novel, historical novel, spiritual autobiography, moral tract, practical advisory, or some mélange of all these forms, *sui generis*? The formal answer matters less than an understanding of the ways in which the *Journal* adapts all these genres to its own complex strategy of mediating the plague.

In 1722, Defoe's book would have found an audience along with a number of other works produced in response to an outbreak of the plague in Marseilles and the subsequent apprehension among the English that the epidemic might spread across the Channel. These publications included journalistic reports on the progress of the plague in France, medical treatises advising due precautions and remedies, and reprints of older works going back to Elizabethan times. The physician Nathaniel Hodge, whose *Loimologia*, a history of the Great Plague, was first published in Latin in 1671 and later translated into English, provided one of Defoe's main sources.[16] A journal "Never made publick before" and purportedly written (as Defoe's title page announces) by "a Citizen who continued all the while in London" during the epidemic would surely have been a marketable addition to this literature, especially as it appeared to promise fresh material rather than a recycled publication, to document "Occurrences, as well Publick as Private" and to offer both practical and moral advice based on an eyewitness account. Thus, it has been possible for F. Bastian to make the classic case that Defoe's "object, after all, was to pass off the *Journal* as a genuine record of the Plague, able to stand the scrutiny of those who could themselves recall those days." To this end, Defoe is careful to ballast the work with "a considerable mass of first-hand information, critically sifted by an acute mind."[17] Nor would the admixture of fiction necessarily jeopardize this intention, for, in the view of a like-minded critic who sees the author working at the "nexus" of fiction and history, Defoe "regularly employed fiction in history; his historical texts suggest that he conceived of fiction as a legitimate strategy in historical representation."[18] Defoe's H. F. dismisses such questions, however, in the service of a more urgent practical purpose, insisting that if his readers should "be brought to the same distress" by another plague, "this account may pass with them rather for a direction to themselves to act by than a history of my actings." Disclaiming any attempt to "pass off" a fictional confection as an authentic record kept by a Londoner in 1665, the *Journal* here imagines itself as a document analogous to the kind of "pass" H. F. refers to on the same page:

---

16. Hodge, *Loimologia, sive, Pestis nuperae apud populum Londinensem*. See Mayer, "The Reception of *A Journal of the Plague Year*," on the plague literature of 1722.

17. Bastian, "Defoe's *Journal of the Plague Year* Reconsidered," 166.

18. Mayer, "The Reception of *A Journal of the Plague Year*," 532.

a certificate of health that allows the bearer to pass safely out of the plague-ridden city.[19] As such, it would be a companion piece to Defoe's *Due Preparations for the Plague*, published in the same year; the two works drew upon the same material and were produced for the same readers eager for guidance under the cloud of a looming epidemic. H. F.'s running commentary on the effects, for better or worse, of public health measures taken in 1665 pointedly addresses the contemporary debate about the government's policy in the face of the threat from Marseilles.[20]

If, in this view, the *Journal* is firmly rooted in the year of its publication—and not without a hint of opportunism on the author's part—an equally compelling case can be made for the importance of its origin in the experience of a child going on six years old. Although the evidence suggests that the family of young Daniel Foe may have removed from London during the plague summer of 1665, that journey in itself would likely have its influence on the themes of flight and of Londoners' reception in the country so prominent in the *Journal*.[21] Daniel's uncle Henry Foe—who shares the initials of his name with Defoe's narrator, H. F.—remained in London. It is very probable, as Bastian concludes, that Henry Foe "must have been the source of some of the anecdotal material" that would ultimately make its way into the *Journal*: "incidents actually involving H.F., or witnessed by, or taking place near his home in Whitechapel High Street, are prima facie those most likely to have had this origin."[22] All this must remain speculative in the absence of direct evidence, but everything we know about the childhood experience of such an event, of its enduring traumatic residue, and of the persistent need for recollection even after many years (and especially in the face of the same recurrent threat) collapses the distance between 1665 and 1722. The *Journal* serves not only to "give order and form to events only vaguely and chaotically remembered," as Defoe's editor Anthony Burgess notes in his introduction to the book, but

---

19. Defoe, *A Journal of the Plague Year*, ed. Burgess and Bristow, 29. All quotations from the *Journal* are from this edition and are cited parenthetically in the text.

20. Defoe "supported the quarantine provisions of the Quarantine Act [promulgated by the Walpole government] while opposing its domestic clauses" (Slack, *Impact of Plague*, 335). Restrictions on foreign trade and the quarantine of ships served the public good, but, as the *Journal* argues by "historical" example, the shutting up of houses and other forcible means of control such as were practiced in France tend to be both ineffective and cruel, as Defoe also argues in *Due Preparations*.

21. Bastian, "Defoe's *Journal of the Plague Year* Reconsidered," 160.

22. Ibid., 165.

to "recover those events in all their chaos from the vagueness of time" (14). What the text represents as a historical event is present to its author in a far more immediate sense. He engages it by returning to the scene in the guise of H. F., a mediating figure of indeterminate age, though as a grown man in 1665 "now" surely dead. At times H. F. seems far removed from the epidemic he has, fortunately, survived, as when he notes that there are still "some ancient persons alive in the parish" who can confirm his observations of a burial pit long covered over (78). At times he seems to be in the very midst of the ca-lamity, as when, in the same passage, he seems to report rather than to recall why the pit was needed "now," even as the decision was being made: "But now, at the beginning of September, the plague raging in a dreadful manner, and the number of burials in our parish increasing . . . they ordered this dreadful gulf to be dug" (78). "I remember," he says, "and while I am writing this story, I think I hear the very sound of it"—the "most dismal shrieks and outcries of the poor people" (74). Wandering the streets of the city, H. F. is at once a reflective adult and an anxious and impressionable man-child, as if "his" nar-rative proceeded from a composite voice blending that of young Daniel, Uncle Henry, and the mature Defoe.

Thus divided in its point of view between 1665 and 1722, the narrative tends to slip between past and present. For example, H. F.'s story of the three men who flee to the countryside will be useful to us "in case the like public deso-lation should happen here" (77). Anachronistically, that very desolation has already happened "here," in the London of fifty-seven years ago. If we try to imagine H. F. as writing some years afterward during "his own" lifetime, then he might be concerned about a possible epidemic in, say, 1670 or 1680. But at the same time (or, rather, at a different time), his warning clearly alludes to the specific event he could not possibly live to see, the Marseilles plague of 1722. Even more disconcertingly, near the end of a list of plague burial grounds that (unlike those remaining "in use until this day") have been "converted into other uses or built upon afterwards" (240), we learn that H. F. himself lies in a certain "piece of ground in Moorfields" (241):

[N.B.—The author of this journal lies buried in that very ground, being at his own desire, his sister having been buried there a few years before.] (242)

More than any other in the *Journal*, this one sentence has proved to be a minor but annoying editorial crux. Some editions follow the early printed texts in setting this comment off in brackets, as here, while others leave it as part of the main narrative. The problem would seem to lie in deciding just who is speaking. Earlier, H. F. tells us that he "had an only sister in Lincolnshire" who would have been "very willing to receive" him if he were to flee from London. When, and by whom, are we now informed that this sister had evidently come down to London some time before her death? And that she lies buried next to her brother? It may be Defoe "himself"—perhaps in the guise of some fictional redactor of the *Journal* who appears only here.[23] If the brackets are removed, it must be H. F. himself speaking from the grave, or beyond (as some carted away before their time were said to do). The whole comment—which reads like a "note to self" that somehow survived into the final draft—may be written off, in the view of some critics, as an instance of Defoe's carelessness or haste, rather than taken as an attempt to produce some conscious, if odd, effect. Apparently unconcerned that the remark breaks the frame of the fiction, Defoe may perhaps have felt it necessary or useful for some reason to supply this particular piece of "information," if only to ground his fictional "Citizen" more firmly in the real London of 1722. Yet such remarks, even if (or especially if) hasty and not consciously intended, may be telling nonetheless, although what they have to tell must remain, like H. F.'s gravesite, largely obscured.

The effect of this floating timeline, the narrative counterpart of H. F.'s wanderings around the city, is to transform H. F. into a vagrant consciousness, restless in space and time, until he is (said to be) laid to rest in Moorfields— the site of the plague pit where Pepys had imagined he might see a "dead Corps going to the grave." In this uncanny sense—uncanny in that he is both a familiar tradesman and a hovering voice, *in* but not *of* his moment, affiliated with, but not identified with, Defoe's uncle Henry, strangely immune to the pandemic felling his neighbors but already interred in a plague burial ground,

---

23. Defoe, born in 1660, had two slightly older sisters, Mary (1657) and Elizabeth (1659), of whom nothing is known except the dates of their birth as recorded in James Foe's parish church in St. Giles, Cripplegate. It would be intriguing to know whether either had died before 1722, and if so, where she lay buried, as a possible clue to the cameo appearance of a "sister" in H. F.'s account.

never really alive but already reported "dead" before the conclusion of his narrative—H. F. haunts the cityscape of the *Journal*. Seen through the eyes of this liminal figure, Defoe's account of the plague, however "factual," presents itself as an apparitional narrative, as Jayne Elizabeth Lewis has argued.[24] Drawing upon a long and contentious history of apparitions to which he had also contributed—for example, in the pamphlet of 1705, attributed to him, titled *A True Relation of the Apparition of one Mrs. Veal*, or in his *Political History of the Devil* (1726)—Defoe himself published *An Essay on the History and Reality of Apparitions* in 1727. Following Michael McKeon, Lewis sees the discourse of the "apparitional" in Defoe's time as negotiating a changing relationship between metaphysics and epistemology—between, that is, a waning belief in the "reality" of the spirit world, often adduced as proof of the existence of God, and a nascent empiricism that has still not abandoned the spirit world but seeks to ground its "appearances" in natural phenomena. For McKeon, this shift is fundamental to the rise of the novel; for Lewis, it also provides the key to the spectral aura of Defoe's narrative in the *Journal*, particularly with regard to the status of the plague. The plague is itself invisible, revealing itself only in the appearance of its tokens on the body of the afflicted; this apparitional status, mysterious at its heart but making itself visible in the material world, allows Defoe to consider the causes as both natural and supernatural without contradiction.[25] Conjured up in the spirit of such ghost writing, H. F. speaks to us as an apparition that, as Defoe will describe such phenomena in his *Essay on the History and Reality of Apparitions*, "assumes the shape and appearance of [a] man himself."[26] As Lewis notes, elsewhere in the *History* Defoe will consider it absurd to believe that apparitions are human souls "remaining in a wandering, unsettled state after life," for if that were so, then "the habited and visible world would have been continually haunted with ghosts, and we should never have been quiet."[27] His reason, however, can only strengthen our sense that H. F.—were he "alive" in the first place—would speak to us as just such a wandering soul, for the plague city he both inhabits and conjures up is, in every sense of the word, unsettled and unquiet. Defoe's apparitional H. F. is

---

24. Lewis, "Spectral Currencies in the Air of Reality."
25. Ibid., 94.
26. Quoted in Lewis, "Spectral Currencies in the Air of Reality," 89.
27. Quoted in Lewis, "Spectral Currencies in the Air of Reality," 86.

less the harbinger of an epistemological shift in the history of the novel than the dystopian heir to More's Raphael Hythloday, the ageless time traveler and seemingly disembodied reporter who has cut all his worldly ties, who is everywhere and nowhere at once in Utopia, and who reports the Utopians' belief that the dead walk among them. Like Hythloday, H. F. is a wanderer and a pilgrim (More's *peregrinus*), but one with no "healing wisdom" to impart and no utopian destination in view.

Lewis's suggestive identification of the *Journal* as an "apparitional" narrative, I would argue, is also symptomatic of a more fundamental traumatic narrative that produces the figure of H. F. as its simulacrum. The depths of that narrative are to be found in the "great pit of our churchyard in the parish of Aldgate," a "terrible pit" forty feet long and fifteen or sixteen feet wide. Just as Pepys is drawn to the burial pit at Moorfields, so H. F. cannot resist his "curiosity to go and see it," although he has the sense that to do so may put him in "apparent danger" (77). Indeed, he goes twice: first in the daytime, just when the pit is opened in the first week of September, and then again "about the 10th of September." This second time, he resolves to go after dark—and in spite of a "strict order to prevent people from coming to those pits"—for during the day the bodies are immediately covered with loose earth, but "in the night" it is possible to "see some of them thrown in" (79). The "danger" of such an expedition lay not only in the risk of infection but in the possibility of arrest, since the "strict order" was also intended to thwart the infected and delirious who would otherwise "run to those pits, wrapt in blankets or rugs, and throw themselves in, and, as they said, bury themselves" (79). Under cover of night, and in the company of those who would "throw themselves in," H. F. seems impelled by a like desire to join (or rejoin) the dead—a desire unacknowledged but more urgent than an idle, or even prurient, "curiosity." Not to be dissuaded from his expedition, H. F. tells the sexton, "I had been pressed in my mind to go" (79). When the dead cart appeared with its gruesome load, H. F. could "no longer resist [his] desire of seeing it, and went in" (80).

This descent into the underworld seems to occur twice, in the same narrative moment. First, there are the two visits in early September of the plague year, between the time when the pit was opened for burials on the sixth and when (having quickly reached its capacity of "1114 bodies") it was filled in again, by the twentieth (78). Immediately following the precise notation of these dates, H. F. seems concerned to certify its present location (in 1722), as well as the veracity of his own account, in the passage I have cited above: "I doubt not but there may be some ancient persons alive in the parish who can justify the fact of this, and are able to show even in what place of the church-yard the pit lay better than I can" (78). It is as if we are asked to return to the scene, now in company with "some ancient persons alive (among them H. F. himself, posthumously "alive"), to exhume the past. From the vantage point of 1722, the churchyard, like Defoe's text, becomes a kind of palimpsest: under a layer no thicker than the six feet of earth concealing the remains of the pit lie those ancient persons of 1665, the horror of their deaths undecomposed by time and fresh for retrieval. In this light, H. F.'s "desire" becomes a rehearsal in both senses of the word—a preparation for, and a reenactment of, his own death, the desire of those "near their end" who would "bury themselves." Presented with our two case studies, H. F.'s narrative and Pepys's dream, an ana-lyst might well discern the symptoms of survivor's guilt and a latent death wish, but her diagnosis would in turn be grounded in, and prepared for by, such pre-Holocaust documents as these plague texts.

Everything about this episode is vastly overdetermined, its urgencies in-visible, or, like the pull of a black hole, visible only in the attraction to it of everything in its orbit. What does it "say" to the third ear? Unable to dis-suade H. F. from entering the churchyard, the sexton advises him that the pit will at least provide "an instructing sight, that might not be without its uses"—in effect, "a sermon," and "the best that ever you heard in your life": "'Tis a speaking sight,' says he, 'and has a voice with it, and a loud one, to call us all to repentance': and with that he opened the door and said, 'Go, if you will'" (80). The "voice" from the pit—the voice of the dead, and of H. F.—says nothing of repentance, however. Instead, the only voice to be heard is that of a distraught man who followed the death cart containing "his wife and several of his children," and he "said nothing as he walked about, but two or three times groaned very deeply and loud, and sighed as he would break his heart" (80). This father, unlike Ben Jonson, will not have the consolation of hearing his son speak from the grave. Having witnessed the bodies of his family "shot into the ground promiscuously," the man "cried out aloud" once more. "I could not hear what he said," H. F. recalls, but the man "fell into a swoon" and was carried off by the buriers to a nearby tavern, where he "was known, and where they took care of him" (80). Rather than the "sermon" anticipated by the sex-ton, the man's unspeakable grief provides the only instruction offered by the pit. Nor is there any call to repentance, or any indication that the bereaved father or husband has anything so grievous to repent as may have provoked the divine vengeance to claim his entire family. In the end the man is carried from the churchyard to a tavern, where human "care," rather than godly ministration, will provide the only comfort to be had. Perhaps coincidentally, this unfortunate man's brief journey from the church to the tavern reverses the course of the Canterbury pilgrims. In the wake of the Black Death, Chaucer's company of survivors wends its way from the *taverna* to the *tabernaculum* (and, symbolically, from the earthly to the heavenly city) to venerate the saint who "hem hath holpen, whan that they were seeke." Beyond any help except human consolation, Defoe's survivor can only return to the ordinary world. The sexton has "opened the door" to a chamber buried in the very heart of H. F.'s narrative where Christian consolation cannot penetrate, and where its failure to do so is itself unspeakable.

The sight of this "dreadful gulf" (78), a sight that H. F. recalls (or relives) as "awful and full of terror" (81), may be said to register a proto-Burkean moment in the history of the sublime. The sexton leads us to expect the pit at Aldgate to be a site of revelation, a "speaking sight . . . to call us all to repentance" (80). That it does not so speak suggests that we regard this moment (like that also suggested in Lewis's "apparitional" narrative) as transitional in the history of Enlightenment secularism. In Defoe's account of the pit, the depleted but still terrifying presence of the divine haunts a landscape where all but the voices of human suffering have fallen silent.[28] If, as James Berger has argued, we are to think in turn of the experience of the "sublime" (in its terror, in its vastness, in its exceeding what can be represented or accommodated to ordinary experience) as a precursor of what we now call the traumatic, we can appreciate the power of this "black hole" to impel the narrator to revisit it.[29] It is unspeakable (as modern horrors are) because the "voice" promised by the sexton, the "sermon" that would draw out its meaning, no longer speaks from its depths (80).

---

28. Gary Hentzi follows Thomas Weiskel (*The Romantic Sublime*, 14) in characterizing the relationship in Defoe between the later, "basically empirical idea [of the sublime] and its religious antecedents" as "a displacement of traditional attributes of the divine, like immensity or infinity, onto the world of sensory experience and especially such natural phenomena as seem to approximate those qualities" ("Sublime Moments," 421).

29. Berger, "Trauma and Literary Theory," 573.

An oddly parallel moment occurs when H. F. moves from the scene of burial to the scene of writing, in a passage marked once more by the "incessant roarings" and "lamentable cries" of the afflicted, now to be heard in the streets:

> Terrified by those frightful objects, I would retire home sometimes and resolve to go out no more; and perhaps I would keep these resolutions for three or four days, which time I spend in the most serious thankfulness for my preservation and the preservation of my family, and the constant confession of my sins, giving myself up to God every day, and applying to him with fasting, humiliation and meditation. Such intervals as I had I employed in reading books and writing down my memorandums of what occurred to me every day, and out of which afterwards I took most of this work as it relates to my observations without doors. What I wrote of my private meditations I reserve for private use, and desire it may not be made public on any account whatever.
>
> I also wrote other meditations upon divine subjects, such as occurred to me at that time and were profitable to myself, but not fit for any other view, and therefore I say no more of that. (94)

H. F. has once again passed through a door, moving from a streetscape of a pain that, as Elaine Scarry reminds us in *The Body in Pain*, has no adequate language to an inner realm of reading and writing—in fact, into the very room where the *Journal* is composed, a retreat into intelligibility. His resolution "to go out no more" characterizes this retreat as a voluntary quarantine and, more darkly, as a voluntary entombment. Spiritual exercises seem to occupy most of his time during these periods of solitude. Such "intervals" as may present themselves between apparently lengthy sessions of thankfulness, meditation, and confession are employed for the purpose of two writing projects, each involving texts we are *not* privileged to see. The first leads to an account of his "observations without doors," in fact the published journal we hold in our hands. Excluded from the published *Journal* ("public" in both its subject and its destination in print), although evidently drawn up from the same "memorandums," are "private meditations" reserved for the author's own use. Although the *Journal* emerges from the memorandums, the two documents are thus not identical, as we are, by the "author's" own account, privileged to see only a censored version. The second project, entirely suppressed, consists of a collection of "other meditations upon divine subjects." These latter writings are apparently not worked up from the rough draft of his daily memorandums but are, rather, such "as occurred to me at that time." Both sets of meditations are hedged with repeated warnings against their exposure: they are for "private use," "not fit for any other view"; unrecounted because, as H. F. insists most vehemently, they are not to "be made public on any account whatever."

Such self-censorship seems all the stranger as the one exception to the advertisement of Defoe's title page: that the *Journal* will offer a record of "Occurrences, as well Publick as Private." The question is less what is withheld in these documents than why, if discretion or some other reason for secrecy were at issue, would H. F. risk the reader's curiosity by alluding to their existence at all? By contrast, Pepys sees no reason to keep secrets from himself (as his only anticipated reader), although Francis Barker would argue that he does so unconsciously; Pepys's shorthand, as we have seen, was largely a stenographic convenience rather than a means of encryption.[30] Donne's devotions were always intended for the press. H. F., however, seems intent on his self-imposed quarantine as a means not only of protecting himself from infection—that is to say, from contact with others out of doors—but of securing an utterly private place, one off-limits to future readers as well. There is something he wants to say that he dare not say, and he wants us to know that he dare not say it. He seems further intent on marking that place *as* private, as if to provoke the same desire in us by which he was himself impelled to ignore the "strict order" warning the curious away from the great pit. Like the pit, this place is a "speaking sight" that does not speak, a place where words are buried, a place-marker for the traumatic crypt. Here, though, there is no sexton to open the door to these "intervals"—gaps in the time of the narrative to match the lacunae in the text. Such a narrative requires an "apparitional" narrator, one who has visited the place of the dead and returned to (not) tell the tale.

I think it is possible to argue, as I have suggested before, that the plague pit prefigures our own conception, and experience, of trauma as a "black hole." To it the *Journal*—otherwise so factual, so reflective, and so complete an account of the events of that doleful summer—consigns everything that can't be said, and the empty interval is the sign of that absence. What has Defoe's text

---

30. Barker, *The Tremulous Private Body*.

"shot into the ground"? As scholars have long recognized, the *Journal* evokes the traditions of Puritan spiritual autobiography and the "Guide" tradition.[31] Yet, as Everett Zimmerman has noted, "when H. F. attempts to find a coherent spiritual purpose governing the physical world, material reality presents itself to him so powerfully that he cannot fully reconcile it with his religious assumptions. The disorienting forces of the plague expose the tensions within him, and we see his conflicts and mounting anxiety. The focus in Defoe is on the narrator; we are left with a character, not a lesson."[32] In the structure of Christian autobiography going back to Augustine, the missing lesson would have been the "sermon" of the great pit, a message delivered *de profundis* that reveals the upward path toward redemption. Instead of fulfilling that generic promise, the pit remains a "dreadful gulf." Absent a "lesson" to set the vector of the text, we are left with a "character" in search of an author, and a novel without a plot except for what is dictated by the needs of survival. Cut loose from the normal rules of time and place that govern fictional narrative, and with no coherent social or providential order to shape his destiny, that character will seem all the more apparitional. He is out of "place" because there is no secure place for him to occupy out of doors. He will, in fact, seem to become an apparition of the plague itself: a miasmal presence that roams the streets and haunts the graveyards, never really laid to rest, and liable to reappear at any moment.

Nor is it merely that the "material reality" of the plague causes H. F. to question his religious assumptions. In moments of adversity, self-interrogation and a chastened humility in the face of God's inscrutable ways had always been a part of the tradition in which Defoe writes. Rather, at the core of the *Journal's* traumatic encounter with the plague lies the meaning of the sexton's "speaking sight" that does not speak, and the meaning of a private meditation that cannot be publicly uttered: the Word of God has fallen silent and is no longer capable of imparting any meaning at all to epidemic catastrophe. Significantly (or, perhaps better, insignificantly), inarticulate groans have supplanted sermons as the lingua franca of the pit. In earlier chapters, I have argued that the vast sermon literature engendered in plague times strains the explanatory

---

31. These lines of criticism were set down by George Starr in *Defoe and Spiritual Autobiography* and by J. Paul Hunter in *The Reluctant Pilgrim*.

32. Zimmerman, "H.F.'s Meditations," 417.

power of the theologian to its limits. In other terms, the coincidence of the word for "plague" and the "Word" itself had seemed to guarantee that a visitation, however calamitous, was a legible event if only the interpreter was sufficiently literate in the language of divinity. Perhaps the crucial difference in legibility between the plagues of 1603 and 1625 on the one hand and the Great Plague on the other is that both earlier epidemics occurred, fortuitously, in the year of a monarch's death. This coincidence is vexing, but its advantage on both occasions is that it supplies a rich discourse in the light of which the plague can be accommodated to an overarching providential design—a metaphysical guarantee, in effect, that however horrendous the epidemic, however many tens of thousands died, plague had its place in the rightful order of things. The argument could be staged in various ways: plague purified the realm for the next monarch, it cleared the nation's debt of accumulated sin, it punished the wicked and sent the virtuous to a better place, it justly reclaimed the "loan" of seven-year-old children, its mercies balanced its harshest judgments (for example, by killing more quickly than famine, or by solving the problem of overpopulation in less desirable neighborhoods), just to summarize the leading arguments. Even when understood as a "tragedy," plague was read as having an ennobling and coherent generic form prescribed for it by the divine Playwright. None of these comforts could be completely satisfying even to those who advanced them, and all such justifications supported each other with the integrity of a house of cards. Arguably, their ultimate failure registers the collapse of political theology itself as a matrix for explaining national events; this is perhaps the plague's most enduring English legacy. In the aftermath of 1665—after England had suffered a humiliating naval defeat and its major city was both depleted by the most serious epidemic yet and then burned to the ground—the theological center could no longer hold, and a new narrative would have to take its place. The *Journal* gives witness to the disintegration of the earlier narrative. Pepys's *Diary* has already given us a glimpse of one version of the new.

Of the two writers considered in this chapter, Pepys is obviously far less preoccupied than Defoe with the ways of providence. Compared with the *Journal*, Pepys's *Diary* reads as an unambiguously secular account of the writer's experience during the Great Plague. Both texts report casual daily encounters with ravages of the epidemic—and in Pepys's case, the veracity of

these observations cannot be in doubt. But as his diary entries for the crucial summer months of 1665 suggest, Pepys manages to disinfect the plague
of much of its terror by indexing it to the two most powerful pleasures in
his life: sex and money. The dream of Lady Castlemaine reported on August 15 brings us closer to Defoe insofar as it seems to display an unspoken and potentially traumatic subtext. The allusion to Shakespeare—to the
ghost of Shakespeare, we might say, hovering over Pepys's recollection of
the dream—raises the specter of the grave even as it allows the dreamer
to dally with the notion of an erotic fantasy life after death.[33] But the "real
pleasure" of the dream, a source of satisfaction for Pepys that seems to have
spilled over from the realm of fantasy to that of physiology, proves the more
potent. Pepys's account even succeeds in metamorphosing *Hamlet* into *A
Midsummer Night's Dream*. This erotic calculus by which pleasure balances
fear, even if it does not completely outweigh it, is replicated in the *Diary* by
its perhaps inadvertent but nonetheless eerily precise tally of plague losses
over against personal financial gains. As we have seen, this version of financial accounting, an area of Pepys's professional expertise, adapts the form but
revises the content of the kind of balance sheet of judgments and mercies,
tribulations and blessings, that is familiar from the procedures of spiritual
autobiography. His procedure has the effect of transferring the whole question of the theodicy to the secular world.

Defoe's *Journal*, by contrast, reflects a more complex engagement between
the hermeneutic tradition of plague writing and the evidence of the material
world. As earnestly as H. F. attempts to discern God's plan for him—the principal question is whether he should remain or flee, a question depending more
on such considerations as the ill-treatment of Londoners in the countryside
than on the theological scruples—he is convinced that the "secret conveyance
of infection, imperceptible and unavoidable, is sufficient to execute the fierce-
ness of Divine vengeance without putting it upon supernaturals and miracle"
(205). Indeed, on this one point he is firm in his conviction: "I must be allowed
to believe that no one in this whole nation ever received the sickness or infection but in the ordinary way of infection from somebody, or the clothes or
touch or stench of somebody that was infected before" (206). With the court in
retirement and the parish clergy largely invisible in the narrative, H. F.'s heroes

---

33. See Harries, *Scare Quotes from Shakespeare*, on the dramatist's "haunting" of later writers.

are the local magistrates of the city who are more concerned with enforcing prudent public health measures than with encouraging repentance. In this and other passages, H. F. uneasily accommodates the rhetoric of earlier plague sermons (emphasizing "Divine vengeance") with a faith in the "ordinary" and a hard-headed suspicion of "supernaturals" that in an earlier time would have marked him as a "mere naturian." His faith, and ours, must be placed in the lord mayor, the aldermen, and the other civic officials who diligently, and at no small risk to themselves, enforce the rules in a world no longer governed by any supervening decree. Providential order gives way to civic government. H. F. also acknowledges the endurance and unexpected charity of ordinary Londoners, despite their often giving way to panic and superstition. These underlying "tensions" in the work enact a double trauma: that of the plague itself, full of "unaccountable things" (119) and symbolized by the "great pit"; and that of the crucial failure of theology to render a satisfying moral or medical account of such things, as symbolized by the pit's silent sermon and H. F.'s quarantined meditations that cannot "be made public on any account whatever."

I began this chapter by noting that in the decade of the 1660s, the combination of war, plague, and fire ravaged London, literally clearing away the London of Jonson and Donne and preparing the ground for the physical (and demographic) reconstruction of the city. The result would be the London of Pepys and Defoe, a city no longer "early" modern either in appearance or ethos, but worldly, pragmatic, the hub of empire. The textbook event associated with this fundamental shift toward modernity is the Glorious Revolution of 1688, with its attendant economic and social changes. I would argue that, after the civil war, the trauma of the 1660s lies buried under that new foundation. In Defoe especially, the ghost of the plague still glides through the "ordinary" world of 1722, accompanied by the mere specter of the theology that had once spoken for it.

The View from

Here

My purpose in this book has been to highlight a series of exemplary texts in the history of early modern English plague writing. They form a series in that each responds, in turn, to the three pandemics that ravaged London between 1603 and 1665. They are exemplary in that they speak immediately to moments of personal crisis—the death of Jonson's son, Donne's recovery from a near-mortal illness—and to the crises of their times. In 1665 Pepys offers something new, the perspective of a walker in the plague city, while Defoe reconstructs the same epidemic many years later from an amalgam of childhood memory and journalistic research, at a moment in 1722 when London seemed again vulnerable to an outbreak of plague. Over the century that separates Jonson's epigram on his son and Defoe's *Journal*, the discourse of infectious disease was gradually, though incompletely, passing from the province of the divine to that of the physician (who was to assume something of the priestly aura of his predecessor, along with the warrant of the new empirical science). Five years before Defoe's *Journal* appeared, Lady Mary Wortley Montagu wrote back from the Levant that "[t]he small-pox, so fatal, and so general amongst us, is here entirely harmless, by the invention of engrafting."[1] In the emergent discourse marked at its inception by this first report of the technique of inoculation, Lady Mary's letter will prove far more significant than all the sermons of the age haplessly ascribing disease to the wrath of God. The *Diary* and the *Journal*, different as they are in perspective and intention, are symptomatic of that shift toward the secular, but also of theology's residual imprint.

I have read these texts against as broad as possible a survey of the other kinds of plague writing published during the same years, including broadsheets, pamphlets, official plague orders, medical advisories, and especially plague sermons, jeremiads, and other writings by divines grappling with, and ultimately defeated by, the attempt to factor the plague into a traditional calculus of God's justice and mercy. As I have argued, the task facing the English divine in the seventeenth century is all the more daunting because he can no longer deploy the legion of plague saints available to Roman Catholicism. St. Sebastian, St. Roche, and their local counterparts all over the Catholic world not only performed miraculous cures when they were invoked in prayer, when *de voto* offerings were made in their name, when their relics

---

1. Montagu, *Letters*, letter 36, to Mrs. S. C. from Adrianople, n.d., 167–69.

were displayed, or when their images were borne aloft in processions or carried for protection on one's person in the form of medallions or *Pestblätter*. Apart from the rich visual and ritual culture centered on their veneration, plague saints acted as advocates for the afflicted, arguing for mercy on their clients' behalf before the court of divine justice. Like Moses interceding for his people in the desert when God can barely contain his temptation to destroy them, the saint buffers heaven's anger. In the judicial structure mirrored by this theology of patronage, the saint acts as mediator for those he represents and is himself the sign of a rational means for the negotiation of infectious disease. However, while Palermo could count on St. Rosalia and Venice on St. Thecla to mitigate or ward off the plague, London could muster only a pale replica of these powerful female saints: the allegorical figure of the city itself. Posted at the gates in Henry Petowe's *The Country Ague*, "London" is a forlorn mother whose only authority is to debar entry to those runaways who have not made their "peace with God" (fig. 12), a reconciliation in which she can offer no assistance. In this light, it is tempting to read Pepys's dream of "my Lady Castlemayne" as the eroticized simulacrum of the saint who can appear to the faithful in a vision, but who in Pepys's case can offer only a fleeting pleasure and the wish that we might be able to dream such dreams in the grave: for "then we should not need to be so fearful of death as we are this plague time."

In England, the long and obsessive attempt to construct a satisfying theodicy out of mass devastation—the attempt over three generations to weave the inexplicable into the fabric of the comprehensible—produces an extended post- (and pre-) traumatic narrative. The same biblical plagues are minutely parsed. The same stories are recycled over the years (revelers fall dead in their cups, "flyers" expire in a ditch), often with an ill-concealed schadenfreude. The ethics of flight are obsessively revisited: does scripture endorse self-preservation, or does it reserve a special punishment for those who thus demonstrate their lack of faith in God's power to spare them even in the midst of the plague, or who by fleeing imagine they can put themselves beyond reach of his arrows? The death of the "innocent" can only be rationalized on the grounds that they will sooner find their heavenly reward, or that their demise will lead others to repentance, or else that a quick death by plague is preferable to a slow death by famine or a violent one in war. Why the "guilty" may escape is an even deeper mystery; perhaps they are left alive to suffer, while the dead have "scap'd worlds, and fleshes rage," in Jonson's words. In the larger scheme of things, an excess of punishment must be balanced by an equal weight of sin, an accumulated debt that must be repaid. But how such an extraordinary debt was incurred, and whether that debt was incurred by the nation as a whole or by the sum of its inhabitants, by heedless courtiers or by "pestiferous" suburbanites, cannot be explained.

The energy driving this system is intensified within a kind of traumatic feedback loop. The greater the suffering, the more profound the guilt required to account for it. The punishment must fit the crime, and the crime the punishment. The greater the presumption of guilt, the more ferocious the divine vengeance is conceived to be, and the more richly deserved. And yet the wave upon wave of pandemics must demonstrate that the guilt cannot be rooted out—and that the "justice" it calls down is as harsh as it is ineffective. The encrypted thought against which this discourse most vigorously defends is that no such justice prevails, and the corollary: that the deity who should administer it is at best impenetrable in his motives and at worst malevolent or nonexistent. That unthinkable thought, as Lacan's formulation understands its effect, returns from the "outside," as the projection of the thought, as the fulfillment in fantasy of the wish that the thought might not be true, and as the agent punishing the subject for having (not) thought it. Arguably, the only way theodicy can continue is through a continual traumatic forgetting of its own repeated failure. After 1665 the debate subsided, not because it had resolved anything, but because, fortunately for the English, the plague was not to recur. The debate continues today, of course, whether as a fruitless attempt to justify the Holocaust to men or, in the case of 9/11, as a parody of its earlier sophistication in the late Reverend Jerry Falwell's pronouncement that the destruction of the twin towers was brought on by God's anger at gay-rights proponents, abortionists, and the American Civil Liberties Union.[2]

In the early seventeenth century, the traumatic question is posed most urgently by Ben Jonson in the extraordinary poem "To Heaven": "O, being euery-where, / How can I doubt to finde thee euer, here?" (8:122, ll. 15–16). The question both rejects and admits the possibility of "doubt." If God is everywhere, then he is surely ever "here" (just as, in Jonson's wordplay, the

---

2. Gustav Niebuhr, "U.S. 'Secular' Groups Set Tone for Terror Attacks, Falwell Says," *New York Times*, September 14, 2001.

one word is embedded in the other); but how can I ever find him *here*—here, in my "fear" and in "my griefs," where "there scarce is ground, / Vpon my flesh t[o]'inflict another wound" (ll. 20–24)? Just concealed in the poet's plaint that he is "destin'd unto iudgment, after all" (l. 20) is the plaintiff's defense that there can be no legal "ground" for judgment "after all" the suffering—including, surely, the loss of a son to the plague—that has already been inflicted upon him. The very fact that he seeks "for ease" (l. 4) may, as he fears, be (unjustly?) "interpreted in me disease" (l. 3). This interpretation *in malo* turns, in turn, on God's own manipulation of the poet's language—the divine judge, as it were, entering the word "*dis*ease" into the record rather than the word "ease" intended by the poet. Nor can the poet "wish for death" lest "it be thought the breath / Of discontent" (ll. 23–25), a diseased thought rejected, but one nonetheless discontented, hinting as it does in the rhyme that God's Word is the "breath" of "death." Jonson's "state" (ll. 10, 17)—his spiritual state, his state of mind, his standing before the court—thus depends equally upon the stated fear of his being *dis*interpreted and upon the unstated fear that the God he imagines as his judge has got him right all along. The prior question, double-edged, lurks in the first line of the poem: can "I not thinke of Thee"?

That the language of his expressed (or suppressed) discontent should be "interpreted" symptomatically—diagnosed, or disdiagnosed, by the divine Physician as a form of "disease," and one that God has himself inflicted, as the poem also implies—takes us back to the epigram "On my first Sonne." Once again, the question of man's "state" on God's "just day" is also double-edged: "For why / Will man lament the state he should enuie?" (ll. 5–6). The father will lament nonetheless, and all the more so because what has been taken from him by the plague—by the infliction that is the Word of God, by the disease whose name means literally both the "blow" and the "word," the breath of death—is his best piece of poetry. The epidemic of 1603 is interpreted as clearing the record of the nation's sins and preparing the way for a new monarch, and his son. Jonson himself contributed to the celebrations and, as we have seen, composed a special entertainment for the new queen and Prince Henry at Althorp. Is Jonson now required to "pay" his own son in order to balance this providential account? The insistent questioning in Jonson's verse implies that the "just day" of his son's death is anything but. That the dead child is enabled, in Jonson's words, to speak for himself is a resurrection of the dead in and through poetry, the breath of life.

Donne's plague writing approaches the dilemma of a theodicy from two complementary points of view. If "there is no health," as the "Anniversaries" would have instructed the reader in 1625, then there can be no reason to ask why people fall ill. Nor would our limited knowledge even of our selves be likely to yield up an answer. In the skeptical light of "The First Anniversary," not only are we born "ruinous" as the descendents of our fallen first parents, but our life span has been abbreviated and our stature diminished ever since the days of Methuselah. An epidemic would thus be understood as a momentary acceleration in the long decline of the race. The withering of the species serves, in turn, as a kind of barometer of the world's general decay. If the "worlds proportion disfigured is" (240, l. 302), then the balance of humors in the body and the order of the cosmos are equally imperiled. Although Donne does not elaborate the argument, the early modern plague ecologist could infer from this account of a "rotten world" that miasmal clouds, ill winds, and foul exhalations from the bowels of the earth are the pestilent symptoms of a world in its death throes. The only remedy is a therapeutic failure of memory appropriate to our decline—"Forget this rotten world" (252, l. 49)—and the injunction to "follow" the liberated soul of Elizabeth Drury on its interplanetary voyage to heaven. But she can only be the object of meditation, not the agent of mediation. Her power in the poem is measured by the extent of her loss, an absence that leaves the world bereft and that will be celebrated every year, according to Donne's unfulfilled plan, on the anniversary of her death—Elizabeth's day. The faint twilight of her memory is the trace of the saint she would have been if it had not been necessary to forget the old religion—a traumatic amnesia for Donne in his apostasy, as critics from John Carey to Dennis Flynn have argued.[3] The meditation supplies a form that compensates for veneration: a salutary but solitary and strenuous exercise that will bear no real fruit until we are as dead as she is.

The second point of view in Donne's plague writing is that of the *Devotions* and the St. Dunstan's sermon, texts written after Donne's own recovery. These regard disease as one of the "translators" that God employs to perfect his heavenly library, as he compiles, over the course of sacred history, a definitive set of "works" that will include all those, body and soul, worthy of entering into the collection. The movement of the plague from house to

---

3. See Carey, *John Donne*; and Flynn, *John Donne and the Ancient Catholic Nobility*.

house epitomizes its broader providential vector, as the sermon has it, from the houses of the Egyptians to our own houses, to the houses of our body, to the house of the church, and ultimately, in its definitive translation, into the book of eternal life. Every plague written into the Bible, and every subsequent plague inscribed by the Word onto the bodies of its successive victims, is thus a work in progress, a promissory note of the resurrection by whose metaphorical language Donne interprets his own recovery. The word (for "word" and "pestilence") itself must be understood as it will stand at the end, translated into the "better language" of the Word. In the *Devotions*, every step in Donne's illness and recovery appears in three successively more accurate versions of his experience. By the time the meditations on his suffering have been revised to disclose their spiritual significance, "disease" is given its final translation as "physic." In the text of the St. Dunstan's sermon, "there was not a house where there was not one dead" must finally be rendered in the opposite sense already implicit in its language: not that there were many dead, but that at the resurrection there will be "not one dead." Read as plague documents, both the "Anniversaries" and these two later works converge in their ability—Donne's ability—to incorporate epidemic disease into a nontraumatic providential narrative. In their approach, they can be seen as a *coincidentia oppositorum*. The earlier poems read disease as a natural and moral symptom of the death of the world; the later works read its occurrences as passages in a text whose correct translation points toward the resurrection. These rhetorics can only "succeed," however, by eliding the intractable questions that preoccupy others who persist in wrestling with the angel of death.

Pepys and Defoe offer a final contrast in their writing of the plague of 1665. Its pious gestures aside, Pepys's *Diary* appropriates the theological discourse of debts and payments (as well as the shorthand method intended for the recording of sermons) to a calculation of his own spiritual and financial well-being during the plague year. He witnesses horror after horror in his peregrinations about the city, yet he declares the year the happiest of his life. In some uncanny and unselfconscious way, he records a balance between the rising number of plague deaths during the hottest months of the epidemic and his own rising fortune in coin and movables at a time when his work in the Naval Office proves to be a source of unexpected profit. The pleasure in this accumulation is akin to that he finds in the number of his amorous conquests, also duly recorded and represented most intensely in the wet dream of Lady Castlemaine, which he takes as a prophylactic against fear in "this plague time." This cross-indexing of accounts produces a spiritual autobiography drained of the spirit but rich in its apparent assurance of the diarist's own good credit with providence. As I have argued, the case of Defoe's *Journal* is more complex. Part factual and part imagined, the narrative stems from the apparitional H. F. who hovers somewhere between the author's childhood experience of 1665 and the aging writer of 1722. He is a figure drawn to a burial pit "now" concealed but which, when still in use, fails to yield up the "sermon" promised by the sexton who admits him to the churchyard. He composes secret meditations in the privacy of his rooms and insists on telling us that we cannot know what they contain. We are directed to his burial place. He moves restlessly through the city, noting the absence of the court, expressing his confidence in the prudence of municipal officials, debating with himself whether to flee or remain, filling his pages with statistics, rumors, anecdotes, and practical advice, worrying about his property, finding the common people sometimes heroic and at other times blindly superstitious—but finding, in the end, little spiritual consolation, and no providential design that would endow the epidemic with meaning or purpose. In the *Journal's* London of 1722, the plague pits and the church burial grounds containing the unnumbered corpses of the 1665 epidemic are both lost to view beneath the eighteenth-century city and are reopened by the narrative, their ghosts set free to haunt their world, and ours.

Today, the West has its own psychic burial pits for pandemic disease. In them we have interred, almost beyond recall, not only the cholera epidemics of the nineteenth century, but the two greatest plagues of the earlier twentieth century: the "Spanish flu" outbreak of 1918 and the persistence of tuberculosis, the "White Plague," a steady killer up until the first generation of antibiotics was introduced after World War II. We forget in part because those who survive must cultivate a self-protective amnesia, learning to "not think" of such pandemics. In part, too, we forget because the immediate generation that fell victim to these diseases has almost completely passed from the scene; in part because the sudden devastation of an event like the Spanish flu has no imaginative referent for most of us alive at the moment (and no chapter in our high school history texts); and in part because we still believe we are conquering the frontiers of medical science. Insofar as AIDS, the most recent "plague," is now seen in the West as a chronic condition rather than a quick death sentence, its earlier career has also begun to fade from memory—as suggested by the current casual attitude toward "safer" sex on the part of the children of the 1980s and 1990s. The mapping of the human genome, current investigations into the properties of stem cells, and advances in immunology spurred largely by AIDS research have taken us to the verge of discovering therapies and modes of prevention that will unarguably advance the frontiers of medical treatment. But even if all these promises should be fulfilled in the next decades (an uncertain prospect at best), it is unlikely that medicine will be able to prevent or stem the spread of an emergent pandemic, whether viral or bacterial in origin. We will need to fall back on more widespread and high-tech (though perhaps less effective) versions of the very same public health measures devised in response to the plagues of the early modern period: quarantine, restrictions on travel and trade, and palliative care for the afflicted, delivered by a medical system stretched to the breaking point. With the imposition of these measures, methods of increased surveillance and control will exact their Foucauldian price. For parts of the world lacking such resources, the prospect is dramatically worse. Despite all our technological advantages, if we extrapolate the number of early modern epidemic deaths to current world population levels, we must conclude grimly that the toll taken by a major uncontained outbreak today would likely be in the tens or hundreds of millions. As if to bring this narrative full circle, the World Health Organization "now classifies plague as 're-emerging'" in areas as widespread as India, Zambia, Mozambique, Madagascar, Kazakhstan, Algeria, and China, and perhaps elsewhere in the near future as a consequence of global warming. It remains, in the words of a plague researcher at the Institut Pasteur, "probably the most pathogenic infectious agent on the planet right now."[4]

If and when such a calamity strikes, we (who are around to reflect on the matter) will tend to regard it as somehow unjust, a violent breach in our contract as the world's thriving and dominant species. We will ask the same questions as the seventeenth-century divines but will not, many of us, be satisfied with their answers. We acknowledge the threat, which is invoked almost daily in the news about the latest avian flu or in speculation about how global warming may have serious pathogenic effects. But we don't understand as

---

4. Dr. Elisabeth Carniel, quoted in Laura Miller, "Return of the Plague," *Time*, February 16, 2008.

readily the longer natural cycles that condition our life on this planet. Just as we are now, the geologists tell us, in an interglacial period, so we may also be in (or near the end of) an era of relative good health. The emergence of new (and the reemergence of old) drug-resistant pathogens, alarming as such developments are, may be the harbingers of a global pandemic borne on the winds, or in the passenger compartments of jetliners—one that will significantly reduce the human population.

The prospect may seem apocalyptic in its vision of a population collapse, although the Black Death and its successor epidemics accomplished just that only five minutes ago on the timeline of human evolution. While any one episode of infectious disease will have its unique circumstances, the demographics of early modern London may well epitomize the prospect facing our hyper-urbanized planet. One constant is that dense populations form the perfect environment for the spread of epidemic disease. As we have seen, during the seventeenth century the population of London nearly tripled (from about 200,000 in 1600 to 550,000 in 1700). As there were upward of 200,000 plague deaths during the same century, the overall increase must be attributed in large part to immigration of new Londoners from the countryside and abroad—many of whom arrived only to provide new tinder for the next epidemic. Each of the century's epidemics claimed about one in five Londoners, a proportion that would represent more than a million deaths in London today. Much, of course, is unpredictable, including the nature and virulence of any future epidemic and the extent to which (ideally) farsighted public health measures might mitigate its effects. What is not in doubt is that the species is due for a Malthusian correction, a conclusion that modern earth science has only confirmed on the indisputable grounds that the world's resources of food and energy cannot sustain a population of ten billion people—the tipping point at which we will arrive by midcentury, or shortly thereafter.[5] In the microbial chronicles, the brief history of *Homo sapiens sapiens* may ultimately be recorded as an interregnum in the kingdom of the pathogens, a race that preceded us in the order of evolution and will likely survive us as well.

In the meanwhile, this study is intended to propose that we backdate our narrative of health and disease to include the epidemics of the early modern

---

5. U.S. Census Bureau, "World Population Information," http://www.census.gov/ipc/www/world
.html (accessed February 22, 2007).

period, not as an ancient enemy over which modern medical science would triumph, but as the symptom of an enduring condition that shadows even the most stunning achievements of that science. The result would be, first, a recovery of the cultural memory of our fragile state—a memory that a positivist history of medicine has needed to repress. Second, a history that begins (and ends) with diseases rather than cures has at least the symbolic advantage of bracketing the progress of infectious-disease treatment between the natural processes that constrain it. The history that might issue from such a revised paradigm might offer a more nuanced, if less optimistic, account of the delicate symbiosis between the macrobial and the microbial residents of the planet, and perhaps even a new account of subjectivity in the postmodern age. At the least, it may be necessary to conclude, with Donne, that "there is no health."

[WORKS CITED]

Primary Sources

Alberti, Leon Battista. *On Painting.* 1435. Translated by John R. Spencer. New Haven, CT: Yale University Press, 1966.

Andrewes, Lancelot. *A Sermon of the Pestilence. Preached at Chiswick 1603 . . . by Lancelot Andrewes Late L. Bishop of Winchester.* London, 1636. Reprinted in Andrewes, *Works.* 11 vols. Oxford, 1854. New York: AMS Press, 1967.

Arber, Edward, ed. *Transcript of the Register of the Company of Stationers of London, 1554–1640.* 5 vols. London, 1875–77.

Bacon, Francis. *Francis Bacon.* Edited by Brian Vickers. Oxford: Oxford University Press, 1996.

Balmford, James. *A Short Dialogue concerning the Plagues Infection. . . .* London, 1603.

B. Ion: *His Part of King Iames His Royall and Magnificent Entertainement through His Honorable Cittie of London, Thurseday the 15. of March. 1603* [i.e., 1604]. London, 1604.

Bostocke, Richard. *The Difference betwene the Auncient Phisicke, First Taught by the Godly Forefathers. . . .* London, 1585.

Browne, Sir Thomas. *The Prose of Sir Thomas Browne.* Edited by Norman Endicott. New York: Doubleday, 1967.

Bullein, William. *Bulleins Bulwarke of Defe[n]ce. . . .* London, 1562.

By the King a Proclamation against Inmates and Multitudes of Dwellers in Strait Roomes and Places in and about the Cities of London, and for the Rasing and Pulling Downe of Certaine New Erected Buildings. London, 1603.

By the King a Proclamation for the Due and Speedy Execution of the Statute against Rogues, Vagabonds, Idle, and Dissolute Persons. London, 1603.

Chettle, Henry. *Englandes Mourning Garment. . . .* London, 1603.

Clapham, Henoch. *Antidoton or a Soueraigne Remedie against Schisme and Heresie. . . .* London, 1600.

———. *Doctor Andros His Prosopopeia Answered. . . .* Middelburg, 1605.

———. *An Epistle Discoursing vpon the Present Pestilence Teaching What It Is, and How the People of God Should Carrie Themselues towards God and Their Neighbour Therein.* London, 1603.

———. *Henoch Clapham His Demaundes and Answeres touching the Pestilence Methodically Handled, as His Time and Meanes Could Permit.* London, 1604.

Crashaw, William. *Londons Lamentation for her Sinnes and Complaint to the Lord Her God. . . .* London, 1625.

Cyprian, Saint. *A Svvete and Deuoute Sermon of Holy Saynt Ciprian of Mortalitie of Man. . . .* Translated by Sir Thomas Elyot. London, 1534.

Davies, John. *Humours Heau'n on Earth with the Ciuile Warres of Death and Fortune. As Also the Triumph of Death: or, the Picture of the Plague, according to the Life; as It Was in Anno Domini. 1603.* London, 1609.

Defoe, Daniel. *Due Preparations for the Plague, as Well for Soul as Body.* Edited by G. H. Maynadier. Boston, 1903.

———. *A Journal of the Plague Year.* Edited by Anthony Burgess and Christopher Bristow. London: Penguin, 1966.

———. *The Life and Adventures of Robinson Crusoe.* Edited by Angus Ross. New York: Penguin, 1985.

Dekker, Thomas. *The Dead Tearme.* 1608. In vol. 4 of *The Non-dramatic Works of Thomas Dekker.* Edited by Alexander B. Grosart. New York: Russell & Russell, 1963.

———. *The Plague Pamphlets of Thomas Dekker.* Edited by F. P. Wilson. Oxford: Clarendon Press, 1925.

Diggs, Thomas. *Humble Motives for Association to Maintaine Religion Established Published as an Antidote against the Pestilent Treatises of Secular Priests.* London, 1601.

Donne, John. *Devotions upon Emergent Occasions.* Ann Arbor: University of Michigan Press, 1959.

———. *The First Sermon Preached to King Charles, at Saint Iames 30. April. 1625.* London, 1625.

———. *Foure Sermons vpon Speciall Occasions.* London, 1625.

———. *John Donne: The Anniversaries.* Edited by Frank Manley. Baltimore: Johns Hopkins University Press, 1963.

———. *Letters to Severall Persons of Honour.* London, 1651.

———. *The Poems of John Donne.* Edited by Herbert J. C. Grierson. 2 vols. 1912. Reprint, Oxford: Oxford University Press, 1968. Page references are to the 1968 edition.

———. *The Sermons of John Donne.* Edited by Evelyn M. Simpson and George R. Potter. 10 vols. Berkeley and Los Angeles: University of California Press, 1953–62.

———. *The Variorum Edition of the Poetry of John Donne.* Edited by Gary A. Stringer. Vol. 6, *The Anniversaries and the Epicedes and Obsequies.* Bloomington: Indiana University Press, 1995.

Dryden, John. *Annus Mirabilis, The Year of Wonders, 1666.* London, 1667.

Elton, Edward. *An Exposition of the Epistle of Saint Paul to the Colossians.* . . . London, 1620.

Elyot, Sir Thomas. *Bibliotheca Eliotae = Eliotes Dictionarie the Second Tyme Enriched, and More Perfectly Corrected, by Thomas Cooper, Schole Maister of Maudlens in Oxforde.* London, 1552.

Evelyn, John. *Diary and Correspondence of John Evelyn.* Edited by William Bray. 4 vols. London, 1859.

Fenton, Roger. *A Perfume against the Noysome Pestilence Prescribed by Moses vnto Aaron. Num. 16. 46.* . . . London, 1603.

A Form of Common Prayer, together with an Order of Fasting, for the Averting of Gods Heavy Visitation upon Many Places of This Realm. London, 1665.

Fracastoro, Girolamo. *Syphilidis sive de Morbo Gallico.* 1525. Translated by Geoffrey Eatough. Liverpool: Francis Cairns, 1984.

Godskall, James. *The Arke of Noah for the Londoners That Remaine in the Cittie.* . . . London, 1604.

Greenham, Richard. *A Fruitful and Godly Sermon.* . . . London, 1595.

Hall, Joseph. *Meditations and Vowes, Diuine and Morall.* . . . London, 1605.

Harman, Thomas. "Caveat for Common Cursitors." In *The Elizabethan Underworld,* edited by A. V. Judges. New York: Octagon, 1965.

Herbert, George. *The Works of George Herbert.* Edited by F. E. Hutchinson. Oxford: Clarendon Press, 1970.

Herring, Francis. *A Modest Defence of the Caueat Giuen to the Wearers of Impoisoned Amulets, as Preseruatiues from the Plague.* London, 1604.

Hobbes, Thomas. *Leviathan, or the Matter, Forme, & Power of a Common-wealth Ecclesiasticall and Civill.* 1651. Edited by Richard E. Flathman and David Johnston. New York: Norton, 1997.

Hodge, Nathaniel. *Loimologia, sive, Pestis nuperae apud populum Londinensem.* . . . London, 1671.

Hooker, Richard. *Of the Laws of Ecclesiasticall Politie.* London, 1593.

Horne, Robert. *A Caueat to Preuent Future Iudgements: or, An Admonition to All England.* . . . London, 1626.

I. H. *This VVorlds Folly Or A Warning-Peece Discharged vpon the Wickednesse Thereof.* London, 1615.

Jacobus de Voragine. *The Golden Legend.* Translated by W. Granger Ryan. 2 vols. Princeton, NJ: Princeton University Press, 1993.

Johnson, Samuel. *The Idler and the Adventurer.* Edited by W. J. Bate, John M. Bullitt, and L. F. Powell. New Haven, CT: Yale University Press, 1963.

Jonson, Ben. *Ben Jonson.* Edited by Charles H. Herford, Percy Simpson, and Evelyn Simpson. 11 vols. Oxford: Clarendon Press, 1947.

Lachrymae Londinenses: or, Londons Lamentations and Teares for Gods Heauie Visitation of the Plague of Pestilence. London, 1626.

Lodge, Thomas. *A Treatise of the Plague.* . . . London, 1603.

Luther, Martin. *On the Bondage of the Will.* In *Martin Luther: Selections from his Writings,* edited by John Dillenberger, 166–206. New York: Anchor/Doubleday, 1961.

Manning, James. *A New Booke, Intituled, I Am for You All, Complexions Castle as Well in the Time of the Pestilence.* . . . Cambridge, 1604.

Martial. *Epigrams.* Translated by Walter C. A. Ker. Rev. ed. 2 vols. London: Heinemann, 1919–20.

Marvell, Andrew. *The Poems and Letters of Andrew Marvell.* Edited by H. M. Margoliouth. 3rd ed., revised by Pierre Legouis with the collaboration of E. E. Duncan-Jones. 2 vols. Oxford: Clarendon Press, 1971.

Montagu, Lady Mary Wortley. *Letters of the Right Honourable Lady M—y W—y M—e: Written during Her Travels in Europe, Asia and Africa.* . . . Vol. 1. Aix: Anthony Henricy, 1796.

Montaigne, Michel de. *The Complete Essays of Montaigne.* Translated by Donald M. Frame. Stanford, CA: Stanford University Press, 1965.

More, Thomas. *Utopia*. Edited and translated by Robert M. Adams. New York: Norton, 1992.

Muggins, William. *Londons Mourning Garment, or Funerall Teares Worne and Shed for the Death of Her Wealthy Cittizens, and Other Her Inhabitants.* . . . London, 1603.

Orders, Thought Meete by His Maiestie . . . *to Be Executed throughout the Counties of This Realme, in Such Townes Villages, and Other Places, as Are, or May Be Infected with the Plague.* London, 1603.

Pepys, Samuel. *The Diary of Samuel Pepys.* Edited by Robert Latham and William Matthews. 10 vols. Berkeley and Los Angeles: University of California Press, 2000.

———. *Letters and the Second Diary of Samuel Pepys.* Edited by R. G. Howarth. London: J. M. Dent & Sons; New York: E. P. Dutton, 1932.

Perkins, William. *A Golden Chaine: or the Description of Theologie.* . . . London, 1600.

Petowe, Henry. *The Countrie Ague. Or, London Her VVelcome Home to Her Retired Children.* . . . London, 1625.

———. *Englands Caesar His Maiesties Most Royall Coronation.* . . . London, 1603.

———. *Londoners Their Entertainment in the Countrie Or the Whipping of Runnawayes.* . . . London, 1604.

Pliny. *Pliny the Younger.* Translated by Betty Radice. 2 vols. Cambridge, MA: Harvard University Press, 1969.

Price, Sampson. *Londons Remembrancer: for the Staying of the Contagious Sicknes of the Plague by Dauids Memoriall.* . . . London, 1626.

Puttenham, George. *The Arte of English Poesie Contriued into Three Bookes: the First of Poets and Poesie, the Second of Proportion, the Third of Ornament.* London, 1589.

S. P. *Two Precious and Divine Antidotes against the Plague of Pestilence.* . . . London, 1625.

Shakespeare, William. *The Riverside Shakespeare.* Edited by J. Blakemore Evans et al. Boston: Houghton Mifflin, 1974.

Shelton, Thomas. *Short Writing the Most Exact Methode.* London, 1630.

Sibbes, Richard. *The Soules Conflict with It Selfe.* . . . London, 1635.

Swift, Jonathan. *The Writings of Jonathan Swift.* Edited by Robert A. Greenberg and William Bowman Piper. New York: Norton, 1973.

T. C. *A Godly and Learned Sermon, vpon the 91. Psalme Declaring How, and to What Place, a Christian Man Ought to Flie in the Daungerous Time of the Pestilence.* . . . London, 1603.

Taylor, John. *The Fearefull Sommer: or Londons Calamitie.* . . . London, 1625.

Thomson, George. *Loimologia: A Consolatory Advice, and Some Brief Observations concerning the Present Pest.* London, 1665.

———. *Loimotomia: or The Pest Anatomized.* London, 1666.

Udall, Nicholas. *The First Tome or Volume of the Paraphrase of Erasmus upon the Newe Testament.* London, 1548.

Vaughan, Henry. *Silex Scintillans: Sacred Poems and Private Ejaculations.* 2nd ed. London, 1655.

Ward, William. *Gods Arrovves, or, Two Sermons, concerning the Visitation of God by the Pestilence.* . . . London: Henry Ballard, 1607.

White, Thomas. *A Sermo[n] Preached at Pawles Crosse on Sunday the Thirde of Nouember 1577. in the Time of the Plague, by T.W.* London, 1578.

Whitney, Geffrey. *A Choice of Emblemes, and Other Deuises. . . .* Leiden, 1586.

Willis, John. *The Art of Stenography: or, Short-Writing, by Spelling Characterie. . . .* 9th ed. London, 1628.

Wilson, Thomas. *The Arte of Rhetorike for the Vse of All Sutche as Are Studious of Eloquence, Sette Foorthe in Englishe.* 1553. Reprint, London, 1580.

Wither, George. *Britain's Remembrancer Containing a Narration of the Plague Lately Past. . . .* London, 1628.

———. *A Memorandum to London Occasioned by the Pestilence There Begun This Present Year* MDCLXV. . . . London, 1665.

Secondary Sources

Abraham, Nicolas, and Maria Torok. *The Shell and the Kernel: Renewals of Psychoanalysis.* Edited by Nicholas T. Rand. Chicago: University of Chicago Press, 1994.

Achinstein, Sharon. "Plagues and Publication: Ballads and the Representation of Disease in the English Renaissance." *Criticism* 34 (1992): 27–49.

Artaud, Antonin. *The Theater and Its Double.* New York: Grove Press, 1958.

Bailey, Gauvin Alexander, et al., eds. *Hope and Healing: Painting in Italy in a Time of Plague, 1500–1800.* Chicago: University of Chicago Press, 2005.

Bald, R. C. *John Donne: A Life.* New York: Oxford University Press, 1970.

Barker, Francis. *The Tremulous Private Body: Essays on Subjection.* London: Methuen, 1984.

Barker, Sheila. "Plague Art in Early Modern Rome: Divine Directives and Temporal Remedies." In Bailey et al., *Hope and Healing,* 45–64.

———. "Poussin, Plague, and Early Modern Medicine." *Art Bulletin* 86 (December 2004): 659–89.

Barroll, Leeds. *Politics, Plague, and Shakespeare's Theater: The Stuart Years.* Ithaca, NY: Cornell University Press, 1991.

Barry, John M. *The Great Influenza: The Epic Story of the Deadliest Plague in History.* New York: Viking, 2004.

Bastien, F. "Defoe's *Journal of the Plague Year* Reconsidered." *Review of English Studies* 16 (1965): 151–73.

Bell, Walter George. *The Great Plague in London in 1665.* 1924. Edited by Belinda Hollyer. London: The Folio Society, 2001.

Berger, James. "Trauma and Literary Theory." *Contemporary Literature* 38 (1997): 569-82.

Bettelheim, Bruno. "Trauma and Reintegration." In *Surviving, and Other Essays.* New York: Knopf, 1979.

Bond, Erik. *Reading London: Urban Speculation and Imaginative Government in Eighteenth-Century Literature.* Columbia: University of Ohio Press, 2007.

Booth, Stephen. *Precious Nonsense: The Gettysburg Address, Ben Jonson's Epitaphs on His Children, and* Twelfth Night. Columbus and Los Angeles: University of California Press, 1998.

Braudel, Fernand. *The Mediterranean and the Mediterranean World in the Age of Philip II*. Translated by Siân Reynolds. Vol. 1. New York: Harper & Row, 1972.

Breithaupt, Fritz. "The Invention of Trauma in German Romanticism." *Critical Inquiry* 32 (2005): 77–101.

Cantor, Norman F. *In the Wake of the Plague: The Black Death and the World It Made*. New York: Free Press, 2001.

Carey, John. *John Donne: Life, Mind, and Art*. New York: Oxford University Press, 1981.

Carmichael, Ann G. "Contagion Theory and Contagion Practice in Fifteenth-Century Milan." *Renaissance Quarterly* 44 (1991): 213–56.

———. "The Last Past Plague: The Uses of Memory in Renaissance Epidemics." *Journal of the History of Medicine and Allied Sciences* 53 (1998): 132–60.

Caruth, Cathy, ed. *Trauma: Explorations in Memory*. Baltimore: Johns Hopkins University Press, 1995.

———. *Unclaimed Experience: Trauma and History*. Baltimore: Johns Hopkins University Press, 1996.

Clericuzio, Antonio. "Thomson, George (1619–1677)." *Oxford Dictionary of National Biography Online*. Oxford: Oxford University Press, 2004. http://www.oxforddnb.com/view/article/27300 (accessed June 18, 2008).

Cohn, Samuel K. *The Black Death Transformed: Disease and Culture in Early Renaissance Europe*. Oxford: Oxford University Press, 2003.

Connor, Steven. *Dumbstruck: A Cultural History of Ventriloquism*. Oxford: Oxford University Press, 2000.

Cormack, Braden, and Carla Mazzio. *Book Use, Book Theory: 1500–1700*. Chicago: University of Chicago Library, 2005.

Deaux, George. *The Black Death, 1347*. New York: Weybright & Talley, 1969.

de Man, Paul. "Autobiography as De-facement." MLN 94 (1979): 919–30.

Derrida, Jacques. *Spectres de Marx: L'État de la Dette, le Travail du Deuil et la Nouvelle Internationale*. Paris: Galilée, 1993.

Dewhurst, Kenneth. *Dr. Thomas Sydenham, 1624–1689: His Life and Original Writings*. London: Wellcome Historical Medical Library, 1966.

Diamond, Jared. *Collapse: How Societies Choose to Fail or Succeed*. New York: Viking, 2005.

———. *Guns, Germs, and Steel: The Fates of Human Societies*. New York: Norton, 1997.

Erikson, Kai. "Notes on Trauma and Community." In *Trauma: Explorations in Memory*, edited by Cathy Caruth. Baltimore: Johns Hopkins University Press, 1995.

Esposito, Anthony L., MD. "AIDS: A Twentieth Century Plague." *Worcester Medicine* 69, no. 1 (Spring 2005): 16–17.

Finberg, Robert W., MD. "A Modern Understanding of the Plague of Fourteenth Century Europe." *Worcester Medicine* 69, no. 1 (Spring 2005): 18–20.

Flynn, Dennis. *John Donne and the Ancient Catholic Nobility*. Bloomington: Indiana University Press, 1995.

———. "John Donne: Survivor." In *The Eagle and the Dove: Reassessing John Donne*, edited by Claude J. Summers and Ted-Larry Pebworth. Columbia: University of Missouri Press, 1986.

Foucault, Michel. *Discipline and Punish: The Birth of the Prison*. Translated by Alan Sheridan. New York: Random House, 1979.

Freedman, Barbara. "Elizabethan Protest, Plague, and Plays: Rereading the 'Documents of Control.'" *English Literary Renaissance* 26 (1996): 17–45.

Freud, Sigmund. *Moses and Monotheism*. Translated by Katherine Jones. New York: Vintage, 1939.

———. *The Standard Edition of the Complete Psychological Works of Sigmund Freud*. Translated under the general editorship of James Strachey, in collaboration with Anna Freud, assisted by Alix Strachey and Alan Tyson. 24 vols. London: Hogarth Press, 1953–74.

Friedländer, Saul. "Trauma, Transference and Working-Through." *History and Memory* 4 (1992): 39–55.

Garrett, Laurie. *The Coming Plague: Newly Emerging Diseases in a World out of Balance*. New York: Penguin, 1994.

Gilman, Ernest B. *Iconoclasm and Poetry in the English Reformation: Down Went Dagon*. Chicago and London: University of Chicago Press, 1986.

———. "Sycorax's 'Thing.'" In *Solon and Thespis: Law and Theater in the English Renaissance*, edited by Dennis Kezar, 99–123. Notre Dame, IN: Notre Dame University Press, 2007.

Gilman, Sander. *Disease and Representation: Images of Illness from Madness to AIDS*. Ithaca, NY: Cornell University Press, 1988.

Girard, René. *"To Double Business Bound": Essays on Literature, Mimesis, and Anthropology*. Baltimore: Johns Hopkins University Press, 1978.

Gomel, Elana. "The Plague of Utopias: Pestilence and the Apocalyptic Body." *Twentieth Century Literature* 46 (2000): 405–33.

Gould, Stephen J. "The Accidental Presence of the Humans in the Age of Bacteria." Irving H. Jurow Lecture, New York University, New York, NY, October 16, 1996.

Grady, Denise. "Ironing Out the Wrinkles in the Prion Strain Problem." *Science*, December 20, 1996, http://www.mad-cow.org/prus_sci.html.

Grell, Ole Peter, and Andrew Cunningham, eds. *Medicine and the Reformation*. London: Routledge, 1993.

Grigsby, Bryon Lee. *Pestilence in Medieval and Early Modern English Literature*. New York: Routledge, 2004.

Groopman, Jerome. "Medicine on Mars." *New Yorker*, February 14, 2000, 36–41.

Gruenberg, Kurt. "Transmission of Trauma of Nazi Persecution: Second Generation Jews in Germany." Panel, "How Trauma Is Transmitted," Forty-third IPA Congress, New Orleans, March 2004.

Halasz, Alexandra. "Lodge, Thomas (1558–1625)." In *Oxford Dictionary of National Biography Online*. Oxford: Oxford University Press, 2004. http://www.oxforddnb.com/view/article/169237 (accessed June 18, 2008).

Harding, Vanessa. "Burial of the Plague Dead in Early Modern London." In *Epidemic Disease in London*, edited by J. A. I. Champion, 19–34. London: Centre for Metropolitan History, 1993.

Harley, David. "Spiritual Physic, Providence and English Medicine." In Grell and Cunningham, *Medicine and the Reformation*, 101–17.

Harries, Martin. *Scare Quotes from Shakespeare: Marx, Keynes, and the Language of Reenchantment*. Palo Alto, CA: Stanford University Press, 2000.

Harris, Jonathan Gil. *Sick Economies: Drama, Mercantilism, and Disease in Shakespeare's England*. Philadelphia: University of Pennsylvania Press, 2004.

Hartman, Geoffrey. "On Traumatic Knowledge and Literary Studies." *New Literary History* 36 (1965): 537–63.

Healy, Margaret. "Discourses of the Plague in Early Modern London." In *Epidemic Disease in London*, edited by J. A. I. Champion, 19–34. London: Centre for Metropolitan History, 1993.

———. *Fictions of Disease in Early Modern England: Bodies, Plagues and Politics*. New York: Palgrave, 2001.

Hentzi, Gary. "Sublime Moments and Social Authority in *Robinson Crusoe* and *A Journal of the Plague Year*." *Eighteenth-Century Studies* 26 (1993): 419–34.

Herendeen, Wyman H. "Camden, William (1551–1623)." In *Oxford Dictionary of National Biography Online*. Oxford University Press, 2004. http://www.oxforddnb.com/view/article/4431 (accessed December 2, 2005).

Herlihy, David. *The Black Death and the Transformation of the West*. Edited by Samuel K. Cohn, Jr. Cambridge, MA: Harvard University Press, 1997.

Hooper, Edward. *The River: A Journey to the Source of HIV and AIDS*. Boston: Little, Brown, 1999.

Hooper, Judith. "A New Germ Theory." *Atlantic Monthly*, February 1999. http://www.theatlantic.com/issues/99feb/germs.htm (accessed June 18, 2008).

Hunter, J. Paul. *The Reluctant Pilgrim: Defoe's Emblematic Method and Quest for Form in Robinson Crusoe*. Baltimore: Johns Hopkins University Press, 1966.

Hutton, Ronald. *The Restoration: A Political History of England and Wales, 1658–1667*. Oxford: Oxford University Press, 1985.

Jones, Pamela M. "San Carlo Borromeo and Plague Imagery in Milan and Rome." In Bailey et al., *Hope and Healing*, 65–96.

Karlen, Arno. *Man and Microbes: Disease and Plagues in History and Modern Times*. New York: Simon & Schuster, 1995.

Kassell, Lauren. *Medicine and Magic in Elizabethan London: Simon Forman: Astrologer, Alchemist, and Physician*. Oxford: Clarendon Press, 2005.

Katritzky, M. A. *Women, Medicine and Theatre, 1500–1750: Literary Mountebanks and Performing Quacks*. Hampshire, UK: Ashgate, 2007.

Kuhn, Thomas S. *The Structure of Scientific Revolutions*. Chicago: University of Chicago Press, 1970.

Lacan, Jacques. *The Psychoses, 1955–1956*. Bk. 3 of *The Seminar of Jacques Lacan*. Translated by Russell Grigg. London: Routledge, 1993.

LaCapra, Dominick. *Representing the Holocaust: History, Theory, Trauma*. Ithaca, NY: Cornell University Press, 1994.

Laub, Dori, and Daniel Podell. "Art and Trauma." *International Journal of Psychoanalysis* 76 (1995): 991–1005.

Lewis, Jayne Elizabeth. "Spectral Currencies in the Air of Reality: *A Journal of the Plague Year* and the History of Apparitions." *Representations* 87 (2004): 82–101.

Lyotard, Jean François. *The Differend: Phrases in Dispute*. Translated by Georges Van Den Abbeele. Minneapolis: University of Minnesota Press, 1991.

Maus, Katharine Eisaman. *Ben Jonson and the Roman Frame of Mind*. Princeton, NJ: Princeton University Press, 1984.

Mayer, Robert. "The Reception of *A Journal of the Plague Year* and the Nexus of Fiction and History in the Novel." ELH 57 (1990): 529–55.

Mazzola, Elizabeth. *The Pathology of the English Renaissance: Sacred Remains and Holy Ghosts*. Leiden: Brill, 1998.

McNeill, William H. *Plagues and Peoples*. New York: Doubleday, 1976.

Meiss, Millard. *Painting in Florence and Siena after the Black Death: The Arts, Religion, and Society in the Mid-Fourteenth Century*. Princeton, NJ: Princeton University Press, 1951.

Mitchell, W. J. T. *Iconology: Image, Text, Ideology*. Chicago: University of Chicago Press, 1986.

Moote, A. Lloyd, and Dorothy C. Moote. *The Great Plague: The Story of London's Most Deadly Year*. Baltimore: Johns Hopkins University Press, 2004.

Mormando, Franco. Introduction to Bailey et al., *Hope and Healing*, 1–44.

Mullett, Charles F. *The Bubonic Plague and England*. Lexington: University of Kentucky Press, 1956.

Munro, Ian. "The City and Its Double: Plague Time in Early Modern London." *English Literary Renaissance* 30 (2002): 241–61.

Neill, Michael. *Issues of Death: Mortality and Identity in English Renaissance Tragedy*. Oxford: Clarendon Press, 1997.

Nicolson, Adam. *God's Secretaries: The Making of the King James Bible*. New York: HarperCollins, 2000.

Orent, Wendy. *Plague: The Mysterious Past and Terrifying Future of the World's Most Dangerous Disease*. New York: Free Press, 2004.

Paracelsus. *Four Treatises of Theophrastus von Hohenheim, Called Paracelsus*. Edited by C. Lilian Temkin et al. Baltimore: Johns Hopkins University Press, 1941.

Phillips, Patrick. "'Fleshes Rage': Ben Jonson and the Plague." PhD diss., New York University, 2006.

Porter, Roy. *Disease, Medicine and Society in England, 1550–1860*. London: The Economic History Society, 1987.

Riggs, David. *Ben Jonson: A Life*. Cambridge, MA: Harvard University Press, 1989.

———. "Marlowe's Quarrel with God." In *Critical Essays on Christopher Marlowe*, edited by E. C. Bartels, 39–58. New York: G. K. Hall, 1997.

———. *The World of Christopher Marlowe*. New York: Holt, 2004.

Ross, Cheryl Lynn. "The Plague of *The Alchemist*." *Renaissance Quarterly* 41 (1988): 434–58.

Saint-Amour, Paul K. "Bombing and the Symptom: Traumatic Earliness and the Nuclear Uncanny." *Diacritics* 30 (2000): 59–82.

Scarry, Elaine. *The Body in Pain: The Making and Unmaking of the World*. Oxford: Oxford University Press, 1985.

Schwyzer, Philip. *Archaeologies of English Renaissance Literature*. Oxford: Oxford University Press, 2007.

Scott, Gordon R. "The Murrain Now Known as Rinderpest." *Newsletter of the Tropical Agriculture Association, U.K.* 20 (2000): 14–16.

Sennet, Richard. *Flesh and Stone: The Body and the City in Western Civilization*. New York: Norton, 1994.

Sharpe, Kevin. *Sir Robert Cotton, 1586–1631: History and Politics in Early Modern England*. Oxford: Oxford University Press, 1979.

Shrewsbury, J. F. D. *A History of the Bubonic Plague in the British Isles*. London: Cambridge University Press, 1970.

Siraisi, Nancy G. *Medieval and Early Renaissance Medicine: An Introduction to Knowledge and Practice*. Chicago: University of Chicago Press, 1990.

Slack, Paul. *The Impact of Plague on Tudor and Stuart England*. Oxford: Clarendon Press, 1985; reprinted with corrections, 1990.

Sloan, A. W. *English Medicine in the Seventeenth Century*. Durham, UK: Durham Academic Press, 1996.

Sontag, Susan. *"Illness as Metaphor" and "AIDS and Its Metaphors."* New York: Doubleday, 1989.

Starr, George. *Defoe and Spiritual Autobiography*. Princeton, NJ: Princeton University Press, 1963.

Sutherland, James. *Defoe*. London: Methuen, 1937.

Theilman, John, and Francis Cate. "A Plague of Plagues: The Problem of Plague Diagnosis in Medieval England." *Journal of Interdisciplinary History* 37 (2007): 371–93.

Tomalin, Claire. *Samuel Pepys: The Unequalled Self*. New York: Viking, 2002.

Totaro, Rebecca. *Suffering in Paradise: The Bubonic Plague in English Literature from More to Milton*. Pittsburgh: Duquesne University Press, 2005.

Traister, Barbara Howard. *The Notorious Astrological Physician of London: Works and Days of Simon Forman*. Chicago: University of Chicago Press, 2001.

Trimpi, Wesley. "'BEN. JONSON his best piece of poetrie.'" *Classical Antiquity* 2 (1983): 144–55.

Twyning, John. *London Dispossessed: Literature and Social Space in the Early Modern City*. New York: St. Martin's, 1998.

U.S. Census Bureau. "World Population Information." http://www.census.gov/ipc/www/world.html (accessed February 22, 2007).

van der Kolk, Bessel A., Alexander C. McFarlane, and Lars Weisaeth, eds. *Traumatic Stress: The Effects of Overwhelming Experience on Mind, Body, and Society*. New York: Guilford, 1996.

van der Kolk, Bessel A., and Onno van der Hart. "The Intrusive Past: the Flexibility of Memory and the Engraving of Trauma." In Caruth, *Trauma*.

Watts, Sheldon. *Epidemics and History: Disease, Power and Imperialism*. New Haven, CT: Yale University Press, 1997.

Weiskel, Thomas. *The Romantic Sublime*. Baltimore: Johns Hopkins University Press, 1976.

Welsby, Paul A. *Lancelot Andrewes, 1555–1626*. London: SPCK, 1964.

White, Hayden V. *The Content of the Form: Narrative Discourse and Historical Representation*. Baltimore: Johns Hopkins University Press, 1987.

———. *Metahistory: The Historical Imagination in Nineteenth-Century Europe*. Baltimore: Johns Hopkins University Press, 1975.

Wilson, F. P. *The Plague in Shakespeare's London*. Oxford: Oxford University Press, 1927.

Ziegler, Philip. *The Black Death*. New York: Harper & Row, 1969.

Zimmerman, Everett. "H.F.'s Meditations: *A Journal of the Plague Year*." PMLA 87 (1972): 417–23.

Zinsser, Hans. *Rats, Lice and History*. Boston: Little, Brown, 1935.

[INDEX]

Page numbers in italics indicate illustrations

Blake, William, 48

blow from Hand of God: death of Jonson's son as, 93, 146, 250; Donne's theology on, 206–7; as God's speech to men, 100; justification of quarantine and, 152; meaning of "plague," 94–95; plague as, 97, 145; promise of renewed life and, 97; speaking of plague inflicting, 181; universality of, 153; victims ability to feel/see/hear, 94

Boccaccio, Carlo, 3, 23, 49, 60

Body in Pain, The (Scarry), 238

Bond, Erik, 217

"Book, The" (Vaughan), 205

Book of Life, 203

Booth, Stephen, 169

Borromeo, Bishop Carlo, 78–79, *81*, *86*

Borrowed Time (Monette), 6n3

Bostocke, Richard, 92–93, 200

bovine spongiform encephalopathy (BSE), 12, 41

Boyle, Robert, 117, 138, 209n26

brazen serpent, 77, 78, *80*, 90–91

breath, 100, 137, 201, 250

Breithaupt, Fritz, 54–55

Bright, Timothy, 226n11

Britain's Remembrancer (Wither), 46, *101*, 101–9

broadsheets. *See* plague broadsheets

Browne, Sir Thomas, 21, 207

Bruno, Giordano, 67

buboes: Berowne's transformation of, 53; displayed in depictions of St. Roche, 77; as evidence of God's anger, 40; Galenic reading of, 142; as inscription of disease/sin, 3, 53, 94–95, 98, 112; seen on victim in *Loimotomia* illustration, *ii*, *118*, 119; as symptom of plague, 34; Thomson's analysis of, 121

bubonic plague: causative agent of, 9; course of in humans, 33–34; critical literary investigations of, 31; cultural construction of, 37–40; epidemiological facts of, 32; global pandemics of, 9; persistence of, 9–10; seventeenth-century divines' view of, 40; spread of, 11; strains of, 11; as summer illness, 193; transmission of, 34. *See also* Black Death; plague

Bullein, William, 44

Bulwarke of Defense (Bullein), 44

Burgess, Anthony, 231

burial of plague victims: in church yards, 58, 178, 202; Donne on, 202, 205; observers of, 222; in unmarked plague pits, 25, 59, 132, 177–78, 232

Burnett (Pepys's physician), 222

Burton, Robert, 181

Calvin, John, 120, 173

Camden, William, 163, 182–87

cancer, infectious causes of, 12n12

"Canonization, The" (Donne), 36, 51, 201

Canterbury Tales (Chaucer), 237

Canzoniere, 3

Carey, John, 201–2, 251

Carlo Borromeo Administers the Sacraments to the Plague-Stricken (Landriani), *86*, 86

Carlo Borromeo Saving Milan from the Plague (Maratti), *81*, 84

Carmichael, Ann G., 39

Carteret, Lady, 223n7

Carteret, Sir G., 224

Caruth, Cathy, 54, 56, 70

Cary, Sir Nicholas, 194

Castel of Health, The (Elyot), 44

Castelvetro, Lodovico, 90, 120

Castiglione di Cervia, Italy, 10

Castlemaine, Lady, 219, 220–21, 229, 248

catastrophe theory, 17

Catholic Europe, 26, 78–79, 122–23

Catholicism: Andrewes's position on, 147; persecution during Reformation, 205;

Council of Constance, 77–78

Counter-Reformation, 78–79

Country Ague, The (Petowe), 109–10, 111, 111

courtiers, 46–47, 159, 248

Crucifixion, 77, 91

Cruise, Tom, 6–7

Crusoe, 51

crypt, 58–60. *See also* burial of plague victims; plague pits

Cynthia's Revels (Jonson), 183

Cyprian, Saint, 65

dancing mania, 60

Danvers, Lady, 194

Danvers, Sir John, 194

David, 142n25, 147, 157

Davies, John, 132, 133, 165, 178

Day, Angel, 209–10

DBR (deber/dabar), 95–97, 99, 121, 181, 207

Dead Tearme, The (Dekker), 7

death: Donne on, 199–200, 205–6, 252; Pepys's fear of, 219, 220–21; as translation, 205–11. *See also* bills of mortality; Jonson, Ben: death of son of; plague: deaths due to

Decameron, The (Boccaccio), 3, 23

Defoe, Daniel: characters of, 179; chronicle of 1665 plague epidemic, 35, 39, 51; contribution to history of apparitions, 234–35; decryption of plague, 60; evocation of Puritan autobiography/ Guide tradition, 240; experience of plague, 62–63; on failure of religion to impart meaning to plague, 238–41, 253; flight during plague of 1665, 231; on God's bookkeeping, 97; on government policies concerning plagues, 231; H. R.'s self-censorship and, 238–41, 243, 253; on inexpressible horror of plague, 51; perspective of the *Journal*, 42, 218;

preoccupation with ways of providence, 241; on process of contagion, 100; reconstruction of 1665 epidemic, 247; recording of mortality figures, 229; recording of plague anecdotes, 229; recounting of trauma memories, 59, 62, 218; shift to secular, 26, 153, 238–41, 252, 253; on sounds of plague, 238; source on plague, 230; on survivors of plague, 236–37; on transmission of plague, 242; treatment of plague, 242–43; use of fiction in history, 230; *Crusoe*, 51; *Due Preparations for the Plague*, 100, 231; *Essay on the History and Reality of Apparitions*, 234; *Journal of the Plague Year*, 35, 36n13, 38, 42, 51, 59, 62, 218, 229–41, 242–43, 253; *Political History of the Devil*, 234; *A True Relation of the Apparition of one Mrs. Veal*, 234

Dekker, Thomas: allegorical figure of Sickness, 180; on Apollo's roles, 181; on burial of dead, 177; on causes of plague, 137, 172; on concealed sickness, 7; on contagion of the book, 97, 99–100, 181; depiction of James, 165; on effects of plague in London, 111, 126, 132–33; on flight from plague, 137, 175–76; on God's bookkeeping, 97–98, 171; graphic imagery of illustrations of, 109–10; on hushed account of plague victims, 170; on means of death, 46, 112; on medicinal value of laughter, 97, 181; on plague body as revelation, 98–99; on plague images, 111; on plague's cleansing of England, 47–48, 135, 157, 159–60; questions concerning plague's selection of victims, 142–43; on reading as prophylaxis, 97, 99–100; record of deaths in 1603, 130, 228; on relationship between state/body, 46, 47–48; stories of plague victims, 34; story of

outbreak during time of, 35; plague writings of, 251–52; on preservation of neutrality in body, 18; publication of devotions, 239; publications of "Anniversaries," 195–97; on quarantine/flight, 201; reading of plague, 212–13, 251; on resurrection, 192, 193, 198, 202–4, 205–11, 212, 252; retreat to Chelsea estate, 194; Saint Dunstan's sermon, 251–52; sections of devotions on his illness, 207; sermon at St. Paul's, 193; on sources of bubonic plague, 36; studies of plague writings of, 37; as survivor of Elizabethan persecution, 170n14; on translation, 192, 205–11, 251–52; view of world, 195, 201–5; on zeal, 212; "Anniversaries," 192, 195–201, 202, 251; "The Broken Heart," 189; "The Canonization," 36, 51, 201; *Devotions upon Emergent Occasions*, 192, 193, 197, 200, 205–11, 251–52; "The Exstasie," 203; "The First Anniversary" (*An Anatomie of the World*), 1, 20, 29, 122, 195–97, 196, 199–201, 251; "First Sermon after Our Dispersion, by the Sickness" (St. Dunstan sermon), 192, 194, 201–5, 206, 211, 217, 251–52; *First Sermon Preached to King Charles*, 193–94, 197; "Holy Sonnet 14," 121; "Hymne to God, My God, in my Sicknesse," 193; "A Hymne to God the Father," 193; "Preached to the King's Majesty at Whitehall," 203; "The Second Anniversary" (*The Progresse of the Soule*), 30, 195–96, 199, 212

Douglas, Mary, 136

Douglas, Michael, 6

Drummond of Hawthornden, William, 129, 156–57, 163, 169, 182

Drury, Elizabeth, 195, 199, 201, 251

Dryden, John, 217

Due Preparations for the Plague (Defoe), 100, 231, 231n20

Dunglison, Robley, 209n26

Dutch wars, 35

dysentery, 33

Ebola, 12, 23

ecology, 17

Egypt, Biblical plagues in, 45, 157, 203–4, 211, 248

Eisenman, Peter, 63

Elizabeth I (queen of England): death of, 132–33; death of as frame to Jonson's poem, 170; death of as prelude to plague, 6, 47, 65–66, 154, 156, 160–61, 241; Dekker's account of death of, 160–61

Elyot, Thomas, 44, 65

emblematist, 104–5

Emma (Austen), 48

empty circle of trauma dream: in dream of child of Holocaust survivors, 63; of Jonson's poem, 170; of plague theodicy, 64–70; in plague writing, 64; in post-Holocaust art/poetry, 63

encephalitis, 10

endemic organisms, 33n8

England: analogy of human body and, 42–48; appeal to biblical plagues, 45–46, 203–4, 211, 248; bubonic plague statistics in, 32; census in, 142n25, 157; cycles of plague in, 3, 32–33, 34–35, 130; deaths due to plague in, 130, 195 (*see also* bills of mortality); defeat at Cádiz, 191; Glorious Revolution in, 217, 243; Great Fire in, 217, 243; imagery of plague in, 26, 100–112, 101, 110, 111, 113, 114, 114, 115, 116, 117–26, 118; influence of French Revolution in, 48; Marvell's depiction of, 217; plague of 1603 in, 35, 47, 65–66, 132, 154–55, 241, 250; plague of 1625 in, 47, 65, 66, 175, 191–92, 217, 241; plague of 1665 in, 35, 241 (*see also*

England (*continued*)

    Diary of Samuel Pepys [Pepys]; *Journal of the Plague Year, A* [Defoe]); preoccupation with empire, 48; response to plague in, 91–94, 125–26; studies of bubonic plague in, 31; Wither's depiction of, 102; Wither's warning to, *101*, 101–9. *See also* London

English plague imagery: of *Britain's Remembrancer* frontispiece, 46, *101*, 101–3, 104–5; compared to Continental plague imagery, 73, 92, 109–10, 114, 117, 122–23; on frontispiece of *A Rod for Run-awaies*, *110*; graphic/linguistic nature of, 92, 109–10, 114, 117; linguistic form of, 114; of *Pest Anatomized, The*, 117–26, *118*; of plague broadsheets, *110*, 110–14, *111*, *113*, *114*, *115*, *116*, 117; on title page of *A Country Ague*, *111*; on title page of *Anatomie of the World*, *196*, 198; verbal nature of, 103

English Reformation, 73, 90–91, 92. *See also* Reformation

environmentalists, 139

Epicurus, 67

epidemics: colonization and, 14–15; Donne's reading of, 200–1; erasure from histories, 16–17; as historical forces, 17; present anomaly in history of, 20–21; of Spanish flu, 4, 12, 19, 30, 35, 253. *See also* AIDS; Black Death; infectious disease; plague

epidemiology: Bible as source of, 92–93, 137–38, 142, 146–48; model for disease narrative, 17; warnings of impending calamity, 15

epigram, 176–77

Epigrammes (Jonson), 177, 182, 184

Epistle Discoursing upon the Present Pestilence (Clapham), 46n33, 94–95, 99–100, 150, 151–52

epitaphs for John Roe, 168

Erikson, Kai, 56

Essay on the History and Reality of Apparitions (Defoe), 234

ethopoeia, 179

eukaryotic bacteria, 40

European literary Renaissance, 3

Evelyn, John, 191

evolution, 9–10, 11, 40–42

evolutionary biologists, 40

Exodus, 45–46

Exodus 12:23, 98

Exodus 12:30, 192, 195, 204–5

"Exstasie, The" (Donne), 203

Eyes Wide Shut (film), 6–7

faith: effect of plague on, 66–69; in God's preserving power, 45, 172; plague as exercise of, 65; as protection from plague, 143–44, 150, 248

Fall of Man, 93, 148, 200–1, 213, 251

Falwell, Reverend Jerry, 249

famine: caused by rinderpest, 14; plague as reprieve from, 112, 157; plague death preferred to, 46, 157–58, 241, 248; threat of during plague, 102, 112, 155; threats of during reign of Elizabeth, 157

"Famous Voyage, The" (Jonson), 47, 51

fast day, 224

Fatal Attraction (film), 6

fear, 89, 144

Fenn, Mr. (Navy paymaster), 224

Fenton, Roger, 100, 157, 158, 174

festaiuolo, 84, *85*, 86–87

"First Anniversary, The" (Donne): on absence of health, 1, 29–30, 39, 40, 200, 251, 256; on decline of human race, 200, 251; on life expectancy/death of world, 20, 200–1; meditations on disease/death, 195, 199–201; publications of, 195–98; title page of 1625 edition, 195–99, *196*

God (*continued*)
   198, 204, 212–13, 247, 249; limitations of
      man's knowledge of, 145–46; mercy of,
      97–98, 135, 204, 211; omnipresence of,
      174–75; plague as test for faithful, 65;
      plagues as cleansing of political scene by,
      47–48, 65–66, 153, 156–61, 250; plagues
      as judgment from, 44–47, 65–70, 71,
      73–74, 85, 136, 137; plague symptoms as
      token of anger of, 40; portrayed as cross/
      crucified, 97–99; questioning of exis-
      tence of, 66–69, 172, 249–50; response to
      prayer, 148–49; as source of healing, 99,
      102–9, 207, 210, 213; as source of plagues,
      16, 24, 26, 43, 74, 94, 102–9, 135, 142, 147,
      158, 203; as translator of believers, 205–6,
      207, 208; ways of speaking through the
      plague, 171; as Word, 71
Godskall, James, 92
Golden Legend, The (Jacobus), 74, 75–76
Gombrich, Ernst, 23
Gomel, Elana, 179
Goodyer, Sir Henry, 194
Gould, Stephen J., 21
government policy on plague: Clapham's
      Epistle and, 150, 152, 155, 158; H. F. on,
      231; plan to contain epidemic, 154–56;
      tension between jurisdictions, 43. *See
      also* burial of plague victims; quarantine
Great Fire, 36n13, 217, 241, 243
Great Influenza, The (Barry), 15n20
Great Plague (1625), 191–92. *See also* plague
Great Plague (1665), 3, 51–52, 130, 217, 230,
      241. *See also* plague
Greco, El, 75
Greek philosophy, 139
Greenham, Richard, 67–69
Gregory the Great, Saint, 74
Grierson, Herbert J. C., 197
Grigsby, Bryon, 37
group denial/evasion, 60

guilty people. *See* wicked people
Gulliver's Travels (Swift), 27

Hall, Joseph, 65
Hamlet (Shakespeare), 43, 49, 138–39,
      178–79, 219, 221, 242
hantavirus, 12
Haring, Keith, 6
Hariot, Thomas, 67
Harris, Jonathan Gil, 37
Hartman, Geoffrey, 55, 56
Harvey, William, 47, 117
Hawkins, John, 156
healing: God as source of, 102–9, 207, 210,
      213; sight of brazen serpent and, 77,
      78, *80*, 90–91; through intercession of
      saints, 75–79, *77, 78, 81, 82*, 82–84, *85,
      86*, 86–88, *88*, 90; through repentance,
      71; by touch of the king, 139
health: *de voto* offerings as assurance of, 83;
      Donne on absence of, 1, 29–30, 39, 40,
      200, 251, 256; God as source of, 99
Healy, Margaret, 37
Hebrews 11:5, 208
Helicobacter pylori, 12n12
Helmont, Jan Baptist van, 120, 121
hemochromatosis, 32n7
hemophiliacs, 40
*Henoch Clapham his demaundes and
      answers touching the pestilence*
      (Clapham), 95, 150
Henry (prince of England), 166–67, 183,
      250
Henry VIII (king of England), 99
Hentzi, Gary, 237n28
Herbert, George, 20, 98, 99, 146, 194, 201
herbs, 138
Hermes Trismegistus, 93
Herring, Francis, 145, 158
H. F.: ambiguous position of, 179; as ap-
      parition, 232–35, 240, 253; attraction of

forbidden sights, 222, 253; gravesite of, 232–33; heroes of, 243; on historicity of *Journal*, 230; identity of, 231, 233; on inexpressible horror of plague, 51; as liminal mediating figure, 232–34; perspective of, 42, 218; principle question of, 243; repeated memories of plague, 59, 62, 218; self-censorship of, 238–41, 243, 253; on transmission of plague, 242; visits to burial pit, 235–37

Hippocratic crisis, 18, 29

Hippocratic discourse, 139, 209

historians, 15–23, 168

history, 70

HIV, 11, 14, 19, 24, 32n7. *See also* AIDS

Hobbes, Thomas, 42

Hodge, Nathaniel, 230

Holbein, Hans, 75

Holocaust: artworks of, 63; authentic witness of, 179n30; imprint in Jewish literature, 48; indescribability of, 51; mass burial of victims, 25; memories of, 60; spokesmen for, 52; testimonies of, 63; theodicy of, 249; trauma of passed on to next generation, 61–62; trauma theory arising from, 54

"Holy Sonnet 14" (Donne), 121

homeland security, 100. *See also* government policy on plague

homosexuality, 40

Hong Kong "chicken virus," 10

Hooke, Robert, 138

Hooker, Richard, 67, 208

Hooper, Edward, 19

Horne, Robert, 66

human genome mapping, 254

humans: analogy between body/body writ, 42; bodies as text, 119–22; body as microbial reservoirs, 43; citizenship in microbial community, 21; as disease in ecological realm, 22; exchange of

pathogens with animals, 8, 10, 11–12, 41; symbiotic relationships with bacteria, 40–42; threat of extinction, 254–55

humors, 18, 139, 142, 209–10, 251

Hungerkünstler (Kafka), 6

"Hymne to God, My God, in my Sicknesse" (Donne), 193

"Hymne to God the Father, A" (Donne), 193

iconophobia, 90–91

Idler (Johnson), 27

idolatry, 83

I. H., 133–34, 154, 173

Iliad (Homer), 75

Illness as Metaphor (Sontag), 6

ill winds, 162, 201, 251

image of Blessed Mary, 74

images of saints. *See* Italian Renaissance art

immigrants/migrants, 32, 130, 134, 155–56

immunology, 254

incense, 148, 149

Indonesia, 25

infant diarrhea, 14

infection, 138, 145, 150

infectious disease: as binary partner of health, 40; crisis in faith in medical science and, 29; cultural construction of, 37–40; deaths due to in world wars, 17; de-theologizing of, 16; Donne on, 192, 195, 199–201, 205, 207, 251–52; emergence of drug-resistant strains, 11, 12, 19, 255; erasure from histories, 16–17; evolution of, 40–42; extinction/transformation of, 8; Gilman on, 38; jump from animal to human populations, 8, 10, 11–12, 41; meaning beyond biological nature of, 3, 39–40; as metaphor, 3, 4; Paracelsian view of, 93; politics of, 42–48; prions causing, 12; re-emergence of, 254–55; relapsing fever (spotted

infectious disease (*continued*)
fever), 192–93; representation of, 21;
revised historical narratives of, 17;
seventeenth-century concept of, 138–39,
145, 150; social discord caused by, 4,
5–6, 13–14; as symptom of infirmity of
all things, 29–30; transfer of discourse
on from divines to physicians, 247;
transformation of pathogens, 8–10;
translation of, 205–11, 209, 251–52. *See
also* bacteria; pandemics; pathogens;
plague; viruses; *specific disease*
influenza: mutations of, 10; pandemics of,
33; shots for, 19; Spanish flu epidemic,
4, 12, 19, 30, 35, 253; threat of avian flu,
10, 12, 41, 254; threat of pandemic, 4
innocent sufferers: condemned by AIDS,
40; Donne's theology concerning, 213;
heavenly reward for, 248; inexplicabil-
ity of, 151; justice of God and, 69, 143;
national guilt and, 45–46, 93, 154, 172;
salvation from worse evil to come, 171;
sins of the fathers visited upon, 172–76;
theological explanation for, 45–46, 123.
See also Jonson, Ben (son)
inoculations, 18, 19, 90, 247
Institut Pasteur, 254
intercession of saints: absence of in
Reformation England, 91, 93–94, 248;
Elizabeth Drury as afterimage of, 199;
for healing, 75–79, 77, 81, 82, 82–84, 85,
86, 86–87, 88, 90, 248
I Promessi Sposi (Manzoni), 35
Iraq, 54, 60
Irene, Saint, 75
Isaiah 9:8, 206–7
isoniazid, 18
Israelites: exodus of, 212; literature of
Holocaust, 48; mercy of plagues in
Egypt, 204; plagues in wilderness,
45–46, 77, 148, 248; political aspect of

Egyptian plagues and, 157; rebellion of
Korah, 158
Issues of Death (Neill), 132n9
Italian Renaissance art: compared to English
plague imagery, 73, 92, 109–10, 114, 117,
122–23; efficacy of saints and, 73; as
material healing images, 82–83; plague-
related resonances in, 49; plague saints
represented in, 74–79, 76, 78, 80, 81, 82,
82–84, 85, 86, 86–87, 88, 90; as record of
plague, 37, 87, 89, 89–90; as spur to devotion, 83–84, 85, 86–87, 88, 90; therapeutic
value of, 84, 85, 86, 86–87, 88, 89, 89–90.
See also specific artist or piece by name
Italy: Black Death in, 34–35; chikungunya
fever outbreak in, 10; cities freed of
plague by saints, 74; fear of anointers
in, 7; plague culture of, 74–90; plague
in, 74, 75–79, 87–88; response to
plague in, 24, 125–26; spread of plague
to England from, 7. *See also* Italian
Renaissance art

Jacob, 178
Jacobean policies. *See* government policy
on plague
James (king of England): arrival in England, 157; death of as prelude to
plague, 102, 191, 193, 241; entry into
London, 48, 166; genealogy of, 183; literary representations of, 165; plague crisis
and, 43; praise of, 162; purification of
England for, 160; reign of, 191; succession of as frame to Jonson's poem, 170;
succession to throne, 65, 102, 133, 250
Jenner, Edward, 19
jeremiads, 110, 165, 247. *See also Britain's
Remembrancer* (Wither); sermons on
plague; theodicy of plague
Jesus Christ: ascension of, 208; Crucifixion
of, 77, 91; Donne on death of, 211–12;

Resurrection of, 77; as source of mercy, 84, 85; as Word made flesh, 77n5, 95, 207

Jews, 39, 74. *See also* Holocaust

John, Saint, 88

John 1:1, 77n5, 95

John of God, Saint, 87

Johnson, Samuel, 27, 31

Jonson, Ben: absence from London during plague, 129, 157, 163, 166, 173, 175, 176, 180, 181; on affliction from God, 93, 153–54, 163; analogy of human body/city, 47; association of suburbs/theater/plague, 134; consolation in death of son, 144, 163; death of first son, 36, 47, 49, 93–94, 100–1, 129–30, 163, 165–66, 250; documentation of bereavement of, 168; dream of son's death, 60, 129, 163, 180, 181, 182; epitaphs for John Roe, 168; exchange of places with son, 179; fantasy of, 175, 183; on God's bookkeeping, 97, 171, 228; key to understanding poetry of, 129; on miseries of old age, 185–87; obsession with disease, 131; omission of plague in poetry of, 49, 50, 60, 168, 170, 177, 181–82; as one with his son/Camden, 184–85; on Penshurst, 50; plague outbreak during time of, 35; on plague's meaning, 123, 248–49; plague writings of, 50–51, 163; planning of welcoming for James, 166, 183, 250; praise of James, 162, 165; question of existence of God, 67, 172, 249–50; questions concerning his sin, 47, 163, 171–73; questions on justness of death of son, 171–73; relationship to Camden, 183; response to theodicy of plague, 153, 163; reversal of roles of son/father, 163, 185; revisit to graveyard, 178–81; Roman frame of mind, 169–70, 186–88; sin of too much love, 169, 172–73; on

social discord of epidemics, 36; son's speech from grave, 179–81, 182, 183, 185, 250; studies of plague writings of, 37; studies on plague origins of his poetry, 168–70; use of Pliny's lines, 186–87; wish for death, 180–81, 186, 187, 250; wish to loose all father, 146, 163, 169, 177, 183; *The Alchemist*, 36, 129, 168, 175; *Cynthia's Revels*, 183; *Epigrammes*, 177, 182, 184; "The Famous Voyage," 47; "The Fantastic Voyage," 51; *Love's Triumph through Callipolis*, 134–35; ode to Cary and Morison, 168, 176; "On my First Davghter," 182; "On my first Sonne," 36, 47, 49, 60, 129, 163, 168–73, 176–77, 182, 183, 250; *Particular Entertainment*, 166–67; "To Doctor Empirick," 184; "To Heaven," 67, 93–94, 153, 186, 187, 249–50; "To King James," 162; "To Penshurst," 165; "To William Camden," 182–87; *Volpone*, 131

Jonson, Ben (son): death of, 36, 47, 49, 93–94, 100–1, 129, 130, 163, 165, 250; escape for old age, 185–87; exchange of places with father, 179; father's dream of, 60, 129, 163, 180, 181, 185; as Jonson's best poetry, 101, 163, 168, 176, 183; naming of characters in *Epigramme*, 184; poem on, 163, 168–70; question of justness of death of, 143, 171–72; as right hand of his father, 177, 185; seen as at resurrection, 163, 166, 171, 180, 182; speech of, 179–81, 182, 183, 184, 250

Jonson, Joseph, 176

Jonson, Mary, 182

Journal of American Medical Association, 10–11

Journal of the Plague Year, A (Defoe): on burial pit at Aldgate, 235–37, 253; divided time frame of, 232; epidemic of 1722 prompting, 36n13; evocation

medical science (*continued*)
mercy/justice, 247; chemical theory, 117–18, 120–22, 125, 141; collapse of victories over infectious diseases, 18–22; cures for plague, 140–41; discovery of inoculations, 18; history of, 18–20; lack of answers to plague, 64; limitations of, 255–56; loss of faith in abilities of, 29, 168n8; meaning of "translation," 209–10; opinions about nature/cause of plagues, 136–39; period of apparent improvement in world health and, 15, 18–20; as province of plague discourse, 16, 247; recent advances in, 254; repression of sense of fragility of human state, 15, 256; revision of narrative of, 15–23; Royal Society and, 27; theories of disease transmission, 137–39, 162; therapies for AIDS, 5; Thomson and, 117–18. *See also* Galenic physicians; Paracelsian physicians

Medieval historical narratives, 16

memento mori, 6

Mercutio's curse, 36

mercy: death by plague as, 157–58; God's bookkeeping and, 97–98, 99, 159; Malthusian correction as, 157–58; plague in suburbs of London as, 135; of plagues in Egypt, 204, 211; prayer/repentance as means to, 92, 103, 112; remembrancer's recording of, 105; representation of in Wither's vision, *101, 102*; resurrection of dead as, 171, 204, 211; saints as intercession for, 83, 90, 218; survival of wicked as, 46, 144; theological balancing of justice and, 247; timing of Elizabeth's death as, 159; Virgin/Christ as source of, 84

metaphor, 16, 100, 208

metastasis, 209–10, 211

metonymy, 16

miasmal medium of infection: as accepted cause of plagues, 47, 138, 139, 200, 251; burial pits of previous plagues and, 59; Clapham's view of, 137; modern theory of, 24; questions raised by, 142; represented in Wither's vision, *101, 102–3*; Shakespeare's reference to, 49; speech causing thickening of, 100

microbes. *See* bacteria; pathogens; viruses

Milan, 75, 78, 79, 81

military histories, 17

Milton, John, 17, 31, 37, 51

ministers: Clapham's criticism of, 100, 144, 150; flight from plague, 146, 150, 151, 152, 153, 173–74, 175; ministry to plague victims, 78; as sinful members of guilty state, 47; as victims of plague, 46, 143. *See also* saints

Miracle of St. John of God, The (Solimena), *87, 88*

Miracle of the Brazen Serpent (Tintoretto), *78, 80*

Mitchell, W. J. T., 104

Modell, A., 70

Monette, Paul, 6

Montagu, Lady Mary Wortley, 52, 247

Montaigne, Michel de, 17, 30, 200

More, Sir Thomas, 37, 50, 99, 235

Moses, 77, 150, 158

Moses and Monotheism (Freud), 56

mosquito-borne diseases, 10

Muggins, William, 165

Munro, Ian, 42

mutation, 8–10, 32n7

Nachträglichkeit, 57–58

Naples, 74, 87

Nashe, Thomas, 67, 127

national guilt, 45–47, 65–66, 154–56, 172, 213

Native Americans, 14

Pepys, Samuel (*continued*)
body, 221n6; dream of Lady Castel-
maine, 219–21, 229, 236, 242, 248, 252;
encounter with corpse, 224; encryption
of *Diary*, 226–27; everyday activities of,
223–24; on God's bookkeeping, 97, 225;
immunity to plague, 223n7; prosperity of, 229, 252; recording of plague
anecdotes, 229; rewriting of will, 223;
as right hand of Navy, 218; sermon on
man's knowledge and, 225–26; shift
to secular with residual theological
influence, 26, 219, 241–42, 247, 252–53;
stenography in *Diary*, 228, 239; studies
of plague writings of, 37; tallying of
dead/financial gains, 223, 224–26, 228,
229, 242, 252; treatment of plague,
217–18, 222, 228, 241–42; view of
Shakespeare's play seen in 1662, 221n5;
Diary of Samuel Pepys, 217–29, 241–42
Perkins, William, 93, 200
Perugino, Pietro, 75
Pest Anatomized, The (Thomson). *See*
Loimotomia (Thomson)
Pestblätter, 79, 82–83, 103, 248
pestilence. *See* Black Death; bubonic
plague; infectious disease; plague;
pneumonic plague; septicemic plague
Peter, Saint, 147
Petowe, Henry: depiction of James, 165;
on flight from plague, 174–75, 180;
on God's mercy toward Elizabeth,
159; graphic imagery of illustrations
of, 109–10; on plague in suburbs of
London, 135–36; praise of James, 162;
representation of London, 111; *The
Country Ague*, 109–10, 111, 111
Petrarch, 3, 32
Philadelphia (film), 5
Philip II (king of Spain), 141
Phillips, Patrick, 168

Phinehas, 147, 148–49, 153
physicians. *See* Baconian physicians;
Galenic physicians; medical science;
Paracelsian physicians; Thomson,
George
Picture of the Plague (Davies), 178
plague: of 1603, 35, 47, 65–66, 132, 154–55,
241, 250; of 1625, 47, 65, 66, 175, 191–92,
241; of 1665, 35, 241; among Israelites, 45–46, 148, 248; as apparition,
234; application of trauma theory to,
55–70; association with AIDS, 23–26;
association with leprosy, 24; as both
universal/selective affliction, 142–43;
as call of good men to joy, 65; causative
agent of (*see Yersinia pestis*); climate
changes increasing chances of outbreak,
13; confluence of new inhabitants
as, 156; connection to plays, 133–36,
154; as contagious/infectious disease,
137–39, 145, 150–51; conversion of, 232;
course of in humans, 7, 33–34; cultural
construction of, 37–40; as cure for
corrupt nation, 107–9; cycles of in
London, 3, 32–33, 34–35, 130; deaths
due to between 1348–1370, 32; deaths
due to between epidemics, 33, 35n11,
130; deaths due to in 1603, 35, 130;
deaths due to in 1625, 35, 130, 191, 195;
deaths due to in 1665, 35, 51–52, 130,
223, 225; Defoe's account of, 229–41,
242–43; Dekker's depiction of, 132–33;
documentation of deaths from, 15;
Donne's view of, 203–4, 251–52; in
Egypt, 45, 157, 203–4, 211, 248; English imagery of, 99–126, *101, 110, 111,
113, 114, 115, 116, 118*; environmental/
demographic factors affecting flares of,
34; erasure from histories, 17; as escape
from evil to come, 144; as escape from
ravages of old age, 144; etymology of

biblical word, 74, 94–97, 250; evocation of contaminating language, 181–82; as force in indistinction/undifferentiation, 20n24; forgetfulness as cause of, 59–60; in fourteenth century, 32; hidden nature of, 145–46; immunity to, 32n7, 33; inexpressible horror of, 51–54, 239–41; Italian Renaissance art representations of saints and, 75–83, 76, 78, 80, 81, 82, 85, 86, 88, 89, 90; in Italy, 7, 74, 75–79, 87–88; justice/mercy of, 64–69, 203–4, 241, 247; justification of, 241, 247; justness of, 66–69, 136, 142–46, 171–72, 196, 198, 204, 212–13, 247, 249; as language event from the Word, 73–74, 94; language of, 5, 171; as Malthusian correction, 46, 112, 157–58, 255; in Marseilles in 1722, 230; means of transmission, 34, 36; medical theories on cause/transmission of, 136–39; as metaphor, 4; as mnemonic, 103; movement through history, 211, 251–52; as natural event, 67; Pepys's account of, 217–19, 222, 242; persistence of, 5, 9, 254; pestering crowds as, 156; on Philistines, 87; as plague writing on flesh, 40, 106–7; politics of, 42–48, 150–53; as preferred death, 46, 112, 144, 157–58, 195, 241, 248–49; as preparation for regime change, 47, 65–66, 153, 156–61, 250; as process of translation, 192; proposed cures for, 125, 140–41, 148–49; as punishment for invention in religion, 147–49; as punishment for sin, 16, 66, 73–74, 101, 101–9, 123, 136–46, 151–52, 212, 241, 248; reading of, 92; re-emergence of, 254; Reformation as, 79, 99–100; reign of James and, 191; retreat from human population, 35–36; return of infectious process as traumatic aftermath, 56; in rodent population of American West, 12–13; said to be

communicable through breath, 36; shaking of theological precepts, 66–69; speech as, 99–100, 158–59; as spiritual physic, 65; spread of, 7, 33, 102; as summer illness, 193; supposed protection from, 138; survivors of, 33–34, 35; as test of faithful, 65; theories on causes of, 137–39, 172–73; transmission of, 34, 82–83, 100; treatment for, 34; unspoken narrative of, 15–16; upheavals in England due to, 36–37; variants of, 9, 11, 34; visual response to in Italy, 75–90; Wither's depiction of, 101, 101–9; as word/Word, 3, 26, 73–74, 92–100, 126, 145–46, 152–53, 206–7, 210, 241, 250, 252. See also Black Death; bubonic plague; government policy on plague; theodicy of plague; theology

"Plague" (Stenseth), 13

plague broadsheets: contents of, 110; images on, 42, 79, 109–14, 110, 111, 113, 114, 115, 116; as pestilence, 99–100; publications in 1625, 192; theodicy of, 110–12, 114, 117, 247

plague discourse, 3, 5–6

plague exegesis: by Andrewes, 146–50, 200; by Clapham, 94–97; by Donne, 200–213

plague gonfaloni, 79

plague houses: as architectural emblem of speechlessness of plague, 53; as prefigure of blood on houses of Israelites, 98; quarantine measures and, 36; red crosses/Lord Have Mercy signs on, 94, 112, 126, 222; as text, 112. See also quarantine

plague imagery. See English plague imagery; Italian Renaissance art

plague memories, 59, 60–63, 108–9

Plague of Ashdod, The (Poussin), 87, 89, 89–90

Plague of Justinian, 9

"Plague of Utopias, The" (Gomel), 179n30

plague orders, 91. *See also* government policy on plague

plague pamphlets: Clapham on plague as Word, 94–97; as contagion, 99–100; as plague, 99–100; on plague of 1625, 191; as source material, 247; stories of plague victims in, 34, 57. *See also Rod for Run-awaies, A* (Dekker); *Wonderfull Yeare, The* (Dekker)

plague pits: Dekker on, 177–78; H. F. on, 232; H. F.'s visits to, 235–37; London mythology of, 58–59; reminders of in article on Indonesia, 25; stories of drunks falling into, 39, 178. *See also* burial of plague victims

plague saints. *See* saints

plague sermons. *See* sermons on plague

plague stories: of drunkard falling into plague pit, 39, 178; as evidence of trauma, 57; recycling of, 38–39, 248; of sudden death, 34; on vanity of flight, 95. *See also Journal of the Plague Year, A* (Defoe)

plague theodicy. *See* theodicy of plague

plague trauma, 54–70

plague writings: on 1625 plague, 192, 197; on afflictions of individuals bound in body politic, 185; confusion of living with dead, 177; connection between plagues/ words in, 97–99; decryption of plague due to trauma, 60; definition/extent of, 48–54; double nature of, 181–82; etymology of word plague in, 94–97; as evidence of survival, 51; on flight from plague, 174; on plague in Marseille in 1722, 230; as psychosocial form of traumatic repetition, 57–65; publica- tion of, 195–98; published in 1603–4, 165; reading of, 26, 61, 70; relevance for

current generations, 4–13; response to epidemics, 247; secular view of plague in *Loimotomia*, 118, 119–23; shift to sec- ular with residual theological influence, 26, 219, 241–42, 247, 252–53 (*see also Diary of Samuel Pepys* [Pepys]; *Journal of the Plague Year, A* [Defoe]); by sur- vivors, 52; traumatic reading of, 64–70; understanding through triangulation of human body/city/kingdom, 42–48. *See also* jeremiads; plague broadsheets; sermons on plague; theodicy of plague; *specific author or work by name*

Plato, 42

plays, 131, 133–36, 154

Pliny, 186–87

pneumonic plague, 11, 34, 138

Poe, Edgar Allen, 7

poets, 21, 103–4, 181. *See also specific poet by name*

polar ice caps, 10

polio vaccine, 19

Political History of the Devil (Defoe), 234

politics: 1666 shift in, 217; Clapham's *Epistle* and, 150–53; of contamination, 157–59; of the plague, 42–48; plague cleansing in preparation for monarch, 47, 65–66, 153, 156–61, 250. *See also* government policy on plague

Pollaiuolo, Piero del, 75

Portia (fict.), 138

postmodern disease historians, 17

post-traumatic stress, 54–57

Poussin, Nicolas, 87, 89, 89–90

Practice of Everyday Life, The (Certeau), 42

prayer, 148–49

"Preached to the King's Majesty at White- hall" (Donne), 203

predella decorations, 119

pre-traumatic stress, 57

Price, Sampson, 73, 172

religious pamphlets, 44–45

remembrancer, 103–4

Renaissance, 30, 35–36. *See also* Italian Renaissance art

Renaissance historical narratives, 16–17

Renaissance pastoral genre, 50

Reni, Guido, 75

Rent (play), 5

repentance: plague pit's silence and, 236–37; as prevention from plagues, 103–9; re-incorporation in Christ through, 202; as remedy for plague, 71, 135, 136–37, 141–42; spiritual rebuilding of church through, 217; suffering of innocents as incentive to, 248; through reading, 112, 114, 117

repetition, 213–14

Republic (Plato), 42

Responsio ad Bellarminum (Andrewes), 147

Restoration, plague epidemics during, 35

resurrection: baptism as metaphor of, 208–9; Donne on, 192, 193, 198, 202–4, 205–8, 211, 212, 252; of Jesus, 77; Jonson's son and, 163, 166, 171, 180, 182; Pepys and, 221; as reward for faithful souls, 198; speech of dead through poetry as, 250; at time of Christ's resurrection, 202

Revelation 16:21, 98

Richard II, 44

Rift Valley fever, 12

Riggs, David, 67, 166, 167, 176

rinderpest (cattle plague), 14

Roche, Saint, 77–78, *78*, 79, 199

Rod for Run-awaies, A (Dekker): on flight from plague, 137, 175; frontispiece of, *110*; graphic nature of illustration in, 109–10; publication of, 192; stories of plague victims, 34

Romana, Saint Francesca, 74

Roman Empire, 9, 14

Rome, 75, 79, 87–88

Romeo and Juliet (Shakespeare), 36

Rosalia, Saint, 74, 248

Ross, Cheryl Lynn, 129, 134

Royal Society, 27, 138

Rwandan genocide, 60

Sabin, Albert, 19, 31

Saint-Amour, Paul, 57

saints: Bishop Carlo Borromeo, 78–79, *81*, *86*; Elizabeth Drury as afterimage of, 199; Saint John, *88*; *Pestblätter of*, 79, 82–83; physician's assistant of *Loimotomia* in place of, 123; Reformation and, 73, 90–94; replaced by official guards in England, 114; replacement with pestilential body in *Loimotomia* frontispiece, 119; Saint Roche, *78*; role in healing, 26, 75–79, *77*, *78*, *81*, *82*, 82–84, 83–84, 85, 86, 86–87, *88*, 90, 247–48; role of in Italian Renaissance, 73, 74–90; Saint Sebastian, 75–77, *76*, *78*, 79, *82*; use of images of, 26, 82–84, 86–87, 90; Wither in role of, 104

Saint Sebastian Altarpiece (del Biondo), 75, *76*, 83

Salk, Jonas, 19, 31

salvation, 207, 210–11, 213

Sandwich, Earl of, 218

sanitation reforms, 154–55

Santa Maria Maggiore Church, 74

Sarah, 96–97

SARS, 12

Satan (Devil): as agent of God fomenting diseases, 65; as agent of pestilence, 52, 92, 96n24, 145; Defoe's history of, 234; eye as doorway of, 120; temptation to deny of God and, 67, 69

Scarry, Elaine, 52, 238

schistosomiasis, 14

Schnitzler, Arthur, 6

Schoen, Erhard, 79

Schreber, Daniel Paul, 69
Schwyzer, Philip, 178
science, 217. *See also* medical science
scientific laboratories, 10
Scripture: Andrewes's use of, 146–50; appeal to plagues of, 45–46, 203–4, 211, 248; conflation with bodies of saints, 202–3; etymology of word for plague, 94–97; on Fall of Man/entrance of disease, 93, 200–1, 213, 251; on flight from plague, 100, 146, 150–51, 173, 174, 248; King James translation of, 206, 208; Methusian years granted to patriarchs, 20; as proof text for understanding plagues, 73, 248; Septuagint translation of DBR, 95–97; as source for study of disease, 92–93, 137–38, 142, 146–48; on susceptibility to plague, 145; translation process, 205–11. *See also specific book of the Bible*
Scuola Grande di San Rocco (Venice), 77–78, *78, 80*
Sebastian, Saint: Biondo altarpiece of, 75, *76,* 83; Elizabeth Drury as afterimage of, 199; engraving of, 79, *82;* Godskall's skepticism about, 92; life/martyring of, 75–77; modern counterpart of, 6; as patron saint of AIDS patients, 75; predella decorations with images of, 119; Tintoretto's work depicting, 78; in *Virgin and Child Enthroned with Saints,* 84, *85,* 86
"Second Anniversary, The" (Donne), 30, 195–96, 199, 212
2 Samuel 24, 157
sectaries, 148
Sennacherib's Plague, 149
Separatists, 148, 152
September 11 terrorist attacks, 51, 54, 55n46, 249
septicemic plague, 11, 34

Septuagint, 95–97
Sermon of the Pestilence, A (Andrews), 146–50
sermons on plague: on 1625 plague, 192; on doubting existence of God, 67–69; on justice/mercy of God, 247; justification of plague, 65–66; as mode of theological decryption, 59; as plague, 99–100; on plague as divine document, 73; on plays as source of plagues, 136; published in 1603–4, 165; published in broadsheets, 110; unspeakable concept and, 66–69; "First Sermon after Our Dispersion, by the Sickness," 192, 194, 201–5, 206, 211, 217; "Preached to the King's Majesty at Whitehall," 203; *A Sermon of the Pestilence,* 146–50. *See also* theodicy of plague; theology
seventeenth-century divines, 40, 59. *See also* Andrewes, Lancelot; Clapham, Henoch; Donne, John; sermons on plague; theodicy of plague; theology
Shakespeare, William: analogy of human body/body politic, 44; Hamlet's imagining of Polonius as convocation of worms, 43; Pepys's allusion to, 219, 220–21, 242; plague outbreak during time of, 17, 35; references to plague houses, 36; on transmission of plague, 139n23; use of plague language, 49; *Coriolanus,* 49; *Hamlet,* 43, 49, 138–39, 178–79, 219, 221; *Julius Caesar,* 46, 138; *Love's Labour's Lost,* 53–54; *Macbeth,* 178–79; *Measure for Measure* , 49; *Othello,* 49; *Richard II,* 44; *Romeo and Juliet,* 36; *Troilus,* 49
Shelley, Mary, 179
Shelton, Thomas, 226–28
Short Dialogue concerning the Plagues Infection (Balmford), 143
Short Writing (Shelton), 226–28